A YEAR IN RED SHIRTS

by JACK BERRY

The Sporting Life

First published in Great Britain 1993

by THE SPORTING LIFE
Orbit House, 1 New Fetter Lane, London EC4A 1AR

© Jack Berry 1993

Edited by Michael Gallemore

ISBN 0 901091 60 X

British Library Cataloguing-in-Publication Data.
A catalogue record for this book is available from the British Library.

Photographs by courtesy of: Bert Butterworth, Kenneth Bright,
John Crofts, The Daily Mail, S. Davies, Robert Elliot, Healy Photography,
Steve Hunt, Alan Johnson, Newcastle Chronicle & Journal,
George Selwyn, The Sporting Life, Colin Turner, Ron Vavasour and
Jack Berry's family, friends and associates.

Printed and bound in Great Britain by
Bath Press Limited, Bath and London

Jacket designed by ReproSharp Limited, London EC1N 8UN
&
Printed by Ark Litho Limited, London SW19

LIST OF ILLUSTRATIONS

After much soul searching who to
dedicate this book to I would have liked
to have given the honours to the Stable
lads and lasses but, seeing there are so
many of them, it isn't possible. So, on
their behalf, I will dedicate this book to
a lovely man who has done so much for
their needs over the years, Wilfred
Sherman – Founder Trustee of the Stable
Lads Welfare Trust.

PREFACE

SINCE writing "It's Tougher At The Bottom" many people asked when am I going to do the follow-up. Rather than do that, I thought it would be better if you tagged along with me for the next twelve months, and be a part of me and my thoughts as I jot down the happenings in some sort of diary. I talk more about the horses than I did in "It's Tougher At The Bottom." People have mentioned to me that I didn't say very much about them but with that kind of a book it was never intended. For a title I have decided on: "A Year In Red Shirts."

During the year I shall visit bloodstock sales, dash to race meetings, attend various functions and even go on holiday. If the coming season is anything like the last eight months when my Toyota Carina diesel car, very kindly sponsored by Terry Holdcroft's garage at Stoke-on-Trent, clocked up 43,019 miles it should be some season. As well as my own transport I had, on occasions, to travel in other people's cars, on planes, trains and in taxis in our relentless search for winners. In fact, our horses visited every racetrack in Britain at some stage of the season.

For the second consecutive season yours truly was the leading trainer numerically, and eighth in the earnings list with prize money included from Italy, France, Germany and Ireland. In Britain from 834 runners we trained 143 winners and had 222 places. Richard Hannon was the only trainer to have more runners than our yard, with 951.

One of the most stressful parts of our life is travelling. Some of the journeys to the Southern tracks can take up to five hours. The opening of the M40 during the summer will hopefully ease our plight somewhat, as we won't need to use the M25 quite as much. That road can be a permanent car park. Inevitably we will still have some hairy journeys on the roads, especially when we are doing the two (a day and an evening meeting) and JC's at the wheel. JC is my jockey, John Carroll, not Jesus Christ. If he ever invites you to share a lift with him and you are of a nervous disposition, bring with you a change of trousers or a packet of Pampers.

There will be ups and downs, hassle, highs and lows and a bit of stress with all the red tape involved in running a business. It's like Gordon Richards, the Greystoke trainer says: "It don't get any easier Jack lad. It's aard y-o-u know."

This recession we are going through is cutting deep into the funding of every aspect of racing. British racing is the best in the world. We have to unite and look after it to get it back on a straight course. Perhaps this new British Racing Board might be the answer if all connected with racing are prepared to give it a chance. Who knows we may see floodlit racing at Southwell and Lingfield. It could be just a matter of time before Sunday racing comes in. We may even get a lottery off the ground to help racing's finances.

In this next twelve months I will try to win as many races as possible without intentionally hurting or riding roughshod over anyone. Let's hope somehow, somewhere, sometime, down the line even the smallest punter in the betting shop can take pleasure from our yard. With our new exciting batch of yearlings, maybe lightning can strike twice in the same place and we are graced with another Paris House.

TUESDAY September 10, 1991

IT'S the first day of Doncaster St Leger Sales-a very exciting time. What yearlings we buy over the next few weeks are crucial to our success next season. This is why I have chosen to start my book today-the first day of the yearling sales.

Seeing I will be missing from the yard for the next five days I'm looking at the injury book to make sure there isn't anything in it to worry about or see to, before I go. Kestrel Foxboxes had sore heels, Heaven-Liegh-Grey a cut jaw but healing well. Dokkha Oyston a bit jarred. Battle of Britain's head is on the mend after having a couple of stitches. Son of Schula sore shins. Great, nothing there looks like snuffing it.

Jo and I set off from Cockerham at 7.0 in the morning with our case packed for the next four nights. We are staying at the Doncaster Moat House. The sales commence at 10.0am prompt so we go straight to the sales yard. After much research and leg work we finally end the day buying five colts and one filly by Belfort, Cyrano de Bergerac, Risk Me, Fayruz, Clantime and Absalom. The prices range from 5,000gns to 15,000gns. I was the brides-maid on several nice lots.

The 15,000gns was for Lot 133, a colt by Fayruz the same sire as Whit-tingham who had won on his three starts for us. This included a Listed win in Italy where we sold him on. He was a ringer for Whittingham, even bred at the same place by Gay O'Callaghan at the Tally-Ho Stud in Ireland.

Hugh O'Donnell, who had horses with Linda Perratt, told me if I liked anything tell him and he would buy a couple for me to train. So I picked out this fellow and a nice sharp looking Belfort colt. True to his word, Hugh bought them.

All today's buys went straight on to get broken at Garry Gosney's, the ex-Flat jockey, at Towton where I was an apprentice. Garry has been breaking in for us for three or four seasons now.

Jo and I move on to the Moat House for our first meal of the day. We have it with Harry Beeby and Richard Hannon. Richard is a bit bullish about Notley's chances and strikes a bet with me that he will beat Food of Love in the five furlong Listed sprint tomorrow.

Four of our horses ran at Carlisle. Palacegate Jewel, ridden by Lindsay Charnock, won the Auction race-Between Two Fires was third of twenty, ridden by Lester Piggott at Leicester. The rest were unplaced.

This takes our season's score to 132, with 84 of them being two-year-olds.

WEDNESDAY September 11

RANG home to do the entries with Alan and confirmed yesterday's runners are okay. At 7.0am went down to the hotel health club for a swim and a sauna. In the sauna was Channel 4 racing personality Derek Thompson. We ran out of water to throw on the coals. Your man Derek, bollock naked, walks with a wooden bucket through the pool area where a nice young lady is swimming. Without batting an eyelid he smiles showing enough teeth you would have thought he was breaking them in for Red Rum-and says good morning to her!

We had two runners today, Food of Love in the Doncaster Bloodstock Sales Scarbrough Stakes won by Richard Hannon's Notley. Needless to say Richard won his wager. Food of Love started at 3-1 favourite. Notley was joint second favourite at 5-1.

Our second runner Heaven-Liegh-Grey ran in the Portland Handicap. In this race a fancied runner, Farfelu, fell. The horse was not badly hurt but the subsequent races ran late. This delayed the start of the sales, making it an even later finish.

There was great concern whether racing would be abandoned because in the same race two years before horses and jockeys got injured quite badly when they fell and false ground was found to be the cause. The incident ended the riding careers of Ian Johnson and Paul Cook. Thankfully after an inspection, racing continued in safety. It must have been a real worry for the Doncaster executive.

At the sales we purchased four colts and one filly, the prices were between 5,200gns and 14,500gns. The most expensive at 14,500gns is by Treasure Kay out of Lala which makes him a half-brother to Dream Talk, who we trained for Prince Yazid Saud. Dream Talk won three races at two and three

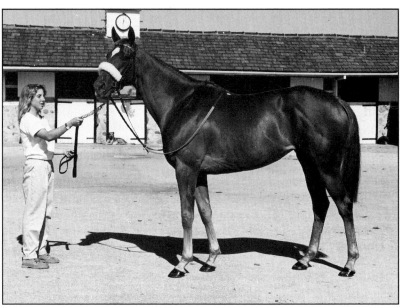

FOOD OF LOVE : A loser
in more ways than one.

for us and was placed four times before he moved to France with his owner. He has since won five more races on the Continent. The other four yearlings are by Mansooj, Mazaad, Governor General and Bold Owl.

THURSDAY September 12

RANG Alan 7.0am to arrange with him what horses to enter and declare.
We had two runners at Folkestone, Rhythmic Echo and Coco Queen, both unplaced. Folkestone being the furthest course from Cockerham in Britain-it was a long way to go for nothing.
The yearling sales didn't start until 5.15pm. We hadn't any runners at Doncaster, so Jo and I spent just about all morning and afternoon looking at the youngsters to be sold in the evening session. There were some nice lots coming up.
The bidding was quite lively-me again being under-bidder for two lovely colts by Belfort and Superlative. The latter was bought by John Wharton for 28,000gns-I bet we see its backside in the coming season.
At the end of the sale we bagged two sharp fillies by Taufan and Sayf El Arab. With all the gloom beforehand people were saying it will be a bad sale. Anything that was really nice quality and well-bred fetched the money. I must say year after year the breeders have improved the turnout of these yearlings. The majority of them have been handled so much when we take them over they are already half broken. It certainly makes our job easier. In fact some yearlings have actually been driven in long reins and are stabled with rugs on. When we buy the yearlings we can have them wind and drug tested by a panel of vets based at the sales.
It would be interesting to know the mileage recorded if a pedometer was attached to me in the course of a day at the sales.
When we went back to our hotel Jo and I went for a swim in the pool where plenty of people had the same thoughts. A quick change followed before a nice meal with a bottle of wine.

FRIDAY September 13

ALTHOUGH we didn't have any runners anywhere today I was invited by BBC Radio to join Peter Bromley on the build-up for the Laurent-Perrier Champagne Stakes. You'd think that the radio racing commentators would have a nice plush seat in a warm cosy box to bring live coverage into the homes of thousands of people. This is not the case at Doncaster, I can assure you. I was led round the back of the stands, up some crummy stairs, over wooden planks, up scaffolding, to a make-shift little den that, I must say, had an absolutely beautiful view of the Town Moor track. After stating the cases for all the runners I tipped Rodrigo de Triano, which duly won. He was so impressive he must have a good chance in the Guineas. It's great to see Robert Sangster with such a nice horse.

Later in the afternoon I was interviewed by Derek Thompson for Channel 4 television along with Jack Greenwood, a retired coach driver and Mary his wife, a former civil servant. They are getting sponsors together for them to visit all the 59 racecourses in Britain, within the year, in aid of the Trinity Hospice for the Fylde. Their aim is to collect in the region of £22,000, as £78,000 has already been donated by the Friends of this worthy cause.

The one hundred thousand pounds is needed to extend the clinic at the day centre of which the Mayor and Mayoress of Wyre and myself are joint patrons.

In the evening session of the sales there were some particularly nice yearlings. We bought for Robert Sangster an Auction Ring colt, the half-brother to It's All Academic, who won three juvenile races, was second in the Molecomb and the Queen Mary and was later sold to Norway.

Other horses bought were by Absalom, Cyrano de Bergerac, Petong and Chilibang. Prices ranged from 8,000 to 28,000gns.

SATURDAY September 14

JO packed our case and put it in the car ready for home after the final day of the sales. We arrived at the sales for 9.0am. I bought a nice Music Boy filly for 5,400gns and a Superlative colt for 5,000gns.

We had four runners this day at Doncaster, all two-year-olds. Langtonian in the Graduation Stakes, Paris House and Diamond Mine in the Group 2 Flying Childers Stakes (which we won last year with Robert Sangster's Distinctly North) and Bit-A-Magic in the Nursery.

Langtonian ran with little zest as if he'd had enough for the year. We will cut him now for next season.

Peter Chandler, the main partner in Paris House, is the highly acclaimed chef of the Paris House Restaurant at Woburn. He wasn't going to come to Doncaster as he had to prepare the food for a wedding reception for 150 guests. To enable Peter to watch the horse run, his staff and friends hired a helicopter to take him to Doncaster and return him to Woburn, three quarters of an hour after the race. Fortunately Paris House, ridden by John Carroll, easily won the £28,200 first prize at 4-6 favourite.

Diamond Mine finished fourth to put £2,067 in Peter Savill's Weatherby bank account.

Last time John rode Paris House on July 20, 1991 he gave JC his eighth winner from his last eight rides.

Paris House deserved this prestigious race. In his previous race at York, the Group 1 Keeneland Nunthorpe Stakes against older horses, he put up an incredible performance when running second to Sheikh Albadou, the champion sprinter.

Toulon, the French horse, ridden by Pat Eddery won the next race, the St Leger. Seeing this fellow win the Chester Vase in May after the trouble he was in during the race made me think he would win a classic.

Our luck ran out with Bit-A-Magic in the last race. He had only travelled a furlong or so, when he was struck into from behind and cut his tendon so badly he had to be put down. A real shame as he was a good horse that had done us proud, winning three times, including a Listed race in Italy.

On arrival home from Doncaster we discovered the water was turned off. The Water Board sent us a big tanker to the yard to enable the horses to be watered until they could get the taps back on.

PARIS HOUSE, our stable standard-bearer,
again shows his rivals a clean pair of heels
in the Flying Childers Stakes, ridden by John Carroll.

SUNDAY September 15

LIVERPOOL Daily Post and Echo had their open day at the yard. About one hundred of the shareholders in Echo-Logical and Echo Domino came. It was a lovely day. We showed them around the yard, looked at all the horses and brought out their two so they could have their photographs taken with them.

Most of the people had arrived in three coaches after having had their lunch in the village. Others came in cars.

We had a bit of a problem, all the water had been turned off as the Water Board hadn't mended the burst pipe yet. On our tannoy system I announced I was very sorry but no one could use the toilets as the water had been temporarily turned off. No doubt the men would have filled their bladders up at the bar at the village hall. Even after saying all that, people were still asking "where are the toilets?" Our lads were sending the men over the road at the back of a hedge. Coming from a city like Liverpool most of them weren't used to being so close to cows. The cows were curious and headed towards the men. Some of them were for diving over the hedge to get back; the urge soon left them. For all that, it was a good day and everyone seemed to have enjoyed it. One of the shareholders wanted to buy one of my books. Pat was up here this weekend as she also has shares in the Echo horses so she got some out of my car boot and ended up selling twenty-seven! If Sir Rupert Mackeson, who published it, had seen her, he would have been proud of her.

After evening stables I walked round the gallops with the dogs and the cattle. This time of night and early in the morning are the best times of the twenty-four hours. Old Bruni (pictured right), the golden labrador is getting on a bit now, he's started to slow up. In fact sometimes he doesn't even want to come for a walk, but the old fellow is about sixteen years old. We named him Bruni after that horse Ryan Price used to train who won the Yorkshire Cup and the Cumberland Lodge Stakes in 1976.

MONDAY September 16

ROAD work for all the horses today except Doublova and Palacegate King. They strode out for two and a half furlongs on grass to blow them out.

Food of Love travelled to Leicester to be picked up from there for a rest, which she has truly earned, at her owner David Abell's place.

John and I travelled to Edinburgh. Greetland Rock ran a good race in the five furlong sprint only beaten a head in a driving finish by Best Effort. The next race Laurel Queen won. The heavens opened as the horses cantered down for the race. It was absolutely belting it down making it nearly impossible to see. Our filly was slow into her stride. Turning into the straight she moved up very quickly, like a hot knife through butter, to fly past horses to take up the running a furlong out. In the finish she won by an easy three lengths. The starting price was 4-1 joint favourite, fourteen ran. The jockeys got so wet in the storm they all weighed in as much as two pounds in weight more than they weighed out. There were a few of the Laurel Racing Syndicate present, they didn't mind the rain. All of them were there in the winning enclosure greeting their game filly in.

Chateau Nord and Laurel Connection were unplaced at Edinburgh. At Leicester Palacegate Racing apparently ran well from a poor draw but also was nowhere. The horses split into two groups. The fast horses were on the other side. This horse is in good heart and should win again before the season is through. He doesn't want many more runs as he would be a nice horse to go with the yearlings and run on the all-weather.

TUESDAY September 17

ALAN has travelled down to Sandown with John as we have Doublova running there today. Palacegate King is at Yarmouth but I am staying at home as we have a lot of fancied runners coming out this week which need to be worked. Also I have to take stock so to speak, as I will be away in Scotland for a few days.

Cantered all the horses round the Moss one mile figure of eight. All except tomorrow's runners that is. They were winged up the middle grass gallop for two and a half furlongs. Our horses are still looking well even if some have had a long season and hopefully we should still have a few more winners before the season is over. Our target of 100 two-year-old winners however is looking about a 100-1 shot at the moment. In fact we have about as much chance of getting a hundred two-year-old winners now as Neil Kinnock has of becoming the next Prime Minister.

Listened to Doublova win by an easy two and a half lengths in the claimer at Sandown at 10-11 favourite on the Racecall phone line. According to the race reader she only had to be pushed out to win. There was no such luck for the Palacegate horse at Yarmouth.

We have a runner at each of those two meetings tomorrow therefore our horseboxes will stay overnight.

Went round the yard for a change at stable time. I say a change because most days I am away racing. Our two head men, Flash and Kevin, go round every evening, anything to report they write in the injury book when they have finished. The first job I do when I come in the house, even if it is two in the morning, is look at the book. If there is anything wrong I go and see the horse there and then.

WEDNESDAY September 18

GREAT weather, an absolute brilliant day with runners all over. Six at four meetings. One of those days though not one of them looks a goodish thing. Although Kestrel Forboxes should run well at Yarmouth.

Worked all the horses on the grass in pairs and threes, very pleased with them.

Jo packed the car up with all the gear we will need for the Western Meeting. We are booked in at the Fairfield House Hotel. We didn't have the pleasure of John's driving as we took our own car seeing as we are there for some length of time. Also he stays with a few of the other jocks and I bet the little beggers let their hair down.

We were a bit late in setting off as I had a lot of last minute things to do like take phone calls. I had to tell Ruby, our secretary, in the end to put the rest on the carphone as I was running late.

The vet is coming to cut Dokkha Oyston and Langtonian. When he arrives to castrate horses our dogs follow him. He puts the horses to sleep in the indoor school. When he appears Bruni, one of our labradors is always the first there to get the testicles and eat them. The other dogs seldom get a chance.

Dashed up to Ayr taking no end of phone calls. Everytime I wanted to get through to home it's engaged. When we eventually arrived at Ayr the amateur jockeys were just going down to the start for the first race. Our little sprinter Greetland Rock is walking round the preliminary paddock. Ayr always gives me a buzz. Not only is it my favourite racecourse, but this Western Meeting, I love it! Every year it gives me another crack at the Ayr Gold Cup.

Ever since I was very young it was my ambition to win the Ayr Gold Cup. After several attempts it wasn't until 1988 when So Careful (Albert) won us the great race. A day of my life I will never forget.

Greetland Rock finished third of the fourteen starters, only he cut a couple of horses up hanging to the left. So the stewards demoted him to fourth.

HERE I am seen collecting the Ayr Gold Cup
after the success of So Careful in 1988.

We ran Ecliptic, owned by Robert Sangster who made one of his rare visits North. We would have loved to have trained him a winner while he was in attendance. But it wasn't to be, Ecliptic finished seventh of the seventeen that went to post.

I went to the stable yard to have a look at the next day's runners. Then Jo and I went to our hotel. A fabulous place it is too with a nice swimming pool and a sauna. Right away half an hour in the sauna, an hour in the pool and a good steak with the bride.

Looked up the form of our declared runners again. Got my declarations sorted out for when I ring Alan up in the morning. None of the other horses came anywhere, we drew a blank even with Kestrel Forboxes, although he was 2-1 favourite. Featured in the Racing Post Profile by Howard Wright. I suppose they have to write about something. Howard is a friend of mine. He worked for the Sheffield Star when we first started training at Doncaster. With it being a fairly local paper he was always ringing us up for news about the horses. Those days winning a seller at Sedgefield was quite something.

THURSDAY September 19

RANG Alan first thing, did the entries and declarations with him. Had a chat about the horses in general.

Yesterday at the races I promised Linda Perratt and John Wilson I would be down for a ride out. I was at Linda's for 7.30am, it was a nice change to be riding somewhere different. I have to keep riding out to keep fit. Sitting in the car for six days out of seven most weeks, sometimes up to eight hours a day, doesn't do me any good at all. Anyway I like riding. I have always been a bit of a saddle tramp.

Afterwards it was back to the hotel for half an hour in the sauna. The sauna was full of Flat jockeys. None of them were staying at the hotel but I could have sworn I recognised John Carroll, Allan Mackay, Geoff Baxter and Richard Fox in the box.

Next, a swim which we had a laugh and a bit of fun about. In the Harry Rosebery two year old Listed race Diamond Mine and Another Episode ran well, finishing fourth and fifth to Richard Hannon's Miss Nosey Parker. Snowgirl was third in the six furlong sprint, and Windpower unplaced.

Dashing about watching our other six runners at Beverley and Lingfield on SIS. Cee-Jay-Ay obliged for us at Beverley by a short head ridden by Lindsay Charnock.

In the evening I went to the Horserace Writers' Association Scottish Branch dinner held at the Western House on the racecourse. Guest of honour was jump jockey Chris Grant. Chris couldn't be there as he was riding elsewhere. His ex-boss Denys Smith, the Bishop Auckland trainer stood in for him to collect his prize, and he was very entertaining speaking on Chris's behalf.

John Penney was the chairman and speakers Graham Goode and Francis Lee were both very amusing. We had a good night.

FRIDAY September 20

TODAY's the day. My day of the year. Ayr Gold Cup Day! Our Fan and Gorinsky have as much chance on paper as Albert had. Did everything the same as yesterday morning, including riding out again for Linda.

With it being the day it was I walked the six furlongs of this great racecourse. I love the place. Many years ago some bloody hooligans burnt the open ditch round the back stretch. With a little guidance from me our owners had partly paid for its rebuilding.

In addition to sponsoring the Ayr Gold Cup Ladbrokes very kindly invited Jo and I for drinks followed by lunch in the Craigie Stand. They did a first class job and looked after us very well. No fairy story for J.Berry today in the Cup, but our two ran well, without troubling the judge.

In the next race, the Nursery, Nil Nisi Nixu (in English means nothing without effort) was third. I must truthfully say everything is an effort for this fellow. He is a bigger rogue than Al Capone. He won't help the jockeys one little bit. I am not proud of it but I bought him at Calder Park, Florida, Breeze-Up Sales. I think he has ability and may be better later on over a few flights of hurdles.

In the sprint Amron finished sixth of the eighteen starters. SIS came into the fore again in between Ayr races, at Newbury and Southwell, where I was pleased to see Laurel Queen win. It was with great delight to learn Richard Hannon recorded his first hundredth winner at Newbury with Knight of Mercy. From my hotel room I sent him a card to congratulate him and told him it was time he pulled his finger out and did something useful.

SATURDAY September 21

RANG Alan to talk the entries through and about working the horses at home. Jo and I rode out for Linda again, only today we had company, John

**MAMMA'S TOO (noseband) seen winning
the Shadwell Estate's sponsored
Firth of Clyde Stakes from Harvest Girl.**

[11]

Carroll, Kieran Fallon and Allan Mackay. My mount today was Ayr Raider, he was really going well. I said to Linda put me a fiver on him next time he runs. Back to our hotel for a swim where we were joined by Linda, John Wilson and Henry Beeby.

Vanessa, Henry's wife, didn't come as she wouldn't get out of bed. Some of the jockeys came also. We had quite a bit of fun. It's so relaxing to do something like this before racing.

It's raining hard as we set off for the races. Catterick and Newbury are well patronised by Berry horses, six in all. Seven here, at Ayr, but Rose of Eire wasn't sound so that reduced it to six.

By the time the £23,000 to the winner feature race, The Shadwell Estate Firth of Clyde Stakes (Listed) was due, the going got heavy as the heavens had truly opened. Although Nifty Fifty is owned by Norma and Roy Peebles who live in Scotland and were looking forward to their filly running, I took her out. She ran in soft going when she was joint favourite with Pat Eddery up at Windsor in April, and she couldn't handle it.

Our other filly, Mamma's Too, owned by John Brown and Tom Bibby, two of our longest-standing owners' and their partners, had already won the St Hugh's Stakes Listed race on August 17 at Newbury. She flew out of the gate in the torrential rain. This was her first run over six furlongs. She made

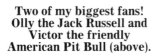
Two of my biggest fans!
Olly the Jack Russell and
Victor the friendly
American Pit Bull (above).

every inch of the running to win by half a length from Harvest Girl giving her 3lb.

Immediately after the race JC and I were presented with lovely silver trophies. Also, unfortunately for JC, he picked up a two-day suspension for a whip offence. I was interviewed on Channel 4 with the rain literally running down my face.

Tino Tere was second at Newbury in the Nursery with top weight of 9st 7lb, beaten three quarters of a length giving the winner 21lbs!

Makeminemusic and Spot the Earlybird were third and fourth in the two-year-old maiden at Catterick. The rest just made up the numbers.

Sporting Life editor Mike Gallemore and his wife Janetta came back to Cockerham with us. The Life had sponsored a race at Ayr and kindly entertained some of our owners and numerous trainers. Jo and I gave them a tour of our gallops with all the dogs and bullocks in tow. It was 2am and chucking it down. I told them the animals would come out of the woodwork to greet us after being away for a few days, and they didn't disappoint us. Our big soft American Pit Bull Victor jumped straight through the passenger window into Mike's lap as we were driving along. If Mike wasn't already wet through before, he was then.

SUNDAY September 22

IT'S a lot better today than it was yesterday in Scotland. Led yesterday's runners out and they are all fine. That Mamma's Too must be a tough nut after slogging through that six furlong bog yesterday. She has come back and eaten every bit of her last night's mash. When she had a lead out she was as fresh as paint. Some of these little fillies we seem to fuss over them as if they are so delicate. Yet they are as tough as old boots.

Tomorrow's Pontefract runners-we just stretched their legs for a couple of furlongs up the middle grass.

CASHTAL DAZZLER wins the Tote Credit Silver Bowl at Haydock Park in May 1990.

When we finished stables we loaded eight horses in two of our horse boxes and sent them on their travels to Doncaster Sales. Leaving some staff to tend them, the boxes returned. This has been part of our annual casting. It's sad in a way as through the year we get to know them. For example Cashtal Dazzler has been good to us. He has won good races but his future looks to be in jumping and we don't keep many of them nowadays. Let's hope they get good homes.

Lots of owners came including John Brown and Tom Bibby with a couple of bottles of champagne to celebrate Mamma's Too winning. The day got going like some sort of party but it was good. In addition to the champers John brought a lovely silver trophy which the filly won at Ayr in the Shadwell Estate Firth of Clyde Stakes. John had been presented with it but after consulting with his partners decided it wouldn't be fair for any one of them to own the trophy. So Jo and I were presented with it. They had added an engraved inscription on top of it "Thanks Jack and Jo, J K Brown, T Bibby, G Tiribocchi".

MONDAY September 23

WE sell 11 horses at Doncaster Sales to make room for the yearlings. Amongst them is Cashtal Dazzler who Nigel Tinkler bought to go jumping for 14,000gns. This being the second highest price of the day to Bright Hour who realised 18,000gns. Dazzler should do well at jumping, I hope he does anyway.

It's always good to sell a few winners otherwise people just think you get rid of your rubbish. We sell quite a few winners, especially abroad.

While I am doing my bit at Doncaster we have four runners at Pontefract where not one of them gave the judge a moment's concern.

Arctic Appeal was second and Laurel Queen was unplaced at Nottingham.

Finished at the sales I have to catch a plane to Ireland for the Fairyhouse Yearling Sales. The traffic was so bad on the M62 I missed my intended flight. Catching the next one which is an hour or so later, gives me the chance to read my Sporting Life. I see Jimmy Bleasdale has had to retire from race riding on medical grounds. Shame that. Jimmy has put quite a lot into racing. He was a good stable lad boxer as a kid. He was also always very polite and well mannered. Good luck in whatever you do now Jimmy!

I was met at Dublin Airport by George Mernagh from Tattersalls to take me to the Station House at Kilmessan. But first I had to meet Jimmy Byrne my Irish agent at Mick Ryans of Rathoath, as it's on the way to the Station. Time to sample again the best pint of Guinness and the best steak in Ireland. Never in my wildest dreams would I ever think of drinking a Guinness. But here in Ireland it tastes so different. Possibly because it's not travelled very far. Or maybe, it's the way the Irish pour it out. Whatever-here it's different class. Tommy Carberry and a few more of the boys were in and in good form too. It's great here. Always busy and friendly like.

TUESDAY September 24

GEORGE picked me up to take me to the sales. Looked around most of the yearlings I had marked off in the catalogue with my man in Ireland, Jimmy Byrne. Only doing it that way is very frustrating as every second person you see wants me to look at his or her yearling. It takes the line of thought or the intended direction of going about my task of trying to pick some winners out. That's why at the sales I devote most of my time to watching the yearlings walk round the preliminary paddock. It gives me a great buzz when I see one that's a good mover, sharp and sound, bred to be a fast runner. In working this way every yearling is seen out and at close range. The first yearling I bought was a colt by Reasonable for 5,000gns. Then a filly by Glenstal and a colt by Nomination.

Frank Dunne had earlier asked Gay O'Callaghan to introduce me to him as he wanted me to train a couple of yearlings this season for him.

My next buy was a Common Grounds colt followed by a lovely Standaan colt nearly white and then a Treasure Kay colt. The prices ranged between 2,000 and 12,500gns.

At the sales Benny Powell very kindly lent me his car for my stay in Ireland. Thanking George for picking me up but now I have got some wheels he can give me a miss in the morning. When the sales finished Jimmy Byrne and myself went to Ryans for a steak and a Guinness. Then I drove to the Station House where Richard and Liz Whitaker were staying along with several other interested parties from over the water. As you may have guessed it was a late night. In the home country, Tenacity was third at Nottingham. Our other runner Flash Bid was unplaced.

WEDNESDAY September 25

JIMMY picked me up for battle at the second day of the sales. On this day I bought four yearlings. A colt by Don't Forget Me. Then a cracking colt by Salt Dome on behalf of Frank Dunne as David Pim the Irish auctioneer would say, "My new man." To secure this lovely colt I was bidding against a telephone, me having the last nod at 32,000 Punts. On the other end of the line was Newmarket trainer Alex Scott. Next purchase was a filly by Drumalis for 7,000. She is by the same sire as Another Episode who won us the Roses Stakes at York, a Listed race, and second in the Philip Cornes Molecomb Stakes. In fact when Pat Eddery rode Another Episode to victory at Windsor in June, Pat said: "that is the fastest two-year-old I have sat on for a very long time."

Finally for 18,000 Punts I bought a very sharp looking filly by Fayruz for John Brown and partners . They owned Whittingham who won his three races for us, including a Listed race in Italy before being sold to race in that country. Jimmy arranged the shipping with agent Eddie Brennan.

After the sales I went on to stay with Benny and Sheila Powell, jump jockey Brendan's parents. They actually bred Another Episode at their Swordlestown Stud. The yearling they own is a full-sister so you can appreciate I am very keen to get my eyes on her. She is entered in the sales at Goffs and I haven't any intentions of going there. I am hoping I might buy her privately if I like her. As we were having something to eat Brendan (left) rang up to tell them he had got buried that day at Ludlow. He was sore but not too bad.

He rang to reassure them as was his procedure after a fall so they don't worry unduly. Not like Mrs B when Candy fell with me at Bogside in the Scottish National at the last fence first time round. The ambulancemen picked me and Jo up. Only I was spark out. It stopped to let the horses by before crossing the course. It's debatable whether the driver did this for safety reasons or was it because Jo wanted to see the finish?

THURSDAY September 26

SHEILA and Benny showed me Another Episode's sister who I liked very much and bought for Palacegate Racing Corporation. Benny took me to see the stud which his son-in-law, the vet, runs. We watched some of the horses working. It was a nice change. Benny's car took me to Fairyhouse Sales yard where I looked at the yearlings.

Picked up Jimmy Byrne and went into Dublin to arrange the shipping and VAT with Eddie Brennan at his office. Then seeing as we had spent 32,000 Irish Punts for one of his offspring the previous day we went to the stud where Salt Dome stands to have a look at him. I wasn't disappointed in him. He was a lovely horse and he is stamping his stock the same way. Dropped Jimmy off, went on, had a meal and stayed the night at Benny's.

Rang up Tommy Stack to see what time to meet him tomorrow as he said he would take me for a day out to Listowel races. I am looking forward to that as I have never been but I have heard so much about it. Years ago when I was an apprentice I used to spend my holidays in Ireland with my long-time pal Paddy Farrell and we went round quite a few of the Irish meetings. Before we went to the meetings we would ride out for Paddy Sleator. You may think, some holiday, but it was great. The Irish lads are good fun so switched off and yet they get there just the same.

There are lots of Berry's in Ireland but I have no relations there at all. I have a great feeling for the place though. One day at Leopardstown a man did say to me: "For all these years you have left the old country you have never lost your Wexford accent!"

FRIDAY September 27

BENNY took me in his car to meet Tommy. Liz had gone ahead to drop her car off at a garage to get it serviced or something. We picked her up en route, and talked about old times when Tommy first came to England to ride for Bobby Renton.

Listowel was great. The ground was soft as it had rained for two days. When we parked the car on the car park it was like a bog. No one seemed to give a monkey's. The crowds at the races were unbelievable. There were droves of them and mainly in a holiday mood. Tommy's horse finished second. It ran a good race though. The atmosphere was grand. Just like at our Cartmel. The prize money was real good as well.

In the bar at the races I sold the Standaan grey colt I bought on Tuesday at Fairyhouse to Seamus Purcell, a cattle dealer. He's very friendly with one of our ex-owners Mick Ward.

It was great crack in the bar. No end of people shook my hand. Some two or three times. We had a great day, didn't back any winners but as the Irish lads say, it was great crack!

After racing we managed to get the car off the car park all right but some didn't. On the way to Tommy's house he was giving us a running commentary. He would make a good courier if ever he packed up training. "See that

farmhouse on the left of those buildings, our blacksmith's father lives there. This is the village Jack White lives in. I once nearly bought a farm over there. The little cottage over there so and so lived there, what a good trainer he was..."

Tommy (left) goes on like this all the time. He knows everyone everywhere. After a lovely meal at Tommy's, we watched the box, talked about racing, his horses, our horses. Then I retired to bed and slept like a log, better than at home.

Talking about home we had five runners at two meetings. Miss Parkes was the nearest we had to a winner. She was second of twenty-one beaten a neck at Redcar. No hard luck stories. She ran very well.

SATURDAY September 28

TOMMY, Liz and I went on a tour of their gallops in a Land Rover driven by Tommy. He was either putting a show on for me, or thought he was at Brands Hatch. The gallops were brilliant though. If Nick Lees, the Newmarket Clerk of the Course saw them he would be embarrassed. It's just like acres of lawns. Tommy was dashing about worse than that Cockerham nutter does, giving orders to his riders on their horses in the pouring rain. Where to go, how fast and so on.

Liz cooked a nice breakfast. I then got bathed, changed and ready for racing at The Curragh. We had Sizzling Saga running in the Testimonial Stakes, a six furlong Listed race. Tommy drove me to the stable yard so I could look at Sizzles to make sure everything was all right. David and Juliana Abell his owners were just arriving at the same time. We saw the horse, Amanda our travelling head girl reported he was well and had eaten up.

Steve Craine rode him. Steve rides most of our Irish runners. It was him who rode Bri Eden to win the Ballyogan Stakes at Leopardstown for us in 1983, our first Group win. No such luck today however. We finished sixth, just out of the money. We can't grumble about this fellow as he has run some tremendous races for us this season. He won the Newcastle Northumberland Sprint with 9st 7lb, a Listed race in Germany and three others.

Tommy Stack and I watched No More the Fool (Jessie) run second on SIS. He jumped awful. I think it was because it was a right-handed track.

We had plenty of runners at Haydock, Carlisle and Redcar with a few places but no winners.

Jimmy Byrne took me to the airport in his car to catch my plane.

On arriving at Manchester, collecting my car, the money it cost for leaving it-I nearly died!

There's no wonder you have to put money in a machine to pay for the parking at airports. No person would dare tell you the amount to one's face!

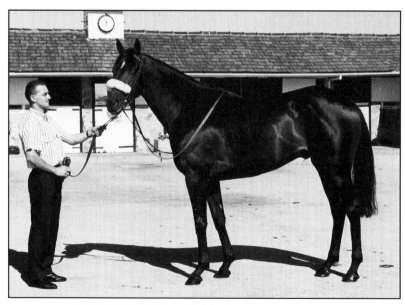

**SIZZLING SAGA . . finished sixth in the Listed
Testimonial Stakes ridden by Stephen Craine.**

SUNDAY September 29

ENJOYED my stay as always in Ireland but it's nice to be home again to catch up with what's happened in my absence.

Let all tomorrow's runners, except Gorinsky who likes to run fresh, sling along for two and a half furlongs up the middle grass gallop where the going is perfect.

Made lots of phone calls to people who had missed me whilst I was away and had left messages for me to ring them on my return.

Had a walk round the gallops with my string of dogs which I enjoy doing. It also gives me space and a chance to think. My main thoughts were-who can I sell or how do I go about selling my recent purchases before I get the brown envelope from Tattersalls or a friendly phone call from the manager of Garstang and District Midland Bank.

Although it's getting near winter it's still very mild and we have lots of grass. The cattle look a picture. They all stand while I stroke them. Blimey they could put you off eating meat.

Walking round with my cattle and dogs I get loads of confidence. This season we have trained here the winners of 86 two-year-old races. So on form if I can't sell the yearlings, then who can? When I got back in the house I started to ring people up to get them motivated to put their names on these, what I aim to be next season's winners.

MONDAY September 30

ALL the horses either went on the walkers or were ridden round the roads. Four runners at Hamilton. Tricycling being the nearest to trouble the judge, he was second. The others I'm afraid were also-rans. As was Stormswept and Master Eurolink at Wolverhampton. Jo went to Hamilton. Alan saw to the Wolverhampton runners.

With the majority of Doncaster and all except three Fairyhouse yearlings not yet sold, Sheikh Mohammed is probably worried I am trying to own more horses than him. To rectify this matter instead of going racing I will swell the profits of BT even further by making more than my usual number of phone calls to anyone who over the past few months has given me the slightest indication they were interested in purchasing a yearling. It won't be long, like all the other years in the past, before we receive brown envelopes requesting a piece of paper with my signature on. If I can get someone else's on first, the sales companies and my bank are delighted. John Carroll's enforced holiday, compliments of the Ayr stewards, starts today.

Boozy went home for a rest via a lift in our box to Wolverhampton. From there she got picked up to take her the rest of her journey. The vet came in the afternoon to castrate Music Dancer. He is a lovely big horse who wants strengthening up and he could do well next year. Bob Heathcote owns him. He's the head of Philip Cornes who sponsor quite a few races. One that comes to mind is the series of Philip Cornes Nickel Alloys Maiden races for two-year-olds. They also sponsor the Houghton Stakes at Newmarket in October.

TUESDAY October 1

CANTERED most of the horses round the Moss quietly. Put about a dozen through the stalls. Gary Carter rode the two Wolverhampton runners Tynron Doon, fourth of 16, and Prohibition (Ben) second of 19, as John is now on one of his two days enforced holiday.

I didn't go racing today as I will be in Newmarket for some time and I have to catch up with entries, declarations and countless other jobs.

At evening stable time I went round all the horses. I can only do this if I don't go racing. Also I took my dogs and had a good look around the gallops. All our 37 cattle followed us. For a townie looking on it must have been a fair spectacle to see 37 cattle and, at one time 59 and eight dogs, all keeping up with me. They are great. With having them in our fold yard in winter, all the stable muck goes in the yards to bed them down. With the lads and lasses carrying their muck from 100 plus horses in there every day and stroking them and talking to them they get real soft.

When I go outside in the field I just shout, "Come on boys!" and they come running from all directions and follow me wherever I go. It's awful when they have to be sold, in fact these should have gone weeks ago as they are all ready for slaughter. Alan, my son, keeps letting a few go to the fat market on Mondays when I go racing. Then, on a Friday when I get the chance, I go to the Lancaster Market and buy more stores.

I love buying them but I hate selling them, especially knowing where they are going to finish up next day when they have gone. When I'm off racing I often wonder if they have killed my bullocks yet. I am sure I would be better off with a suckler herd and sell the young ones off as stores.

WEDNESDAY October 2

WORKED all the horses before setting off to Newmarket Highflyer Sales which start at 5.30pm after the races. Minimum bid is 10,000 guineas. At these prices no doubt there will not be many of them travelling up the M6 to Cockerham.

At the sales there is a message to look at a couple for Frank Dunne. Most of the yearlings at this sale are by sires with a bit more strength in their pedigree than I like. Just not sharp enough for me as I like them so they can win yesterday rather than tomorrow. If I wanted to buy stores I would buy this type. The ones I buy you would think I only had a year to live. For what good I did today my time would have been better spent treading footings in at home after the horses had worked. Anything I fancied the bidding went through the roof. Still, I stayed the trip as good as Desert Orchid, watching the last of the yearlings through. Then I went to my second home, Gerry and Bridget Blum's, whom I have stayed with for years.

Having a good chat there over a nice steak and a bottle of wine and listening to Gerry, like I have done for the past five or six years, saying if he doesn't get some more horses it looks like being his last year.

Gerry is a star man. I have known him since I was an apprentice. One day, when I was hitching a lift at Halls to go to Tadcaster, he stopped and gave

me one. It was the very day he was taking up the post as travelling head lad for Captain Bill Elsey, the Malton trainer's father.

GERRY BLUM . . . the owner
of my second home!

THURSDAY October 3

AS always, when I go to Newmarket I ride out every morning, mainly for Mark Tompkins. Today I rode Father Time who went a mile and a quarter at a nice pace. His first bit of work for a while as he has been off for some time. Last year in the Children In Need Charity Race at Sedgefield I rode Father Time to finish second.

Rang Alan to go through the entries and declarations on my car phone. Went on to the Moat House for breakfast with Pat Knight and her parents, who always stay there for this meeting.

Heather Bank was our only runner here at Newmarket in the Nursery, finishing fifth of nine with top weight 9st 7lb. J.C.was back on board, having served out his suspension. The handicapper thinks a lot of this fellow. I hope he's at the sales buying horses at the end of the season. The only problem is Norman Harper, his owner thinks a bit of him too and he may bottle out sending him to the sales.

Rodrigo de Triano came good again to win the Middle Park Stakes, Group 1, a furlong shorter than the Champagne Stakes he won at Doncaster. For my money he has to be the best two-year-old around.

At Lingfield, Battle of Britain was the only runner we had there and finished third of 20. I got to train Battle of Britain through a Sporting Life/Sunday

Mirror competition (which raised £5,000 for the RAF Benevolent Fund). I chose the horse myself at Doncaster. The man who won the horse to own for a year is a lovely chap. It's good for an enthusiast like Michael Goddard to win such a prize. We'll win a race or two for him, he'll be chuffed to bits.

I was in attendance again at the sales for the evening session. Not troubling the auctioneers too much, I had a few goes at a couple with no luck. They went for far too much money than I was prepared to go to, in view of the fact we had no owners to pass them on to.

MICHAEL GODDARD, competition horse Battle of Britain
and myself.

FRIDAY October 4

RODE my old horse Father Time out again. Had a bit of a chat to my old mate Johnny East. We used to ride jumping together. Johnny is now Mark's head lad.

I like riding when I come to Newmarket. People up North say horses get bored at Newmarket as they do the same thing every day. Although I am a Northerner, I won't have that. There are lots of different routes to take the horses. Not that I have intentions of doing so but I could train at Newmarket. It fascinates me, seeing the many different strings out and watching the horses work.

Our son, Sam, has gone to Tenerife today for the winter. Ruby, our secretary, has taken him. She's staying there for a week's holiday.

Did the declarations and entries again with Alan on the carphone.

Snowgirl was the only runner we had today at Newmarket, finishing third of 21 to Stack Rock, trained near us in Lancashire by the much under-rated Eric Alston. Snowy ran a big race as Stack Rock is a fair tool.

Wore out quite a bit more shoe leather at the sales without putting my hand in my pocket.

Gerry invited Pat and her parents up for an evening meal at their house. We had a lovely night with a couple of bottles of wine. The food, as always, was good, cooked by Gerry's other half, Bridget.

SATURDAY October 5

FIRST thing, I rang Alan up regarding working, entering and declaring the horses.

Left Gerry's 6.30am. Picked my Sporting Life and Racing Post up from the shop. Rode my old pal Father Time nine furlongs work. He went well enough but was in need of the gallop.

Went to Newmarket races where our sole runner was Elton Ledger, who ran unplaced in the six furlong Nursery to Richard Hannon's Merlins Wish. It was still a good day for the North. Mellottie, with John Lowe aboard, trained by Mary Reveley, beat home Lynda Ramsden's pair, High Premium and Vague Dancer in the Cambridgeshire.

Up at Kelso, Peter Niven (below left) rode five of the six winners. Only a strand of red tape prevented him riding the lot, as Graham McCourt the jockey and Nigel Tinkler the trainer offered Peter the ride on Rawaan, the

2-7 favourite. But the stewards, in their infinite wisdom, wouldn't allow it. A short-sighted decision to say the least.

It was a long, miserable haul back home. No winners and no buys at the sales from three days of trudging around Suffolk.

My dogs went bananas when they saw the car draw up in the car park. First job, looked at the injury book to make sure everything is well with the horses. Just a knock or two.

A couple of the yearlings have a touch of ringworm and Flash has put them on Fulcin medication and isolated them. One with slight over-reach, one with a sore girth. That's not bad, nothing serious.

Caught up with the mail and messages which had piled up in my absence, and by the time that had been accomplished it was very late when I got to bed.

SUNDAY October 6

PICKED John Carroll up at the Manor car park 6.15am on the first leg of our journey to Longchamp as Paris House runs in the Ciga Prix de l'Abbaye. Caught the 8.0am flight from Manchester to Paris. Arriving at Charles de Gaulle Airport we met Michael Kinane who kindly offered to give John and me a lift to the racecourse in the chauffeur-driven car laid on for him. Whether it was because when we have runners in Ireland and Mick has the odd ride for our yard, or whether it was because he didn't trust John Carroll sat next to his Mrs. But Mick elected me to ride shotgun with the chauffeur. In doing so I got some great views on the way to the races.

There are some very noble looking buildings in France. One year Jo and I went to the Arc and before racing we went on a bus tour of Paris. We saw the Bastille, Eiffel Tower, Champs Elysees and lots more places. It was great.

John walked the course as I went to see Paris House at the stables. Wally reported him well. There is a marvellous atmosphere and buzz to the Arc meeting. One in three seem to be British. Bands are playing, people are beautifully turned out, lots of glamour, it's great.

In the paddock area I spotted Mike Dillon from Ladbrokes who kindly invited me for a drink and a bite to eat in their box. He pointed out the box to me. It was so far away and high up in the stands, I thought I had better not. I might not get back through all that crowd in time to see Paris House race, let alone saddle him up.

Going out of the paddock a crowd of British supporters were chanting "There's only one Jack Berry."

Paris House jumped out smartly and was travelling well until weakening just over a furlong out. John sensibly caught hold of him and let him come home in his own time to finish last of the fourteen runners. No one can grumble though. This was his ninth race of the season. He won at the first meeting at Doncaster-his career earnings to date total somewhere in the region of £140,000. Not bad when you think he cost only 5,000gns. We could do with a few more like him.

After all the travelling and excitement I was back in our house for nine o'clock.

MONDAY October 7

MY birthday, 54 today! Opening a present from Pat it is a personalised car number plate J888 ACK. That's great! All I need now is a car to put it on.

Tomorrow's runners slung along for a couple of furlongs to blow the cobwebs away. The rest cantered steady round the top moss for a change from road work.

There was quite a lot of traffic on the road travelling to Pontefract where the going is on the firm side and it's a nice warm day. Greetland Rock ran out the back in the sprint. Tenacity was second to 2-7 hotpot Tamim, of Tom Jones'. Our only other runner, Soba Guest at Warwick, trying his little heart out to give me a birthday winner, finished fourth of eighteen, beaten less than two lengths.

To celebrate this annual occasion we put on the answer phone then Jo, Alan, Neville and myself had a very nice meal at the Orchard, an Italian restaurant near Preston. The waiter came carrying a cake with one candle and put it on our table and sang "Happy Birthday". To add more embarrassment the silly buggers from the surrounding tables also joined in the sing-along with my trio.

TUESDAY October 8

TODAY we put five two-year-olds in the stalls, up the straight, on grass. We cantered all the horses on the all-weather, except Wednesday's runners. They did a couple of furlongs sharp on the grass straight.

Seven runners at three meetings, Folkestone, Warwick and Redcar. The only one who came nearest to earning a crust was Cee-Jay-Ay who finished fourth of eighteen at Redcar. John Carroll, being the great judge he is, asked to get off him to ride Red Rosein. Needless to say he finished in the rear.

Mind you, I mustn't blow about that too much. Our sole runner, Master Eurolink at Folkestone over three hundred miles away, was sent there thinking it was a nice cosy little race to pick for him, finished fifth of eight. He was 10-11 favourite but never looked like winning.

It's never a formality winning races. No matter how short-priced the horses are they are flesh and blood. So much depends on how they feel on the day. The mood they are in, or often things go wrong for them during the race.

 With a motor car it's consistent. If it's capable of doing 120 mph it will do it every day. With horses a lot depends on circumstances and feelings to produce their best. The yearlings are settling in all right and on the whole look a nice bunch. The first batch we bought are still at Garry Gosney's (left). Speaking to him on the phone he is also very pleased with the ones he is breaking. So we have some very nice yearlings to start next season off with. We certainly had some good ones this year. If the new ones are as good they will do for me.

WEDNESDAY October 9

GALLOPED most of the horses on grass. The ground here is perfect. In preparation for tomorrow's race we put Bold Mood in the stalls to sharpen him up a bit.

See in The Sporting Life, Bryan Marshall has died aged seventy-five. What a good jockey he was.

Jo, John and I went to York. John drove us. Jo and I were kindly invited for lunch in Ladbroke's box, in the Melrose Stand, which was very nice.

Our Fan (Gordon) ran seventh in the seller with a claiming price of 10,000gns on him. To our amazement someone put in a claim for him to race in Sweden. Ruth Dix, the girlfriend of John Barrett was very upset as they

OUR FAN. . . memories of a happy day
at Hamilton Park when 'Gordon' became our 100th winner
of the 1991 Flat season.

have owned him since he was a yearling. Being realistic she should have actually taken the man for a drink. Although he has won five races this season there are limitations regarding his abilities. He is very small but real gutsy. No doubt we will miss him. All the kids rode Gordon as he was such a good ride. He wouldn't pull a hen off the nest. At Hamilton on the 17th of July he won giving our yard its 100th winner of the season with 10st 3lb in the handicap sprint.

Heaven-Liegh-Grey was third in the York sprint. Oddly enough she gave the yard its 100th winner at Brighton last year.

No success to report from Amron and Between Two Fires, our two runners at Haydock.

Plenty of runners, but a blank day. Although it's getting late on in the season the horses in the main are still running well. The mileage is piling up on some of their clocks.

As for the horses we keep next season-the colts we will farm out to livery yards. The geldings and fillies will be turned out in water-proofs in our sixteen-acre field. We put tumbrils in for them to eat out of and fetch them in at night. They really enjoy their break.

THURSDAY October 10

JEFF BAINS, the vet came to cut Cranfield Comet. Most of the two-year-olds we keep on for next season get castrated around this time of year. This horse has done well for us winning four races out of nine runs. Even so, he's a bit of a thinker and should benefit greatly from being gelded. It isn't cruel to geld these horses. If they were left as entires they tend to get difficult and bad to manage in the stables. They also have limited freedom as they cannot be turned out with other horses in the field during their off season time, as they kick and play up. I don't have to add what they do to mares and fillies. If they have been very good racehorses and won some good races, then they have a fair chance of going to stud and are priviledged to keep their manhood. At the stud they will have a big stallion box with their own paddock. You could say, they have got it made.

Haydock Park is John's and my venue today. Only forty-six miles down the road. A nice change to some of the meetings that can take hours to get to. That is a great problem running the volume of horses we do in a season. It would be fair to say we spend a quarter of our day travelling by car to see the horses run. The only consolation is, if I am not driving, I can catch up with my paper work.

Bold Mood, from the unfavoured box one, ran third of twenty-three in the maiden which was a very pleasing run.

Made my way to the course betting shop to see Fylde Flyer, ridden by Lester (below), win the Nursery at York to give us our first winner since

Mamma's Too at Ayr on September 21. In the seller at Haydock Park, Tri-cycling ran fourth of eighteen.

Echo-Logical also ran a brilliant race in the Nursery, finishing second to Walking Possession, the favourite, giving him seventeen pounds. I like this fellow and he should train on as a three-year-old, but I doubt if he is up to Group or Listed class. So I hope the handicapper gives him a chance, otherwise he would have been better going to the Newmarket sales.

[27]

FRIDAY October 11

IT'S a lovely warm autumn day. First thing, Mamma's Too, Snowgirl, Tino Tere, tomorrow's Ascot runners, breezed for a couple of furlongs so Amanda could set off in good time, as Friday's traffic is always the heaviest of the week.

Diamond Mine cantered for a couple of furlongs as he runs tomorrow at York but he galloped yesterday and sometimes he gets a bit crutchy afterwards. A quiet canter tends to loosen him up.

Gorinsky was merely led out as he also runs at York. He prefers to run fresh and does not take kindly to having the edge taken off him.

Roughed Amron off and turned him out for a well earned rest. This time of year the horses that are turned out are brought into the indoor school for the night. Although the weather is quite mild at the moment it can get very cold in the evening. The horses are always pleased to go out in the mornings but by the same rule are happy to come back in at night, where it's warm.

It's nice to have a day at a jump meeting. Miami Bear runs at Carlisle but unfortunately today I gave it a miss. I sent Neville in my place to give him a day out. With Ascot and York on tomorrow and me going to Ascot I have a lot of work to catch up with. My bank manager would appreciate it if I got off my butt and tried to sell some of these yearlings.

Neale Doughty rode the Bear who finished last on the firm ground. Neale reported to me that he hated it and would be all right on better going. Also the Bear felt as good as ever.

All the yearlings have now got used to the horse walkers. One or two at first resented it but seem all right now.

SATURDAY October 12

LEFT Alan to work the horses at home as I went to Ascot in my car. That journey can take hours. The roads weren't too busy and we had a good run. John took his own car as he has a ride in Spain tomorrow and needs his to get to the airport and back.

Snowgirl 10-1 joint favourite ran a close up fifth of twenty-three to the Mark Tompkins-trained Gilt Throne in the Bovis Handicap. We won this race with Bri-Eden in 1982.

Tino Tere and Mamma's Too ran in the Group 3 Cornwallis Stakes to see if we could get some black types on those two year pedigrees. Unfortunately it wasn't to be. Mamma's finished fourth, the other fellow ran sixth to the useful Magic Ring. I should add Pat came with me to Ascot. I was glad of her company. It's a long haul down there and back in the same day. Plus the fact we shared the driving. She also gives me some help with this book as she did with the other one I wrote - "It's Tougher at the Bottom".

Diamond Mine was unplaced in the Listed Rockingham Stakes at York. Watching him on the telly he looked unsettled. He was lathered down at the start. It was a very warm day, horses often boil over walking from the stable yard. Knowing this I wouldn't be too concerned about Diamond as he's had to walk over the vast open Knavesmire to the racecourse. This little fellow is in the Racecall Trophy in a couple of weeks time. With a light weight he must have a good chance. Peter Savill, his owner, is very keen for him to run. So I hope he isn't over the top. He's in the Newmarket Sales the following day. Having won five races for us he will be impossible to place in handicaps. With the likes of Paris House and Magic Ring about he would be hard-pressed to beat the likes of them.

In the Coral Sprint Trophy, Gorinsky ran a much better race to finish second to course specialist Cumbrian Waltzer.

SUNDAY October 13

HAD a walk round the yards to see the horses. On Sundays we only do what we have to. It's a day off for the horses unless they are running within the next couple of days. It's also the weekend off for half of the staff. They are then given the chance to go home to see their parents.

Young Derek McGaffin, a little fellow from Scotland who sometimes comes down to spend his holidays with us, arrived today. I bought two Jack Russell pups over the phone. So Pat, young Derek and myself went to Southport to pick them up. I remembered on the way that I promised our Sam I would ring him in Tenerife as I do most Sundays. I couldn't get through to him on the carphone so I had to ring Jo and ask her to ring him instead. Knowing Sam he would be walking his box waiting for a call.

After we picked the pups up we were trying to think of names for them coming back in the car. They are really super. We finally decided on Roy and Rodgers.

Jo likes animals but not too much. Well, let's say she doesn't go a bundle on too many dogs around. Taking the bull by the horns we brought them straight into the house to show her.

"What do you think of these mate?" I said.

"They're all right. I hope you are going to clean up after them" she replied. But it wasn't too long before she had one in her arms. Her bark is worse than her bite. She's not unlike Jenny Pitman.

MONDAY October 14

THE horses either went on the walkers or were ridden round the roads. The likely runners in the next couple of days were given a canter.

7.30am: Jo and I set off for Newmarket Sales with our cases packed as we are staying at my Newmarket home, Gerry and Bridget Blum's. Left Alan enough jobs to do to last him until Christmas. Also instructions not to forget to feed the pups four times a day.

The traffic is plentiful on the roads. But we have time on our side for a change as the sales don't start until noon.

Our first buy was a Bit-A-Magic half-sister by Bairn, for Christine and Ray Robinson, owners of ours.

Of our only two runners today, Tenacity ran third at Leicester to the useful Distinct Thatcher, Prohibition ran in the rear at Newcastle.

When Jo and I got to Gerry's, Bridget told us the old boy was in hospital. Something amiss with his plumbing system. The three of us had a meal out. Doing that was best as knowing Gerry he would have been ringing for news every couple of hours.

Loves the phone does Gerry. The nurses will have their work cut out keeping him in bed. He is never still for a minute. He's worse than me.

TUESDAY October 15

6.20am-Drive to Newmarket paper shop to collect my Sporting Life and Racing Post, as I do every morning, when I stay here. I rang Alan on the car phone to declare tomorrow's horses. Next, I called into my mate Mark Tompkins yard to ride out first lot. Then went back to Gerry's to collect Jo and change. We then visited Cheveley Park Stud to see my old pal Music Boy, a thing I often do when in Newmarket. The staff think the world of him especially Jimmy Elington who looks after him.

He is now nineteen years of age and looks nothing like it when you see him tearing around his paddock. We have been lucky enough to have trained stacks of his winners. It pleased me no end when we trained Northern Commander to win at Newcastle on March 27, 1989 to give Music Boy his 500th winner. Cheveley Park presented me with a super photo of the old boy in a silver frame to commemorate the occasion.

At the sales I drew a blank. There were a couple that interested me, a Superlative that went for 36,000gns. Another by Petong, but it looked rather unfurnished so I bottled out on that one. It was in this ring last year when I bought a Petong for 5,000-Paris House-what a star he turned out to be!

Most of the other yearlings had quite a lot of stamina in their pedigrees and when I buy that type of horse invariably they end up going round places like Bangor or Sedgefield in selling hurdles.

At the sales I was asked to do a Racing Video on how to pick a yearling interview with Steve Cauthen. It was freezing cold. I bet when it comes out I look more like Julian Wilson. Our Leicester runner Cashtal Queen ran a fair race to finish fifth of the twenty starters.

In the evening rang Alan to discuss tomorrow's work arrangements for the horses.

WEDNESDAY October 16

RODE Father Time out again for Mark. Rang Alan to declare and enter the horses from the carphone.

The yearlings look a lot racier than yesterdays. Bought five, prices ranging from 6,200gns for a colt by Glow to 17,500gns for a lovely colt by Salt Dome.

Richard Hannon is about sixteen winners behind us in the table of leading trainers and seems to be training winners every day. Our yards' horses are running well but they are not the force they were.

Richard Hannon's travelling head lad Taffy (below) has bet me a tenner  they will beat us for the number of winners. But I don't think all of the money was Taffy's. I think he was having a bit on for his guv'nor too.

Looking at the Wolverhampton card you can see we are quite desperate having seven runners. In the first race Ellebanna is sixth of seventeen. Then Tricycling is fifth of thirteen. In the third race, Soba Guest wins the Nursery in a field of twenty. Having a good look for R Hannon. I see him with a couple of his henchmen, Tony Murray and John Corbett, at the parade ring before the horses enter the arena. I nip smartly round to the room where the gentleman calls with messages and ask him if he would announce, for the benefit of Richard Hannon, to please note Jack Berry has just won the two-year-old race at Wolverhampton. Only give me a minute to get out so I can see the Marlborough maestro's face when he hears it. Richard took it in the spirit intended and had a good laugh.

In the next race, a claimer, we had the second, Laurel Queen and the fourth, Kestrel Forboxes, who was claimed for £5,250. Kestrel Forboxes did us proud winning six races for us. He would have been sold at the end of the season so we mustn't grumble. The remaining two were not sighted.

THURSDAY October 17

WENT to Mark's and rode out. Father Time looks at me as if to say, "When is he going back?"

At home it's a road work day. Told Alan on my carphone what to do with Friday's runners and had a chat in general about the horses. Had a quick shower and changed at Mark's before wearing out more shoe leather at the Park Paddock Sales ground.

It's work all right at the sales but it's good as well to see the old faces. Some we may have bought from in the past, others congratulate me for doing well or say they thought that colt they nearly gave me would have won races. Whatever it's good crack.

We only bought one yearling today, a lovely grey filly by first season sire Common Grounds out of an unraced American-bred mare who had bred seven winners.

In the evening Bridget, Pat, Jo and myself all went for a Chinese at The Fountain in the town. We had the banquet. It was great. It's no good going in there expecting to be served quick. It's a long meal as they keep on bringing different things. Very relaxing but time consuming. Anyone who has ever been there will tell you, it's good.

I drew the short straw again and had to drive so I only had one glass of wine. When Jo tosses the coin she does it that fast and shouts "heads". For the future I think it will be fairer if we take turns.

FRIDAY October 18

RODE out at Mark's as usual. Saw quite a few faces I know including Julie Cecil. They all have a smile when they see me ride out on my Newmarket trips.

Got in touch with Alan for the decs, entries and a chat about the horses, including the Catterick runners. Both agreeing a winner today would be a bonus. The horses all have a chance but have live dangers to beat.

It's a sharp morning at the sales, commencing at 9.30am. Some of the yearlings are just starting to go in their coats. Having seen some thirty odd yearlings with less than half of them sold, there's plenty more sales still to go, so unless they are jumping out of the ring pleading with me to buy them I am definitely saving myself for lot number 870 tonight!

Arthur Slack, Snowgirl's owner is on the bridge. I've told him this half brother to her is a real good sort. Hopefully, we will be fetching him home as Arthur is as keen as mustard to add this lovely grey colt to our string.

When the morning session had finished Jo and I, instead of going racing at Newmarket, went for lunch in Cambridge and did some shopping there. We called into a Ladbroke shop and watched our three runners in the claimer at Catterick on SIS. What a result our Palacegate Racing beat the odds-on Sense of Priority by three quarters of a length. Our other two finished fourth and sixth. In the next race Greetland Rock was third of the seventeen that went to post. From a very poor draw, sixteen, he ran a big race. We watched Alan Munro ride his 100th winner of the season on Petite D'Argent. Alan is a good young jockey. Given any luck he will ride many more centuries.

Back to the evening sales for 5.15pm start. Thirty-five lots on. Here comes my boy looking an absolute picture under the lights. The bidding opens up at 5,000gns. I go in at 12,000. Around 16,000 it looks as if he could be mine. A few more bids take it up to 21,000, it's my bid. Knock him down you prat I'm thinking.

The auctioneer takes a bid to someone out of sight, high up the stairs. The bidding got very spirited at 36,000gns. Yes, I will have one more bid. Arthur will probably have to sell the farm. No chance, 38,000 right away. The auctioneer announced James Delahooke - Good! He buys mainly for Peter Savill, I may still get a chance to train him, as Peter has one or two horses with most of us Northern trainers.

There was a Primo Dominie filly I had an interest in later on which again made too much money.

SATURDAY October 19

RODE out as usual at Mark's. Had a read of the sporting papers, a cup of tea and a chat with Johnny East in Mark's office. Showered, changed, had breakfast, rang Alan before going onto Newmarket races. Our cases are already packed in the car ready for the off.

Sizzling Saga ran seventh of ten. A little bit flat, Lester said, so we will send him home for his winter break. Sizzles has done us proud, winning five of his 11 starts. This includes him reaching our fastest 50th winner and a Listed winner in Germany where I was presented with a very nice stopwatch.

Spot the Earlybird and Tynron Doon failed at Catterick to trouble the Judge. Tel Quel, the French horse, won the Champion Stakes and Go South at 33-1 with Nicky Carlisle on board won the Cesarewitch.

Jo and I stopped to watch On Tiptoes win the Bentinck Stakes. After which we jumped in my jalopy and headed North.

On reaching home I discover, looking at the work sheet, that Elton Ledger and Echo-Logical have both worked very well.

SUNDAY October 20

SOMETIMES it's nice to get away for a few days. But it's great to get back home too!

Looking at the injury book, we only have four casualties, one with a nick, one with a bang on a joint and two, Tino Tere and Cranfield Comet, have a little bit of swelling from being castrated. Which isn't too bad really!

There were quite a few owners who called to see their horses. Many come on a Sunday, especially those who live in towns.

Walked and looked round the horses. For the time of year and with the racing lots of them have had, they looked remarkably well.

Took all the dogs for a walk, they were really excited. With being away at Newmarket it's the first opportunity I've had for a while to get the dogs out. Olly, one of my Jack Russells, often goes to a nearby caravan site in the afternoons as people feed him and the kids throw balls for him. Seeing I have been away for a bit, the little monkey won't let me out of his sight. I often take him in the car with me and he doesn't want to be missing out on that through absconding today!

[33]

MONDAY October 21

IT'S difficult now for trainers, even in Newmarket. Just read this morning that Lord John FitzGerald is quitting Graham Lodge at Newmarket to train in Germany.

It's very sad to hear of anyone packing up. Looking at John's list in the Horses in Training, he has got 25. With wages, poll tax, phone, water, electric, feed and a thousand other things to pay for living in Newmarket, I would imagine he'd need a lot more than that number of horses to make it pay.

It's getting late on in the season and we now have no chance in reaching 100 two-year-old winners, although we should still have a few winners before the season closes. It's quite mild riding out today, we still have quite a big string going out round the roads.

TUESDAY October 22

WE just cantered the horses round the Moss today, except for tomorrow's runners which were breezed up for a couple of furlongs.

Tynron Doon is going well. Although his last run at Catterick was moderate because he missed the break and, when he got behind, he didn't go out of his way to try. He is certainly playing the right notes at the moment and it would be no surprise for him to be our 142nd winner!

At Chester, Arctic Appeal was third of six from a poor draw-number six in the six furlong race. She was beaten by Yafill of Michael Stoute's.

Gorinsky was 13-2 joint favourite. He disputed the lead from halfway but then faded.

Wednesday October 23

TOLD Alan to work the horses on the grass in the middle gallop.

We have four runners today at Edinburgh. Tynron Doon was the only one with a payday. He was third in the seven furlong claimer.

Bold Mood and Cee-Jay-Ay both ran fifth at Chester. Cee-Jay missed the break like he often does. He was just running up horses' backsides. Trying to weave your way through as tight a track as Chester isn't easy. If the fool would jump out and get straight into the race he would visit the winner's enclosure more often.

We are definitely not getting the best out of him. Probably a run or two over hurdles would do him good.

Right after Chester, I go onto Doncaster, my bags are already packed and in the car.

Four of tomorrow's sales horses are also being sent to Doncaster overnight. Learnt that Sussex Stud sent a Petong yearling filly today to train.

The Jockey Club's new ruling on walkovers came in force today. Races with only one horse declared have to be reopened. The last horse to have a walkover was Diamond Mine, trained by yours truly, at Newcastle on July 27, putting £4,905 into Peter Savill's racing account. I agree entirely with the new rules. Walkovers are a farce. It certainly isn't sport.

Personally, I would go further and allow racecourses concerned to keep the place prize money if they don't receive entries or when, in jump races, horses don't finish. Years ago at Perth, Cannobie Key of ours walked over to take the Tamerrosion Cup Steeple Chase. The Clerk of the Course did a presentation to me. I never felt such a dick in my life. After that, I vowed I would do a bunk if the occasion ever arose again.

THURSDAY October 24

BACK in the Doncaster routine: First thing had a sauna and a swim. Rang home, then onto sales. It's all very well every year buying lots of yearlings, but to make room for them we have to sell some of the older horses.

Today at the Doncaster Sales we are selling Tricycling, Palacegate Gold, Make Music, Mariecurie Express and Fivesevenfiveo.

The second half of today's sales are yearlings. Tomorrow and Saturday are for yearlings only.

Our horses sold quite well considering the market wasn't great. Palacegate Gold fetched the most at 6,000 guineas. All of the horses we sold should go on to win races, as they have won or been placed often enough.

The yearlings I looked at did not turn me on at all. Most of them looked small and had more faults than I cared to live with.

Seeing as no yearlings caught my eye, and as I intended listening to Doublova's race at Pontefract, I left the sales.

Eddie O'Leary, the Irish breeder, spotted me and asked where I was galloping off to. I told him. He said to hold on, he'd come with me. We got there in plenty of time. Doublova was 4-6 favourite, she ran a good race to finish third to Reg Hollinshead's Metal Boys. After the race, we both went straight back to the sales. Still nothing caught my eye. However, like a true stayer, I remained until the last horse was sold.

Back at the Moat House, I had a quick shower and change of clothes before joining Liz and Harry Beeby for a nice steak. The waiter kept filling my wine glass up as we were talking away. I don't recall how much white wine I drank but it was more than a couple of glasses and more than I would normally have with any dinner!

FRIDAY October 25

WOKE up with a bit of a headache. My own fault. Tonight I will keep my eye on the waiter. Had a shower then rang Alan for entries, declarations and chat about working the horses. At 7.15am went down to the Moat House Health Centre for a nice swim and sauna. No sign of Derek Thompson. After his last escapade he has probably had to change hotels. Felt much better, had some breakfast then onto the sales in pursuit of some Cockerham-based winners.

The first blow I struck was an early lot - a sharp, smallish filly by Belfort, three parts sister to Defence Call, a very good two-year-old. She was a mere 700gns. Derek Ayres from the Isle of Man liked her and said he would have her straight away.

Geraldine Rees and I bought a sharp Doc Marten colt that looked a runner. He'll do for the breeze-up sales in March. Geraldine took him home to break and get ready.

Then I bought a Lochnager filly that looked just a bit backward but I liked her. She will look different in three months' time. Hughie Harris, the Northern stall handler, took this one home to break for us.

In the afternoon at Doncaster we ran Threepence first time in blinkers. He ran a big race finishing fourth to the highly rated Wolfhound.

Back to battle at the sales after racing for the evening session where there were some real nice middle-of-the-road type yearlings. Finished up buying six - five colts and one filly. First yearling bought was a grey colt by Skyliner, same sire as our Mamma's Too who was one of my last year buys and is pictured on the front page of the Doncaster October Sales Catalogue winning the Shadwell Estate Firth of Clyde Stakes at Ayr. She also won another Listed race at Newbury, the St Hugh's Stakes. Her cost price was 4,400gns.

I bought a very nice King of Spain colt, absolutely jet black in colour.

Then I acquired a Prince Rupert colt who was quite a late foal, having been born on the 20th May. He is, however, a good strong lad who will make the time up and looks like running well.

After that, a Cragador first foal from the mare, looks a nice plating type.

Grand Time, who was the first winner of her sire Clantime (who we also trained) had her full-sister ending up Cockerham bound.

Finally, a lovely cheap colt by Dreams to Reality only costing 2,000gns. This fellow is a dead ringer for Dream Talk who we trained a couple of seasons ago for Prince Yazid Saud.

Jimmy Byrne, who works for Eddie Brennan, the Irish shipping agent, looks after our horses at all the sales. He gets them wind tested, arranges transport with our office, sees to passports, etc. I left the arranging to him and went back to the Moat House for a sauna and a swim, then dinner with two glasses of white wine!

SATURDAY October 26

LAST day of the sales. There weren't many people down there. The main bunch of the yearlings looked moderate. But there was one though that stood out like a beacon above the rest-No 599, the second last one in. In this portion of the sale I must be having two birthdays this month. Days like this, there is always a bargain to be had. Most people I talked to kept saying what a bad lot they all were.

I bought a Clantime filly for 2,800gns and a Petong colt for 2,400gns. I continued looking at every yearling as they walked round the preliminary sale ring until my man of the match came in. He looked tremendous. By Mansingh, who isn't everyone's favourite sire, this fellow walked around the ring as if he owned it. Full brother to three two-year-old winners. Bidding eased up at 5,000, it was my bid. Just as Harry Beeby looked like he was going to knock him down to me David Minton, who must have been hiding in the woodwork, came in. I finished up buying the horse for 10,500gns, which was the highest price of the day.

Hugh O'Donnell, who had previously bought some nice yearlings at the Leger Sales, decided to sell them at this sale. Our Fayruz and Belfort colts, who he bought for us, were at Garry Gosney's getting broken. We did a deal that we would keep them. I told one of our owners Robert Aird about the Fayruz and he said he would like to see him.

Garry was coming to Doncaster anyway, with the Raceaid William Hill Mazaad filly. She was to be filmed walking round the paddock at Doncaster racecourse for a future televised edition of Channel-4 where Hills would promote her in the way of a raffle for a very worthy cause, the Royal Marsden Cancer Fund.

I rang Garry up and arranged for him to also bring the Fayruz colt along in his box to the sales paddock in order that Robert could see him. Robert

HILLS RACEAID
- seen here at work
on the gallops at
Cockerham.

[37]

liked the colt and bought him. Racing that afternoon, Echo-Logical was second in the Doncaster Stakes, a Listed race. Spot the Earlybird and Snowgirl ran without troubling the judge.

At Newbury in the Nursery, Fylde Flyer ran a creditable fifth of 18, giving 29lb to Don't Smile, the winner!!

SUNDAY October 27

TOOK Miami Bear and No More The Fool schooling over Gordon Richards' fences at Greystoke, and Cee-Jay-Ay over the hurdles. All the horses jumped well.

Jessie (No More The Fool) was a bit delicate but he will get better. As nice a horse as he is certainly not the most courageous horse I've ever seen. Gordon says we can bring them again. That's a better job doing it there away from home, as Jessie just sails over ours but that's because he knows them too well.

On a Sunday afternoon when it's a nice day like today, you can always rely

My old pal O.I.OYSTON, now fourteen years of age.
We often have a chat together about the good times.
You can see from the mud on him Olly loves a roll
and always picks the wettest place.

on it bringing the owners out to see their horse. Today is no exception. Yesterday's yearlings bought from Doncaster have settled in well. We have had them out ready for potential clients. It's a fairly hot seat to sit on buying as many yearlings on spec like we do, as sometimes it isn't easy to sell them on. The temperature is only luke warm with this recession. In fact, to be honest, it's cold. We have no trouble filling our yard up, thank God, but this year we seem as if we have far more people wanting to bring their home breds to us. Especially fillies as they make little money in the sales unless they are outstanding lookers and bred real well. Personally I like fillies as well as colts. If a colt has a 7lb penalty for winning a race and a filly has a 5lb sex allowance it needs to be a very good colt to give a good filly 12lbs.

In the afternoon took my dogs for a walk round the gallops and to see Olly. The old boy is in great heart. Looking at him even at his age I bet he would still win races.

MONDAY October 28

ON a very foggy day John and myself travelled down to Bath for Doublova, Grand Time and Luvly Jubly. It was so bad you could only see the last 100 yards or so. We didn't have any luck but the horses ran well enough.

Doublova went off at 2-1 favourite in the very competitive claimer, finishing sixth of the 14 to Love Returned. This filly has done us proud, she has raced for the Moss Side Racing Group for the last two seasons, winning ten of her 17 races. She has given this bunch of owners no end of pleasure. Granted, most of her races she has won have been in claimers but the filly has a 100 rating. That means she's only eligible to run at the group one courses. Places like Hamilton, Carlisle and the like have mainly a rating band of 0-70. On occasions they may stretch to 0-80. If we ran the filly in 0-100 she has an automatic top weight of ten stone. You wouldn't find her with a pair of binoculars if I were to run her in these type of races. I have no intention of running such horses for 12 months until the handicapper relents on them. Plus the fact fillies blow their minds and it's hard to keep them sweet. Like a lot of women, fillies have to be humoured and not knocked about. If they are chasing horses' backsides time after time it isn't long before they get mulish and throw the towel in.

Anyway, Doublova will now be sold at Newmarket Sales on Wednesday. Although she has a fair bit of mileage on her clock, when her racing days are over she will make a cracking brood mare.

Completed a deal with The Sporting Life to have their advert painted on the backs of our three horse-boxes. Nice to be associated with the Life again after so many years. Our boxes were the first ones to carry advertisements. I thought of the idea in 1965 when I was laid up in Lincoln Hospital with back injuries from a fall at Market Rasen.

TUESDAY October 29

CANTERED all the horses round our peat moss gallop. John Carroll and I went to Redcar. Master Eurolink was third in the maiden two-year-old race. Diamond Mine ran a big race in the £100,000 Racecall Trophy to finish fifth of 25 runners. Only beaten three and a half lengths. It's a cracking race this, Distinctly North was second in it last year. It's a race very high on my agenda to take back to Cockerham. This is only the race's second year of running so no doubt I will be back. The race was thought up by Lord Zetland and his son with J Berry written all over it.

After the race Diamond Mine was put in a Newmarket horsebox as he's been put up for public auction tomorrow at Newmarket Sales. Hilary Kerr asked me to sign some injured jockey calendars, they sell like hot cakes for Christmas.

At Leicester Laurel Queen won her sixth race of the season ridden by Gary Carter. She has been a good filly for Laurel Racing Club. Bill Sutcliffe, a local farmer and horse hater pleaded guilty today to driving and not stopping when causing one of our girls, Jo Webster, to get dropped from Laurel Queen a few weeks ago. He was fined £100. I wonder if he had a few bob on her at Leicester today. I doubt it. I would think he would rather bet his Mrs half a dozen eggs which cow was going to calf first.

Back home the vet came and cut Tynron Doon and Chateau Nord.

It was great to see Loki win at Redcar for Geoff Lewis and his team to record their 40th win of the season and land a touch of some £100,000. Well done! Just about everyone in racing was rooting for them.

WEDNESDAY October 30

WE haven't got an owner for Caesar yet, the two-year-old I bought from Phil Canty to run on the all-weather. Over these past three weeks we have galloped him a few times. Some horses can't help being slow but this bugger abuses it. Working him with some of our most moderate performers Caesar never showed us much speed. I rang up Steve Wiles to come and collect him and put him in the sales with a single fare. At least he is a decent ride and would probably make a jumper. We don't have the time to hang on to these types of horses.

Finally completed the sale of Prohibition (Ben) to Geoff Lewis. He took him when he only wanted a couple more winners to reach the forty. Although Geoff had his 40th winner yesterday we have been negotiating this deal for a few days and it's still gone ahead. A couple of Geoff's winners were on the all-weather surface and there may be a doubt about them counting. Hopefully Ben will add to Geoff's total.

Drove to Newmarket Sales. We sold Castle Cloud, Doublova, Ellebanna, Luvly Jubly, Spot the Earlybird, Diamond Mine and Tenacity. Top price fetched 41,000gns, bottom 5,200gns, so all in all we had a good sale.

Mr Massimi, the Italian trainer, asked me if we had a horse in the sale as good as Whittingham because he knew we had trained him. We only ran him twice here and he won them both. After that we took him to Italy where he won a Listed race for us, only to be sold to stay in that country afterwards.

Diamond Mine is a better horse than him. It was only yesterday he ran fifth at Redcar in the £100,000 Racecall Trophy. At least the man listened and bought him. I hope he proves what I say about him being a better horse ability-wise, although Whittingham has won some good races in Italy since we sold him, and that's good. When you sell people good horses and they turn out to produce what you tell them they will always come back.

Looking at the film The Godfather, one wouldn't be wanting to tell those people untruths!

THURSDAY October 31

THIS morning is a real struggle as it's raining like the clappers. In this part of the world when it rains it never knows when to stop.

Now, after our culling of horses at Newmarket yesterday, and the end of the season in sight, we have quite a few empty boxes. This will give us an opportunity to keep up with painting and disinfecting the stables before collecting some of our yearlings and bringing them to Cockerham. We can then get on with them.

We have no runners today. Heather Bank runs tomorrow at Newmarket but he is already down there as he went with the sale horses. Amanda rang at 7 o'clock and I told her to give him a bit of work over a couple of furlongs. I placed an advert in the papers to try and get a few punters to relieve us of some of these yearlings. I would love to be leading trainer, but I have no intentions of becoming leading owner.

Sharp Anne has been a good servant to us. She went to Reg and Jenny Leah's home as she is now retired and going to stud. We are sending Another Episode to keep her company for the winter.

It rained so hard we walked and trotted the horses round the indoor school before we cantered. By doing this we held the yearlings up. The "breaking" team wanted to work with them in the school out of the rain too.

Had a shower when we finished work, I was wet right through to my underpants.

It was still raining at stable time. To be fair though we can do with it. Lots of the racecourses are riding firm and that is particularly bad for the jumpers. Our gallops can do with the rain also.

FRIDAY November 1

NOW the Flat season is winding down we have several empty boxes and it gives us a chance to wash, disinfect and paint them. That's what we are doing now. With the weather still mild thankfully they are drying out well. In the post came a statement for the horse Fivesevenfiveo we sold at Doncaster Sales in October. With all the additional charges, the end result was the very same figure as the horse's name.

Graham Lyle the Leeds bookmaker is a game fellow. He once laid me 100-1 for £50 our yard wouldn't train a hundred seconds in a season. Lucky for me we did. Graham presented me with the cheque in the second enclosure at York. What odds would he have laid on our filly fetching £5,750 in the Sales ring on behalf of her owners Clayton Engineering Ltd?-How about 5,750-1!. The filly was a good buy for racing or breeding. She won five races worth £18,835 and was also placed six times.

SATURDAY November 2

THE yearlings are coming on nicely. We are driving them all over, down the lane, round the gallops, through open stalls. I'm very pleased with them. Nowadays they are a lot better to handle. In fact some of the yearlings are very near broken when we buy them at the sales.

Breeders' Cup day from Churchill Downs live on TV. What a treat for us. The prize money is mind-boggling. It makes our prizes look like chicken feed.

Alex Scott's top sprinter, Sheikh Albadou gets a peach of a ride from our champion jockey Pat Eddery in the Breeders' Cup Sprint, winning in the most impressive style. This is only the second win for Britain since the Breeders' Cup series started in 1984.

Learning Sheikh Albadou stays in training next year I shall have to be having a word or two with our Paris House about him pulling his finger out.

Shadayid, ridden by Willie Carson, ran well enough in the Mile.

Arazi, in the Juvenile was nothing short of brilliant. Until today I thought Rodrigo de Triano was the better of the two. For me, Arazi's run today first time on dirt must be the performance of the year. Without a shadow of doubt that was the best performance I have ever seen a two-year-old put up. If I ever see it again I hope it's trained by J Berry.

Arazi would most certainly get my vote for Horse of the Year and I watched Generous win the Epsom Derby!

It's the first mash night in the new month. We worm all the yearlings every month until Spring time when they start running. It's very important to worm horses. You can give the horses the best food available but if they are not wormed on a regular basis, it's no good. In fact, if it wasn't for the fear of showing up positive in tests at the races I would worm my horses once a month throughout their lives. It's great to feed horses. It's no good feeding worms.

ARAZI and Pat Valenzuela
winning the Breeders' Cup Juvenile.
It was the best performance I have ever seen from a two-year-old.

SUNDAY November 3

MET Phil Tuck and Neale Doughty at Gordon Richards' with Cee-Jay-Ay, Jessie and the Bear. Off we go over Gordon's hurdles, tyres, all sorts of obstacles. The three horses were jumping out of their skins and loving it, and so were we. Phil and Neale popped the Bear and Jessie twice over fences. They were brilliant, never put a foot wrong. I would have loved to have gone over them with Cee-Jay-Ay, but he is only a four-year-old hurdler.

We rode them all back to the horsebox talking about what a performance Arazi put up and comparing him with such good horses in the past. Neale was reckoning how many novice hurdle winners around Catterick he'd have to ride to equal Arazi's Breeders' Cup prize of £269,430! We also discussed Sheikh Albadou winning the big sprint and Phil's new role of stewarding. How Gordon gave them bollockings from time to time but we had some good laughs, it was great. Phil can even imitate Gordon to a tee!

Our dogs seem to know when it's Sunday. They were all waiting for me to take them for a walk on my return from Gordon's. So off I go, loaded up with polos for O I Oyston and his pal, Tiny Tim. It's very mild still for the time of year and the going on our gallops is perfect.

Here's Olly and his best friend Tiny Tim,
enjoying the quiet life.

On the top moss gallop it is so open with very little shelter. I have mentally picked out a few places where some trees can be planted. John Nixon, the builder, has a nursery. I will have a word with him and see if he can plant a few for me.

This ground up here is great for the horses to work on. It's solid peat. When we first came to Cockerham the land was really wet. We put in drains everywhere and it's very good now. On this West coast we get more than our share of rain so the going never gets any real jar to it. In summer, it's the best going anywhere. Tony Dickinson, when he was training at Guisburn, used to bring his jumpers down to work when the going was firm on his own gallops.

MONDAY November 4

BIG headlines in The Sporting Life-Arazi accolade. Jockey Club handicapper Geoffrey Gibbs paid the ultimate compliment to Arazi's brilliant display by saying it was the best performance from a two-year-old he has ever seen and he will never see it bettered. It is good for racing, or any sport, when something crops up like this. Similar tributes flooded in when Cassius Clay came into boxing.

Most of our yearlings have hind shoes on now and are going well enough for them to be allowed round the roads. Riding Palacegate King I led them the long way on the roads to a farm down our lanes called Baxters. We mainly walk them as too much trotting on the hard surface does their legs no good. I like them to walk on, trot steady, canter slow and gallop fast.

This time of year on the Lancashire coast we get plenty of wind and rain. To help keep the yearlings as warm as possible we trace clip them so they don't sweat too much. If it's raining we ride them out in waterproof hoods and if it's very heavy they're ridden out in waterproof sheets. I am not a great believer in mollycoddling them too much by giving them a lot of indoor work. When we get them ridden off and going well I like them outside in the fresh air, not indoors. I also like them ridden in boots in front, as they are often not very mature at this stage and very easily knock their joints.

All the old horses went round to Baxters for road work except for tomorrow's runners at Hamilton. To liven them up, we let them jump out of the stalls for a couple of furlongs.

Nil Nisi Nixu goes well at home but when he gets on the racecourse he doesn't show a lot of bottle. When I bought this fellow for Robert Aird at Calder Park Sales in Florida I was so excited. He was doing a good time when he breezed out, coverering the two furlongs in 23 seconds. It nearly takes him that in minutes now. We just seem to have lost him unless he hasn't acclimatised properly yet. If he doesn't pull his finger out tomorrow, he can do his acclimatising somewhere else. It takes the same amount of money to keep a bad horse as a good one.

The clipping machines are flat out clipping the yearlings at the moment. Jo is busy getting them all fitted out in their new rugs. One little monkey has chewed two rugs to shreds so Jo has put him in a bib. That way he can't get hold of it. They are just like naughty kids, some of them.

TUESDAY November 5

CANTERED all the old horses round our top moss and some of the yearlings cantered quietly round the ring. At the moment they are all at different stages of their education. Some are lunged and some are driven but all in all they are coming good. We have put them on another course of

Fulcin as a bit of ringworm is breaking out here and there. If they get Fulcin in their systems it helps to build up an immunity to it. Although a ten-day course is quite expensive, it's cheap if it keeps ringworm away.

John and I set off for Hamilton today at 9.00am. Although J Berry is leading trainer and John Carroll's leading jockey at Hamilton, I can't see Bold Mood or Nil Nisi Nixu setting Hamilton Park turf alight today, even with it being Bonfire Night.

Prohibition, who we sold to Geoff Lewis, looks nailed on in the five furlong seller, 4-6 in the betting and every single tipster tips him. I hope he wins for Geoff and his staff. It's a long miserable journey up that A74 and the police are very keen on that road. Mind, it's no wonder, there have been some awful accidents on it.

No luck with Bold Mood. He ran in the middle and the other fellow was an also ran. Prohibition also got well stuffed and only finished third. Just shows there are no certainties.

John and I stopped at Southwaite Service area on the way back for a tea and a fag for John, as I won't allow smoking in my car.

WEDNESDAY November 6

WORKED the horses that are left to run but, from now on, things taper off as the season comes to an end. At one time, we looked to reach 100 two-year-old winners. From now on, we haven't many runners left, but we will be back battling next year!

I rode Miami Bear and No More The Fool strode out with John Carroll for six furlongs to get them in trim for Friday at Hexham. They are to compete in a charity race for the BBC Children In Need. The reason these two are in is because the race didn't fill and I put our two jumpers in to make up the numbers.

My pitbull terrier Victor was taken to a vet in Chorley by Ruby, our secretary. If you happen to see a dog with ED2845B tattooed on the inside of his near hind leg wandering about, soft as a brush, answering to Victor, give me a ring and I will come and collect him.

It looks as if Sherlock Holmes will have to make a comeback to sort out the mystery surrounding Robert Maxwell's body, found in the sea.

We have had another schooling day with the yearlings on the horse walkers. We lead them round in sixes then gradually clip them onto the walkers, still walking alongside them, until they are used to being tied up to the machine. They are all pretty good now so, in future, they can be clipped straight on. Lots of people don't agree with walkers but I like them. Our horses would go on them an average of twice a week. In summer, when we have worked the horses and they are sweaty, we wash them off and put them on the walkers until they have dried. Then afterwards we take them for a pick of grass. The walkers are good for horses with knocks or injuries if one doesn't want weight on their backs.

THURSDAY November 7

MOST of the horses did road work. Just a few of the older ones that are likely to run shortly had a canter.

John and I travelled up to Edinburgh. Palacegate King ran fifth in a moderate contest but I like this horse. I think he needs a bit more time. I'll keep him in training for the all-weather in the New Year. He has a bit of foot but he's weak. Edinburgh racecourse presented me with a trophy and champagne for being the season's leading trainer there.

Watched Battle of Britain win at Lingfield on SIS, beating Palacegate Racing, also ours, by a neck in a ding-dong finish. The betting in this race, 11-4 and 3-1, our two being the market leaders. These same two horses ran together at Catterick and they finished the other way round. This win gave us our 90th two-year-old winner of the season.

After the race, Battle of Britain was claimed for 6,200 guineas by Mr Geoff Davies. The horse was a competition prize, to be owned for one year (put up by The Sunday Mirror and The Sporting Life as a moneyraiser for the RAF). The lease, keep and all expense paid. It was won by Mike Goddard who worked in computers. The prize could not have been won by a more deserving bloke. Mike really got into it and enjoyed the horse and all the build-up to the races. He called a few times to see him at the yard and always had a day off work to see him run. Mike had a lot of fun with him.

FRIDAY November 8

HERE at Hexham racecourse, The National Association of Bookmakers very kindly sponsored the BBC Children In Need Appeal Celebrity Race. Jonjo O'Neill, Tom O'Ryan, Bob Champion, Frazer Hines, Mark Todd, Lord Oaksey, Nigel Tinkler, Ron Barry, Phil Tuck and myself all rode in it. No More The Fool won the prize for the best turned out horse, which was a holiday for four to the Wonderwest World of Ayr. The race was won by Rock Face, ridden by Nigel Tinkler and trained by Sir Mark Prescott.

After the fifth race, I was asked to auction for the appeal a magnum of Croft Distinction Port. Ken Oliver, the Scottish trainer, very kindly gave £150 for it. The same amount of money was generously given by Brian Dunn, the Northern bookmaker, for a signed and framed photograph of the previous year's riders when the race was run at Sedgefield.

There was a 'Talk-In' Show after racing. We had a bit of fun and raised over £6,000 for the kids.

Kinlet Vision, a horse owned by a few of us which includes A K Collins, of Gay Future Cartmel fame, Bob Willis, David Brown and myself, ran a good race to finish third.

Alan flew off today to stay with Sam in Tenerife for a week. The Marchioness of Tavistock travelled up to Cockerham with her driver in their horsebox to deliver one of her yearlings to us. Martin, Amanda and Linda, our travelling head people, needn't worry. She didn't ask for their jobs.

Here I am pictured whilst conducting an auction for the BBC Children In Need Appeal at Hexham.

SATURDAY November 9

TODAY is the last day of Flat racing in the North and we have no runners. Folkestone next Monday is the very last meeting of the season.

We have had a cracking season, having won 143 races. I suppose if we have a next target it will have to be 150 winners in a season. Seeing this amount of winners is still only second to Henry Cecil's 180 it will be very hard to equal that, never mind beat it.

Next season, if we are lucky enough to train a Group 1 winner and reach the hundred, I will be delighted. It's a nice feeling now to know we don't have to tear away every day racing. To spend time with these yearlings is great. They are so innocent. It's so exciting to school them and bring them along, especially when they win first time out on a racecourse. You can have a look at them in the winning enclosure and be proud. Just like parents would be when their kids have done something clever.

Lots of the horses have been roughed off. Some have gone home for the winter and quite a few that we are going to keep on as three-year-olds have been cut.

A nice Music Boy colt of Heathavon Stud came today. I love those Music

Boys. Fylde Flyer is a Music Boy and could be a nice three-year-old next year.

The horses that are in at Doncaster Sales did a long steady canter with Miami Bear and (Jessie) No More The Fool. So they will keep looking well and stop them getting too fresh.

Miami Bear is going really well. With a bit of luck, himself and Jessie should give their owners quite a lot of fun this winter. Come to that, me too, as I love a day's jumping.

SUNDAY November 10

THIS morning is really fresh and sunny. For the third Sunday on the trot we have schooled Miami Bear and No More The Fool at Gordon's. Like last week ridden by Phil Tuck and Neale Doughty, they jumped like bucks. If these two go on and win chases I will have to tell the Press they are trained jointly by G W Richards and J Berry!

I arranged to drop them both off at Phil Tuck's yard as we have permission for the pair of them to have a pop around Carlisle after racing on Tuesday. Phil only lives a few miles from Carlisle. It was mid-afternoon when I got home. We had quite a few owners down to look at their horses. A nice day always brings them out.

Later in the afternoon I walked my pack of dogs round the farm and the gallops. It's great doing this, one of the best parts of my life. I get time to think and the dogs don't keep talking. Sometimes a hare gets up and we have a bit of fun. In the evening I treated Jo to a meal at The Orchard, an Italian restaurant at Broughton. That's about eight miles from Cockerham. Ivan Bragagnini, the boss man there, had a filly in training with us called Miss Pinocchio. She won him a couple of races. The waiters are all racing mad. They follow our yard and are chuffed to bits when we are on a roll.

MONDAY November 11

THIS evening yours truly is guest of honour at the Stable Lads' Amateur Boxing National Championship Finals.

It's a fairly quiet day with the horses. Just breaking yearlings. Some are having road work, some are being driven in long reins, others are being lunged and so on.

Around mid-morning I met Colin Nutter, John Brown and Tom Bibby in order to catch the London train to take us to the finals at the London Hilton Hotel. We got a cab at Euston Station to the Park International Hotel, Cromwell Road, Kensington, where being very English and civilised we had afternoon tea. Colin and myself went for a walk afterwards.

[49]

Back at the hotel I had a bath and started to get changed for the highlight of the evening. Jo as usual had packed my gear. She had put everything in except my dickie-bow. Ringing down to reception I asked whether they sold dickie-bows. On being told they didn't I enquired if one of the waiters could lend me one but they couldn't. Fortunately Colin Nutter carried a spare.

The trustees met us in the Coronation Room at the Hilton at 6.30 where we had a couple of drinks before going in for dinner.

After dinner Harry Beeby, the Boxing Chairman, made a speech in which I had a few mentions. He also presented me with a beautifully hand-made

Steve Williams receives his award from me after his victory in the Stable Lads' Boxing contest.

red shirt. Unknown to me Jo had sent him one of my own red shirts to get a fitting from. Following this my turn came to have a little go on the mike. Peter O'Sullevan took it in turns with Harry at doing a very important job as part of the evening's proceedings; auctioneering the items people had donated. Some of the items were really good and were worth a lot of money. The fifteen auctioned items realised in the region of £30,000!

A few years ago the whip Lester Piggott snatched, or borrowed, in a hurry from Alain Lequeux whilst riding in France, was auctioned twice, raising £8,000. Bjorn Borg's broken tennis racquet raised over £1,000.

Then came the boxing. It was, as always, brilliant. The bouts ranged from

6st 7lb juniors to 10st 7lb seniors. All the boxers gave 100 per cent. There was some excellent boxing. I am sure some of these lads could box for a living.

TUESDAY November 12

CAUGHT the early morning train from Euston to Lancaster. Read The Sporting Life and The Racing Post on the train. See Steve Smith Eccles rode his eight hundreth winner yesterday. Well done, Steve.

Both papers gave the previous night's boxing a good and fair account of the programme. I must say I felt sorry for Stewart Pair who had announced earlier he was to retire from the ring. In a real battle from the word go, he and Michael Carter, both Southern pairs, fought really well. It was a shame there had to be a loser. In my reckoning it was very close. The issue was possibly swayed in Michael's direction because he may have just finished the stronger.

Colin Nutter did a bit of boxing, he also was a promoter for a time. John and Tom are very keen on boxing. We all four go down every year, so you can imagine the crack was good on the way home. We said our farewells at Lancaster, then I collected my car from the station car park.

At stable time, I looked at all the horses.

In the evening, Jo and I went to the Cock of the North dinner dance in the Shirley Heights Suite at York racecourse. On the way there I rang Phil Tuck from the carphone to see how our potential chasers fared round Carlisle. Phil was over the moon. They both had jumped very well.

The Cock of the North Champion this year was none other than our own John Carroll. Most of the Northern jockeys were there at York as well as other notable racing personalities. Mark Birch who has held the title himself a number of times did a presentation to John. I also presented him with a trophy as a small token of our appreciation.

Unfortunately I drew the short straw for the driving home. So I only had two glasses of white wine. Poor old John wasn't feeling well with a tummy upset and had to leave quite early.

WEDNESDAY November 13

JO drove a couple of yearlings then she went to her mother's at Beverley and stayed overnight to help her pack her things up as she is coming to live in one of our bungalows. It must be sad for her in a way as she has lived all her life over there. But she is getting on and Jo can keep an eye on her over here.

I rode Palacegate Gold and gave the yearlings a lead round to Smiths, a farm half an hour down the road. Then we had a hack round the indoor school. They are coming together nicely. All of them whether they are led, driven or ridden come through the open starting stalls that we have at the entrance into the yard easy. Just as if you or I are walking through a door. A lot of the yearlings have been trace clipped. Only the odd one gives us any problems. But mainly they are good. As we get riding them our farrier, Alan Worthington, shoes them up behind. They all arrive with fronts on but very seldom with hinds.

THURSDAY November 14

IT'S very busy at the yard at the moment with the yearlings. For me it's as good a time of year as any. Some horses are being ridden, some lunged, some driven. They are going all directions until we pack up at lunch time. The clipping machines are flat out. The blacksmiths are hammering away. There always seems more people about, this is probably because there is hardly any racing on for us. Vets are in the yards writing up the naming forms. The place is sure busy.

In the afternoon Martin brings back Jo's mum's belongings in one of our horseboxes. Jo comes back in her car with her mum and her mother's black labrador Sam, that I gave her about twelve years ago. Three or four times he has nearly left us. They must have a good vet in Beverley, as Sam has made some remarkable recoveries.

FRIDAY November 15

ALAN arrived back today from Sam's in Tenerife looking nice and brown. John Corbett, the bloodstock agent rang asking if we have a three-year-old for sale to race in Macau. Ken Oliver and Jo own Down the Middle between them. He has won them five races trained by us. We sent him up to Ken's to go hurdling. That very day Ken said he wasn't taking to jumping. I told John about this fellow. He said he could come on Saturday night along with Noel Barrett-Morton, book into a hotel near us and come Sunday morning to see him. That seemed fine to me, it will give us a chance to get the horse down from Scotland. I arranged with Ken for him to take the horse to Catterick tomorrow where our box could pick him up.

Chateau Nord had a touch of colic but was all right after having medication and a lead out.

Gwen and Fred Viner travelled up from Lightwater near Ascot and arrived in the afternoon. They are staying with us along with Bridget and Gerry Blum for our end of season party tomorrow night. The last time Fred came up in March, when we went to Andrea Campion's party, he forgot his shoes and came up in slippers. I'm glad to say he's in shoes today!

Bill Sutcliffe, the local farmer, has hit Flash's wife Heather's car with his trailer. He seems to go out of his way to cause trouble. Flash went down to his farm to see him but it's impossible to reason with him. One of these days someone will give him a crack.

We had an evening meal at the Crofters, a restaurant near us, with Nan and Bill Robertson, Elaine and Robert Aird and Gwen and Fred Viner. Tricia Harrison and Pat Knight are also staying at the Crofters this weekend because of our party tomorrow night. They joined us for a drink before we went in for our meal. It was well after 9.00pm before we actually sat down. Bill and I both ordered a medium rump stake. When they arrived they were nearly burnt, not a bit of moisture was left in them. Honestly they were just like leather. The manager said it was because the waiter hadn't told the chef how we wanted the stakes cooked.

"That's an excuse," I said, "the prat must have fallen asleep when he put them under the grill."

"We don't employ prats, sir," he replied.

"You must have another name for them," I said, and we left it at that.

It was a shame really because everybody else had a lovely meal and normally the food IS good there!

SATURDAY November 16

RODE out with two lots of yearlings. Hacked them in figure of eights in one of the paddocks.

Picked Tricia and Pat up at the Manor pub car park before going onto Leeds for a book-signing session to promote my book "It's Tougher At The Bottom." My publisher, Rupert Mackeson has arranged the event at Austicks book shop from 12.30pm. It was nice to see one of the characters from the book there-my old pal Eddie Foster. He came and bought a book for me to sign. I wouldn't have known him only he said: "Would you sign it to Eddie Foster?"

We did have intentions of going onto Catterick races, as Kinlet Vision, the horse I have a small investment in was running in the 2.45pm. Time however passed and it gave us little hope of getting to Catterick for our race. (Luckily for us we didn't set off as we found out later that racing was abandoned after the second). That gave us more of a chance to get organised for the party.

Our party started at 8.00pm in Cockerham Village Hall. We had about 300 guests. People came from as far afield as Ascot and Scotland. We booked up most of the local accommodation for their overnight stay.

We had a really good disco which kept going non-stop. Our lads and lasses definitely seemed to put more energy into their dancing than they do when they are mucking out. Some of them are great movers. Everybody appeared to enjoy themselves and only one, that I saw, was ill with drink. I am not telling tales, but he was up the following morning at 5.20am feeding the horses.

The party finished about 1.00am but Jo and I stayed back and tidied up as this is part of the contract for renting the hall. The next day an antiques fair was to be held there and it had to be left as it was found for the next event.

SUNDAY November 17

JO and I finally got to bed at 3.30am.

I got up after about four hours sleep, Jo followed a bit later.

We have Miami Bear in at Bangor-on-Dee, Monday, so I rode him three furlongs on the grass. He's flying, never felt better. I'm looking forward to this fellow running tomorrow in his first novice chase. Neale Doughty rang to say his boss Gordon Richards is sending him to Leicester. I asked my old mate Steve Smith Eccles to ride him but he's at Leicester too. So Mark Perrett came in for the ride.

We have a busy day ahead with owners calling. Gerry and Bridget left early before breakfast. Gwen and Fred after breakfast. John Corbett and Noel Barrett-Morton liked Down the Middle and bought him. Nan and Bill Robertson, and Elaine and Robert Aird came to look at the yearlings again. They have decided to have the big strong Ballad Rock chesnut colt and also the Absalom colt who looks sharp. They decided on two names for the Ballad Rock yearling and Robert's Fayruz yearling bought in September. They will be very appropriate if they get them; Time Will Tell and Make It Happen!

There's a phone call from Jim Naughton's wife. He was having a nice Mazaad colt which I bought at Fairyhouse but he's changed his mind after he got the bill. Jo said he was a timewaster at the offset.

Gary Moss, one of our ex-lads who is now helping to run the Wells Springs public house in the Pendle Hills, stayed overnight at the hostel following the party. On his way home this morning he met one of our apprentices Willie Hollick driving to work and crashed into each other. Luckily no one was hurt. Gary made a mess of his nice car. Willie's old banger hadn't a mark on it!

MONDAY November 18

DONCASTER November Sales are held from today until November 21, but I won't be going until tomorrow. On the front cover of their catalogue is a photo of our horse, Another Episode, who was bought at Doncaster the previous year at the Breeze-Up sales for 12,000gns. He went on to win five races, including a Listed race and was Group placed. He was timed at

9.51sec for the third furlong of his run in the Molecomb Stakes at Goodwood. This means he was travelling at 47mph. On this time he surely should
rank as the world's speediest horse. In the Guinness Book of Records Klute
has this title. But Klute had a match with two of our horses So Careful at
Haydock and Valdermoza at Catterick. Neither of them broke sweat to beat
Klute out of sight. So that horse's time has to be iffy!

Funnily enough the day I bought Another Episode I sold him to one of
Barnsley trainer Steve Norton's owners to stay in our yard. The man rang
the following day to say he had been drinking and had got carried away,
would I send him his cheque back.

The bride and I went to Bangor-on-Dee to see Miami Bear in his first run in
a novice chase.

The first race on the card was won by one of our former inmates, Whippers
Delight who had won a couple of races for us. He's now trained by Gareth
Charles-Jones. It's nice to see he's still winning.

The Bear, in his race, gave an exhibition of
jumping leading all the way round until the
second last fence, where he jumped well
but landed a bit steep. For this he paid the
penalty by ending up on the deck. I was
standing down at the last fence and walked
back with Mark Perrett. Poor old Mark
(left) was sick as the Bear had been jumping so well for him and was certain to have
been in the frame.

TUESDAY November 19

I WENT to Doncaster Sales. We had nine horses in. I let them all be sold
except for Echo-Logical who I bought in for 10,000gns. He is a newspaper
owned horse. We didn't really want to sell him but he had to go to public
auction so the readers could get paid out or reinvest in a share.

Echo had won two races and been placed in a Listed race on his final run of
the season at Doncaster.

I would have liked to have gone to Wetherby as our yard sponsored the first
race, the Jack Berry Selling Hurdle race, in aid of the International Spinal
Research Trust. Jo went in my place to present the trophy. The race was
won by Palacegate Corporation Ltd., who own Abigail's Dream. They have
several horses in training with us for the Flat.

In the evening John Carroll, Tracy, Jo and myself went to Blackpool for a
dinner organised by the Blackpool Evening Gazette to celebrate their horse
Fylde Flyer winning four races. It was a first class night. There were 300
members present to enjoy it. We watched videos of the horse's wins and I
talked them through the races as it was happening. They were cheering like

mad when he won. It's nice when ordinary people like these get a good horse. They get involved and are so appreciative.

During the course of the evening Mary and Jack Greenwood held a raffle in aid of the Poulton-Le-Fylde Hospice.

WEDNESDAY November 20

AT 7.30am John Carroll rode Cee-Jay-Ay and I rode No More The Fool (Jessie) up the last four furlongs of the all-weather, to blow them out as Jessie runs in the novice chase at Haydock tomorrow.

The yearlings did a steady canter in pairs twice round the three furlong ring. Our yard sponsors the amateur boxing which is to be held tonight at the Imperial Hotel in Blackpool. I am looking forward to that, those little fellows are like tigers in the ring.

The chairman of the Blackpool Sportsmans Aid Society asked me today if I would be prepared to serve on their committee. I had to decline because of my racing commitments. I didn't feel I could give it 100 per cent.

The boxing was very good. All our owners who were present enjoyed themselves. When the boxing finished at about 11.15pm we went to the Castle Casino to have a little flutter and some breakfast. I've just got home, it's 2.10am and I'm making myself a cup of tea.

THURSDAY November 21

A LOVELY day at Cockerham. We had our yearlings hacking around the all-weather gallop in pairs. They are a lovely sight, for sure. At this stage I could not be more pleased with them.

Today there's a nice photo and write-up about John Carroll in Julian Armfield's Jockey Column in The Sporting Life.

What do you think happened at Haydock?

There were only six runners in "Jessie's" race. Perfectly Possible and Wayside Boy fell at the second fence and Jessie was second or third most of the way, jumping for fun. He was upsides going to the last when he got a bit too close, and for doing so, finished up on his backside. Poor old lad didn't deserve that. Thankfully he's all right. The only consolation was that he had won the prize for the best turned out. At least he was sensible and ran to the paddock entrance to be caught. Not like a few years ago when Nerine, a chaser of ours, fell at Ludlow. She crossed a railway line and galloped for a few miles on the roads. Her feet were worn right down nearly to the coronet band. All the next day she lay on her side in her stable moaning and groaning. She couldn't put her feet on the floor with the pain.

FRIDAY November 22

JESSIE is just a little bit stiff but not too bad. He soon walked it off.

Jo has taken her mother out for the day to Preston as it's her 82nd birthday. By the look of her today she'll out-stay me. There's no wonder Jo keeps on to me to make my will out if she takes after her mum.

I went to Lancaster cattle market when we finished riding out. I didn't buy any. The stores were quite dear and they were mainly heifers and we only keep bullocks on. Children in Need was on the television in the evening. We watched it until the early hours of the morning. It shows there are some nice people around the way they rallied round for the kids.

SATURDAY November 23

JOHN Carroll has gone on his holidays to America for three weeks with Tracy, his wife and Danielle, their young daughter.

It will do him good to recharge his batteries. When he comes back he will be raring to go. A good man John, he works his pants off to ride winners. It isn't often he throws a race away. If he rides a moderate race, which at times all jockeys do, you don't have to tell him. He knows, but he learns from it. The last thing jockeys want is stupid owners and trainers laying into them over riding a bad race. That doesn't do their confidence any good at all. The majority of the time, the people are talking out of their pockets anyway.

I rode Jessie round the roads for an hour. He has got over his race now.

Alan and I had a meeting with John Nixon to sort out a couple of drains in the middle yard that have been blocking up ever since we built the hostel and the bungalows. We came to the conclusion that new drains will have to be put in and routed a different way. In due course, we are going to have new horse walkers and a covered-in ring to ride the yearlings round in bad weather. Now our string has got bigger, the indoor school gets congested when we collect the horses up before we set off to ride round the roads. The covered ring will be much safer. In view of these extensions taking place shortly, we have decided the drains should be re-routed to where the new walkers will go. The drains from that area will be piped away the same route.

Our yearlings are going well. We have quite a few ridden away and hacking in figures of eight. When we get to the stage of cantering them, we trace clip them to minimise the risks of colds from sweating too much. It also stops them getting sore around their girths. A few of them are already a bit sore there now where the girths chafe. Sometimes it can be caused by a kind of pox and, if one's not careful, it can pass from one to another unless the girths are disinfected and scrubbed every time they are used. When the horses have this condition, it's advisable to give them a course of Fulcin.

[57]

SUNDAY November 24

MR and Mrs Darlington called to take some photos of the Race Aid horse. Mrs Darlington wrote to me some time ago asking if she could visit the yard. As it turned out, she works for William Hill in Blackpool and wanted to have some photos of the horse to promote the cause in her shop.

Terry Holdcroft, who is responsible for my sponsored car, rang about the car going back as our contract is up. Jo mentioned she is not at all happy with her new car. She wants some wider wheels on like she had on the other one and some spoilers fitted.

The Domynsky colt is down with a touch of colic. The vet was called and has given him an injection.

A set of starting stalls arrived today. We were only going to be allowed £600 in part exchange so we had the old ones done up for £1,553.80. Like brand new they are now. In all, we have four sets of stalls. One set is placed outside the yard so the yearlings walk through them daily. The others are on different parts of the gallops. The majority of the time these are open while the horses are driven in strings through them so they can get used to them. After 1.00pm the owners start arriving to see their horses. Mike Burrows came to draw up the plans to build the new horse walkers with an indoor cantering ring around them. More expense!

MONDAY November 25

GOT up early as I had a few things to do before setting off for Newmarket Sales at 6.00am. As I went to fetch the car, my shadow Olly (the dog) jumped in as soon as I opened the door and sat on the passenger seat, ready to ride shotgun. I told him he wasn't coming all the way to Newmarket. His eyes pleaded with me. The poor little bugger would go through fire and water for me so what can I do?

The roads were very busy even that early in the morning. My main objective for going to the sales was to see Paris House's half-sister. Really, I need more yearlings like I need a hole in my head. I still have to sell some from previous sales. It's a good job I have an understanding wife and bank manager.

Seeing the filly, there was a lot to like about her and there was also a fair bit not to like her for. She was small and turned her near-fore out. Paris House is by Petong. This filly is by Presidium. Still, she moved well and had a bit of presence. Yes, I will have a go. I kicked on and bought her for 7,000 guineas. No owner in mind. Like I said, it seems to suit me living dangerously.

Derek Ayres, one of our owners from the Isle of Man, liked a Belfort filly of Noel Souter's. We trained her half-sister, Tamara's Twinkle, to win a couple of races. This filly, unfortunately, has only sight in one eye, but she also finished up in a red, white and blue horsebox, Cockerham bound.

On my return home, I fed Olly and went into the office to get something. I discovered some berk had locked Sol, our Labrador, in there accidentally. Although he is seven or eight years old, Sol flaps if he is on his own for any length of time. He had pulled the curtains down, chewed up a table and made a right mess scratching on the inside door that had only recently been renewed. The whole office, in fact, has only just been done up. There couldn't have been a bigger mess if we'd been burgled.

SOL : Seen here in a more relaxed pose.

TUESDAY November 26

THIS morning I had to set off early, 5.30am, to go to Ascot Sales to sell Elton Ledger and Crestwood Lad. Olly always comes to the car with me in the hope of coming with me. Not today old pal. You had enough yesterday. At 5.45am, driving onto junction 33 of the M6 motorway, it's just like yesterday, very busy. Where on earth is all the traffic going? If there's a recession now, what will the roads be like if we ever see a boom again? Thank goodness that's the last of the sales for us this season.

At times it's awful selling some of the horses. Elton Ledger was a partnership horse. The lads who owned him didn't want to sell him, they were forced to as their businesses are going bad. Pat, one of the partners, had an appointment with the VAT man so he couldn't go to see Elton sold. Gerry, the other partner, went but he couldn't watch. He was absolutely gutted. It's a shame in business when you are having a rough time and things need pruning. The first things to go are the pleasures. In this instance, their horses. He was bought by the BBA for Alex Scott, for 14,500 guineas. The fourth highest of the day. He was cheap at that as he had won and was placed this season. The whole family train on. Next season, he will be an even better three-year-old.

The other fellow, Crestwood Lad, didn't fetch his reserve. We could have done with the punter at Ascot in the 'Trainer' TV series, who bought that horse for 525,000 guineas there.

On my return from Ascot, I rang lots of people to ask if anyone had seen Olly, as he was still missing; to no avail. After making all my other phone calls, I went into the sitting room at 8.30pm to watch Question of Sport on the telly. Settling down in my Parker Knoll chair I thought I heard a moan. There was Olly. He'd been under the chair all that time. Was I glad to see him!

The builder, John Nixon, has finished putting in the new drains from the middle yard right down the side of the indoor school into a drain where we piped a dyke. Hopefully, our drainage troubles are over now.

WEDNESDAY November 27

7.30am. Had a ride on Miami Bear over the jumps. He was brilliant. Makes one feel like riding in earnest again. Steady cantered three lots of yearlings in pairs, four furlongs on the back side of the all-weather.

A message from Mrs Hobby, the lady who bred Paris House, to give her a ring. At Newmarket Sales she told me she would like to buy 50 per cent of Paris House's half-sister, who I bought that day. Sign of the times, her and her husband had second thoughts.

After lunch, when we finished the horses, Jo asked me if I would like to go with her to Lancaster to get a few things for our young son, Sam, who is in Tenerife, as I have to take them to him on December 8. Jo parked her car in the multi-storey car park. She then put some money in the machine to get a ticket. When we got back, Warden 156 had put her a ticket on the windscreen. If we pay £3 more for another ticket within the next eight hours it's all right. Otherwise, she could get a £40 fine. It might be cheaper for us if our local Council took up shares in our place.

8.30pm. Jo and I were invited to the Hamilton Arms near Garstang for a night out with the winners of a Ladbroke competition, which involved all their local shops in the Lancashire area. It was a nice evening out. We got back in at 2.00am.

THURSDAY November 28

FIRST thing this morning, 15 of our fat bullocks went to Longtown Cattle Market, near Carlisle. They were sent there because Arthur Slack, Snowgirl's owner who deals in cattle and sheep, swears this is the best market to take them. Knowing Arthur, he's probably got shares in it!

First lot rode out Jessie with the yearlings for half an hour on the roads then led them round the all-weather ring.

Second lot rode out Gorinsky with the next bunch of yearlings. On our return, 100 yards or so from our lane, Bill Sutcliffe, a local farmer nicknamed by our lads Basher Bill, was driving from his farm in the opposite direction. Instead of stopping and waiting until we had reached our lane, he drove towards us on the narrowest part of the road, bearing no regard for us or the horses. Not looking in my direction, he doesn't stop and, by doing so frightened the yearlings. They went scatty. Some finished up in the hedge, others were whipping round all over the place.

For years we have had trouble with this fellow. He was fined £100 only a few weeks ago for frightening a horse ridden by one of our girls, Jo Webster, and getting her dropped. For the same offence, he was awarded four penalty points on his licence for driving a car and a tractor without due care and attention.

On the 15th of this month, he hit Heather's (our head lad's wife) car. He is renowned for being a bully. Sutcliffe is a huge ignorant bugger who everyone appears to be frightened of. He has hounded us for years. Many times we have reported him to the police, regarding his reckless driving towards the horses. Today, enough was enough!

Turning Gorinsky round, I hacked up to Sutcliffe's car, jumped off the horse, opened the car door and let fly my fist into his face. When he got out of his car, still lipping, I gave him another crack. He said: "You haven't bought the road yet", and added the inevitable, "I will report you to the police".

True enough, just as I'm going out of the house after shaving and changing, the phone rings; the police. The soft sod's reported me for assault.

I told the officer I was about to go to Carlisle races and asked if I could give a statement the following day.

Cee-Jay-Ay ran in the first at Carlisle. He finished seventh of 21. First time over hurdles, he jumped well. The poor fellow gave his all. He was absolutely cooked when he came in. On this run I think he will win us a race somewhere.

I was wearing a lovely tie I bought on my way to France when Paris House ran in the Prix de l'Abbaye. It's of lots of people going down the entrance to the London Underground. Ray Gilpin of the Racing Post said to me: "If you put that tie on tomorrow, Jack, wear it as a belt."

In the third race we ran Miami Bear, ridden by Michael Moloney (left), the

good 3lb claimer from Gordon Richards's stable. The Bear popped out in front. Jumping well he only pecked a couple of times but nothing serious. He led until approaching the last where he was passed by the odds-on favourite Danny Connors and Military Secret. Danny Connors won last season's Coral Final at Cheltenham.

That was an excellent run by the Bear. It shouldn't be too long before we are patting him on the neck in the winning enclosure.

In the evening, Jo and I went to the Opera House Theatre in Manchester with Brian and Sonia Durkin to see Buddy. We met up in the Greyhound Hotel on the East Lancs Road at 5.45pm.

The show was absolutely brilliant. Afterwards, we went to meet the cast at the Pavilion for eats and drinks.

FRIDAY November 29

LED three lots of yearlings on Jessie, Gorinsky and Palacegate King. We hacked them in single file up the centre grass gallop. Walked them all through open stalls on their way home. This year's yearlings are coming to hand faster than I have ever known them. We will have to be careful we don't get them ready for Boxing Day!

Sent two bullocks to Lancaster Market. These didn't go to Longtown yesterday as they had horns on. They have to travel separate to avoid injuries. They fetched £600 each.

At 11.30 I went to Lancaster Police Station to give an account of the assault I made on Basher Bill yesterday. Not only did I have to make a statement I got the whole works, finger printed and mugshot taken.

In the afternoon I went out and traced clipped Gorinsky. He's a grand little chap that. I'm sure he will win this winter on the all-weather.

Cee-Jay-Ay looked a bit distressed after his run yesterday. When led out today he was fine and had eaten up. Two and a quarter miles in soft ground on a stiff course like Carlisle proved too much for him.

Neville, our feed man, wormed all the horses.

SATURDAY November 30

SET off for Sandown Park races at 6.45 am. Today is the launch of William Hill's Race Aid horse. She is a filly I bought at the St Leger Sales by Mazaad out of a mare that was full sister to Sandford Lad, the champion three-year old sprinter in 1973. So we are quite confident that the filly will trap.

The idea is to raffle the filly. William Hill saddle themselves with all costs of buying and running the horse, training fees, everything. The lucky owner gets badges to the meetings, Timeform Race Cards, the whole works. They don't have to pay one penny for anything for the whole season.

The draw takes place on William Hill Lincoln Day at Doncaster on 21st March 1992. All proceeds for this very worthy cause go to the Royal Marsden Cancer Appeal. The aim is to reach one million pounds. I would like even money they will do it. Jimmy Lindley, Don Payne and many more people who are connected with this fund are determined to make it work.

I drove the car until Keele Service Area, there I dived into the shop to purchase The Sporting Life, Racing Post and The Star. I buy The Star as I tip the televised racing every Saturday in the Flat season. Gordon Richards tips the jumpers so I like to see how he's doing. Jo took over the driving while I read the papers. Going along the M40 we saw a car which had just overturned and rolled down the enbankment. Two cars had already pulled up. There were three or four people going to the car so there was no need for us to stop. I hope whoever was in the car is alright, but it looked bad. We had a good run for the rest of the journey and landed at the course 10.45am. We met everyone in the Ardross Suite for drinks before lunch at 12noon. Looked at the table plan to see where Jo and I were drawn. Seeing some of the names on the plan we were in very good company.

When we were seated at our table a video of Race Aid which was taken in October at Doncaster was shown. She looked tremendous on film, real photogenic and a proper poser. Henry Cecil was asked to make a speech. He said the filly looked real good and if she didn't win it's Jack Berry's fault. Next speaker was Geoff Lester of The Sporting Life. He gave us a run down on all Sandown's races. For starters he openly admitted the last time he tipped a winner John Oaksey rode it.

In the first race he gave us Knight Oil; he was so far behind you couldn't see him through binoculars.

Fill your boots he told us for Deadly Charm in the second; a short favourite, it finished second.

Listen to this for the third race. He said "I am one of David's owners (he didn't mention Elsworth as he wanted it more personal) so I know a bit about Muse. It stays as well as my mother-in-law and it's just as fast. So it has got no chance. Muse was the easiest winner of the day winning by twenty lengths.

Geoff went through the rest of the card and tipped only one winner. But he's a great fellow and we had a lot of fun. I think he will have to keep his day job though.

The weather was pleasant, it was great racing. The lunch went extremely well. We had a lovely day.

Arrived back home at 9.45pm.

MUSE : David Elsworth's charge who confounded Geoff Lester of The Sporting Life by running a lot better than he had forecast!

SUNDAY December 1

RODE out Jessie for half an hour. He is entered at Kelso tomorrow in the same race as Dick Allan's Clay County, who has cantered-up in his last three races. There's no point in taking Jessie all the way up to Scotland just to see Clay County's backside for two miles, so I won't run him.

John Brown, the part owner of Mamma's Too came to see his horse. He stayed and had a drink. John has had horses here now for nine years.

George Atkinson also came to see his yearling by Treasure Kay. George and his friend Brian Todd owned Cashtal Dazzler with us, who won some races including a £25,000 one mile handicap at Haydock Park.

On the phone I sold Dokkha Oyston to Murray Grubb, one of our Scottish owners. Last season he leased him from us.

At 6.30pm I rang Sam in Tenerife as I do every Sunday. Next Sunday I have arranged to go and have a week with him. He tells me it's been raining there this week. That's all I need.

Looking at the injury book Flash has entered in a few yearlings with sore girths.

Syd and Sally Wild, who own the caravan site near us, came round for a drink. They have a very old farm cart that in the past was pulled by a horse. I mentioned to them that it wanted doing up as it's rotting away. Both of them said I could have it so I will get it done up. In the summer it will look real good in a corner somewhere with flowers in it.

MONDAY December 2

JO and I have very kindly been invited as guests of Mike Gallemore, Editor of The Sporting Life, to the Horserace Writers' Association Derby Awards twenty-fifth annual luncheon in London. To eliminate some road work we caught the 8.10am train to the city.

As we were waiting on the platform at Lancaster station a message came over the tannoy about five minutes before post time.

"Will the person who has left a blue bag outside the buffet room please pick it up immediately."

Fortunately someone had genuinely forgotten it and it wasn't a bomb scare.

For once Ruby our secretary hadn't booked our seats. The train was packed. However, we eventually managed to find two seats. I sat opposite a fellow with the biggest feet you ever did see. On that three hour twenty minute journey the prat must have kicked me a dozen times. If all of his body is in proportion to his feet-God help his wife!

From Euston station we got a cab to take us to the Royal Garden Hotel where the luncheon was being held. Prince Fahd the owner of Generous was awarded Owner of the Year. His racing manager Anthony Penfold spoke on his behalf. The bold speech he gave regarding Generous not being voted the Cartier Racehorse of the Year will no doubt be mentioned in tomorrow's papers.

The Flat Race Trainer prize, which incidently was won last year by yours truly, went to Paul Cole, the trainer of Generous.

Alan Munro was voted Jockey of the Year on the flat.

The National Hunt Trainer for the third time in succession was Martin Pipe. That is an amazing feat.

Peter Scudamore won the National Hunt Jockey honour for the sixth time I believe. This is truly a remarkable achievement. Peter certainly deserves his successes, he is so dedicated.

John Sexton was the top journalist and the Arundel handler John Dunlop received the Services to International Racing Award.

Steven Rose, head lad for Ron Smyth for 32 years and Harvey Ewart who works for Chris Thornton were the Stable Staff of the Year.

After having a most enjoyable day. Steve Simpson of the Blackpool Gazette, Jo and myself got a taxi to catch the 4.30pm train home. Making sure I didn't sit opposite the man with the feet like small boats, we chatted all the way back about racing, football, boxing, hunting and snooker until Steve got off at Preston. Brilliant!

It's 10.10pm Stan Newman one of my partners in our greyhound Lisnakill Wish has just rung me up. The dog did a solo trial 460 metres over hurdles at Wimbledon this morning in 28.36 seconds. He is a two-year-old black dog trained at Wimbledon by Phil Rees. He won two races in Ireland from only three runs and has won three here for us. Sonia, Stan's wife, and I have something to look forward to there, that's for sure.

TUESDAY December 3

IT was a lovely day at Cockerham, nice and mild. I rode Jessie over a couple of jumps as he runs at Catterick tomorrow. Then took Miami Bear for a seven furlong steady canter. With the second lot of yearlings, I rode Gorinsky round the roads for half an hour. We hacked down the middle of the grass, 16 of them upsides for three furlongs. What a beautiful sight that was. It's a super time of year, breaking these yearlings and getting them going. This season they look so good. We have most of them trace clipped. I don't want to wish my life away, but I'm really looking forward to next season to see these on the tracks.

As predicted, Anthony Penfold's bold speech got a big mention in the sporting papers.

It was such a nice day at 11 o'clock, I went to Newcastle races. I took Neville Hill, our lead man. For most of his life he stays in the yard, getting feeds ready. For a change I thought I would let him see a bit of daylight.

Ken Oliver runs Kinlet Vision in the three-year-old claimer here at 2pm.

David Brown, Bob Willis, me and a few more own her. Neville and I had a good run getting to Newcastle just as they were jumping off for the first race. The second race is a three mile novice chase. I like to see the horses jump, so I went down to the last fence. Pollibrig had jumped like a buck, making the running all the way, only to be collared approaching the last by Lupy Minstrel and finished second.

Our filly ran a sound race to finish 5th of the 16 runners. She should pick up a small event somewhere soon.

On my return from Newcastle, Andy Hoyle, the boss man of Laurel Racing, confirmed with Jo he will buy Paris House's half-sister. Tattersalls and our bank manager will be pleased.

**HERE I am enjoying the atmosphere
of a day's jumping at Newcastle.**

WEDNESDAY December 4

ANOTHER lovely mild day here at Cockerham. I had the yearlings put on the walkers with tack on for half an hour or so. Then we took them off to do a nice steady canter in one of our fields for a change. On the way home, we walked them through a set of open starting stalls.

One third of our national hunt string runs in the Novice Chase at Catterick-No More The Fool (Jessie).

Jo and I arrive at Catterick just before the start of the first race at 12.50pm. Jessie's race is the third on the card, The Bobby Faulkner Memorial Challenge Trophy. I knew Bobby very well, he was a very keen amateur and later became an inspector of courses. He died at quite a young age.

We were a bit unlucky to meet the Jimmy FitzGerald trained and Tony Budge owned Blacksburg, who had won four of his last five races. Ridden by Mark Dwyer, Blacksburg set off at a good clip. Jessie was second most of the way. Both horses jumped well and that's how they finished. There was a bit of grief at the last fence as two horses came down. They were behind Jessie at the time. On this run, our fellow should win soon. In the paddock he looked a million dollars. Beth, his lass, collected the £50 prize for the best turned out. If she's late in for work tomorrow, I'll know why.

Mrs Sarah York, a northern steward, has a yearling with us. The filly just needs a bit of time, so I arranged to send her home for a while. Trying to earn my corn for the day I sold, to stay in the yard, a very nice Governor General colt to Kath and John Hibbert, owners of ours who last season had an interest in our Moss Side Racing Group. We are doing well with the sales of the yearlings. Eight left from about 75 I bought.

Neville Crump was at Catterick. Talking to him brought many jumping memories back. What a good trainer he was, quite a character too. I felt honoured when he asked me to sign one of my "It's Tougher At The Bottom" books for him. I hope he doesn't light his fire with it.

Kirkby Stephen is on our way back, so we called to see Mel and Sheila Haughey. They owned Bri-Eden with us a few years ago. Mel gave me a lovely old print of St Simon for Christmas. Instead of Jo cooking, we called on Colonel Sanders in Lancaster for our tea.

THURSDAY December 5

IT'S 3.05am. I often get up at this time of a morning. It gives me chance to take stock. I seem to get more done when it's quiet like this, no phones ringing or any other disturbances. This morning I am going through the yearlings. We have named a few recently and sold a lot of them to new owners. Instead of referring to the Clantime Doncaster St Leger colt, that yearling now could have a name and an owner. So I have to put them all together. It isn't always easy when we have so many along with the other yearlings we have had sent to us. Especially when in the yard, the only name the yearling is known as is Ben or Fred.

Some get leased to other owners. Others are divided into partnerships, syndicates, Racing Clubs and so on. It's got to be all registered and above board. We have also got to get the new owners registered, plus their colours etc. Every single item costs money to do but fail to miss just one could entail expensive fines or visits to the disciplinary committee at Portman Square, London.

We are about three-quarters of the way through repairing, washing, disinfecting and painting all the stables. Another two weeks should see us finished. It's a tedious job that we do every year. It's a joke when people say to us in the off-season 'You must be quite slack now!'

Today, Jo has taken her mother to Beverley. Her brother (Jo's uncle) died and it's the funeral today.

I sent the yearlings solo one furlong apart down the back side of the all-weather for a steady canter about four furlongs. Doing this is to educate them to go on their own and teach them to grow up.

John Nixon the builder and one of our owners has started his men putting new drains in the middle yard. It's all dug up but it has to be done as the last heavy rain had flooded the yard.

Jessie is all right and has eaten up after running yesterday.

Richard Lanni has just rung (8pm) to say he is coming to see me in the morning. He owns Skyline Racing, and also bought some nice yearlings this season. Hope he's going to drop us a couple of them off.

FRIDAY December 6

WORKED Gorinsky with Palacegate Racing over five furlongs. This was Gorinsky's first strong work since he was gelded six weeks ago. He went well, hopefully he should keep the wolves away from the door on the all-weather during the winter.

The yard looks a bit of a tip at the moment. John Nixon and his merry men are still on with the drains. Men are working on the all-weather gallops putting new wood fibre down. Building is going on with the renovating of three boxes. We have contractors in, draining some land near the three furlong all-weather ring. Our lot are painting the rest of the boxes. It's a hive of activity. Mind, I like it that way. You can't beat progress. Only thing is I will never be a rich man as I spend, spend, spend on the place. I could never see the logic in some people seventy and eighty years of age still saving. As soon as the poor bugger croaks, the tax man grabs it. Or failing that his progeny blow it.

Richard Lanni of Skyline Racing came in the afternoon to see his yearling by Domynsky. He bought some nice yearlings this season. He also owns Palatial Style, the best middle distance horse in the North who won the Tetley Handicap and the Andy Capp Handicap at York, and the £24,000 Courage Handicap at Newbury carrying 9st 7lb. Richard apparently hasn't been seeing eye-to-eye with Peter Easterby of late. I don't want to poach anyone's horses. I thank God, at the moment we are full. However, for a horse of his calibre, he could have my bedroom. On Sunday I'm going to Tenerife for a week to see our youngest son Sam as he isn't coming over for Christmas. Richard said when I returned could I go to see him.

Ian Bolland our accountant came to pick up all the things required to finish the yearly accounts.

Andy Smith, the bloodstock agent, rang to ask would we be interested in selling Paris House. He has a client prepared to give a fair price for him to stand as a stallion in Ireland. Hopefully, there should be some more mileage in him before he goes off to stud, he's only two.

The farmer Jim Mitchell is putting slurry on the big field opposite us today-what a bloody stink!

SATURDAY December 7

ON page 7 of The Sporting Life, "It's Tougher At The Bottom" has its first of two extracts. The other is to appear on Monday. There is half a page dedicated to the book, this should sell a few copies.

Like the song in Oklahoma "Oh What A Beautiful Morning", there is a lovely white frost and the sun is shining. I rode the Bear with the first lot of yearlings round the backside of the all-weather, three lengths apart in single file. Then we came back down the inside grass gallop all in a nice bunch. When we pulled up, I could hear the lads and lasses chatting away about how good the yearlings are. It's always nice when the staff are chatty and pleased with their lot. It rubs off on the horses.

Frank Dunne rang from Ireland. He is sending a yearling and a two-year-old over for us to train.

Flash asked me this morning which horse did I want to ride first lot, the Bear, Jessie, or my war horse-because of the Basher Bill incident. Gorinsky! In between lots I just had a mosey to see how John Nixon was getting on as he and his men are concreting the part of the yard they have dug up for the new drains. Wherever I go all the dogs follow me. Victor my pit bull terrier with his great big paws has walked the full length of the newly laid concrete. I won't bother to write what John said but you can imagine. Before I left I heard him going on about it being Saturday. His men were on double time. He was still wittering on as I got out of earshot.

Watched racing on TV from Cheltenham and Doncaster. Peter Niven went mad riding five winners. John Francome gave our horse Race Aid a mention, also showed a film of her at Doncaster racecourse.

Saturday is mash night. While Kevin the second head man went round the horses with dressings, seeing Neville and Flash are off this weekend, I did the feed. This time of year it's great to get more involved with the horses at home. In the season racing every day doesn't allow me to.

Went to Wally Haggers twenty-first party in our village hall. Wally origi-nates from London. He has been coming here since he was twelve years old. He, like me, left home early, lived here, and went to our local school. So Wally is like one of our own sons. The party was really good. Wally's mum and dad did him proud, one hundred and fifty people attended. There was a nice disco and a bar and a buffet. Lots of our owners and all of our staff were there. Jo, Pat and I got back home just after midnight. No doubt it will still be in full swing at 2am. It was nice to walk out of the village hall with Jo and not have the thought of cleaning it up.

Just as I got through the door Sam phoned from Tenerife to make sure everything was in order and that I was still going out to see him.

SUNDAY December 8

THERE was a phone call at 5.40am-the Frank Dunne horses are on their way from Ireland. Jo tells the driver of the box how to get to the yard. Half an hour later he rings again-he's lost. I told him to go back to the Manor pub, where I will meet him and guide him to our yard.

Stan rang to let me know Lisnakill Wish, our greyhound, won a 475 metres hurdle trial at Wimbledon last night in near record time 28 seconds.

Ian Bolland our accountant called in this morning to ride out with me and do a bit of business. It's the only chance I have to talk with him really without being disturbed by the phone ringing. I rode Jessie again-he's very fresh and full of himself. We met up with our friend "Basher Bill" on our travels, but nothing happened.

Olly is sticking to me like glue today-he seems to sense I'm going away.

Pat took me to Manchester Airport in her car to catch the 2.50pm flight to Tenerife. She had been invited by Wally to his party and stayed the night at our house. Pat lives on the Wirral so it isn't very far out of her way going to the airport. We arrived shortly after 1pm so we walked around the shops. I bought a couple of papers for the journey. Also, I had a look in the Tie Rack shop-that's my weakness, buying ties. Every country I visit I make a point of bringing a tie back. One day when I was travelling back from Italy with Lester Piggott even he bought me one on the plane. Mind you he probably thought the same as Ray Gilpin about the one I was wearing, but honestly I have dozens. The plane landed in Tenerife just gone 7pm. Waiting at the luggage roundabout for my case, although I wasn't wearing a red shirt, I heard: "Hello, Jack, having a bit of a break in the off-season?"

It was one of Brian McMahon's owners, Garry Roberts. I then hailed a cab to the Hotel Paradise Park.

On arriving at the hotel, the only money I had with me were the Spanish pesetas Ruby, our secretary, had got from the bank. I hadn't got to grips with the currency yet so I said to the cabbie, who spoke perfect English: "What would you say is a fair tip for you?"

"One thousand pesetas." he said without hesitation.

After I had paid him he set off burning up the rubber as if he'd robbed a bank, not me. I bet it had been a fair while since he'd been bunged one thousand pesetas for bringing someone from the airport to the Hotel Paradise Park.

I checked in and put my case in the room. Then I asked the girl at reception if she would please get me another cab to take me to Sam's flat at Mar-Y-Sol. Sam looked well. I then took him for a nice meal in the restaurant in the complex. There they cater for people in wheelchairs. The swimming pool is really warm with bars to hold onto to get in and out and lots more facilities for the likes of Sam and some much worse. He has bought a flat there and he stays for most of the winter. It keeps him out of the cold and he loves it. What's more they have a very caring and understanding staff. It's a bit like sheltered accommodation.

It would be nice if the likes of Cliff Boothman, Jonathon Hayes, Sharron  Murgatroyd (pictured left), Paddy Farrell, Jessica Charles-Jones and other wheelchair-bound racing casualties could come here for a couple of weeks holiday. I might just have a word with Hilary Kerr of the Injured Jockeys Fund, as she is a good friend of mine, to see what she can do for them.

MONDAY December 9

I HAVE just finished my breakfast, it's 10.10am. Since I have landed in Tenerife I have seen nearly as many falls as I did watching racing on TV from Cheltenham and Doncaster last Saturday. A man fell at the airport last night, another just outside the restaurant went a right purler.

Sitting here at the breakfast table, I must say, I feel a bit of a charlie with shorts and a T-shirt on. Looking around I must be the only new punter at this hotel, everyone else is nice and brown. Mind you I don't know where they have been to get their tans as I was reading in the paper the past two weeks they have had torrential rain and storms. It's been the worst weather here for 22 years. My cab has just arrived to take me to see our Sam.

Great here, laid on the sunlounger by the edge of the swimming pool. No sign of the German gentleman I pulled out of the pool last year. If the Ministry of Transport saw the tyres on Sam's wheelchair they would ban it from the roads. The canvas is coming through the rubber. After telling Sam I will pay to get his wheels re-shod, he has set off in the direction where the maintenance for such things is done.

In the afternoon Sam and I went to a small supermarket to stock him up. It was about half a mile down a steep hill. The boy kept putting things in the trolley I was pushing until he had in it nearly as much as when Jo shopped when we had lads living in our house. I'm not convinced he needed all this lot, like two tubes of toothpaste-or was it because I was paying. Sam wanted me to ask if the man delivered. Finally we put all the gear in a big box I found in a corner of the shop and sat it on Sam's knees on his chair. He could barely see over the box and only just get his arms round it. Muggins here pushed the lot back up the hill to Mar-Y-Sol thinking if we have a blow out now I shall scream. Sam told me he was struggling up this very same hill once on his return from the bank where he had just drawn £600 out as he was coming home to England for the summer. Crossing a kerb he tipped his chair up. A man stopped, put him back in his chair and pushed him to the top of the hill. The man had seen Sam's wallet-he quickly grabbed it, took the money out, threw the wallet back towards Sam and ran off.

TUESDAY December 10

ANOTHER lovely sunny day. It's not so at home, apparently. I have just heard racing at Plumpton and Sedgefield has been abandoned because of frost. There's no sign of that here as Sam and I are flat out at the pool edge on sunloungers with just our shorts on. Sam's got it made here for definite. I have just come back from down the beach to get The Sporting Life. There is a woman walking Sam around the pool. Most of the people here walk him. Whatever nationality they are, most don't speak English but they communicate with him all right. When they order drinks at the poolside they often count him in. Sam and I had a meal at Mar-Y-Sol. About 9pm I went back to my hotel. With having two days in the sun I am getting a nice tan, being dark I tan quite easily.

Rang Jo to make sure everything is all right and ask if she's sold any more yearlings. We have about eight or nine to sell yet. There are a couple of people dithering whether to or not. Some people need to wear a belt as well as braces. Last year we struggled to sell some until after Christmas, it's all a sign of the times.

WEDNESDAY December 11

AFTER having a bath at 7am I went for breakfast, then came back to watch the English news on television. No racing today I see because of frost. On Wednesdays Sam goes to the gym so I am not going to his place this morning. Instead I will test out the swimming facilities at Paradise Park then go to the beach for my Sporting Life and a walk.

Sam and Alan (Polaris) seen enjoying the delights of the pool at Mar-Y-Sol.

Went to Sam's about 2.30pm. He's got to know a man called Alan Shaw who is there for two weeks holiday. Alan is retired now but his old job was making ejector seats for aircraft. He got polio in one leg when he was 18 months old. Sam calls him the "human polaris" because at the Mar-Y-Sol they have two overhead six inch pipes in the pool that release water at 9am, 3pm and 5pm. Alan bobs up and down towards the water holding the side rail.

Came back to my hotel late afternoon. Sam has got friendly with a little bird. I am taking them out for dinner at 8 o'clock. Met the two of them as planned and took them to a very nice place at Cruce De Arona about twenty minutes away by taxi-Restaurante Velazquez. The young lady's name is Andrea Contreras. She was born in Tenerife. She met Sam when she was at Mar-Y-Sol visiting her sister who was paralysed in a car crash in which their mother was killed. Andrea is a student teacher and speaks quite a bit of English-a very nice girl too.

THURSDAY December 12

AS I am having breakfast looking at the rest of the inmates here, I have caught most of them up with my tan. When I come back from Barbados in January hopefully I will be the colour of Frank Bruno.

Went down to the seafront for my Sporting Life, it's 11.15am and it hasn't come in yet. I have been talking to a couple who are friends of Alan the ejector seat man. They are going on a boat trip. We have been talking and waiting outside the Bahia Cafe drinking coffee until it's coming out of my ears. Alf and his Mrs have gone to catch their boat. No "Life" yet-to hell with it. There won't be much in it anyway as there's no racing with the bad weather. I'll go to Sam's and have a swim in that nice warm pool.

These young people are a damned nuisance trying to sell time-shares. They are a persistent lot into the bargain. I ought to employ some of them to sell our yearlings for us.

Called for Sam at 8pm to take him for dinner. We had a super T-bone steak at a place called Victoria Court Two.

FRIDAY December 13

THIS is a bad day for the superstitious. However, my day started all right. I nearly ended up in heaven as one of the swimming pools is on the top floor of this Paradise Hotel. When I finished my breakfast I sunbathed there until around 1 o'clock. Looking over the left hand side the view is about level with a mountain not far away. On the right side looking downwards the people bathing in the ground floor pool look no bigger than babies.

I thought I would give Britannia Airways more of a chance to deliver The Sporting Life this morning by going to pick it up later. As I'm striding out towards the paperstand a voice from a hairy face in dark glasses said: "What are YOU doing here then?"

It was Albert Wake with his wife Joan from Lancashire. Albert owned Home Cliff, a horse I rode for him a couple of times when trained by Don Charlesworth before I started training.

Over a couple of cups of coffee I am pleased to announce racing now has no problems. We reduced the VAT on bloodstock to a more manageable rate of 2.7 per-cent, the same as the Irish. Thought it was time our Government realised racing is a very big industry employing countless people, providing jobs to lots of other people from the spin-offs. I bet Don McCain's ear's were burning too. Albert is quite friendly with Don. My friendship has definitely taken off with Albert since our meeting today especially since he's told me I don't look any older than when he first remembered me over twenty years ago.

Tonight at 7.30pm we had a lovely barbeque at Sam's place in real Christmas festive mood. A choir from the Swedish sector dressed in white robes. The little kids had torch crowns on their heads and were each holding a lit candle. They made their entrance in pairs singing carols from a room across the pool. As it was in darkness it looked and sounded splendid.

SATURDAY December 14

TODAY Sam is going by taxi to Andrea's other sister's house. They both take it in turns at looking after the sister staying in Sam's complex because with her injuries she is not capable of looking after herself.

Mike Gallemore, The Sporting Life editor, would be impressed with me if he saw me going down town everyday for my Sporting Life. That's where I am going now.

Whilst reading the "Life" on the sea front a nice old boy sat on my bench telling me he wrote a book four years ago about politics. Two thousand copies were published but they have not all been sold yet. He also wrote the follow up and was proud to tell me he had 35 rejections! I wonder if he was any relation to Eddie the Eagle ski-jumper!

I see in today's Life Alex Bird has died aged seventy five. He was a gentleman if ever I met one-always had a minute for a chat. I had a lot of time for Alex.

All these people passing are holding hands no matter how old they are. It must be the sun. They certainly don't go on like this in Cockerham.

I'm getting to like the coffee here. Finished my paper. I'm off-God, some of our young lads would get excited if they walked along this beach seeing all these tits. Walking to the pier to see the fishermen I spotted one small but very fat Spaniard fishing in the best position of all, right at the front. He was about forty or so, a noisy little beggar with a lot of rattle towards the other men fishing. All of a sudden he stood up and bent over looking at the water. I had to go for a walk as I got the urge to give him a little push with my foot. What a splash he would have made, dropping in from some twenty feet. Did a bit of shopping for presents. Also bought a nice silk tie. I am going to get a bath now as Albert and Joan Wake have invited me out for dinner with them.

I met Albert and Joan at their hotel, the Princess Dacol. We had a drink there then went onto a nice restaurant with live music called Charlies. It was good food, everything was fine except the damned drummer, who was too noisy. You couldn't hear the female vocalist for the daft prat. She should have broken his sticks in half, but it was a good night for all that.

SUNDAY December 15

THIS is my last day here in Tenerife. It's been nice to see our Sam and take him out a few times. To be honest though Tenerife isn't my scene. Except for dogs and cats I haven't seen a single animal or a bird in flight. I can appreciate how Terry Waite must have felt when those terrorists told him he was being released.

Its 9.30am I have just come up from having breakfast to pack my case. Watching some of these people eat dirty big platefulls I thought if our horses ate like some of them I would have to put the fees up.

The weather is a bit overcast today. I have changed after having a swim. I will go to reception to pay my bill, then I'm taking Sam out for lunch. After lunch I'll be on that big bird home.

Took Sam to Christys Bar for a proper English Sunday lunch of roast beef and Yorkshire pudding. It was a nice place, too. While we were eating outside really good country and western tapes were being played. The likes of Kenny Rogers (Lucille) Billie Jo Spears (Blanket On The Ground) Johnny Cash (A Boy Named Sue) and many more. I really enjoy good country music.

After lunch I took Sam home to Mar-y-Sol, kept enough money for the cab to the airport and gave him the rest of my pesetas.

At the airport the planes were running an hour late. I saw Garry on his return and had a chat in the aircraft. He and some of his pals are thinking of having a yearling with us. He said he would be in touch.

MONDAY December 16

JO picked me up at the airport. When we got to bed after reading through the mail and the messages it was 4am. The dogs were pleased to see me. John Carroll has come back from his holiday in the States looking nice and brown.

The yearlings are looking great. First lot I rode the Bear. Second lot I rode out Jessie with them. We just walked to Smiths, that takes twenty-five minutes. Then we steadily cantered them in pairs four lengths apart all the way round the backside of the all-weather. We then hacked both lots in nice tight bunches of sixteen for about three furlongs. Three or four gave a few coughs. That's not serious, though. This time of the year that happens. It's better that they get any ailment now than during the season. We have a cough mix that we make up, it's a black treacle base. It seems to ease the tickle. If they continue coughing I will put them round the roads for a week to ten days as they are all going well enough.

That Jessie is flying. I will enter him today for Uttoxeter on Saturday.

I must say it's good to be back among the yearlings. Leonardo Da Vinci, Rambrandt, Picasso and the rest of our painters have only about a dozen boxes to finish off down Hillside, our bottom yard.

Today we have started mucking out the fold yard. We have three spreaders on the go and one tractor loading them up. A good smell they are creating I can tell you. All this muck is spread on our grass gallops and believe me, it does them a world of good.

Alan, our son, was knocked over by one of the horses that was turned out, and broke his collarbone. We were changing them from one field to another when they rushed through a gateway. Alan was waving like mad to stop them, holding his ground. Unfortunately, he got flattened.

One of the horse walkers broke down but we got it mended in the afternoon. Simon Giles one of our apprentices came back to work today. He has been off six weeks with an ankle injury. Peter Dodd from Doncaster, the owner of Heaven-Liegh-Grey, the filly that gave us our first one hundred winners in a season, rang to say she won't be with us next season.

Shame that, win some, lose some.

TUESDAY December 17

READING this morning's Racing Post I see Peter Savill has thirty-three yearlings with various trainers for next season, but he's excluding me this year. For a number of years I have trained an odd one or two for Peter with a fair amount of success. Probably this has happened because he told me at Doncaster September Sales that he would like to send our yard ten yearlings. He insists on his horses being ridden by his retained jockey. I said it wasn't fair on John Carroll to have this many horses in a yard not eligible for him to ride. Shame, because Peter is a good owner. I'm sure loyalty will prevail in the long term.

This morning we cantered four lots of yearlings round the three furlong ring led by Jessie, the Bear, Gorinsky and Cee-Jay-Ay. All ridden by me. We chose this route as the fold yard is half-a-day off finishing and and we don't want to get in the tractor's way with the horses.

Miami Bear had a bit of a temperature at evening stables. When I rang

Arthur Campbell his owner to tell him the Bear had a temperature of 102 degrees. I think Arthur's possibly went up a few degrees more. He absolutely idolises the horse. The race he is in at Edinburgh looks poor. Better see how he is over the next couple of days.

It started to rain at about 10.30am and it was still raining at 5.30pm when I set off to go to the 221st Annual Gimcrack Dinner at York.

This season's Gimcrack race was won by Tony Budge's River Falls, trained by Richard Hannon. Tony and Richard have won the race three times out of the last four years. That is an impressive record. No one could begrudge Tony this splendid achievement as he has done so much for racing and he deserves his successes. The same also can be said for Richard.

It was, as always, a really nice evening. Without doubt it is the racing dinner of the year, and I am flattered to have been invited to the last three. Hopefully one day I may train the winner of the race, as it is high on my agenda for races I would like to win.

After the dinner Mike Gallemore and I had a drink in the bar with Mick Easterby, putting racing to rights. I had been on Perrier water all night as I was to drive home afterwards.

About ten of us took part in the five pound pool game in which you had to predict the time of the speech. Mine was 1hr 32min. Doug Moscroft of the Newcastle Journal beat me by 3 minutes. Apparently he won the pool last year, too. I think Doug must be getting inside information. I should add the speakers were far from boring and were very entertaining.

It was very wet and windy travelling back from York in the early hours. It's now 3.32am Wednesday. Goodnight...or rather,...Good morning!

WEDNESDAY December 18

7.30am C and C Transport have just come to pick a Hard Fought yearling of Sarah York's that's going back home.

John Carroll on Cee-Jay-Ay, me on Jessie worked ten furlongs. Jessie again worked particularly well.

The yearlings went round the roads and walked through the open stalls on their return. John on Palacegate King, me on Gorinsky winged up that straight five all-weather, and both worked well.

Sold the filly by Clantime out of Moorhill to Solid Gold Racing Club. This is the first horse we have trained for them.

Peter the joiner has just put the finishing touches to the three garages being restored on our car park-they look really good.

Martin, John and Wally are putting some half round rails on the lane side of our moss grass gallop. In summer when contractors were doing the job, they ran out of railings. These rails only came the other day, so our resident joiners are putting up this last one and a half furlongs.

Kinlet Vision runs at Bangor-on-Dee today. I can't go as I have an appointment with a man this afternoon regarding Jo's and my will. Kinlet

Vision ran last at Newcastle. It's two and a half miles today and that should suit her, particularly as she only has 10st 2lb. For a change I will invest a few pounds each-way in the "Life's" price at 10-1.

Came in the house to listen to Kinlet Vision's race. The little cracker has gone in at 12-1. Great, I am ever so pleased for Ken and Rhona Oliver. It's a seller, so I hope we still own her. The Bear's temperature hasn't dropped. Rang Arthur Campbell to tell him he can't run at Edinburgh. Arthur was a bit disappointed. I told him when I saw the entries he had an excellent chance of winning.

Peter the joiner is now mending the doors in the front yard as some have got a bit rotten at the bottom.

Went to Bede and Anges Rogerson's restaurant called The Cottage, built in 1771. They invited a few of us over, who are members of Laurel Racing Club, for a meal, just as he did last year. The place is renowned for its venison and this year was no exception. Beautifully prepared, food fit for a king.

At 6.35pm had a live interview with Radio Lancashire regarding my thoughts on the proposed new British Racing Board.

I agree to allow the Animal Health Trust to monitor the blood of ten of our horses through the coming season. Our vet took the first lot today. It will be good for us as well as them to give us a picture.

THURSDAY December 19

NOT a very nice morning to start with, windy and raining. We rode some of the horses for a good trot in the indoor school, the rest round the roads.

Gave Jessie and Cee-Jay-Ay a one mile swinging canter. Wagon and trailer load of straw came just at breakfast time. All the stable boxes are finally finished being painted. Our artists have now started on the indoor school.

Dave Bamber, the footballer from Blackpool, came with a film crew from Granada TV to do some filming of him with the Nomination colt he owns a quarter share in.

Miami Bear is still a bit under the weather. It's the first time he has been ill from the day we bought him as a yearling.

I went through the debts owing to us with Ruby, our secretary. She has given me the hit list of names for me to hopefully recover the amounts. This part of training is a constant worry.

The lovely Beveled yearling filly I bought at Doncaster, then sent to Bearstone Stud for breaking, has caught the eye of Terry Holdcroft, the boss. He rang to say they liked her so much that he and John Forsythe were thinking of buying her for Christmas presents for their wives, both named Margaret. Jo and I went to Liverpool to see Oklahoma at the Liverpool Playhouse. The weather was terrible on the way. We drove through blizzards and snow. Real Arctic conditions. On reaching Liverpool we didn't know where the theatre was so we parked the car in a multi-storey car park and hailed a cab. The cabbie seemed a smashing fellow. He told us he had been a cabbie in Liverpool for twenty-two years. He dropped us off at another theatre called the Everyman and scarpered. The prat, I'm certain he did it on purpose. Hailing another taxi and telling our new pilot what happened, he said in a Willie Newnes accent: "Oh! You have to watch these boys, Sir". I must say I couldn't help wondering where this bloke was going to drop us. Oklahoma was great, even though we were over half an hour late. We were to have met Pat Knight, her mum Ida and Tricia Harrison beforehand but they had already gone in.

After the show, travelling back in the pouring rain, Jo and I sang "Oh What A Beautiful Morning", "Poor Jud Is Dead" and all the other lovely songs from the show.

FRIDAY December 20

JOHN CARROLL on Cee-Jay-Ay and myself on Jessie had a good blow over three furlongs. They are declared at Uttoxeter tomorrow, but both are in danger of being balloted out.

That Jessie is flying-he has never been better in his life. With the weather still being wet, wild and windy we are walking and trotting the yearlings in the indoor school and on the walkers. It doesn't do the poor little mites a lot of good working in weather conditions like they are at the moment. They duck and dive about when the wind blows up their skirts.

Bob, our gardener, has just told me that John, our white rabbit, has died.

Henry Hughes from Wales came to see his home-bred Beveled yearling. I finished up buying Cashtal Queen from him as he can't afford to keep the two in training. If I am not careful I will own more horses than Sheikh Mohammed.

Jo's mum came flying out of her bungalow chasing after the dustbin man as he had forgotten her bin. Like in the Lonnie Donegan song "My Old Man's A Dustman", the part which goes "you've missed me, am I too late?"-"No...jump up on the cart". The turn of foot she showed I'd better get her entered in the Cockerham District Pensioners Stakes. She wouldn't be much of a price coming from our yard though, even at 82.

Jo took her to Beverley in the afternoon to see her other daughter and her offspring to exchange Christmas presents and have a good chin wag.

I'm happy to report Miami Bear is back to normal. Ian Bolland our accountant came to go through some things with me.

The television man returned our TV. He had it for a couple of weeks getting it sorted. The one he left for us as a replacement until ours was mended was something else. To see it properly from my armchair I needed binoculars. Which reminds me Dave Bamber, the Blackpool striker who was filmed in our yard yesterday was shown on Granada TV in Kick Off. My mate from the village Andy Campion rang for a half hour chat.

Paul Shanahan of Coolmore rang to tell me some good news, Distinctly

North is coming back from the States to stand at Kilsheelan Stud, part of the Coolmore empire. Sid, as we called him, was an absolute flying machine. He could really trap. He won for us first time out on a racecourse at Goodwood on owner Robert Sangster's birthday. He won the Group Two Flying Childers Stakes at Doncaster. In the Group One Middle Park Stakes he was only beaten half a length by Lycius in record time, and was beaten in a photo by Mac's Imp in the Group One Heinz 57 at Phoenix Park. He has to be the fastest horse I have trained. Although Paris House must be close on his heels.

DISTINCTLY NORTH . . the fastest horse I have ever trained.
Here's "Sid" winning the 1990 Flying Childers Stakes
at Doncaster from Mujadil and Line Engaged.

SATURDAY December 21

IT'S absolutely soaking wet everywhere, it's rained all through the night. Rode the horses in the indoor school. Just cantered the few older horses except the Bear. He got well wrapped up in a waterproof and I had Little Rachel, one of the girls, ride him down the road for half an hour.

Jo and I set off to go to Uttoxeter just gone 9.0am. In the paper the going is heavy and there's an inspection. Jessie wouldn't want it heavy and the other little fellow, Cee-Jay-Ay wouldn't get the trip. Max, Cee-Jay's part owner rings on the car phone to tell me it's pouring hard and he doesn't live far from the course. Right, I said to him, we won't run. Jessie's owner, Reg Leah, is told the same. I turned the car round and came back home. Seeing as Jo was changed and all geared up to go out for the day on our return home, she got her car out and pursued her favourite pastime-shopping.

Got hold of Martin Stanner, our travelling head lad, and told him not to run the horses but to stay put until twelve o'clock as a yearling filly by Governor General, is being delivered there for us to pick up and train for a Mr Rivenaes, a first time owner for us.

Watched racing from Chepstow on TV. Carvill's Hill won the Coral Welsh National. What a trainer that Martin Pipe is to get the first, third and fourth in the race with today's gruelling conditions.

Uttoxeter ran the first race, a Novice Hurdle, then abandoned the remainder of the meeting.

Terry Holdcroft rang to say he had just come in from a day's hunting. He told me he had never been so wet in his life. Could he and John Forsythe buy the Beveled yearling for their wives as a Christmas present. He said he was having to speak on his portable phone in the next room and had to keep his voice down for fear Margaret would hear him.

Angela, from Pride and Place Bookstall, brought me forty "Tougher at the Bottom" books for me to sign.

If Harry Beeby, the auctioneer of Doncaster Sales, could see me now he would be proud of me.

I have just sold the Bold Owl colt to Tony Williams, from Yeovil. He is the full-brother to Miss Ellie Pea, who won two races as a two-year-old for us. Tony and Carol have had plenty of successes with us. They owned Timewaster and were also in our Moss Side Racing Group who had sixteen winners in the '91 season.

SUNDAY December 22

JESSIE and Cee-Jay-Ay were put on the walker for half an hour. It's still very windy and showery.

Peter Teesdale, who has a livery yard near York, delivered the Lochnager yearling filly we bought at Doncaster Sales in October from Hughie Harris, the stall handler, who has broken her. We have given Peter Almost Blue to ride round the roads for a few weeks, for a change.

Now the shops are open on a Sunday, Jo's gone to Lancaster to do a bit more. She was out all day yesterday shopping and brought so much gear back. You would have wondered how on earth she got it all in her car. If it wasn't so difficult parking in Lancaster town, I'm sure she would have taken one of the horse boxes.

We had the staff who were on duty this afternoon in for a Christmas drink. The carol singers always come here to the yard the last Sunday before Christmas. They come in for a warm, a drink and a mince pie after singing a couple of carols. We have left the money and the drink for them with Alan, as Jo and I won't be able to greet them tonight because we have been invited to a company staff dinner dance at the Crofters at 8.0pm.

I didn't put my red shirt on just in case the chef there recognised me. It was a real good do. The disco was loud though, but that could be me getting old. We came home at 12.15am.

MONDAY December 23

6.45am-it's still very wet and windy at Cockerham. Left instructions to ride the yearlings in the indoor school for a good trot so they can keep dry and to canter Jessie, Cee-Jay and Gorinsky.

Jo, John Carroll and myself set off at 7.0am for Richard Lanni's at Malton. It was very wild travelling, especially on that M62 over the Pennines. Arrived at Richard's just gone nine o'clock. He showed us all the horses-looked well they did too.

John rode a nice sharp looking Efisio yearling along with a couple of other yearlings, both by Midyan, led by one of our ex-horses, Spot The Earlybird, who Richard bought out of our yard at the Newmarket Sales. They walked and jogged round a covered-in ride. We then watched them canter up a steepish, wood-chip all-weather gallop that ran parallel with the Beverley Road for about three furlongs. The yearlings were well-behaved and did their job well. In watching this we got absolutely soaked. John then had a sit on a two-year-old by The Noble Player.

At lunch time we went for a drink at a pub in Malton, followed by a nice meal at the Italian restaurant. Here it comes, the good news. The man said, "Would you like to train Palatial Style for me?" I didn't do any backward flips or forward rolls. Restraining myself the best I could I told him I would love to. "Yes sir, I will be delighted to have him."

To save her going to the shops tomorrow, Jo thought she would go to Lancaster to get the vegetables and cream from Asda on the way home.

Tom Thompson, of Findon Transport, delivered a Salt Dome yearling colt belonging to Eurolink Ltd from near Brighton. Tom and his mate came in the house for a meal and a beer. We offered them a bed for the night but they declined. After an hour or so they kicked on.

Jo has been giving Jim Barnes, the TV man from Satelight Ltd, Preston, a hard time. Our television still isn't going well. The poor fellow has just rolled up with a new one. It's 9.55pm and he has another call yet!

TUESDAY December 24

IT'S a nice day, best one we have had for a while. The cough in the yearlings is clearing up. Only just an odd one now and then.

Cantered Jessie, Cee-Jay-Ay, Palacegate Gold, Palacegate Racing and

Gorinsky on the all-weather. How on earth did we ever train horses before we had all-weather gallops? For the amount of rain we have had over this past week, this gallop is still riding good. It's truly amazing.

All the yearlings went on the roads and on walkers. The few days off from cantering won't hurt them at all. In fact, it will do them good. They are all well without being too fresh and silly. Although the Christmas hols are coming up, the horses still have to be exercised. If a horse goes out for one hour per day there are still twenty-three hours for the horses stuck in a box. Not much different to being in jail. I like them out even during holidays even if it's just to stretch their legs.

Noel Souter, from the Isle of Man, popped in on his way back home. He had with him a lovely Christmas cake his mother had made. We had a sherry, a coffee and a piece of the Christmas cake-good it was, too.

When everything was finished at the yard, about 12.30pm, all the staff went down to the Manor, our local pub where, traditionally, I buy them a drink. I have always done it, it's about the only time I go in our local. I feel it's their pub and it doesn't need me to cramp their style. They have to let their hair down and don't need the hassle, knowing that the Old Man's in the next room. So I keep out.

Jo's taken her Mum to do the last minute shopping. God knows what for. There appears enough food and drink here to keep everybody going for a fortnight and, for clothes, it's a work of art getting anything in her wardrobe. We have got lots of carrots, polo mints and apples for the horses' treats tomorrow.

John and Jo Cousins arrived with a piece of pork as they have done for the last 19 years. John and his brother Eric both trained for years in Lancashire and Cheshire. In fact, Eric was a bit of a handicap specialist.

Our Jo has just put the turkey in the bottom of the Aga oven. All the staff who don't go home for Christmas come and have their dinner with us. By the size of this year's turkey, most of them must be staying. The slaughter-man must have shot this one, it's that big.

In the late afternoon, I took my mate Andrea Campion her present. Andy is the girl I dedicated "It's Tougher At The Bottom" to. She is 21 but unfortunately handicapped in a wheelchair and blind. In the past, I used to have a small recorder I carried with me almost everywhere, recording items of news for her. Then I used to send the tape down to her house. She had a machine that she played it on. I would tell her how and which horses had worked. Play it whenever we were having a bit of crack or whatever. I even took it racing one day when we were buying in one of our sellers.

I remember one day we were putting some two-year-olds through the stalls on the grass gallop. There was a particular lad who was mauling the horse. I was telling him to settle the horse down as he had the poor little fellow all wound up. When the gates opened my man got left. The horse's head was up in the air though the lad was fighting with him. Well, you can imagine, there were a few choice words on the tape. Recording for Andy was automatic and I never played them back. Andy rang me up-she loved it. She said, "Bet you got a bit mad down at the stalls Jack, didn't you?"

Now I seem to get so busy I just don't get the time. More often now Andy has to ring me for the news.

John Carroll came round with his little daughter Danielle. She's a lovely little thing, only 14 months old. A pity she hadn't come sooner, she could have had a ride on that turkey.

Jo and I went to go to midnight Mass in the village, only we were a bit late-they had already started. The old girl bottled out, so we came home and watched the telly.

WEDNESDAY December 25

A MERRY Christmas. First thing we put the yearlings on the walkers then rode out the few older horses we have entered, and gave them a canter. The three or four yearlings that won't accept the walker are lunged. We were all done and dusted by 10.30 am. All of us went into the house and had quite a skinful. The staff who were staying on got changed and went to the pub returning back for their Christmas lunch beautifully made by Jo. We opened some wine and two magnums of champagne we had collected up in the season for various achievements.

John Carroll, the two Head Men, Flash and Kevin, along with Simon Brooks, an ex-box driver, all brought their kids to see us and had a drink.

I watched the Queen's speech like I have for as long as I can remember. Come stable time every single person who was on duty turned out, even if they weren't in a perfect state. We just worked around like we would on any normal Sunday afternoon.

Jo, her mum and myself settled down in the evening to watch telly. During the programmes Jo's mum gave us a running commentary on what was happening although we were all watching the same television set. When Crocodile Dundee Two came on at 8.0 pm I put my foot down. Let's just watch and enjoy this and no talking, I said. It was brilliant-some man that Paul Hogan. We then watched The Sound of Music. I have seen it a few times before but it's still good. The "outlaw" went home. No, she's not bad really. If I was anyway near as good at her age I would settle for that. Jo went for a bath. I stayed up and watched a circus spectacular on Channel 4 with a nice glass of port. The open fire roaring up the chimney and the dogs sprawled out in front of it on the rug-Peace.

THURSDAY December 26

JESSIE and Gorinsky cantered. Except for exercising the rest of the horses for about three quarters of an hour each in the school and on the walkers, we worked around the yards like we would on a Sunday.

Kevin drove Gorinsky to Lingfield for tomorrow, as the box drivers are away for Christmas.

Went down to see Olly (O I Oyston) with his Christmas treat. He's got it made in his seven-acre paddock with a big double box, bedded up to his belly in straw. For company there's Tiny Tim the Pallerbella pony, who stands 36 inches high, with his nice warm rug on. Neville feeds him everyday. He gets wormed every month, shod regularly in front and trimmed up behind. He is as fit as a butcher's dog. I am telling you all this as people often ask me: "How is Olly?" His paddock is on the bend before the straight on our all-weather gallop so he is very much in the know. Honestly, he takes a big interest in everything that happens and often watches the horses work. When we put horses in the stalls, he always comes over to the fence. Whether he gives them any advice I don't know, but most of ours come out of the boxes fairly fast-just like he did. The old boy won twenty four races for us, we are now just paying him back a bit.

I went to Wetherby races when we got finished. Didn't have any runners but it's great to have a day's jumping, especially on a lovely sunny day like today. It was packed at Wetherby. Cars were still coming in the car park after the second race. It was nice to see the old faces of the jump world. Mr Proos, the owner of Rinus, asked me to fax him the details of any yearlings for sale as he fancied a Flat horse.

At 3.15pm I went into the members' to watch the most famous horse in training to see if he could win the King George again for his thousands of fans. It wasn't to be and what a shock seeing Desert Orchid fall. Adam Kondrat, the French jockey who rode The Fellow to victory at Kempton, spent a summer in our yard on an apprentice exchange course a few years ago. He loved it here. In fact, he didn't want to go back!

I see on Teletext Peter Niven has ridden yet another five-timer, at Sedgefield. Well done, Peter.

FRIDAY December 27

IT'S a beautiful frosty morning here at Cockerham. Just as I am getting in my car to go to Lingfield at nearly 9.0am, about 100 geese came flying very low over the car park making a lot of noise. It's a lovely sight, one I never tire of seeing. It happens every day here as they come down to feed off Mitchells grass in the field opposite our house.

About four years ago, as we were eating our Christmas dinner looking out of our window over the field across our lane there were THOUSANDS of them eating grass. There couldn't have been a yard's space in between each of them.

Travelling to Lingfield it was a bit foggy around Charnock Richard. Arrived just gone 1.0pm. The paddock and the course looked super. There was a good crowd there which was nice. Lingfield could certainly lend itself to have the all-weather there for floodlit evening meetings. It is such a picturesque little place. Gorinsky in his race jumped out fast from the worst draw and was in front within a furlong. Turning into the straight our little fellow was a good length in front. However, Mac's Fighter of Bill O'Gorman's, ridden by his dashing daughter Emma, was making good headway. The two horses ran on right to the line, the judge called for a photo, but I knew we were second. It was a good run for Gorinsky. On that run he should win a race somewhere.

The Racing Post reporter told me at Lingfield that Desert Orchid had been retired by Richard Burridge, his owner. On behalf of all your thousands of fans Dessie, thanks for the pleasure you have given us these past few seasons. Enjoy many years of retirement.

On the way home from Lingfield the motorways were very busy, M25, M40, M42 and M6. It was well over a hundred miles before we pulled up at the first service area on the M6-Hilton park. It was so crowded we couldn't park the car so we had to go onto Keele. That was very busy too. John and I were talking about young Philip Barnard's crashing fall yesterday at Wincanton. He was taken to hospital with head injuries.

The first thing I did when I got in was to put the Teletext on. Philip had died, he was only 24.

Derek McGaffin, the young lad from Glasgow who stays with us on holidays, came today.

SATURDAY December 28

FOR a change, we let the yearlings go a steady canter on the backside of our all-weather gallop, a furlong apart to teach them to be on their own. I didn't want to do too much yet as the occasional horse is still giving the odd cough, but they are mainly over it now. We tested the blood of a few of them and they are all right. The Bear is almost right again. He was ridden round the roads for an hour. Hopefully on Tuesday he will start cantering again.

Worked Jessie and Cee-Jay-Ay, one mile. Worked Palacegate Gold with Palacegate Racing, five furlongs.

Watched racing from Newbury on the box. Jenny Pitman has a nice horse in the making with Triple Witching. Also I see that Clay County won the Northumbrian Gold Cup, the £25,000 Novice Chase at Newcastle. Good horse that. It's nice to see someone in a small way as Dick Allan training such a talented young chaser.

In our field we have twenty one geldings and fillies with waterproof rugs on. They are fed in six tumbrils in a line about twenty yards apart first thing in the morning, then they are brought in later in the afternoon into the indoor school to hay and shelter.

On the first of January all these horses come into training. They walk and trot round the roads for five weeks then we put them in steady work. Some of them we send to various people for these preliminaries. Jo and I sorted out which and where some of them are going.

Sam rang from Tenerife, normally we ring him on a Sunday night, but he's going out tomorrow so he's rung tonight instead.

SUNDAY December 29

MADE the breakfast today for a change; the whole works, egg, bacon, mushrooms, sausages, beans, toast-the lot.

It's a lovely mild day. Took my eight dogs for a walk all the way round the gallops. Sorry seven, Dick the sheepdog wasn't around.

Joe Heler, one of our owners normally rings up for a chat on a Sunday. In the mid-seventies he was a Master of the Cheshire Hunt for several seasons. He now owns a cheese factory in Cheshire. For the record he was telling me it takes 17,600 pints of milk to make one ton of cheese.

Pat and Derek cleaned out my sponsored car as the contract has expired and it goes back tomorrow. It was a bigger job then it sounds, coats, hats, binoculars, waterproofs, books, tapes, racecards, all sorts of things. This is the second year I have had a sponsored car from Terry Holdcroft. At the moment I am negotiating with a car firm in Kirkcaldy, Scotland for another. I think I am the only trainer with a sponsored car, certainly with a firm's name plastered all over it.

Tomorrow will be the first day I have been without a car for years. Hopefully, I will get a new one shortly. I am keen to get my number plate on-J888 ACK, which Pat Knight bought me for my birthday.

MONDAY December 30

JESSIE is flying in preperation for tomorrow. All the horses did road work with the exception of Palacegate Racing, Palacegate King and Cee-Jay-Ay. They went to Smiths-we then put them through the stalls ready for Southwell on Wednesday.

Derek and David Bowker came to see their Superlative colt, now named Super Seve, bought at the Leger Sales.

Very busy today moving horses around getting ready to farm out for road work starting on Wednesday.

Martin took two to Cumbria for Phil Tuck first thing. When he returned, he and Amanda took four each to Garry Gosney and brought seven yearlings back.

The Taufan filly we bought at the St Leger Sales came up from David Brown's Furnace Mill Stud and he took four back for his girls to ride.

Geraldine Rees sent her box up for four. A Belfort filly came from Devon, two fillies by Sayf El Arab and Beveled came from the Bearstone Stud, already broken.

The two Margarets have picked a lovely name for the Beveled filly which was their Christmas box-Margaret's Gift.

All day I was wondering why our Jo wasn't walking her box to go shopping. Then when Ruby delivered a whacking big parcel from Grattans Catalogue full of all sorts of stuff for her hols, silver shoes, blouses, shorts, etc, I realised why. She had no reason to go out, the shops were being sent to her.

TUESDAY December 31

7.10am-It's a lovely sight looking out of our kitchen window into the main yard lit up with all the verandah lights on. The lads and lasses are dashing about carrying muck sacks, water buckets, pitch forks, brushes, bales of straw and so on.

Big day today-Jessie running at Catterick. He has just had a lead out and he's fine. Martin is taking two other horses with Jessie for Chris Morris, wife of Flat jockey Stuart, to ride them round the roads for a few weeks. Chris used to work for us before she married. The rugs the horses have been turned out in are to be washed and mended. Anna Tompkins is to pick them up at Catterick.

My greyhound Lisnakill Wish, owned in partnership with Sonia Newman, has hit the front page headlines in the greyhound section of The Sporting Life, with a picture of me instead of the dog-he runs at Wimbledon Friday. Just rode Cee-Jay-Ay along with two Palacegate horses to blow them out for tomorrow. He flew-that run over hurdles has put him just right. Yesterday he came out of the stalls better than I've seen him, as sometimes he misses the break.

Second lot I rode the Bear to lead the yearlings for three-and-a-half furlongs in pairs about four lengths apart. Then back in a nice bunch. The crack from the lads was great. You can tell the yearlings are all firing-no coughs. The Bear is as fresh as paint again. As we were riding up our lane there was one magpie sat on the hedge. God, I hope it isn't bad luck.

In the paddock at Catterick Jessie looks a bomb. Thirteen runners in the race. Reg Leah, Jessie's owner, finally got here. He thought it was doubtful due to commitments.

The favourite, Just Frankie, trained by Mary Reveley (left), strode off in

front, jumping well. Jessie was always second and that's how they finished. It was a good run as I am sure Mary's horse is useful. Jessie met the water all wrong. From then on his jumping wasn't as fluent as it could have been. Take nothing away from the winner though-he is a good horse.

Came back from Catterick and watched A Question of Sport then a great film, Back to School, on the television.

Kevin and Flash can't get a babysitter so they are having a party in Kevin's house. It's 10.30pm-I have been invited so I'll go for an hour or so.

Reading in today's Racing Post I see that Sawdust Jack of Mick Easterby's has been put down. A few years ago I named a horse Spitting Mick after Mick. There was no malice in doing this. Mick's always game for a laugh or a bit of fun. Seeing what I had done Mick said "I'll name a horse after you-Yer Bugger!"

WEDNESDAY January 1 1992

HAPPY NEW YEAR, and Many Happy Returns to all the horses.
The staff have swapped shifts. We now have the Christmas crew off. On the way to Southwell I saw my first lamb of the year in a farm just outside Cockerham. Also, just before arriving at the entry to the motorway I spotted two magpies for luck. For a change the roads were quiet.
Three runners today. Cee-Jay-Ay ran in the fourth race, a one mile handicap. He missed the break again but soon got back into the race. He ran fair to finish third of the eight runners. Probably could do with a bit further now as he just stayed on. Palacegate Racing's race was next, he also finished third. He had every chance and was beaten by that bit better horses. But he should win a small race or two before long.
Next of our trio was Palacegate King. He was bottom weight in this six furlong handicap. Unlike Cee-Jay, this fellow pinged the stalls and kept racing right to the line to win by a length. It certainly was Palacegate King's birthday. This was his first win from six other attempts. Now he is more mature he should have no trouble again in similar company. It was nice for Palacegate Racing Corporation as the boss of the outfit, David Spencer, runs the syndicate well. He hired a box to entertain the members who were there in full force. It was great for them as they are so good for the game.
Two yearlings, sorry two-year-olds, came today, both broken, one by Evelyn Slack and the other by Jeff Ewbanks.

THURSDAY January 2

VERY windy, in fact gale force. Riding the Bear for a mile canter I could hardly breathe with the force of the wind in my face. All the two-year-olds were lunged or went on walkers. It was too windy for roadwork.
Jo thinks writing this diary is a bit of an ego trip and I should stick to training horses-she could be right. But like Magnus Magnusson on Master-mind says: "I've started, so I'll finish."
Took the New Year staff to a pub for a drink to even things up with the Christmas workers. We went to the Stork at Conder Green as The Manor was closed.
Jo is packing our cases ready for our holidays. If she puts in everything she has recently bought on her shopping expeditions she ought to get Geoffrey Gibbs and Nigel Gray, the handicappers to carry them for her. The other day a couple of new cases came up our stairs. I hope they're the new jobs with wheels on.
It's 8.0pm and it's still very windy. On the news there are reports of damage, especially up in Scotland. About three years ago we had some new wooden boxes put up by Hodgsons of Cotherstone, near Barnard Castle. After just a

few months the wind got under the roofs of three of the boxes, lifted them up right across the main yard and into the orchard. Since then the wind has always been a bit of a worry to me. The next morning when we opened the box doors to feed the horses and discovered there were no roofs-what a sight. It took us half an hour to find them.

FRIDAY January 3

I LED the two-year-olds round the three furlong on the Bear, nice and steady three times. Same again next lot, this time on Gorinsky. All the horses are fine, looking good and running well.

Jo and I are getting ready now for our three week holiday in Barbados. I have just fetched a case down from upstairs. It's very heavy but has got wheels on it. What a berk I'm going to look leading that up at Gatwick Airport. Mind you, I suppose it's better than finishing up in hospital with a hernia trying to carry it.

Alan took us to Manchester Airport in his car as we are catching the shuttle to Gatwick. Fred Viner and Stan Newman are picking us up there because we are going on to Wimbledon to see Charlie (Lisnakill Wish) run.

On the way to Manchester I was asking Alan if we had any chance of him

**LISNAKILL WISH : Charlie was absolutely brilliant
in beating some of the best dogs around
to win at Wimbledon.**

getting clipped out whilst we were away. His hair is a cross between Billy Two Rivers, the all-in wrestler, and John Francome. I suppose we'll have to wait and see. Travelling on the M6 in the opposite direction going towards Cockerham we saw the Findon Horse Transport box.

It's occupants are Paris House and Memsahb who are coming back to us to restart training.

When we eventually arrived at Wimbledon we had a really nice table to have dinner with a beautiful view of the track. Just messing about with forecasts and trios I had a couple up. The sixth race on the card at 8.45pm was our race. Lisnakill Wish, number two with a blue jacket. This is Charlie's first run over hurdles. The number four dog Tramps Ball is one of the best hurdlers about. Our fellow has been thrown in at the deep end. Phil Rees the trainer, and Stan the other owner's husband, are very hopeful of the boy running well. Off they go-our chap is close-up fourth going to the first hurdle. He checks a little and then on the first bend he accelerates to go a close third on the inside. Jumping like a buck, he's making up ground with every stride. Into the last bend he takes up the running and goes on to win by a length and a half-he was 2/1 joint favourite.

Charlie was absolutely brilliant. In fact, brilliant isn't the word for it-first run over hurdles and to beat some of the best dogs around. I don't have to tell you I was chuffed. We had a marvellous night. On this run we shall hear more of Lisnakill Wish.

Jo and I went and stayed the night at Fred and Gwen Viner's, who were coming on holiday with us.

SATURDAY January 4

HAVING a cup of tea and reading Fred's Sporting Life I see old Red Rum is poorly. What a great horse he has been and a great ambassador for National Hunt racing. Although the old fellow is 27 I hope he's alright. The Jockey Club should give an honour to these great horses. The likes of him, Dessie, Sheikh Albadou, Generous-they are so good for the game.

Stan Newman took us to the airport. When we got on the plane it was delayed an hour because there was something loose. The cabin crew stuffed us passengers with food and drink for nine hours. In between, we watched a couple of films. On arriving at Barbados everyone seems so friendly. It's the only time I have ever seen complimentary drinks being offered at an airport. Peter Manning, who I knew quite well from his visits to England and through him being an owner of Steve Norton's, sent a car to meet us at the airport driven by one of his staff named Nicholas. He took us to our hotel, the Asta, right on the beach front. Peter is the Manager of this hotel. There we unpacked, had a shower and then a nice meal with a couple of cool lagers in the open air restaurant. While we were in there a whacking great frog hopped through. It must have weighed in at around half a pound.

It looks a nice place, plenty of lawns, two swimming pools, trees and shrubs, a big fish pond with hundreds of fish, lots of wild birds flying around. At the rear entrance to our apartment there are some trees with monkeys living in them.

BEACH BUM : It's a grand life here, soaking up the sun outside the Asta Hotel, Barbados.

SUNDAY January 5

FED the birds from our balcony with a sliced loaf of bread that was in our fridge.

Nicholas arrived as arranged at 7.0am to take us to watch the horses swim in the sea. The horses loved it. It's so warm and refreshing for them. Totally different from the horse swimming pools.

A girl called Julie Liddle, who worked for us and had previously worked in Australia for Colin Hayes, told us an amazing story about swimming all their horses. Julie did a yearling filly and the first time they swam her, she entered the pool and just kept on walking until she was under water. Apparently she couldn't swim. There was a bit of a flap on to get her out.

Back to Barbados-Peter Manning was there on the beach. He introduced us to Wes Hall, the West Indies fast bowler who was watching his horses swim. He has them in partnership with ex-team mate Gary Sobers. Wes is the Minister of Sport and Tourism. His son Sean is a jockey here and I'm told quite a good one. Wes was chuffed when I told him David Brown, Bob Willis and Fred Truman were owners of ours. He asked to be remembered to them and then went on to reminisce about the old times they had together. David Brown had told me of the fearsome sight he faced batting when Wes came running towards him with a ruddy great big crucifix swinging from side to side on his hairy chest. Wes and the Australian Geoff Thompson were rated by David as two of the fastest bowlers he had met.

When we came back to the hotel, the four of us went for a swim in the sea. Fred had to borrow a pair of swimming shorts as Gwen hadn't packed him any. There was quite a bit of surplus material in them.

At mid-day Peter invited us for lunch at his house on the east side of the coast, some 15 miles or so away. Again Nicholas picked us up in the car. The views from Peter's house were breathtaking. Built near a cliff edge overlooking the noisy raging sea with the warm breeze blowing. His house and a lighthouse are the only buildings in sight. We had some rum and cokes and an absolutely brilliant meal cooked by Peter. We arrived back at our hotel around 8.0pm.

MONDAY January 6

IT'S just gone 5.0am. Not light enough to feed the birds and yet I can hear them singing away. These damn mosquitoes don't half bite. My arms are covered in lumps from the buggers. All the shopping my Mrs does, rummaging through the toiletries I can't see anything to put on bites though.

6.0am Peter came and picked me up to go and see the horses work on the track. It was good to see Bill Marshall and Scobie Breasley. I was introduced to all the other trainers. It was great watching the horses and listening to the banter from the trainers up on their stand. Looking at the horses it's very hard for them to hold condition with the continuous heat. Yet I saw two yearlings of Peter's at his place yesterday and they had long coats like ours get in the winter.

Garrison Savannah, St Michael, is the home of the racecourse and stables. There are about 140 horses in training there. You know now where Jenny Pitman's Gold Cup horse gets his name from. It was formerly used by the

British regiment stationed here in colonial times. It's a very sharp grass track with training facilities on the inside comprising of a dirt and a sand track.

In the evening we went to a dinner show at the Plantation Garden Theatre. It was great. A marvellous dinner, unlimited drinks, a live show and dancing afterwards. In the mini coach we had a sing song. If our next eighteen nights are like this one we shall have had a nice holiday.

TUESDAY January 7

FRED and I walked up to the Garrison to see the horses work down the back stretch. Later on we had a walk round Queens Park, St Michaels, where we saw a baobab tree estimated to be over one thousand years old. It is sixty-one-and-a-half feet in circumference. An African tree-but no one knows how it got to Barbados!

In the afternoon we sunbathed and went snorkelling in the sea-that was great fun.

That evening our hotel was having a rum punch party and a barbecue-so we had some of that. Good it was, too. There was a five piece band-they were tremendous. The lead singer was out of this world. If a Lionel Ritchie, Michael Jackson, Chris de Burgh or whoever's song came up, this fellow could sing it just like them. He was a marvellous mimic, or impressionist, call him what you like. The thing was he didn't realise he did it. He just sang one after the other, just like they would. Whereas you would normally only see these great singers at different times, we saw them all together here.

WEDNESDAY January 8

UP AGAIN watching work at 6.0am. You would think I got enough of it at home. It's the crack. Today the trainers were full of it about Tony Murray found dead in bed. News travels fast. Strange how bad news often travels faster than good.

Ronnie Burke, a trainer from Canada who used to train here in Barbados, is over on holiday. He was telling me he trained one of our ex-horses, Navarro Secondo.

We won two races with him as a two-year-old then sold him on. He won races for Ronnie but later broke a leg and was buried at his owners' farm.

I went snorkeling on the coral near the Asta. This is good fun and very easy to do. Seeing the life underwater is so fascinating.

Around lunchtime we had a phone call from John Forsythe, Terry Holdcroft and their wives, some of our owners who are over here on holiday. They were in the lobby of our hotel so they spent the afternoon with us, drinking

rum punches. We sat around the poolside, chatting about racing.
In the evening we booked a dinner show at the Plantation Restaurant and
Garden Theatre.

THURSDAY January 9

7.0am by the look of the sun already, it looks as if it will be real hot later. I
am giving the horses a rest today. Bill Marshall told me yesterday that a
nice little grey he worked, called Master Dancer, could possibly win the first
race on Saturday. Mind, I am not rushing around changing more English
money into Barbados dollars on the strength of that yet.
A few years ago in Hong Kong, two ex-English trainers, Frank Carr and Eric
Collingwood, trying to tip Jo and I winners were worse than The Life's Geoff
Lester.
Sunning ourselves on the beach, two mounted police came riding past. In
the heat the horses were absolutely lathered.
Sent a fax home for details of the Taufan filly, as Peter seems keen to have a
2-year-old with us.
The fish in that pond always look hungry. They look up at you and are not a
bit frightened. I took two slices of bread to them in the afternoon. Within
seconds of putting them on the surface the slices were gone and what a
noise the fish made. They are that greedy they are probably piranhas.
Jo, Gwen and I went to Treasure Beach Hotel to meet up with Terry, John
and the two Margarets to have a meal at their place in Holetown. Fred
didn't come. Can you believe it, he's got a cold. The taxi man who took us
bought the vehicle two years and two months ago. It was his pride and joy-
immaculate. It looked brand new. The food on this island is very good
everywhere. Tonight was no exception.

FRIDAY January 10

LOOKING at the Barbados Advocate, that's a newspaper, I see we have
Palacegate King running at Southwell.
We have hired a car to drive round the island. I don't mind a one-off in cars.
If they go in it tomorrow, though, it will be without me. I can get enough of
cars at home-it's the sun I want!
The first stop we had was Folkestone Park at Church Point where there was
a lovely beach with excellent coral. We went snorkeling. The unusual fish
formation and different depths at sea was fascinating. We moved on then to
a shell shop. I didn't go a bundle on this, though.
Animal Flower Cave and Pirates Tavern came next at St Lucy. This is on the
most northern point of the island with a super view. You can see the

powerful Atlantic Ocean thrashing the cliffs with huge waves, sending water high in the air.

In the Pirates Tavern there were thousands of business cards and paper currencies from all over the world, decorating every part of the walls and ceiling. Very interesting this, I could only see one old English pound note though, and no Scottish money. Whether it's because we are mean, or the sign of the times, or what-but it's true. It's probably a good thing trainer Mick Easterby didn't see that English pound note or he might have pocketed it.

Finally we visited St Nicholas Abbey in the parish of St Peter, built in 1650. It's one of the oldest plantations in the Caribbean. It fascinated me. Out in the rear, in a kind of stable or courtyard, there used to be a toilet without flushing water, with seats for four people to sit upsides each other. There were lots of guinea fowl wandering about making a heck of a noise.

Inside the Abbey was a room in which sugar accounts, wages and the likes were stuck on a wall in the most beautiful hand writing you ever did see.

One of the sheets valued the slaves. A top man was £150, a top woman £140. Some were valued as little as £20. One poor old man named John didn't have a price at all. The lady showing us around said as the slaves grew older they devalued. Poor old John, therefore, was worthless. As the children grew older, their value increased.

In the evening we went to the Bamboo Bar, famous for their lobster. Sitting in the open air listening to the sea thrashing about, brought the day to a really nice end.

SATURDAY January 11

Big day today-the Garrison's opening meet. Only five races on the card. One of the races didn't fill so it was abandoned. The racing authorites here don't reopen races through lack of initial entries like ours do now. Everywhere looks spick and span. On days when I have been up to the course watching the horses work, there have been ground staff cutting grass and jobbing all the time. It rained through the night, and although the going still is firm, the rain has freshened the vegetation up. Everywhere looks good and there's a great buzz.

The Governor General, Dame Nita Barrow, unfortunately couldn't attend the meeting and our party was kindly invited by the Turf Club to occupy her box for the day. We had a super time being so well looked after, and wined and dined to perfection. I was asked to judge the best turned out in the first race, post time 2.30pm, in which Bill Marshall's horse was placed third, beaten two short heads in a photo. I was also invited to watch the third race in the Stewards' box. Unfortunately, in that race, Butch Cassidy collapsed as he was being pulled up after finishing third. His jockey Brett Callaghan was taken to hospital with concussion.

There was a good crowd and some excellent racing. We had a couple of rum punches after racing and enjoyed a really good day. Bill Marshall, without doubt was the hero of the hour, training three of the five winners in Pisces, Stylish Dance and Credit Note. Gwen and Jo left just before the last race to pick Pat Knight up from the airport.

We had a get together, Peter, Terry and his crowd, and our crowd for a meal in the evening. Of course, I wanted all the news from England off Pat. First she told me Palacegate King had won again at Southwell-great. Red Rum was a lot better. Tony Murray, it appeared, had taken an overdose. Then Jo said I have some bad news. Andy Campion had been taken into hospital last Sunday and had died. Ruby our secretary rang Pat up to tell her as she didn't want to fax or phone to let me know. Pat told Jo travelling in the car from the airport. Isn't that awful.

At least she didn't suffer long. Jo and I only sent her a card yesterday and a few days before we came here, Andy was in our house and in such good form.

Just as Jo had got back from the airport Stan Newman rang to let us know Charlie (Lisnakill Wish) had won again last Friday at Wimbledon by no less than five lengths.

SUNDAY January 12

THE BIRDS are getting to know me now, seeing as I feed them every morning.

Some of the beach bums would make good car salesmen. One of them carries a small suitcase full of rubbish jewellery and greets you with his arm out to shake your hand, "Hello sir, they tell me you have been looking for me."

Another is called Dusty-he's the best. Earlier in the week when I was on the beach swimming, he said to me, "Can you help me sir? I'm looking for a loan, my wallet is clean empty."

Today he came up to me as I'm flat out on my sunbed soaking up the sun. I asked him if he had filled his wallet up yet and did he manage to get a loan. He replied, "No man, I did not and I don't look as if I am going to."

I didn't have any money with me the other day because I'd been swimming. So today I ask him when did he last eat. He tells me, "yesterday tea-time, man." Giving him a ten dollar note he thanks me and says he'll now go and get one litre of milk, a loaf and some cheese.

Chally Jones and Peter came down to the poolside to have a bit of banter. We had two or three rum punches and a few laughs. It's always good crack with racing folk, whatever part of the world you're in. Asking after Brett Callaghan, Chally informs me he's out of his concussion but still detained in hospital. Thankfully, he's going to be all right.

We were conned at the Tastebuds Restaurant at the Golden Beach Hotel. It was advertised as "West Indian Floor Show, Limbo, Fire-Eating, Dancing on broken glass." It was all of that-performed by just one man. We had a good laugh though, and that's what it's all about.

HERE I am talking to Chally Jones, who rode an incredible 38 Classic winners in Barbados and Trinidad.

MONDAY January 13

PAT, Fred and myself went out for an early morning swim. Before we managed to get there we met up with the monkeys. They were in good form. When I leave this place it will be a good idea to send for Neville, our feed man, to take over looking after the fish and birds and the rest of the animals.

When on holiday I try not to ring home. However, since Friday was an up and down day, I broke the rule. Ruby told me our local church was crammed full at Andy's service. Ray Cochrane rode Palacegate King as John Carroll, Kevin Ryan, Wally and Steve Porritt from our yard, were coffin bearers. Our Alan went on our behalf. Roy and Norma Peebles from Scotland, John Brown, Brian Durkin and lots more of our owners were there from different parts of the country.

In the afternoon we went in a submarine named Atlantis. To get to the sub we had a fifteen minute journey by motor launch, during which our guide pointed out to us various places of interest. Before we were allowed to board Atlantis we had to allow the previous voyagers to disembark. Jimmy Savile was among them.

To be honest, I had a few reservations about going on the sub as I get a bit claustrophobic. I'm not at all keen on cramped conditions. Well down there I was anybody's-it was absolutely great. The fish were there in millions. At different depths the shapes and colours of the coral was mind boggling. A sight you should never miss if the chance comes your way. Raffles at Holetown was the venue for our evening meal where we met up with Terry Holdcroft's crew. We had a super meal. It finished up with a racing quiz-of course, for money! One question, what won the 1937 Grand National? My money was on Royal Mail. Terry Holdcroft bet me quite a sum it wasn't Royal Mail. John Forsythe also had the same bet with me. My thinking was that the only two horses it could be is Reynoldstown or Battleship if it isn't Royal Mail. I asked if I could nominate all three for that year but Terry wouldn't hear of it. Tomorrow, I will have to see if Peter Manning has some means of proof. It's great to have a quiz but it's better with someone asking the questions who has a book with the answers. Especially with all the rum punches that float around on an evening in Barbados.

Margaret Holdcroft said her mother was getting married again at the grand age of 74! She's been courting her friend for ten years or more. Margaret wouldn't take money on her not having any half brothers or sisters.

TUESDAY January 14

AT 6.0am I went in our hired car to watch the horses work at the track and have a bit of crack with the trainers. We had to listen to the hard luck story from Bill about the horse he thought would win.

What a day Fred and I had. We went on the Jolly Roger. That's a pirate boat. We, and everyone else, could drink as much rum punch as we wanted. Most people wanted plenty-it was a real fun day.

Some walked the plank. Naturally I had to have a go. Fred didn't because he said in jest that he saw a shark. (I hope he was joking). We had a great time dancing around. Everyone really let their hair down. If ever you're over there, it's the thing to do. I can recommend it. Bob Willis once told me he got married on the Jolly Roger in 1974. It was consummated there but I bet there ain't a lot of people know that.

Peter Manning has just shown me a fax confirming Royal Mail won the 1937 Grand National. That's a good job as Terry and John went in that strong, they made me have my doubts. To be truthful, my head has felt better and its only 4.55pm-later we are off to a barbecue.

The barbecue was great. We danced until the early hours. I got legless on that awful rum punch. It was only this afternoon after the Jolly Roger trip when I vowed I wouldn't drink the stuff again. Mind you, my man Fred didn't get the trip at all. He didn't even turn up for evening stable. He went to bed in the afternoon and he is still there!

Most of us were a bit the worse for wear. In our party was a New York pediatrician, John Reveley, the Northern trainer's son, with his girl friend Judy. We had a competition-whoever drew the cigarette out of the packet without the filter on was the first in the pool. Peter Manning was the lucky one. Man of his word Peter-jumped in fully clothed.

WEDNESDAY January 15

HAVE been known to have felt better than I did this morning. Chally Jones invited us to lunch at his Blue Ribbon Farms. Peter took Fred and me in his car. On the way we stopped at a Supermarket. Next to the car park there was a church with its doors wide open. As Peter was getting his goods the congregation in the church burst out with the hymn "We Thank Thee Lord, Our God". It was the nicest singing you ever did hear.

Arriving at Chally's I had a fresh coconut drink. Peter cooked a lovely curry with chicken, pigs' tails, a vegetable called squosh, rice, the whole works. It was real good. Joining us for lunch were Elan Lord, a Director of the Turf Club and a Steward, Alan Storey the vet and George Hedghill the trainer and ex-Barbados football player. Apparently, they have lunches like this periodically in each other's houses for men only and have a good talk about things. It's great. Chally's Mrs doesn't approve of them. Chally showed us his horses and one of his lads called Sprinter referred to a staying horse as a journeyman-this tickled me.

WORKING HOLIDAY : Here I am tinkling the ivories at the Buccaneer Bay Hotel, accompanying the singer. I won't pack up the day job just yet.

Just heard on the grapevine that Palacegate Racing has won at Southwell. Jim Marsden, a new owner of ours, invited us to a meal at the Buccaneer Bay Hotel which he owns. It was like dining somewhere in Newmarket. Bill and Pat Watts, Tony Collins, Gavin Hunter, Charles Benson and a host of other familiar faces were there. The music was a one man show. He had a music box, played steel drums and sang. Fred spotted the piano on stage and as he's seen me perform before he got me an invite to accompany the soloist, which I did. I think the man appreciated a bit of company but I will keep the day job. Plus the fact that I am on holiday and I don't want to be taking work on.

THURSDAY January 16

DROVE up to the track to watch the horses work. Peter Manning's horse, Back Raise, worked well. He runs on Saturday. I may just have my pound on that one. Geoff Lewis, who is over here on holiday, rang and left a message to ring him. Bill Marshall invited Jo and me out for lunch at the Yacht Club. It was very enjoyable. We even managed a few rum punches. We got a taxi to Bridgetown to meet up with Fred, Gwen and Pat for a helicopter tour of the island. On the way in the taxi I quietly pushed the gear lever of the car into neutral. The engine was racing like mad for ages before he noticed and put the lever into gear. Next time I did it, the driver says-: "Man this car is running fast and missing gears. I will just have to get it mended."
The view from up there in the helicopter was really stunning. We saw our hotel, the racecourse and other places of interest we have got to know.
In the evening, we met up with Terry and his crew for a trip on the Bajan Queen. We had a feed on board and danced to a very good live band. It looks as if we may have to rest Fred for a few days. He is on the verge of breaking down. His ankle has swollen up quite a bit recently. He wasn't turning out for many dances tonight on the Bajan Queen. He'll need a holiday to get over this one when we get back.

FRIDAY January 17

WOULD you believe it-we are going riding today.
Eleven of us, all boots and saddles ready for a 2.15pm start. Unfortunately, there are two non runners. We have a vets certificate for Fred but Peter has just plain jibbed. I thought we may have to hire a block and tackle to load up John Reveley as he's a big lad.
Riding the horses on the beach we had some fun. My mount was an ex-Bill Marshall racehorse that wouldn't come out of the stalls.
Our horses at home are doing very well. Palacegate King has just won again at Southwell. Peter here rings a town bookie to keep us informed. Punters bet on British racing here every day and have commentaries on them just like we have at home.
We stayed in our hotel for our evening meal for a change-and a rest.

SATURDAY January 18

STAN NEWMAN, my dog partner's husband rang. He's staying at the

Treasure Beach Hotel-the same place as Terry and Co. We are all meeting up to go racing later on.

Rang Geoff Lewis to arrange a barbecue with him for next Tuesday.

Jessie and the Bear run at Haydock in the Steel Plate Young Chasers event. Looking at the race it looks fairly hot. It will be a bonus if either of them win but in a Novice Chase you never know. My man Peter has informed me neither of them were in the frame.

Terry's crew and our lot all went to the races, Peter getting us all complimentary tickets. It was a lovely day and the racing was good. Bill Marshall's Master Dancer got it right today and won by an easy three lengths carrying my money on him again. I judged the best turned out in the 3rd and 4th races and had a good crack with Scobie.

Fred and I played about having forecasts and trifectas. In the finish we

WHAT A THREESOME : Fred Viner, Scobie Breasley and Me
at the races.

came away about even, having had loads of fun seeing no end of people from England on holiday. It was great. It poured with rain after the 5th race and we got soaked getting our car from the car park.

We had the whole team out-thirteen in all-for a meal at the Tamarine Cove Neptune Restaurant. Great food and plenty of laughs, although I thought I might have to do a bit of washing up when the bill came. It's a good job I was sat down when he gave it to me.

SUNDAY January 19

YOUNG piglets for sale. Nine weeks old, price negotiable. For details ring, and then a phone number. That's the first thing that came up on the TV screen at 7.05am. Good isn't it?

It's been raining all night-just like being back at Cockerham.

David Seale rang and invited us up to his Hopefield Stud at Charnock near the airport. The big house is a really beautiful place, steeped in history. David is the vice-President of the Turf Club and a Steward. He is also the biggest producer of rum in Barbados-even bigger than Cockspur, the firm who sponsor the Cockspur Gold Cup, the most valuable race run at the Garrison Savannah track. For the record, all rum is white, they add caramel to change the colour for dark rum.

In England, David has horses in training with Richard Hannon. On his stud farm he stands four stallions. The place is beautifully well kept. Scobie Breasley is one of his trainers here in Barbados. While we were there Richard and Jo Hannon joined us. They had flown in the previous day.

After looking around all the stallions, mares, horses in training and year-lings, we had a nice lunch down at David's beach house. While we were there four elderly people came up the driveway and walked into the house. There was a language problem because they were Italian and were under the impression that David's house was a hotel and they wanted to be served with tea. Nobody minded too much although after they had their tea they were pretty embarrassed when it was explained they didn't have to pay. All our lot were cracking up. After our Italian friends had gone we had a swim in the sea which virtually comes into David's garden. Back in the house then for another couple of rum punches, a bit more chat about horses then off in our hired job to our hotel.

We were joined there by Stan and Sonia Newman. We had a meal and danced to a live band to finish off yet another nice day.

MONDAY January 20

SPENT most of today sunbathing and swimming as it was very hot. Ronnie Burke the Canadian trainer came to see me for a chat. Wherever I am in the world it's nice to talk about racing. I learnt something here this week-Bill Marshall told me when they have a difficult horse to break, they put the tack on the horse in the dark and they don't buck or play about at all. They behave like Christians. They do that for a couple of days then there is no problem.

Met up with Stan and Sonia at the Treasure Beach Hotel. Terry Holdcroft, John Forsythe and the two Margarets were there ready to leave for England. They had a good time but they would have enjoyed another week.

We had a great meal with a few drinks. Then we went on to the Bamboo Bar where Bill and Pat Watts, A K Collins and a load more were enjoying themselves.

We had a sing-song in the car on the way home driven by me. The end of yet another brilliant day.

TUESDAY January 21

JO, Fred and myself went to David Seale's stud to meet up with Richard Hannon, Edward and Sue Hide and see the two-year-olds. Whenever R Hannon and I get together there is always some sort of a bet struck. Today's bet was 1,000 Barbadian dollars. We each picked out three of David's two-year-olds to run this season. The winner is the one with the most wins at the end of it.

OLD PAL'S ACT: Richard Hannon and me watching the two-year-olds work, just like back home. Whenever we get together there has to be a bet struck. Nothing changes, even when we're on holiday. Today's wager is on David Seale's youngsters.

Today in Barbados is a public holiday in celebration of the birthday of Errol Walton Barrows who led Barbados to independence. He died in 1987.

Fred, Gwen, Stan, Sonia, Jo and myself went to see the Flower Forest at Richmond, St Joseph in our car. Pat went horse riding with John Reveley and his girlfriend Judy. They got it right I must say. It was as exciting as watching paint dry. All these stupid names, impossible to pronounce on little bushes and trees. The sun was belting down with us stuck there sweltering in a damned wood. I know now where the Maktoum family get their horses' names from.

Stan has just rung up Wimbledon dog track. Charlie has only won again. He has now won all his three starts over hurdles and beaten good dogs in the bargain. What a star.

I'm driving again tonight. Thought I'd been given the red card after last night. The Pisces Restaurant was where they had to put up with us tonight. Lovely place it was too. Situated right on the sea front. When the tide comes in the water comes up to the restaurant walls. The food was very good. The only low spot was there was no music. Stan, Fred and myself talked boxing as all three of us love it.

WEDNESDAY January 22

THIS morning Jo came with me to see the horses exercise. It all operates very smoothly with the different trainers. They work just like they do in the States. Sandford Prince, owned by David Seale, was out this morning getting ready, hopefully, to win his third Cockspur Cup-a big race here at the

TONY, the jewellery salesman with the
voice of Paul Robeson, entertains us with a sing-song on the beach.

Garrison. After which he is to be retired to stud. Bill Marshall has invited Jo and I for lunch again on Thursday at the Yacht Club-that sounds like another headache coming on.

This morning, sunning ourselves on the beach, two of the sellers were there. They were in good form. Fred, Stan, Jo, Pat, Gwen and myself all bought hats made out of palm leaves from one called Jimmy.

Tony, the one with the jewellery who says "they tell me you have been looking for me," has a very deep rich voice and sounds very much like Paul Robeson. When I mentioned this to him he told me he could sing like him too. So we had a singalong on the sand. Two patrolling police guards were laughing like mad along with the rest of the Asta punters. It was great fun. We were like the Black and White Minstrels.

Jo, Gwen, Fred, Peter and myself went to the Gunners for the biggest lobster you ever did see. It was brill. God knows what time we got to bed but it was late. I know we have to be up early in the morning to go fishing.

THURSDAY January 23

I WAS right about the headache. These rum punches are real rocket fuel.

Went fishing first thing. John Reveley, Fred, Stan and myself had a 20 dollar bet who could catch the first fish and who could catch the biggest. I don't want to gloat but I caught the first, weighing around 24lb. I'm also ashamed to say I caught a kingfish. We all managed to catch something. We had a great morning. Pat came with us to take photos of any whoppers we caught. She didn't fish-just fed them. I did warn her to put a rope round her teeth before we set off. The other ladies took a lead from Jo's book and went shopping.

It was just as I had predicted regarding the headache at the Yacht Club. Bill Marshall received the DFC for flying aircraft. The way he handles the rum, he should have been a sailor in the Navy.

We had a nice lunch and a bit of crack. Came back to the Asta for a kip for an hour. Then we set off to Sandy Lane to watch the polo match between the home team, the Caribs against San Dominico. It was a very good game producing a win for the locals 3.5 goals to 5.

In the evening we all went to the Ho Kwong Chinese restaurant for a banquet. It was really good with enough spare food to have fed another eight. I kept on water all night. Thankfully Bill Marshall wasn't there.

FRIDAY January 24

WE are going home tomorrow evening so we all thought we would have a day on the beach and laze around our pool. We even had a game of cricket which was fun, plenty of laughs.

At the poolside we opened a couple of bottles of Moet, that Fred had bought in the Duty Free shop on our way in. We brought out our bottle of white wine and Peter produced some more wine. So you could say we had a celebration pool party.

A great surprise came when Peter presented Jo and me with a lovely mahogany horse for our contribution to racing. It was made in Barbados from the local trees. The authentic origin of the figure made me appreciate the award even more.

Peter took us all to a barbecue at the Stowaway in the hotel mini-bus where we saw Richard Hannon and David Seale who very kindly gave me a fairly recent Sporting Life to read.

Then we went on to the Cari Beach Bar where we danced until very late. Fred is a really good sport and always game for a bit of fun. While he was dancing with Stan's wife Sonia he had both his arms in the air so I pulled his pants down to his ankles. The lady singer in the band had to stop singing. She couldn't go on for laughing. We had an absolutely fabulous night, with a few rum punches inside of us followed by a rousing sing-song on the bus all the way to the Asta.

SATURDAY January 25

ON our final day of the holiday, Fred and I had a swim and lay on the beach for an hour before going off to the races.

We have had an absolutely wonderful holiday. I can't remember having one bad day. Bad heads, yes, but bad days, no!

Peter packed six of us in his car like sardines and took us to the track. As soon as we got there we saw more fresh faces from England. These included Michael Stoute and Neville Callaghan. Bill Marshall trained the first two winners. Bill told me he did fancy them. But I was so busy doing trifectas and superfectas attempting to earn big money for little outlay, that I failed to back them as straight wins. I never visited the tote windows once for a payout.

There was an announcement over the Tannoy system, Brett Callaghan who had a fall a fortnight ago is still in hospital with some paralysis down one side. He's only young, time's on his side. They are very hopeful he will make a full recovery. During the afternoon David Seale arranged with me to send over a two-year-old filly by Bentom for me to train. I took a shine to the horse when Richard Hannon and I viewed David's horses last Wednesday. Complimentary badges were very kindly provided for the third week running for all members of our party by the Barbados Turf Club, which included tickets for afternoon tea. The food was set fair on a long table where everybody helped themselves. Every visit we have made to the Garrison track we have been taken care of very well.

After racing we still had a few hours before our flight. David Seale invited us all back to his beach house to join Richard Hannon and Co., in a chicken and chip barbecue which Edward Hide had collected from the shop. Before we actually met up with them we checked our cases into the airport. It was a good job too.

Peter Manning ought to have known better, being an ex-pilot, to leave it until the last minute getting us all to the plane. It was only twenty-five minutes before take off. We managed a quick cheerio to Sonia and Stan who still have another week to go. Thanking Peter for all his kindness he'd shown us over the past three weeks-we boarded the plane for the flight home.

SUNDAY January 26

LANDED at Gatwick around 11.0am. Bags had to be taken off the luggage carousel because our connecting flight wasn't until 7.30pm.

Jo and I were pulled up by the customs officer but he let us go when I told him we didn't even have a chance to get our duty frees.

Fred's son Brian had ordered a taxi to take us to their house so we wouldn't be hanging around the airport all day.

Rang Alan up from Fred's to make sure everything was all right.

It's soon 5.30pm and we are getting into another taxi to take us back to Gatwick to catch our Manchester flight.

The captain announces that the first mate is going to fly the plane. I suppose it's like apprentice jockeys. They have got to start somewhere. Next year he might be taking us to the Arc.

Alan met us. True to his word the old lad had had a hair cut. Not exactly down to the wood. Nevertheless he had one.

As soon as we stopped the car in the car park at home Olly, Sol and Dainty (the dogs) saw me and went wild. It was 2.0am when we got to bed after reading all the messages, letters and catching up with things. We had a great time. It's now back to work.

MONDAY January 27

RODE out Miami Bear. Dear me, it doesn't half feel cold after all that heat. It's a very keen frost, nothing like the weather I've been used to for the last three weeks. Had a chat to Olly (O I Oyston) over the fence while on the Bear. All the horses look well, the staff have done a good job in my absence. Three winners from half a dozen runners on the all-weather. They probably think what's he come back for-we were doing all right without him.

The dogs are all laying up with me this morning just in case I nip off again.

Went to see Lynn Campion, Andy's mum in the afternoon. On the way back I noticed our owl had come back. He has lived in the top of a hollow tree in Crimbles Lane for years, but has been missing for a few weeks. James

Kearsley my old army pal and partner, rang to tell me his mother died yesterday.

Signed dozens of horses' passports and training agreements and the like that had piled up in the office waiting for my return. Our A Team are finishing off renovating the fencing on our long all-weather gallop.

Richard Lanni rang me up. He has had a substantial offer for Palatial Style to race in the States. Wants my advice. It was easy-take it.

Tonight I am going to light the fire in the front room and read my three week's Sporting Lifes and Racing Posts to catch up with the racing news.

TUESDAY January 28

1.0am when I got finished reading my papers. Read that Angel Penna, who trained the brilliant filly Allez France, had died. Steve Cauthen had got married. Red Rum is just about better. Martin Pipe has recorded his sixth consecutive century of winners. Looks like Sunday racing will be with us in the not too distant future and much more.

It's very frosty and work is going on repairing the bottom boards on the back stretch of the all-weather. This morning we are just cantering up in pairs on the near straight all-weather. We recently had that part done up with new woodchip, therefore the frost hasn't got right in. The grass is frozen solid. The two Palacegate horses are in tomorrow at Southwell. They just breezed for two furlongs and both went well.

See in the Racing Post that Arazi is the US champion by 5lb. I would go along with that. On Breeders' Cup day he was unbelieveable.

Reg Leah, Jessie's owner, is a very understanding man and thinks a lot about his horse. In the conversation I had with him this morning on the phone, I told him it would benefit Jessie if he was roughed off now and brought back novice chasing after a spring and summer at grass, as he's only five. If that's what is best for the horse, do it, he said. Can't be fairer than that.

9.35pm just sold the Taufan two-year-old to Andy Hoyle on the phone.

WEDNESDAY January 29

IT'S still very frostly but it's a lovely sunny morning. Rode Miami Bear just to blow him out for Edinburgh, weather permitting. All the two-year-olds cantered in pairs for four furlongs on the all-weather after being ridden round the indoor school or off the horse walkers, as the roads are very icy. I see in the Post, Catterick are to stage a £1,000 bumper. That's sad, and a really backward step in prize-money. It would be better if they didn't have the race.

Weather is poor travelling to Southwell, quite thick fog on the M62. John and I are travelling in his car. I haven't got a car now. My sponsor has called his car in.

Passing Clumber Park, part of Sherwood Forest, Robin Hood's old country, the trees were all white with frost. They look a really pretty sight, just like a Christmas card.

There was a fair crowd at Southwell. The all-weather course comes in for a lot of unfair criticism. Nottingham was off. Towcester and Edinburgh meetings are abandoned. Lingfield is the only course in Britain with racing tomorrow. Even if they don't attract massive crowds, the all-weather generates levy in the betting shops.

Palacegate Racing, in the first race, had the worst draw on the outside where the track rides the slowest. He ran well enough finishing fourth, to suggest he could win again. Palacegate King was attempting to win his fourth consecutive race in as many weeks. The little fellow ran a good race finishing third to Pop To Stans, who on his day is not a bad sort.

At 3.30pm I had an appointment to meet a Mr Ransley with a view to buying some hay from him. Last summer wasn't a good year for making good hay. With the amount of horses we have a load of hay doesn't last us very long. However, the hay wasn't top class and it was fairly pricey so I am not wading in. We have two and a half bays on stock so we are far from desperate. It's very important to put the best possible feed down a horses neck. Unlike a cow a horse cannot regurgitate. That means it can't be sick so what goes into its stomach has to be good or it makes him poorly.

I had an appointment at 6.30pm at Lancaster Police Station regarding my brush with basher Bill, a few weeks ago. John Carroll thought in my spare time I might have to serve a few hours doing community work. In fact, I was given the red card-a warning to keep the peace. Except for a couple of speeding offences that's the only time I have stepped out of line. The man is such a bully around here the locals would have given me an award.

THURSDAY January 30

CAUGHT the 8.10am train to London from Lancaster as Jo and I have been invited by David Brown to attend a National Sporting Club luncheon at the Cafe Royal. Normally, we wouldn't have gone, seeing as we have just recently come back from our hols. But it was David's 50th birthday and he was keen for us to go.

On arriving at Euston Station I went to the Tie Shop to buy David one. Lord Whitelaw was there on the station. I passed the time of day with him as I have had the pleasure of meeting him on a few occasions.

At the Cafe Royal people were asking David to let them see his tie. "Give me a pound first," he said. David collected their money then gave it to me for any charity I thought fit. (When I got home I put it in our office blind box). Bob Willis was doing the introductions and Harry Carpenter was the guest of honour. Harry made a speech that was so funny most of the people in the room were howling with laughter. A cake was brought to our table with one candle on for David. Bob, David, myself and our wives went for a drink to the Glass Blowers.

At half past five Jo and I sought a cab to Euston to catch the train home.

Lisnakill Wish runs at Wimbledon in the 8.45pm. We were all contemplating going but we couldn't get a connecting train back to Lancaster. Staying over was out of the question as we have to get home to do some work.

The train was a bit late getting into Lancaster. Saw Alan first thing, horses and everything else is all right. Dashed into the house to put Ceefax on. There he was, number three dog, Charlie, went in 1/2 favourite, in the Springbok Trial Stakes at Wimbledon. Great-what a dog. Ringing up my Wimbledon spy, I heard that Charlie had won by five and a half lengths and took up the running after the first bend. I would have had to give him a ticking off if he'd got beat going as early as that.

FRIDAY January 31

EVERYWHERE is frozen solid. Neville, the feeder, who looks after the horses on the walker, has a big shed down there. We keep tools and things that need to be repaired and the like. Neville has hidden somewhere among this stuff a bottle of whisky and on cold mornings he takes a swig.

"You will have had a drop today, Neville?"-I said.

"Not arf, boss," he replied.

Last year before Neville came back from his holidays someone found his horde, emptied the bottle and filled it with ... well, you can guess! When Neville found out he came galloping into the main yard as we were all riding round with the bottle in his hand. The swear words just flowed out. I don't know if it was Jeff King or Ryan Price who held the previous record. But I think Neville has it now.

We have put a set of stalls in the indoor school for a change. Now after the horses have been walked or trotted for three quarters of an hour we will ride them through the open stalls.

Palacegate Racing runs again at Southwell. He is running a bit quick after his last race because there isn't a suitable one for him for the next few weeks. If he wins it's a bonus. If he gets beat then the handicapper will surely drop him as he has 9st 7lb top weight, and there isn't much of him.

Went to the cattle market at Lancaster in the afternoon. It was good to have a bit of a banter with the old farmers. After two hours down there I start talking slow and feel about ninety. With the exception of Bill Sutcliffe, they love to talk about the horses.

Eleven bullocks finished up on the road to Cockerham. Steve the wagon driver wormed them for me while they were in a pen at the mart. They are easier to do there. No good feeding worms. That's the best first feed they can get. When they arrived home and we were putting them in our fold yard there was a big patch of ice. The first two out of the cattle truck went skating along with perfect balance like Torville and Dean.

SATURDAY February 1

ALL the two-year-olds went up the straight of the all-weather at a good pace for three furlongs. It is the first bit of proper work they have done, and very pleasing it was too. They all got the three without blowing unduly.

There was a smallish filly I was not impressed with. I think she needs a bit more time so I'm afraid she will have to go back home to her owners. Either that, or I will get her in a livery yard to keep her going to see if she comes to in a few weeks' time. Unfortunately, I can't afford the time to let her get too comfortable here.

While we were working the horses we could hear gunfire in the distance. Wild geese were being shot. I'm not against a bit of sport but this frosty, foggy weather is hardly the time to be shooting geese. It must be hard enough for them to survive these weather conditions.

When we were coming off the gallops three swans flew over. The sound of their wings in flight is a real thrill. Every year swans breed at the bottom of Crimbles Lane, the road to our yard. The swans probably got lost on their way to the stream that runs into the sea by way of opening flood gates after the water has been collected up from the surrounding dykes.

Gorinsky and the Bear worked on their own. The rest did plenty of walking and trotting on the walkers, as it's still too frosty and foggy for the roads. It's safer this way. One of the walkers broke down at breakfast time, but we managed to get it put right by lunchtime.

I kicked on so I could get finished to watch racing at Sandown and Chepstow on the telly.

First race was won by Montebel ridden by Peter Scudamore. It was nice to see Peter ride his seventh 100 winners in a season yesterday. Imagine the miles he must have ridden and the number of fences and hurdles he must have jumped on courses and in schooling practises-thousands.

It was also good to see Alex Greaves had ridden fifty winners on the Fibresand track at Southwell. But what a shock, Morley Street getting beat at Leopardstown. That won't do any good for his confidence in the Champion Hurdle.

Jo has rung Anthea Farrell to cry off going to a dance at York in aid of Sharon Murgatroyd, on account of the fog. Some of our Yorkshire owners are going though. I hope they have a good night and make plenty for Sharon. If ever there was a brave lady-it's her. Sharon is paralysed from a fall she had at Bangor-on-Dee some months ago. Well done my home team Leeds United. They're back on top of the First Division, where they belong. Keep it up fellows. Just because I have left Leeds don't think I'm not keeping my eye on you.

Watched the Chris Eubank-Sugar Boy Malinga fight on telly from Birmingham. Eubank was always on top, especially after knocking Malinga down in the fifth round with a beautiful right hook to the chin. After that Eubank coasted home. But I must admit it looked as though he had the

Michael Watson fight on his mind, as he wouldn't go in and bring the fight to an end.

SUNDAY February 2

FROST has gone. Rode out the Bear one-and-a-half miles steady on the all-weather.

Rupert Mackeson, my publisher of "It's Tougher At The Bottom", came with some books for me to sign. He stayed for breakfast. While he was here Rupert said he would like to see Olly (O I Oyston), so I took him down to see the old boy and his pals, Tiny Tim and Pearl. John Brown came with my Parker Knoll chair he had taken away to get mended.

Jo rang Anthea Farrell about how last night's dance fared. Anthea had stayed over at York. Her father reported it was a very good evening and was well attended.

A couple from Beverley, Frank Carr the ex-trainer had put onto me, brought a sample of hay. Good stuff it was. It's difficult to get good hay this year. He had around 80 tons, so I bought it.

Stan Newman rang to report on Lisnakill Wish, who he had been to see this morning and reported he was as fresh as paint. Brian Harrison, a knowledgeable dog owner had offered Stan £20,000 for Charlie. Stan told him Sonia and I, quite rightly, wouldn't want to sell.

Neville has this weekend off. With me being at home I fed the horses tonight. Doing that is great. At the moment we have over one hundred horses in. It takes ages to feed. Getting round them all is like feeding elephants with strawberries.

Peter Chandler, of Paris House fame, rang to invite us to a Spring party in Paris House's honour at his restaurant at Woburn.

You should hear Jo and her mum singing along in the front room to Songs of Praise on TV, while I'm trying to speak to Sam on the phone in Tenerife. Next week I will ask them if they want to go to church. They could do with some singers there.

Jo and I went to Campions for an hour. They own the fattest dogs we have ever seen. Two Jack Russells, a cross-bred labrador and a poodle.

MONDAY February 3

ALL the frost has gone and it's a lovely day. During the past week or so the poor weather has meant the horses have missed a bit of long steady cantering. Today, instead of road work, we hacked the two-year-olds for six furlongs on the all-weather and cantered them back in pairs.

Flash, our head man, has just told me his Mrs is in foal again. It's not been caused by his telly going on the blink because I asked him. Next thing, he will be asking me if I can swap him his three bedroomed bungalow for the hostel.

Just before lunch, a ruddy great load of straw arrived. Our A Team unloaded it in record time.

In the afternoon, I was looking out of our front kitchen window into our neighbouring farmer's field, and saw hundreds of geese grazing.

Watched this month's racing video with Jo and Ted Voute, who came to stay with us from the Adstock Manor Stud. I stayed up to watch the snooker and it was well worth missing sleep for. Doug Mountjoy looked like beating Jimmy White as he was well ahead. Jimmy showed a lot of bottle to smash the balls all over the table to win the final leg by 5-4.

TUESDAY February 4

CANTERED all the two-year-olds in pairs for two-and-a-half furlongs to stretch their legs after all the time they've spent on the walkers. On their way back from the gallops we shut up all 86 of them in pairs in a set of stalls placed in the indoor school. They were as good as gold. Our stall programme started at 8.5am and finished at 11.10am, without a hitch.

Eight Charolais bullocks arrived from Frank Clarkson near Pilling. I bought them from him last Friday at Lancaster Mart. Bought 20 Charolais and Simmental cross store bullocks from Richard Whitton. That makes 59 now in the fold yard to trample the muck down. That will most probably be the best job they will do. It's very difficult to make money from cattle at the moment.

Lots of yards have empty boxes at the present time. It's therefore nice to be in a position to turn two horses away like I did today, as we just haven't got the room. Let's hope our luck continues.

Charlie (Lisnakill Wish) was awarded dog of the month for January. I'm absolutely delighted.

Yorkshire Racing Club asked me if I would give them a talk about racing. Seeing I was born in Yorkshire I agreed. What a good night it turned out to be. There were lots of people. The venue, a Leeds Working Mens' Club, was just about full of good people out to enjoy themselves. Most of the night they were in stitches laughing. At these kind of functions someone always asks for a winner. Tonight was no exception. Sticking my neck out I said, Miami Bear. He was outclassed in his last race at Haydock, but there is nothing of that calibre in the race he's in tomorrow and he's run some good races. Yes, he should win.

It was a great night, arrived home 12.15am. Things I have to do to earn a crust.

Watched the end of the Steve Davies-Dennis Taylor match on the box before I dived in between the sheets. It was a close win for Steve, 5-4, but I have seen him play better.

WEDNESDAY February 5

JUST as it was getting light, I tried the gallop out on Gorinsky-perfect. Today is the first gallop for the two-year-olds. It was hard getting to sleep last night, or early this morning, thinking about them.

This time of the year is so exciting. Worked them in threes up the back stretch. Some were gawping a bit but others looked good. When they have had three or four more gallops they will start getting their act together. Then we will have a fair idea of what we have got.

Preston Guild, a colt by Mazaad, flew. He is entered in the breeze-up at Doncaster as I haven't managed to sell him and another half dozen yet. If we have to keep one, the way this fellow went it may as well be him.

John Budden, the Northern Sporting Life reporter, came to the yard with Colin Turner to take a photo of Preston Guild, the two-year-old I have nominated as one to follow. A weekly report on his progress will appear in John's column in the Life.

Wally has taken our Alan to catch his plane. He's going to Miami for three weeks, he stays with his pal, Niall, who trains there.

After seeing the two-year-olds work, it's made me a bit pushed for Southwell as the Bear runs in the first, at 2.10pm. Had a good run, Olly, my dog, beats me to the car. As soon as I open the door he's in. Got to Southwell in plenty of time. In fact, I walked down the course to have a look at the last fence as this is the first time we have run a chaser on the all-weather.

There's also time for a cup of tea and a read of the complimentary Sporting Life we are all kindly given at Southwell.

I see Lisnakill Wish has a poor draw, trap five for the Springbok quarter final on Saturday, but he's only even money to win the final. Can't be bad.

Miami Bear, ridden by Neale Doughty, was always in the first two. Jumping well, a clear leader from halfway, he won by a very easy 15 lengths at odds of 11-4. Great, our first jump winner this season.

The Yorkshire Racing Club members will have hopefully relieved their local bookies of a few bob.

Jo, John and myself are meeting at 8.0pm to discuss how the youngsters went. We're meeting at the Patten Arms, a pub quite near to us. We will shuffle the two-year-olds about to match them up for their next piece of work on Saturday. It's a case of teamwork.

On the way back from Southwell the police were active on the M62. Three cars had been pulled up, no doubt for speeding.

Jo and I met John and Kevin at the Pattern. Last year we unanimously came up with Paris House as the one to follow. This year we have come up with Preston Guild. Let's see how right we are.

It's now nearly 11.0pm, I'm going to see what happened racing-wise on Ceefax and watch a bit of football. Jo's already gone to bed. What a good game the Aston Villa - Derby County match was. Good football every minute of it, with lots of goals, 4-3 in Aston Villa's favour.

THURSDAY February 6

HEADLINES in the Life-"Berry's Bear Mauls His Rivals". We did quite a lot with the two-year-olds yesterday and I want to work them again on Saturday. It would be foolish to have them coming out that day on flat tyres. So today, we closed them up in the stalls in the indoor school for a little more education and an easier sort of day. All the rest did road work. Miami Bear is fine from yesterday and was led out.

During the afternoon Jo and I went to Derek Naylor's, the saddler's, at Rochdale for some new tack and things for the yard.

Brian Durkin came to see us about Tino Tere's future as his partner isn't going too well. Subject to the other partner, we have sorted the job out.

Jo, Brian and myself, and a can or two of beer, watched the BBC 1 programme on Elizabeth R. It was really good, showing the human, natural side of The Queen and the Royal Family in their work and leisure. It was charming stuff-I thoroughly enjoyed it.

FRIDAY February 7

IT'S a lovely spring-like day, nice and mild and the birds are singing away. Our two-year-olds went twice each way round the three furlong canter ring, nice and steady in pairs, four lengths apart. The first lot led by me on Gorinsky. Second lot the same led by Palacegate Racing and yours truly. Third lot I was on Palacegate King.

A very nice photograph appears on page three of The Sporting Life of Preston Guild, the Mazaad colt who I nominated as the one to follow this season. At the moment he is owned by Midland Bank and J and J M Berry as he hasn't been sold yet. He is entered in the Breeze-Up Sale at Doncaster. Hopefully I can get someone to buy him there and keep him to train.

Last week Frank Dunne told me even Wayne Lukas has entered horses in sales like our Breeze-Ups. It's difficult to get clients who can afford to keep horses in training. This recession is affecting other countries as well as Britain. But I would be disappointed if this chap isn't a good horse and I am writing this down on Friday February 7, 1992 and not the day before the Brocklesby. Once Preston Guild was used to describe an event that only occured once in a blue moon. The real Preston Guild actually happens once every twenty years and for the record there is a Preston Guild this year. Let's hope this is also the year of Preston Guild, the horse.

Another load of hay came at 12.10pm to brighten the lads' day up. People have been ringing up regarding Preston Guild, after seeing the write-up in the Life, wanting to buy him.

Mike Gallemore, Editor of The Sporting Life, has just rung. Arthur Camp-

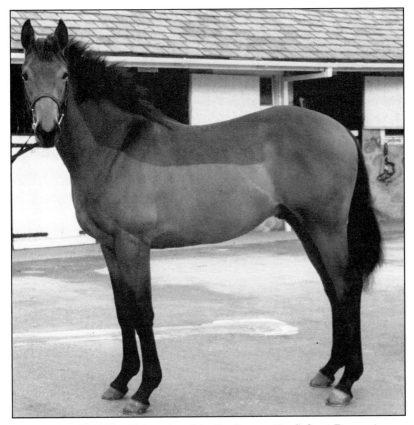

PRESTON GUILD : He's entered in the Breeze-Up Sale at Doncaster, but I hope I can get someone to buy him so I get to keep him at Cockerham. It could just be his year.

bell, the owner of Miami Bear, has written a strong letter to him about the Bear's write-up in yesterday's paper. Steve Boggett called Arthur, Jack. God it's funny isn't it when I read it in The Life I knew Arthur would be pleased. When I see him I will have to call him Jack. I bet he goes up the wall. I don't know what he's beefing about, I have to live with the name!

If I'm not careful we may have an empty box here at Cockerham, and I like the Bear.

One of Ladbrokes managers rang to see if I would open one of their new betting shops in Lancaster. It's probably because Red Rum isn't fit to travel yet.

Neville, John, Flash, Kevin and myself met Tom Bibby and John Brown to go to a sportsman's dinner at Kirkham Grammar School near Preston. The event was organised to raise money to send the school's senior hockey squad on an educational and cultural tour of Australia, New Zealand and the USA.

Jim Watts, the former world lightweight boxing champion, was the guest speaker. The dinner was well attended and I think they will have done well financially.

Neville (pictured right) managed to win a champagne reception before taking a trip in a hot air balloon. I don't know about the balloon but Neville's certainly not short of hot air.

It was fascinating reading how the electric and water meters went up with people putting the kettle on for a cuppa and flushing the toilet as soon as the Elizabeth R programme finished last night. Anti-Royalists were in the minority.

SATURDAY February 8

WORKED the two-year-olds in the same trios as last Wednesday, but changed all the jockeys around. They are going well. You would think it would be easy but some of them differ by as much as six lengths. By the time we have had three or four more workouts we will have them properly sussed out.

This morning at 5.30am a load of woodchip came delivered by Hardman of Oswestry. The poor man came early to get off to a flyer. The engine on the wagon packed up. The driver and his mate ended up shovelling the whole eighteen tons out themselves, and didn't get away until 4.30pm.

While the weather is fair we are again mucking out the fold yard. We have put the cattle in the paddock whilst it's being done and the muck will be spread on some land that was recently redrained and which is going to be ploughed up and re-seeded. It will take three or four days to finish. Muck from over one hundred horses and half as many cattle soon builds up.

John Curwen, the drainage contractor, came to discuss the plans for the new walker.

Mike and Jeanetta Gallemore came to stay the weekend with their point-to-pointer Duskey Comic. We were going to go to an Irish evening at Garry Mosses. With them being late we settled for home. Jo cooked a leg of lamb, we had a couple of bottles of wine. I got out the video tape Oklahoma that Pat Knight bought me for Christmas and we all had a good old singalong. With a little bit of country dancing inserted between songs.

Just after 9.15 we rang Wimbledon greyhound stadium to see how Sonia and my star dog had performed in the quarter final of the Springbok from the difficult draw number, trap 5, he'd got. Charlie had won by five lengths so we opened a bottle of champagne to celebrate. What a dog. Within half an hour of Charlie winning Stan and Sonia were on the phone to tell me all about him. On Thursday he goes for the semi-final from the favoured trap 1.

SUNDAY February 9

RODE out Palacegate Racing with Mike on his horse. What a performance. We hacked to the start of the nine furlong. Came back at a good half speed. Then let them stride on the last four furlongs of the straight. Mike and his horse surprisingly got the trip as both of them looked big and well. When we pulled up Mike said: "Blast!" Only it began with F. "I've lost one of my contact lenses." I told him I hoped he didn't think I was going to look for it as he continued to explain where abouts he thought he'd lost it.

Our A team are working like the clappers getting the muck out of the fold yard. It started to rain so we put the cattle in the indoor school so they don't get wet.

Jo and I went to church this morning. After the service was the burial of Andrea's ashes. The vicar was making his apologies as the church boiler had packed up. It was freezing. We shall have to have a whip round to get a new one.

It was very sad at the burial service. Roger, our vicar, is such a nice fellow. I know vicars have to bury people and one would think they got hardened to it. It may be that because our village is such a close-knit community and Roger knew everyone or maybe it was that Andy was such a nice young girl but he was so upset.

Only the family, the boyfriends of Jill and Nicola, Andy's sisters, Jo and myself were there. Afterwards we all came to our house for a drink. Andy used to love to come to our yard. I could just imagine her saying: "Jack mate, you haven't got your red shirt on."

Quite a few owners came to see their horses.

Rang Sam up. The lad was in good form. He wants half a share in a two-year-old. I plumped for Andrea's Girl for him, a Faustus filly.

Treated Jo to dinner at the Orchard Italian restaurant near Garstang and met Norma and Roy Peebles there. They are owners of ours from Scotland who own a flat at St Anne's.

We galloped back to see the closing stages of the Benson & Hedges Masters final at Wembley where Stephen Hendry beat John Parrott 9-4 to collect a cool £105,000.

MONDAY February 10

ON the front page of the Greyhound Life there is a good photo of Charlie winning at Wimbledon last Saturday and a nice write-up in the Life and Post. Corals quote him 4-6 to win the David Richardson Springbok Final on Saturday, February 15.

Richard Vines popped in to see Duchess de Belfort, his two-year-old filly, as he was in the area.

I led three lots off around the roads on Miami Bear, Palacegate Racing and Laurel Queen. All the horses did road work except Gorinsky and Palacegate King. They cantered five furlongs.

To cheer the lads up, once again a wagon and trailer load of straw came. This will be the last of the season as we change over to shavings next week. Jeff Nichols, the man I once bought a wallaby from, arrived at the yard. He has a part-time job travelling for Spillers horse foods and called to see if we wanted to buy anything. I thought he might have a lion to sell or something.

In the afternoon, Yvonne Carr, daughter of Joe, the former jockey and trainer, came with Nan Broderick, the wife of Paddy, Arthur Stephenson's ex-jockey, to talk about a Racing and Thoroughbred Breeding Training Board for staff.

John Carroll and I were invited to the Liverpool Daily Post and Echo Sports Personality of the Year Award Dinner, at the St George's Hotel. Would you believe it, John and I went in our suits? Honestly, I never looked at the ticket. Ruby just left them out for us and I picked John up on the way. When we got to the St George's and I saw the people in evening dress, I thought, what a berk. It's either a formal dress do or there's a blooming big band on. There was no band.

The world featherweight champion boxer, Paul Hodkinson, was the Personality of the Year, and the guest speaker was Fred Eyre with Alan Minter giving his tribute. In the room were lots of celebrities, too many to mention. We had a very good night-got home about 1.0am.

TUESDAY February 11

MORNINGS like this it's a pleasure to get out. There is a sharp, white ground frost, it's slightly foggy and the sun is shining. The ground is perfect. All the two-year-olds cantered on the middle grass in a big circle, twice each way. To keep an edge on Gorinsky he was led out. Palacegate King was allowed to sling along for two furlongs to blow him out for battle tomorrow. The three swans we saw recently flew over the gallops again, but not as low as before.

Ian Bolland, our accountant, came to go through a few queries he wanted clearing up.

In the afternoon I went to have a haircut to get myself ready for the new season.

Palatial Style has been sold to go to the States. We have had the vet in this afternoon to give him his final check over. Martin, our travelling head man, is taking him later tonight to East Midlands airport. His flight is scheduled for 2.30am. He is a lovely horse and I wish him well.

Rang my old pal Jack Allen up from Pontefract as he has just come out of hospital. The old boy's not very well.

WEDNESDAY February 12

AS soon as it became light I rode the Bear ten furlongs at a nice swinging canter. We then worked the two-year-olds in sets of threes. To enable John to ride as many as possible and to get the feel of them, we had a lad waiting to take his horse from him at the end of the gallop and a car to take him back to the start for his next ride, which was one in every third set.

Before setting off for Southwell at 9.30am, we had worked 69 two-year-olds. John will certainly be fit at Southwell. In fact, he may be fit to drop.

Jo drove us to Southwell in her car. John's already scheming how to save time when we are driving to two meetings a day in the summer. He suggested we buy an orange beacon light and a motorway maintenance sticker, so we can drive down the hard shoulder and in between the cones at the roadworks. I hope he's not serious.

Gorinsky ran second, beaten a length-and-a-half, to Maid Welcome in the sprint. Palacegate King was fourth in the seven furlong claimer. Both our races were won by lady jockeys Madeline Smith and the Queen of Southwell, Alex Greaves, Well done, girls.

There are some good lady jockeys about, only there should be more chances for them. It would be a sorry state for racing if they all left it. If a nervy or a miserable horse goes to a yard the owner invariably asks for you to give it to a girl to look after, so she can settle it down. Ring the owner up and say I would like to put a girl up on it at the races, then that's different.

Ron Muddle asked me up to his box for a tea and a sandwich. He showed me his plans for Wolverhampton Racecourse. Man, when they are finished, it's going to be some course. Those two Muddles, Ron and Richard, may not always be flavour of the month but they get things moving. I think they deserve more credit than they get for keeping things going.

On my return, looking at our injury book, we have a couple with nicks. Andrea's Girl has a back joint up a bit. Not bad from the 102 horses that worked today. If you were to take 102 out of the London Marathon there would be more knocks and sore shins than that.

THURSDAY February 13

WITH the exception of Miami Bear, who had a long steady canter, the rest of the horses did roadwork or were put on the walkers.

Headlines in both racing papers and a picture in each of our star dog as he runs in the Springbok semi-final tonight at Wimbledon.

Two painters came to put the transfers of The Sporting Life on the rear ramps of our horse boxes.

John Budden came to do a report for The Life on Preston Guild, the two-year-old I nominated for the one to follow for the coming season.

Jack Wilkins came to see his horse, Greetland Glory.

Our A team are putting new wood fibre on the all-weather gallop now that we've finished mucking out the fold yard. A man from the Country Land-owners Association came regarding some rights of way.

Sizzling Saga, Food of Love and a Belfort filly named Coffee Mint came today. They arrived looking soft, they are supposed to have been going round the roads for six weeks. The agricultural machinery salesman, John Cornthwaite, came about 6.15. I bought a new tractor and trailer from him and he took in part-exchange an old tractor, trailer and muck spreader.

John Carroll, Flash and Kevin came to the house at 7.30pm so we can go through all the two-year-olds' work and compare it with the two previous work days. We also had to shuffle some about and sadly send a couple home that are slow or need time.

Charlie runs in the Springbok semi-final at 9.0pm at Wimbledon. Sonia and Stan Newman ring up about 9.10pm. Charlie has won easily, 1/5 favourite by eight lengths and he is in the final on Saturday.

What a dog! He is absolutely unbelievable.

Flash has a whippet with a deformed leg that swings when it runs. After hearing Lisnakill Wish had won, Flash says that it's a pity he's not a bitch we could have had a mating with Crumble.

When we finished discussing the horses we had a friendly game of Nap (cards) with a plate full of cheese and biscuits, some cake and a few cans of beer.

FRIDAY February 14

PUT all the two-year-olds in stalls and bounced them out for the first time. Every single one was good. Only a couple had to be manually pushed in, and that was the biggest problem we had. Some were a little slow coming out but they will quicken up with practice. Their attitude was right and that's what is important. All the time we were doing stalls work, which was over three hours, Olly was looking over the fence from his paddock onto the gallop. Hopefully giving them good advice.

At breakfast time a man from the Department of Transport rang up to make arrangements to serve a summons, sometime today, on Martin, Linda and myself, for driving over their stated hours without stopping. Looking at it logically, you may say, why don't the silly beggers stop for a break? Well, when the boxes go to the London tracks, after Hilton Park Services, which is only just over two hours down the M6, you go onto the M42, the M40, then the M25. There is not one service area to stop at and it's well over a hundred miles. On the M25 alone you could be held up for hours. The horses are agitated and want to get out, not be parked up. Try explaining that kind of reasoning to these fellows, who wouldn't know a horse if it kicked them.

All the older horses cantered steady for six furlongs. Jeff, one of our vets, came to castrate Palacegate Racing, Palacegate King and a two-year-old that's been acting colty. They were laid down in the indoor school recovering. When Flash suggested that when the man from the transport office arives we should close the door and let Jeff have a chat with him.

When the man came in the afternoon, he wasn't a bad fellow. Rules are rules, like it or not. We have got nine charges (charges remind me of my King's Troop days) or summons for drivers not taking breaks. With our place being a partnership between the Bride and myself, we have got one each. That's a bit steep, we could have managed with the one. Friday, February 28 at 3.0pm at Lancaster is post time for the hearing. I will plead guilty, let's hope the judge looks on us leniently. In future, we will put two drivers on the southern trips. It will just have to cost me twice as much in Yorkie bars.

Lisnakill Wish had a whole page on Teletext for his build-up for the Spingbok final tomorrow with odds of 4-9.

Pat, Jo and I went to the Grapevine Restaurant at the Crofters for a meal with Nan and Bill Robinson, Elaine and Robert Aird, who are staying there overnight so they can come and see their horses tomorrow.

SATURDAY February 15

HAVING re-grouped the two-year-olds I worked them in threes for four furlongs, allowing them to stride on going as fast as the slowest rather than chase their heads off them.

Our owners who stayed overnight at the Crofters, along with Mr and Mrs Hughes who own Sabre Rattler, came to see their horses work. It was a real cold, fresh morning but very nice.

Jack Clayton, one of our long standing owners, came to see his two-year-old as I had told him she wasn't much. That one is going down the road. It costs the same to keep a bad horse as a good one.

David Brown rang to wish us "Good Luck" with the dog tonight. Lisnakill Wish's big day. It's the £2,000 David Richardson Springbok Final at Wimbledon. Pat, Jo and I are just setting off to see him. He had photos and write ups in The Sporting Life and Racing Post today. He is 4-9 favourite in the betting. The race is at 9.30pm, so the three of us will drive the car home in shifts as it looks like being a late night.

Arrived at Fred and Gwen's at Lightwater to meet up with Sonia and Stan Newman and go on to the dogs.

Great start I had having the first two forecasts up. Charlie's odds on for his race in the worst draw, number 4-known as the coffin box. He ran a great race only to be beaten a neck by his stable companion Double Rack at 25-1. We had a good run back with hardly a soul about. Mind you, this time of the morning you would only expect to see burglars.

Got home at quarter to four. Although Charlie got beat we had a great night. See on the Ceefax that Royal Gait won the City Trial at Nottingham. He probably didn't beat anything special but I think he could well win the Champion Hurdle. Seeing Morley Street on telly from Leopardstown gave me doubts whether he wanted to win.

SUNDAY February 16

IAN BOLLAND came first thing to finally nail me down to make out my will. It will be a bit of a laugh when that's read out.

It was a lovely day here and it brought lots of owners out to see their horses. Nan and Tom Bibby invited Jo and I to lunch, along with a few more of their friends. Tom has some very nice Suffolk sheep. One of the ewes died and left two ewe lambs. In another week or so they will be totally on dry food and weaned off milk. While Jo was dishing out the verbals with the other females in the kitchen I bought these two orphans from Tom to be delivered to our place next week.

6.30pm, as on most Sundays, I rang Sam up. He was in good form playing cards with a pal of his. Carvill's Hill I see won the Irish Hennessy Cognac Gold Cup at Leopardstown. It would have been nice to see it live on the telly though. I haven't seen anything around to beat him in the Gold Cup this year and will look forward to watching him run as I always attend Cheltenham that day.

MONDAY February 17

TODAY we start to let the straw in the stables wear down by not putting any new straw in. We do this to stop the horses eating it, to prevent them getting big guts and impair their fitness. We then put them on shavings. The change over from straw to shavings takes three to four days at a cost of £6,000. To subsidise that amount we make a one-off charge to our owners of £20.

It's a lovely sunny day with a very keen frost. Jo has just rung Wolverhampton up to make sure racing takes place as the Bear runs there in the Novice Chase. There is an inspection at 11.15am but they are hopeful.

Just as we pull into the car park at Wolverhampton the Racecourse Technical Services camera patrol van is pulling out. Presumeably going home. Racing has been abandoned.

Apparently, there was a patch on the chase course where the frost had not come out of the ground and it was still slippery. As we are driving off the car park my pal David Brown, a steward at the meeting, is walking to his car to go home. We all drove to the first cafe and had a tea and natter.

On the way back home listening to the radio someone in America is suggesting putting nappies on the horses pulling landaus through the streets. I'm not too keen on the new ruling on overnight jockeys but I'm definitely opposed to this idiotic suggestion.

On our return home we were greeted with a load of wood fibre which had just arrived on the car park.

The vet had been to cut the Efisio, the two-year-old who was a bit too randy. Lucky those rapists we keep reading about are not stabled here.

TUESDAY February 18

SNOW is the order of the day. Everywhere is white. It looks super. Only an inch or so thick and very mild so it will probably be gone by lunchtime.

Our two-year-olds were ridden to Smith's, twenty minutes down the road. On their return we cantered them in pairs on the all-weather for four furlongs. Then we hacked them back in bunches of a dozen. The older horses cantered various distances after forty five minutes of road work.

Looking out into the yard it looks a bit of a tip as we are wearing the straw down in the stables. There are eight big bales of shavings stacked outside each box ready for tomorrow and Thursday's transfer.

Straight after breakfast I rode the Bear just about six furlongs. With him touring the Midlands yesterday I thought he may be a bit tired. Hacking back he gave a squeal and an almighty buck. So much for me being kind to him.

Mike Gallemore, Editor of The Sporting Life, rang up and asked if I would write a column every week for the Weekender. Why not-I have a Saturday slot with the Daily Star. As Arthur Daley would say, "another nice little earner." You never know, I might get the chance of a metal Press badge to get me into the racecourses.

John Hoyles, a local contractor, and I walked round the thirty or so acres we are going to make into more gallops. We wanted to get an idea of how to plan it all out and get the job moving. While we were up there a hare got up. All the dogs gave chase. Victor, my pit bull terrier, very nearly caught him. It's nice to see hares about again in plenty. A few years ago they seemed to drop out. Around here they all but disappeared.

Peter Chandler, of Paris House fame, rang. He has bought out yet another partner. Only he and his brother own the horse now. Peter has paid the ex-shareholders a great deal more than they originally paid for him. For Pete's sake and loyalty to the horse, I hope he is repaid. He is calling in tomorrow as he has an appointment in Liverpool.

WEDNESDAY February 19

WORKED the two-year-olds. Most of them are improving now they have had a few gallops.

While I was on the gallops working the horses, Blackpool's centre forward,

Dave Bamber, who owns part of Oscars Quest, came to see him work. Dave, full of smiles, said if Blackpool won on Tuesday night he would be up on Wednesday to see the horse work. Not only did Blackpool beat Barnet 4-2, Dave scored a goal. Mind you, this is nothing new as he is the leading scorer in the whole of the football league with 28 of them in the net. If the team gets beat, I believe they all have to turn in the following day.

Dived into our office as I was called in to see a man about my new carphone- for when I get a car to go with it. Helen, one of our secretaries, was doing the scrap book up. The horse scene is fairly quiet at the moment. All our write-ups are about Lisnakill Wish. Helen has made up the heading, The Boss Has Gone To The Dogs.

Opening the mail is always done in the office by our secretaries. As we get quite a lot, they only show me what is important. Today I received a card from Spain with two beautiful girls on, absolutely starkers. Whoever sent it was having a bit of fun and I appreciated it. He was asking for a job for himself and a cook's job for his mamma, who makes good pasta. His sisters on the front of the card would also like to come. He said they are good at everything. Like I often say, you have to have a laugh. I don't know a better medicine.

Peter Chandler came to see his good horse Paris House mid-morning. He gave me three brow bands with the names, Paris House, Beanshoot and Allegrissima on. The Marchioness of Tavistock had made them for the horses that she, her son Lord Howland and Peter have interests in.

When we finished working the horses, Jo and I took Peter and his young lady for lunch at Bumbles, a restaurant in our village.

Ashley Granger, who read in The Sporting Life about Preston Guild, came as he asked me if he could see him work.

Our A team put the load of wood fibre on the gallop and topped up the area around the walkers where they get worn out with the horses going round and round.

That was a fair performance at Warwick by the mare Springaleak of Oliver Sherwood's, winning her fifth novice chase of the season and eighth race on the trot. In doing so, she must be in with a shout for the Sun Alliance at the Cheltenham Festival.

SPRINGALEAK : Oliver Sherwood's mare, who is a contender for the staying novices' crown at the Cheltenham festival.

THURSDAY February 20

BIG day today. We put all the horses on the walkers, except the odd few who resent them. They were ridden round the roads. Three muck spreaders went round the yard collecting the muck from all the horse boxes. It got spread on the 30 acres we are to have reseeded, so it can be ploughed in. A tractor and trailer was busy unloading muck into the fold yard to bed down the cattle.

By putting in eight bales of shavings per box, it takes over 1,000 bales to bed down 112 boxes. Some of our big boxes need 12 or 14. It's a costly job.

Imagine the rubbish we make. All these plastic wrappers, dozens and dozens of paper feed sacks per week, lots of containers, packets, cartons, at least a sack of hay bands. The problems trainers in towns or smokeless zones have to face must be colossal. It must cost a fortune to get it carted away. We have a metal burner which, every single day, is lit to burn our rubbish. The office alone has a bag burnt every day. We would have no chance of our local 'Lonnie Donegan' taking it all away.

TNT overnight carriers have delivered my new hand carphone. All I need now is the car, as I don't intend carting the phone around all day like a yuppie.

It's gone 12.0 noon and we have unloaded another load of shavings. The lads have volunteered to work through their afternoon so we can get all the horses on shavings today, instead of doing half today and half tomorrow.

Jo has rung the fish and chip shop and put a shipping order in for 28 times either fish, meat pies, sausage, cheese and onion pie, all with chips and peas. She is picking a crate of beer up from the pub.

Read in the morning's Racing Post that if we'd had one more best turned out horse award at the races, we would have been sharing the Tetley Bitter/Racing Post Trophy.

Every year, Tetley Bitter, in conjunction with the Racing Post, very kindly sponsor the award. In addition to the beer, the top stable receives £2,500 and a trophy. David Chapman's yard won this year with 49 'best turned-outs'. Our crew were second with 48. On behalf of all the stable staff, I thank the sponsors for their support. The staff really do appreciate it.

FRIDAY February 21

TODAY we closed the two-year-olds up in the stalls and bounced them out in pairs up the straight all-weather. They have sharpened up well from last week. They all went in-not one single problem from 86 horses with five handlers. The whole operation took three hours and ten minutes.

I came in the house for a cuppa and a quick peep at The Sporting Life's big headlines-'Stewards Whip Into Action'.

It went on to say five jockeys were called in at Catterick. This kind of publicity doesn't do any good at all for racing. Year after year it's making out that jockeys are beating up the horses.

Standards of riding have never been better. Jockeys don't know whether they are coming or going. Only last week there were big headlines about non-triers! To get racing back on its feet, it's action, not words, we want. Cut the length of the whip by a few more inches and leave the jocks alone to do their job.

When we had a Donkey Derby on one of our charity days, the Stipendary Steward, Captain Hibbert-Foy's whip was that long when he rode his donkey, if he had needed to use it he would have hit the donkey following five lengths behind!

Tom Bibby brought the two lambs I had bought from him last Sunday when we were at his house for lunch. Hopefully, I will breed from them later on. A few years ago, the Farmers Guardian advertised two ewes with tup lambs each for sale-I bought them. Every day I fed them, they were great. In those days most of the lads lived-in and needed to be fed by us. Jack Smith, a local farmer, kept telling me he would take the lambs and have them butchered for me. One day, I softened up and let him take them. He brought the meat back in joints in plastic bags. Jo put them in the freezer. As I was about to pay him for his troubles, he produced a paper bag. He tipped it up and my four lambs heads rolled out. I felt sick. "You can boil these up for you dogs", he said. I had fed them dozens and dozens of times. I knew them so well. It was a long time before I ate lamb again and I never did eat any of that out of our freezer.

Colonel Sir Piers Bengough, the Queen's Royal Ascot representative, was coming at 5.0pm to see his horse. He was on his way to a wedding near Carlisle, but phoned up to say he was held up in a traffic jam. He would call instead on his way back on Sunday morning. Pity about that, it was a lovely afternoon. The lads made an extra effort tidying the place up, as they didn't want him reporting back to Her Majesty that the place was a tip.

It was nice to see my old mate Neale Doughty ride a treble at Kelso and even better for Gordon Richards, who had an unusual run of a month without training a winner.

SATURDAY February 22

IT'S very wet and windy and had been all night. Not a nice day at all. Instead of working the two-year-olds, we bunched them up in dozens and cantered steady for five furlongs.

From yesterday's stall work we have three injuries, two a bit shouldery and one with sore shins. These knocks and bumps are bound to happen occasionally. The rest of the horses just had a nice canter.

Some of our Scottish contingent, the Grubbs and the Peebles, were down to watch their horses work. It was absolutely pouring down. They went back to their hotel looking a bit bedraggled. When the horses were put back into their stables, they were rolling like mad in their lovely new shavings beds. There is some great racing on the telly today. Five graded races from Kempton and the Eddie Brennan National Trial from Punchestown. I watched the Irish race from my armchair in our front room with the fire roaring up the chimney and listening to the wind howling outside. A ding-dong battle is on from the second last between Zeta's Lad and Bishop's Staff, the latter holding on by a head for the Irish super-star trainer Mick O'Toole. It was nice to hear the applause from the crowd when the Nineofus rose to his feet after being winded in the Novice Chase, won by Tinryland. Just as the horses are lining up to jump off in the Racing Post Handicap, the blasted phone rings. It's Mick Easterby wanting to have a chat.

"Haven't you got a telly Mick?"

"Yes, I'm watching it", he says.

So we watched the race, won by top weight Docklands Express, with Mick giving me a running commentary. We both agreed Mr Entertainer was unlucky, falling at the third last when in front.

"Has ee paid yer fur yer training yet?"

"Who?"

So Mick tells me who.

"Watch im, I tell yer, watch im. The only stable left ee asn't bin in is Bethlehem. Ee's like the three wise men in one. In fact, if ee could catch them e'd ave em mucking is osses out to save costs. It's bad finding that gas, jobs gone. He'll poison us f-----s with it, tha knows".

Telling me Cab on Target is a cert in the next. Him still on the phone, he gets beat by Forest Sun.

The gas Mick was talking about has been found underground somewhere in or around Malton. I believe they intend drilling for it.

In the evening, Jo and I were invited to dinner by the Grubbs and the Peebles at Broughton Park, a plush hotel very near Preston. It was fantastic food. We were in good company and enjoyed the night.

SUNDAY February 23

THE weather today is absolutely beautiful. The sun is shining-no wind, not a bit like yesterday.

Lady Lonsdale, Colonel and Mrs Piers Bengough came to see their horse. I gave them a quick look round the yards. He was telling me he was concerned with the lack of rain down South, especially at Ascot.

There has been a lot said about watering courses for the benefit of Flat horses. A few years ago, I complained about Royal Ascot being firm. Nicky Beaumont, the Clerk of the Course, wrote me a not very nice letter. Afterwards I thought he was right. York's Ebor meeting and Goodwood's early August card both came in for criticism regarding watering. The grass was looking a picture before they watered and the growth was good.

Personally, if I were a Clerk of the Course and my grass was getting burned and going brown then I would certainly water. If the grass is a lush green then I wouldn't. There are lots of horses who love to hear their feet rattle while others prefer a bit of cut in the ground. Clerks of Courses should have their ground as natural as possible and water only to promote growth. Clerks who do water to alter the going make it false and patchy. That's bad for all types of horses.

Now that we have a couple of all-weather courses, trainers who do the most complaining about firm going seldom have runners at Lingfield and Southwell. They may not like an unnatural surface but at least there's no jar. In the States, they run Group 1 races on an artificial surface and, mark my words, there will be Group races run on all-weather tracks in Britain one day.

At 11.30am, Jo and I left to go to the Kinlet Vision luncheon at Brendon and Barbara O'Brien's lovely house in Cleobury Mortimer, near Bridgnorth. We have done this for the past three years. Ten of us share a horse. Last year we trained Kinlet Vision. This season, when she went jumping, Ken Oliver, who also owns a share, trained her.

She is no world beater, in fact she is only a plater, but we have a lot of fun with her. David Brown and Bob Willis were also at the luncheon. We had a sing-song round the piano. It was all good fun. I had a little go before the pianist arrived. We had a great day.

MONDAY February 24

TRAVELLING on the M6 to Doncaster to see Miami Bear run, a car and trailer had spun completely round. The boys in blue were just going up to the driver, no doubt to give him a ticking off.

I had my first call on the new phone. We went in Jo's car and it was someone wanting to know where they could buy white plastic running rails. There was a good crowd at the races and they were treated to a dry, mild day. Fibreguide Tech, once trained by yours truly, won the hunt chase which I was delighted to see. The novice chase, the Bear's race, had two fancied runners reported as non-runners in the morning's papers, Flight Hill and Lake Mission. Even so the Bear could only finish fourth. In the chases there was quite a lot of grief with a number of falls. It's difficult to know what's for the best-soft fences you could very near ride a bike round, like here, where the horses have little or no respect for, or big stiff fences that horses have to measure up and jump properly and cannot take liberties with. Maybe it's because there is so much speed bred into jumpers nowadays. Last Saturday at Kempton Park, the winners of the first three races-Qualitair Sound, Young Snugfit and Tinryland were sired by horses that had won five and six furlong sprints. Imagine sires a few years ago like Arctic Slave, Menelek, Vulgan, Deep Run and the like. You couldn't have sighted them in a five or six furlong sprint with a pair of binoculars!

TUESDAY February 25

TODAY is the Bride's 50th birthday. Happy birthday Jo. I'm taking her to Rycroft Hall for a meal tonight. She doesn't know, but I have hired a white Rolls Royce and chauffeur to drive us there. I shall have to keep an eye on her. She is more popular than I knew. She's received 35 birthday cards. On Saturday night we are having a party at Mamma's Too at St Anne's.

Pat Knight and I were going to buy Jo an Airedale dog for her birthday. It's her favourite breed. As we were arranging on the phone to view the Airedale at a kennel in Manchester, Jo got a whiff of what was going on. "Don't buy a dog for me", she said, "we have enough with eight of them around." When Jo opened Pat's card, Pat had painted on the inside a weeping Airedale dog wearing her colours, a red, white and blue ribbon tied round his neck. We had planned to have him delivered with this. Fortunately, Pat lost her bottle and opted to get something for Jo's car instead, else we would both have been in the doghouse.

Reading the Life I see Brendan Powell broke his thigh yesterday at Doncaster. I am very friendly with his parents. Sheila, his mum, will be upset. She worries like hell about him.

It's a lovely mild day, all the horses have cantered in pairs in the ring. The two-year-olds look tremendous. I couldn't be more pleased with them. Let's hope I am saying that in a few weeks time, when we see if they're as good as they look.

Stan and Sonia Newman, Fred and Gwen Viner rang to sing Happy Birthday to Jo on their carphone as they were travelling to Walthamstow greyhound track.

The white Rolls Royce came. I think at first Jo thought it was a little over the top. Both Jo and I have been to Rycroft Hall before and without doubt they have the best spare ribs of anywhere I know. We both went for the ribs. It was brilliant. Andrea Sands brought Jo a cake with one candle into the restaurant, singing Happy Birthday. We had a lovely night. Martin, the bossman, got his guitar out and played away.

The white Roller picked us up at 10.40pm. We went home to watch Tina Turner to end, for Jo, a perfect day.

PS: The old girl only rode out two lots today.

WEDNESDAY February 26

IT'S workday and it's pouring down with rain. Weather like this makes life difficult, as the horses have to be ridden out in waterproof hoods and sheets. The riders are in similar gear. Still, we have brought these youngsters up through the winter fighting off coughs, ringworm, dirty noses and in worse weather than this. With three weeks and a bit to go before the Flat starts, a drop of rain won't defeat us. I have already turned the volume up on the radio which is piped round all the yards during stable time to try and keep everyone's spirits up. I've loaded my pockets with sweets to give them away here and there and will see I soak up as much rain as anyone to keep the job running.

On Wednesdays and Saturdays, work days, it's not so much the riders who get the thin end of the wedge. Think of the staff who tack the horses up, getting them ready for the work riders only to be handed back their charges all wet and sweaty to clean them up all over again. Halfway through the morning the rain eased off. The two-year-olds are definitely coming on and looking good. We did a nice swinging canter for the older horses led by me on Fylde Flyer. Next week I will ask them to go a bit faster.

At 12.30pm I went to Lancaster to open a new Ladbrokes betting shop, and pick a horse for charity in the Champion Hurdle. I chose Royal Gait for a £50 bet at 6-1. The shop was very nice-quite different to the unofficial betting shop of Ray and Jeff Westmorlands at Tadcaster when I was a kid before betting shops were legalised. This one is fitted out better than a lot of people's houses. They were having sandwiches and drinking coffee. It was really comfortable and homely. When we get night racing Ladbrokes will have to add on living quarters for the punters. Part of my duty was to talk live on the phone on broadcast to all the Ladbrokes' shops throughout the country.

When I went for Jo's car at 3.5pm I discovered a nice traffic warden had stuck on the windscreen a fixed penalty notice for £16, for being three minutes late. I should not have stayed there any longer than an hour. Hopefully Mike Dillon of Ladbrokes will buy this book and reimburse me the £16 fine.

This incident reminded me of the time when our Sam had just come out of hospital. Jo's mother was taken for an emergency operation at a hospital in Beverley. Sheila, Jo's sister, rang up to tell Jo that her mother had gone in with that old dressing gown. Jo said not to worry she would get her a new one that afternoon and take it to her. So off we went to Preston. We had to take Sam as he couldn't be left on his own. I parked the car outside this shop while Jo and I went in, only for a few minutes. As I was driving away a traffic warden was sticking a parking fine on a car near the bus station. "That's right mate," I shouted, "make the buggers have it." Sam was sat next to me and he was cracking up. Tears were rolling down his cheeks and he was making all sorts of funny noises as he couldn't talk. He then pointed to a piece of paper stuck on our windscreen which I hadn't seen.

It's nearly 9.30pm. Amanda has just returned with her box. She has been to pick up our four horses who have been at Dave Browns working on the roads. She's late because the box had a blow-out at Sandbach on the M6. Fortunately Amanda wasn't too far from a garage and managed to get someone to change the wheel for her. It's always a worry when the horseboxes are late back.

On the front page of the Lancashire Post tonight were the headlines "Guild is up for sale". There was a lovely photo of Amanda holding Preston Guild.

Later on I watched the snooker from Derby on the box between Stephen Hendry and Gary Wilkinson. It was great that the young Thai James Wattana scored a maximum 147 break yesterday. But how sad it was to hear about his father getting shot dead the same day. It's certainly a day he won't forget.

THURSDAY February 27

ANOTHER rainy day at Cockerham. All the horses did road work or were put on the walkers. First lot led by me on Fylde Flyer. A load of wood fibre was delivered and tipped on the car park. It's for the three furlong canter ring, just to top it up. A load of hay came at 10.30am as James Kearsley and John Hibbert arrived in a Bentley to pick me up to go to the second day of the Waterloo Coursing Meeting at Altcar near Southport. That's the second time in a week I have been in such a car. Although it was cold and raining, Lancashire's oldest sporting event was good. Irrespective of the antis, there were hundreds of people supporting the biggest meeting in the coursing calendar.

My appointment with Doctor John must be kept today. I have put it off continually with always having better things to do. However, it's a medical for a Jockey Club certificate to ride in a celebrity race at Worcester next month. As the riders are all over 50 it has to be a proper examination as the Jockey Club don't want anyone having a wobbler in the paddock or, even more so, on the track. The doctor told me I was perfect. So it must be the beatings Jo gives me while I'm asleep that makes me feel so bad some mornings.

FRIDAY February 28

THERE'S a touch of frost this morning but underfoot conditions are still wet from yesterday's rain.

Stall work again for all the two-year-olds, except three or four who have a few bits of things wrong with them. No major problems. In fact, they were all good. Some of the fillies are just a little bit keyed up but now they know their job we won't ask them to go in so often. The older horses are just given a long steady canter. Today Neville stepped up their food by starting to feed them at lunch time. This now puts all the horses on full rations.

Alan has returned from his holiday in the States looking nice and brown.

11.30am, Alan, John and myself went in John's car to Southwell. We have left it this late as Gorinsky doesn't run until 4.10pm, and to enable me to get fit for my scrub at Worcester, I rode four lots of canters this morning.

On our way to Southwell John had a phone call to tell him all three lanes on the M61 are closed between junctions 8 and 6 on account of a car crash. We have therefore chosen the scenic route via the East Lancs Road past Haydock Park after which we'll join the M62 to put us back on course. We heard on the car radio that one man had been killed and fifteen injured in the crash. Apparently there is fog there.

Jet lag must have got hold of Alan, he's fast asleep in the back.

Gorinsky finished fourth. To be honest I am not so sure whether he wants to win now. He hasn't won since he was two. I've run him in claimers and he still gets big weights in handicaps. I may as well sell him. Someone like John Hill can get him for little money, give him a couple of runs out of his distance, come down a stack in the weights and in he goes. Just like Grand Time did. He won two races, one maiden and a claimer. In nurseries he carried top weight for us. We sold him at Doncaster for only 2,000gns. He had a couple of runs for his new trainer and won. If this isn't asking one to cheat I don't know what is.

John dropped me off at the Novotel near Preston where I met up with Jo, Fred and Gwen Viner, Stan and Sonia Newman. We all went to the 12th running of the North West Racing Club's annual dinner. George Harris was Master of Ceremonies, David Hillyard was a guest speaker. Dick Pitman was the other guest speaker, who as always, was good. Neale Doughty earned the title North West Jockey of the Year. Dudley Moffatt received the National Hunt Horse of the Year for Deb's Ball. Gordon Richards won the Peter Marsh Jump Trainers Award. Our Paris House was voted Flat Horse of the Year. It was an absolutely brilliant night. When we arrived home it was very late but we still watched a tape of Sonia's and my flying machine, Lisnakill Wish.

DUDLEY MOFFATT received the National Hunt Horse of the Year award for his mare Deb's Ball, at a brilliant annual dinner held by the North West Racing Club.

SATURDAY February 29

KRIBENSIS getting beat yesterday at Haydock by Bank View doesn't augur well for his Champion Hurdle hopes. Even though Kribensis has been off the course for a long while he should have been able to win this event coming out of a grass field if he's going to stand any sort of chance at

Cheltenham. Royal Gait still looks good to me.

Except for the dozen we are working tomorrow, five with sore shins or knocks, all the two-year-olds worked up the near side gallop in threes at a nice three quarter speed. They went well. I was more than pleased with them. The older horses went off in nice bunches at a good strong canter at various distances. Some of the older horses look a bit woolly in their coats, and are sweating up quite a lot. As late on as this I don't like clipping horses out. I just hope we can get a longish warm dry spell, then their hair will come out.

Lots of our owners came to watch their horses work, including a party of thirty from Solid Gold Racing.

Stan, Fred and I went to Haydock Park races for the afternoon, where there was some top class racing. Cool Ground ran a great race to win the Greenalls Gold Cup from Kildimo. Last year's winner, Twin Oaks, was third. He just wasn't as fast as I have seen him. We were in Terry Holdcroft and Tony Ball's box most of the afternoon. We had a great day and so did the huge crowd. Willie Jenks, a Haydock steward, said he was sorry to see I'd got fined for the boxes yesterday. That was the first I had heard of it. With tearing about at home to get finished in time to get to Haydock I hadn't had chance to read the papers. Jo and I were each fined £1,000 and £35 costs for failing to observe regulation breaks while transporting horses to racecourses. Our three drivers were fined £100 and £35 costs each. The total amount was £2,600. With us living out in the sticks, miles from the meetings, we only charge 38p per mile and our boxes are not bangers. This season, to keep transport costs at the same price, we have put The Sporting Life name on the rear ramps, to help defray the running costs. Rules are rules, however, and are made to be obeyed. I didn't want people thinking we had murdered someone or robbed a bank so I have made this point as anyone seeing the write-up in the papers will know precisely what happened. On a much happier note, at 7.30pm, the coach arrived at the yard to take the staff and Olly, the dog, who wouldn't get off, plus anyone else who had been invited to travel in the coach to Mamma's Too at St Anne's, the venue for Jo's birthday party.

We had around eighty people. The buffet Mamma's staff put on was brilliant. There was enough food to feed a regiment and a gorgeous birthday fruit cake all done up in the shape of a horse's head. We had a karaoke and disco. A policeman arrived at 9.30 pm and asked for Jo. You've guessed-a stripper policeman who eventually got down to his underpants. But it was all good clean fun. We danced and sang to the Karaoke machine. It was absolutely brilliant . The most important thing was it was Jo's party and she thoroughly enjoyed it. I doubt if she will ever forget it. It was certainly the best birthday party I have been to.

On the way back to Cockerham some of us were still in fine form and had a good sing song. We disembarked in the early hours of Sunday morning. Neville got off the coach looking like Nat King Cole. While he had been asleep some of our lot had blackened his face.

SUNDAY March 1

IT'S been raining all night. We had an early start this morning as we took twelve two-year-olds to Haydock Park to work out. Not to gallop but to give them a taste of racecourse experience and a ride in the horsebox. Most of the owners of the horses were there, many coming from miles away.

As late as we all got to bed all the staff on duty were there, including John "Jockey" Carroll. With having an early start today John thought it better to go to Jo's party in his own car as he was going to leave early. I am certain that was JC though I saw on the dance floor when the Mamma's team chucked us out, in the small hours of the morning. Someone gave Jo a gas balloon with "Happy Birthday" printed on. I stuck a label with a £5 reward written on it. The last open day we had I did this and the balloon was found by a lady near Catterick in Yorkshire! At Haydock the ground was heavy and it was still raining. The twelve horses were split into three fours. They went really well. Honestly I could not be more pleased. They showed not the

One of the groups of four horses out of the twelve
two-year-olds we galloped at Haydock Park to give them
a feel of the racecourse and a ride in the horsebox.
They couldn't have gone better.

slightest sign of greenness. Everyone stayed the trip without being in any way distressed. Looking at this season's crop they look every bit as good as any we have had in the past.

On the way home the three horseboxes and all the cars stopped for breakfast at Charnock Richard Service Station on the M6.

With all our lot in there, one would have thought we had the green light for Sunday racing.

Did my first write-up for The Sporting Life Weekender today. Let's hope there's more.

MONDAY March 2

8.0am-just come in from riding the Bear. He's entered in a race at Southwell on Wednesday. After that I think we will give the old boy a rest and get a bit of spring grass down his neck.

Second lot I rode Fylde Flyer, leading the string to Baxters. It was brilliant. With the excessive rain we have had over the past few days all the dykes were full of water. Our wildlife was out in full force. The owl was peeping out of his hole in the tree at us when we rode past him. Hundreds of geese settled down to eat the grass in Thorntons field. Plenty of hares and lots of partridges. Mornings like this give one a chance to forget any bad days. Thankfully, the two-year-olds all ate up and came back sound from their experience at Haydock Park yesterday.

The owl, a regular spectator as we exercise our string on the Cockerham gallops.

Another load of woodshavings has just arrived. Keeping up with shavings for these boxes is like feeding elephants strawberries. We also had two loads of hay delivered. Watching the stacking of the bales, you can see some of our lads never played with lego as kids.

After Jo had ridden out, Flasher's wife, Heather, asked her for the phone number of the stripping policeman.

This afternoon, I bought a wagon and trailer load of hay to be delivered a week on Thursday. It was good stuff and well worth getting as this year's hay crop hasn't been as good as some other years. Looking at Teletext it was sad to see old Davy Jones had died at 84. A great character he was. He rode Red Rower to win the Cheltenham Gold Cup in 1945 and rode in races until he was 63 years old.

TUESDAY March 3

7.0am, having a quick cup of tea and glancing at The Life and the Post. I see it's all hotting up on the Cheltenham front. With the Festival next week and the start of the Flat shortly after it's a very exciting time.

Although we only train the odd jumper nowadays I am still in love with the jumpers. Nothing gives me more pleasure in winter than a day at the races. For as long as I can remember I have gone to Cheltenham on Gold Cup day and to Aintree to watch the National, two marvellous days of the year.

Reading on, I see my fancy Royal Gait is 3-1 joint favourite with Ladbrokes, following Gran Alba's injury last Sunday. It's also looking a bit bleak for the North at the moment with Mary Reveley's team down with a virus and Gorden Richards' horses not firing on all cylinders. Our main hopes at the moment look like coming from Jonjo O'Neill, Peter Easterby and Jimmy FitzGerald. Martin Pipe must be the envy of every jump trainer in the land with his ammunition in the form of Carvill's Hill, Granville Again, Miinnehoma and twenty or so more runners at Cheltenham.

On a lovely sunny day at Cockerham we had the pleasure of a stable visit from the Racegoers Club. About thirty people in all travelled from as far afield as Hertfordshire and Bournemouth. Very noble of them. We took them on the gallops to watch two lots of two-year-olds canter in pairs and hack back in bunches. Some of the older horses did a piece of long, steady work. Showing them round the stables, answering questions, telling them all about the horses in general, their stay lasted a couple of hours and I think they enjoyed it. Unless they were telling porkies.

Peter Scudamore rode his 1,500th winner of his career on Slavi at Warwick. What an achievement being the first jump jockey to ride that amount-and he's still going strong.

About 5.0pm I took my string of dogs round the gallops to see if we could work on the grass tomorrow, but it wouldn't be feasible as the going is still soft after the recent rain. The all-weather gallops have all been harrowed and rolled and they are in brilliant nick so we will have to work on them. How on earth we ever trained winners before we got all-weather strips I don't know!

WEDNESDAY March 4

WORKED the two-year-olds in threes up the all-weather straight. It's made my mind up now as next week we will have to enter for Doncaster's opening meeting. So today, without being too hard on them, I want to see a few results from the gallops. The form has stood up for the last two or three gallops. The older horses we let stride on for the first time. Paris House is absolutely flying. Look out Sheikh Albadou.

Reading in The Life it was sad to see Sharpen Up had to be put down at Gainesway Stud, Lexington. But at 23 years old, like Davy Jones, he'd had a good innings.

Derek Ayres came to see his fillies work. He's from the Isle of Man. Mr and Mrs Joe Heler from Cheshire also came. Jo and I were setting off for Southwell to see Miami Bear run when John Curwen the contractor arrived. He's starting to put the footings in for the new horsewalkers we are installing.

When we pulled into the car park at Southwell the first trainer we saw was Peter Bevan. They reckon the first trainer you see usually has a winner. Peter is just recovering from a heart attack so let's hope it's right. He could do with it. If Miami Bear gets beaten I hope it's by Peter's D'Or's Gem.

In the race Miami Bear was always well placed. He made a couple of mistakes, took up the running entering the straight with three to jump. He kept on well to win easily by twelve lengths. Two minutes after the Bear had won our flying machine Lisnakill Wish won at Hove, having had his picture on the front page of the Greyhound Life yet again.

I will rough the Bear off for the season so he can get some spring grass inside him and send him to Peter Teasdale's, a pal of mine who lives in Yorkshire, for the spring and summer. He came back from him looking as big as a bullock for this season. Next season he could be a nice horse.

THURSDAY March 5

I HAVE just come in from riding out and it's a beautiful spring-like day. The daffodils are bursting forth, dandelions are showing and the hedges are just starting to leaf. Who would have an office job?

The Bear is a bit stiff but, thankfully, not too bad. He will have plenty of time to get over it where he is going.

The contractors are getting on well with the foundations for the new walkers.

Roly Daniels, the Irish Country and Western singer I met in Ireland at the Fairyhouse Sales, has sent me his new album on cassette. He knows it's my scene.

Second lot I rode out Fylde Flyer. What a lovely horse he is. Those punters from the Blackpool Gazette and Chronicle are in for some fun this season with him.

Had a luncheon appointment at Bumbles in our village with Philip Curwen, General Manager of Speeds Mercedes Benz, about a promotion scheme on our gallops. Also seeing I still have no wheels, hopefully about getting me a car. When I do get one I have a couple of sponsors lined up. We are sorting a deal out at the moment. Yorkshire Television rang to do some filming before the start of the Flat season.

Wasn't that Ian Botham a star man by taking four Australian wickets for 3 runs and hitting a half century in Sydney? His critics want to have a think before they spout. I think he is brilliant. Jo, Alan, Kevin, John and myself went to The Patten Arms to sort out yesterday's work and re-arrange the horses to work on Saturday. Got the list ready, jocked them up, had a pizza, a couple of Murphys and then back home. As I have said before we do the sorting out at the Patten to concentrate away from "Buzby!" It's also a nice change. Once we've finished talking work we have a game of dominoes. We all put a fiver in a kitty, the first to win two games takes the pot. I won one. Alan won the other two, so he took the pot.

FRIDAY March 6

A BEAUTIFUL sunny morning again. To further the two-year-olds education this morning's programme was to ride each horse individually out of the indoor school at one minute intervals to walk down the paths to the gallops and canter five furlongs steady, pull up at the top, walk off the gallops, out through a gate down the lane and then into our yard the back way. By doing this, if they are lucky enough to get to the front in a race, they will hopefully keep going, instead of waiting for company. Doing this exercise, as you should appreciate, can sometimes be a bit hairy. Some can be a bit soft and want a lead. Doing this makes them more independent.

The whole operation went like a dream, except for one young lad who got dropped walking down to the gallop. Out of eighty-two involved in the exercise, we can't grumble.

The older horses just did a long, steady canter after a spell of road work. The hair is coming out of the horse's coats nicely now and they are getting a bit of bloom. If the weather stays like today come Doncaster's opening meet, our horses will look real good.

John Curwen's men have been very busy all day putting down the drains and foundations for the walkers. Wagons have been rolling up with concrete, hardcore and crusher run all afternoon.

Watching Teletext it's very unfortunate that, in his testimonial year, Steve Smith Eccles cannot get his broken ankle right for the Festival meeting and he may be out for the rest of the season. It's a tough game this jumping business.

SATURDAY March 7

ALL the plans we made last night horsewise have gone to pot as it's raining heavily. We were to work the horses round our moss gallop. Abandoning that idea, as the horses will cut it up too much, we are, therefore, back on the old favourite all-weather.

We let the two-year-olds stride on at a nice three parts speed in threes. The older horses were paired up to do five furlongs at a good pace. Some of the older horses seem as though they are hanging onto their coats and to be honest most of them don't look ready. Especially the fillies, they probably want some sun on their backs. Paris House, Amron, Amber Mill and Echo-Logical look the best. It was great watching racing on telly from Chepstow and Sandown. Carobee, the winner of the £20,000 Swish Hurdle was most impressive. It just shows how jockeys have to earn their corn. Having ridden in the two previous races, and no doubt ridden out before racing, Richard Dunwoody is next riding in a helicopter to fly off to Sandown Park to win on Brown Windsor in the three mile chase. But what a sickener in that race. The marvellous old campaigner Pegwell Bay broke a leg when falling at the first fence.

The Sunderlands Imperial Cup in the past always attracted lots of runners. Only ten went to post today, but what a good race it proved to be. Rodeo Star, for the North, looked home and dry between the last two hurdles, only to be collared close home by King Credo. R.Dunwoody rode in the next two races also. It makes one wonder what that poor man Iain Vallance has to do to earn his £450,000 per annum from B.T. as Richard won't earn anything like that amount.

SUNDAY March 8

TODAY is a lovely sunny day, not a bit like yesterday's awful rain. Peter Teasdale came to collect Miami Bear for his well-earned vacation. He is all right now after his Southwell knock. In fact, he must think he has a bad home as he fair shot into Peter's horsebox as if he knew where he was going.

When we finished doing the horses up I took all my dogs for a walk round the farm. It's great this time of year, everything is starting to grow. The ducks have now paired up as they scuttle out of the dykes, frightened by the Moss Side pack of dogs. It's great, really great to have this free time to walk round the farm and the gallops. I love it.

In the past before I retired Olly (O I Oyston) I always rode around the place on him. We used to stay out for hours. There were always things to do. One day a sheep got over the netting onto the dyke side. Her lambs were bleating for their mum. I jumped off Olly, undid the buckle of the reins and put them round a post to tether him until I sorted the sheep out. Sheep are not gifted with a lot of brains. This one went a long way down the side of the dyke before I caught her. After I had managed to get yet another sheep out I looked round to make sure there were no more in the dyke. I went in the house stinking like a polecat and had a bath, ate my tea and sat down to watch telly. Suddenly I remembered, Olly was still up on the top moss. I vaulted on his back, rode him back, and put him in his box. Just another day to Olly, he loved every minute.

Quite a few owners came with it being such a nice day. The sun gets them out. I wrote my story for the Weekender, which was about the death of veteran Davy Jones and Royal Gait, my fancy for the Champion Hurdle.

Pat Knight and Tricia Harrison have just returned from a Canary Isles cruise. During one of the stop-offs, they visited Sam and took him some bits and pieces Jo and I had got together for him. Both of these girls gave me valuable help in getting my book "It's Tougher At The Bottom" off the ground.

Pat is coming up to stay the night to catch up on the goings on at Jo's party, and see the dogs. She has a room here and comes and goes when she pleases.

I have nearly clinched the car deal on the telephone with Terry Holdcroft for an Audi car. With himself and Andrew Hoyle of Laurel Racing as sponsors it looks as if at long last I am going to get a set of wheels.

MONDAY March 9

IT'S 5.40am on a very sharp pitch black morning. I have just come in the house from giving Neville Hill and Linda Porter a hand feeding the horses. I can feel it's going to be another nice day.

First job at around 5.0am Neville and Linda open the top doors of the boxes and put the stable lights on in all the yards. They have a look inside to make sure the horses are all right. Sometimes rugs are hanging off, or occasionally are completely off, maybe a water bucket has been kicked into the middle of the box. There is the dreaded moment, the odd time, we find a horse cast in a corner. Whatever problems there are we put right. The horses are then fed a bowl of nuts from a big metal barrow that is pushed around the yards. Any horses who may have left some of their overnight feed have it taken out. Later on we feed it to the cattle in the fold yard. The cattle thankfully don't have to rely on this supply totally, as Neville is one of the best feeders in the game and he doesn't have many horses leaving their feed. It's a real good sight first thing in the morning seeing all the horses with their heads over the doors taking their first gulps of the morning's fresh air and looking so pleased to see us. Jo has gone to Ragdale Hall Health Farm in Leicestershire for five days with her friend Gwen Viner to pay a fortune to live on lettuce. Hopefully, when she comes back our horses will notice the difference.

TUESDAY March 10

AT the moment, weatherwise, we never seem to get two days alike. It's absolutely throwing it down. With all the modern waterproofs for humans and equines, riding out in the rain isn't as bad as it used to be. That's my story anyway. With less than two weeks before we line up for the starter at Doncaster's opening Flat meeting, staff and horses will have to do a lot more wriggling before I let them off the hook.

Today is the first day of the Cheltenham Festival. I have already set my fire in the room to watch the telly. I shall be there with my Life and Post and my dogs laid down beside me. I will pull the plugs out of the phones. So unless there is a murder in the yard, don't disturb me today, thank you. Blimey I'm getting all revved up just thinking about Cheltenham. It's so exciting. I will say it again before the event, Royal Gait for the Champion Hurdle.

Budget day as well today. I'm glad those politicians don't have this yard. It wouldn't take them long before they got the boxes emptied.

Because of Cheltenham on the box we groomed the horses when they came in last lot in order that our crew could watch all the racing on the telly. We do this throughout the Festival.

Wasn't it great to see the old boys on parade, Sea Pigeon, Night Nurse, Burrough Hill Lad, Gaye Brief, Desert Orchid and See You Then?

It certainly was a nailbiting Champion Hurdle. I won't make a meal of it but wouldn't Royal Gait have been unlucky to have lost the race for running about. Especially after he got disqualified at Royal Ascot for bumping Sadeem's pacemaker. In that race he won easily by five lengths and broke the course record. As big a fan as I am of Cash Asmussen's the stewards did perfectly right to send him for seven days in the sunshine.

It was good for trainer James Fanshawe to win a race like the Champion Hurdle with his first runner. Although when James was assistant at Michael Stoute's he had quite a bit to do with Kribensis when he won the Champion Hurdle.

What a great day for young Jamie Osborne. To ride three winners on the first day at the Festival is fantastic. I must say there are some good young jump jockeys about at the moment.

Stan Newman rang me to tell me Lisnakill Wish had been to Hall Green for a trial over 475 metres and had done a good time 29.72 sec. His ante-post price now is 6-1 for the Daily Mirror / Sporting Life Grand National. Double Rock, his kennel mate who conquered him in the Springbok Final, clocked 30.22 sec.

WEDNESDAY March 11

THAT was good news for racing, the Home Secretary giving racing £12,500,000. It was a timely boost to say the least. There was lots of overnight rain although the ground was still good on the all-weather. Lots of owners came to see their horses work today. With it being close to the start of the season they all want to see their steeds before we get busy.

After the work I decide that Sabre Rattler will be our Brocklesby horse-let's hope I have got it right.

I have definitely done a deal with Terry Holdcroft for a silver Audi 1900 fuel injected turbo diesel, hopefully coming by the weekend, all painted up with my sponsor's logo. I am going into the room to watch Cheltenham on the box, only I am not going to light the fire today. Yesterday, shouting for Royal Gait and with all the excitement, I was sweating cobs. To watch Cheltenham on telly for three days is worth the cost of the licence.

Seeing Charles Haughey, the ex-Irish Prime Minister, interviewed in his roll as an owner as well as a breeder was great. More the pity our Prime Ministers are not as sporting as him. The last one we had who was as keen must have been Sir Winston Churchill and that was a while since. The Queen Mother Champion Chase was a dream to watch. Remittance Man showed what a very good horse he is by winning well. He is a worthy champion. A touch of sadness that the Queen Mum wasn't there to present the trophy to Mr Collins the winning owner. Let's hope she makes a speedy recovery from her cold.

There was a false start to the Coral Hurdle Final-a red flag was waved to let the jockeys know of the no go. The man waving like mad as 31 horses were charging towards him, held his ground like a true soldier. For doing so he should have been awarded a medal as big as a frying pan. The race was eventually won by My View at 33-1.

With racing on the box I have a £1 Heinz bet on every day of the meeting with Francis Habbershaw of Yorkshire. Not that I need an interest as Cheltenham is surely interesting enough but mainly for a fun bet. The first day I only came up with Royal Gait but today I fared much better. My selections were Bollin Patrick, Waterloo Boy, My View, Miinnehoma, Keep Talking and Sword Beach. Three of them won, at 33-1, 7-2 and 5-2. With money from my winnings I have no intentions of giving up the day job, although I have earned my spending money for tomorrow. The Radio Lancashire listeners who were switched on at 6.30pm would have heard me do a live slot about the Cheltenham Gold Cup.

THURSDAY March 12

IT's been raining all night here and a filthy morning it is too. Olly, my dog, and I are setting off for Cheltenham, it's nearly 7.0am.

I have been invited to the Tote Box and have to be there for 12.0 noon, so I don't want to be troubled with motorway poachers wanting to relieve me of my cash or give me points. I have borrowed Alan's car and it can't half trap. Got to the course at 11.30. The lady at the owners and trainers entrance made me pay £30 for admission which goes down in history as the first time in my life I have ever paid.Chris Leigh of the Weekender asked me if I would do an interview with Ronnie Beggan, the jump jockey, live on radio on the course, which I did.

Met Mike and Janetta Gallemore and went for lunch in the Tote Box. This must be the best box there, it has an absolutely brilliant view of the racecourse.

The finish in the Gold Cup was nailbiting, hammer and tongs right to the line between Cool Ground, The Fellow and Docklands Express. Cool Ground just beat The Fellow a short-head. What a race. That narrow margin made all the difference between winning and losing £60,000.

It was so sad to see Carvill's Hill finish distressed like he did, only able to walk past the post in fifth place.

The crowd was not as great I have seen it in the past. This recession is definitely biting.

It's worth mentioning the brave official with the red flag at Cheltenham yesterday was Don Faulkner, an 81 year-old Dunkirk veteran. He has been doing his duty at Cheltenham for twenty years. So unlike the official at Newcastle last season when there was a false start. Yer man bolted so fast, he could have beaten the horses home. He dived under the running rail so dramatically he very nearly got knocked over by the ambulance. If I was in a house and it was on fire, I know which of the two officials I would vote to pull me out.

Looking at the injury book on my return, nothing serious has happened during my day's absence. A couple with sore shins, one has got a kick. These casualties are from yesterday's work. Today we're only giving the horses road work, so it was a good day to have off.

FRIDAY March 13

PUT the two-year-olds in the stalls from up the near straight. They are all going in easily and certainly coming out fast. The odd one is getting edgy as now they know what it's all about.

While down at the stalls, the lads told me Kevin's little girl Amy went into hospital yesterday with an asthma attack. Her mum, Jill, housekeeps for us and brings little Amy up with her as she's only four. Poor little mite. I hope she's all right.

Lee, one of the girls got kicked on her arm as she was walking back from the stall work. The bruise was quite nasty so we sent her away for a week's holiday to recover. The older horses are being cantered in pairs at varying distances. We have had such a lot of rain over this past 48 hours even the all-weather is riding deep today. It's also very wild and windy. Our secretary, Ruby, has just informed me that we have been fined £60 by Weatherbys for a training agreement that didn't get registered before an entry was made for the owner. Weatherbys must have thought they'd better get in quick and have a bite of our cake in case those Ministry boys came back, and there's none left!

We have Sober Lad entered at Leopardstown in Ireland next week. Nearly every newspaper in the country has rung about Sober Lad, including the Irish boys. They can't make out why we are going over there so early on in the season.

In the past racecourses in Britain were compelled to stage a two-year-old race on every card. Now they don't have to. In the first five meetings of the new season here, three of the courses decided not to list a juvenile race. At Cockerham we have in training more than eighty two-year-olds. Twenty of them are queueing up to run. If this is going to be the norm, there are just not enough races for our team. It would not make sense to buy so many yearlings in the future, as I am not keen on running more than one in a race. Plus the fact that the race in Ireland is an £8,000 maiden. There is no chance of that kind of money being on offer so early in the season over here. At Lingfield Park all-weather track, on Saturday, March 21 four races are being run for £1,200 each, and three of these are sponsored. The big race of the day is the sponsored £2,000 Abbey Life Handicap. Ironically, one of the races that isn't sponsored is the Lancaster Maiden Stakes. Lingfield should have asked those gentleman at Lancaster Courthouse who dealt with our box offences for a sub-they'd already got it named after them.

SATURDAY March 14

READING my Life it says "Taps on at Ascot". For the past three days at Cockerham I can't remember it raining more. Nicky Beaumont, the Clerk of the Course, should send his men up here with some buckets.

For a change, all the older horses worked first lot. Some of these are going great.

The Daily Mail came to do a write-up about 8.30am. They saw the two-year-olds work in threes. Everything went well. Sober Lad our first juvenile runner at Leopardstown went particularly well with John up, as did our Brocklesby entry Sabre Rattler. When the lads were leading the two-year-olds home after their work Palacegate Prince, who is a real playful character, turned round sharp and bit Steve Porritt one of our apprentices on his private part. Steve let out such a yell. The girls were asking him to let them have a look and after breakfast one of them even asked him if there were any teeth marks on it.

Sometimes you have to laugh out loud in the yard. Young Alan "Paddy" Daly, another apprentice, says to Flash: "Fylde Flyer, *he's* just bit a big hole in *her* rug."

"Oh, yes," says Flash, "and I suppose Miss Parkes is a gelding as well."

12.20pm and the lads are just lashing up and finishing off. Five races on the box from Uttoxeter to look forward to-great.

What a bonus before racing started-the fight on BBC 1 between Italy's Sambu Kalambay and our southpaw Herol Graham, for the European middleweight title. These two brave men amazingly kept up a really fast pace for the whole of the 12 rounds. The highlights from the Cheltenham Festival followed. I had already seen them quite a few times, and hopefully will see a few more as I have them safely on video.

In the first race from Uttoxeter, Northern Jinks looked to have the novice chase sewn up only to come down at the last, giving Richard Dunwoody a horrible-looking fall. Thankfully, the cameras showed Richard walking away.

**IT'S A DOG'S LIFE : I am watching the horses parade
round the yard, surrounded by the Cockerham dog pack.
You can't keep them away from the action,
particularly when there's a camera about.**

In the next race, another novice chase, would you believe it poor old Richard, in with every chance, falls again, at the third last this time on Peajade. The race was won by Meat The Foulkes at 50-1.

Jenny Pitman was interviewed by Brough Scott about her Gold Cup tactics with Golden Freeze taking on Carvill's Hill. At the start of the interview I got the impression he was trying to give Jenny a bit of a hard time. However, the bold Brough failed to get the better of Jenny. In fact, I thought any minute he will get a Jamie Osborne, right across the chops. If Channel 4 announces that they're replaying the interview it will get a bigger viewing audience than Coronation Street. It was the best programme I have watched for a while. I am grateful for our Jo being a bit on the quiet side by comparison to Jenny.

I was pleased to see my namesake Frank Berry, the ex-Irish champion jump jockey, win the Ansells National with Laura's Beau.

Jo came back about 5.0pm looking a different model for her Ragdale Hall visit.

SUNDAY March 15

8.0am, Doug Francis's horsebox arrives, driven by the ex-trainer Colin Whiston, to take Sober Lad to Ireland. Sober Lad looked an absolute picture going in the box. It's a nice mild morning and the winds have settled down. Last night was the first sailing to Ireland for a couple of days. We were getting worried about being able to travel our fellow over there.

John and Tracy Carroll, Jo and I travelled in John's car to the Paris House restaurant at Woburn Abbey, as the four of us have been invited to lunch by Peter Chandler, the owner of our good horse Paris House.

The Marquis and Marchioness of Tavistock, their son Lord Howland, Reg Griffin, Jim McGrath, Julie Cecil, Clive and Maureen Brittain were among the guests. Jim McGrath said a few words and told a few tales. Very good he was, too. Andrew Howland auctioned various prints, wine and a Sunday lunch prepared by the Paris House staff who will travel to the home of the successful bidders to cook and serve it up to fourteen diners, which I bought.

The object of the lunch was to raise money for racing charities. With the auction some £6,000 was raised for the cause. Paris House is situated in the beautiful grounds of Woburn Abbey where there are some very rare deer. The house was originally built in 1878 for the Paris exhibition. It was then dismantled and brought piece by piece to be rebuilt on the Woburn Estate. It fell into disrepair and wasn't restored until 1983 when it was opened as a restaurant.

On our return home the diary contained nearly a page of phone calls. The most interesting one was from Doug Francis informing us Sober Lad had landed at his destination in Ireland and had travelled well.

MONDAY March 16

YORKSHIRE Television crew are here today. It's 4.20am and Neville has gone out feeding. He starts at 5.20am normally, only with this lot arriving so early all the dogs started barking so I got Neville up and came down with him. With strangers about you don't know what the dogs would do. Neville, first thing in the morning can be a bit sour. When he finds out he has gone out an hour early, those boys from the television had better look out. He can be more vicious than the dogs.

That is the trouble when you let people like that come. Instead of waiting out of bounds until the scheduled time they invariably come halfway through the night and upset our programme. It's a one-off for them but every day for us.

On Monday it's road work except for Tuesday and Wednesday runners or anything that may be a bit stuffy or thick in its wind. For the camera crew's benefit we put six of the horses together and gave them a canter for them to film. I did an interview before leading the first lot round the roads on Gorinsky.

The phones are red hot today with the new season a few days away and our first five-day entries are in The Sporting Life and Racing Post.

The Daily Mail had a nice centre page on us after their visit on Saturday in which they refer to me as a hobgoblin. As I'm in leprechaun country tomorrow I hope it's a good omen.

Phil Rostron of the Daily Star rang to make sure I am prepared to continue writing for them every Saturday as I did last season. Also if I would give them a preview for the opening meet at Doncaster.

2.30pm-I had an interview with Dee Ford for the Lancashire Life about how a Yorkshireman came to train racehorses in Lancashire.

Jo and I went to The Crofters to meet and have a meal with Ben Allen, one of our London owners, who has the two-year-olds Sefio and Trentesimo. He is going to have a look at his horses tomorrow. Would you believe, when we got to The Crofters, Blackburn Rovers Football Club were having a night out. None other than Kenny Dalglish was guest speaker in the next function room.

I was approached a few years ago to sponsor a football match at Blackburn Rovers. We were to be allowed a box and so many complimentary tickets, banners on four sides of the pitch advertising Moss Side racing stables with guaranteed spin-offs, sure to pull some owners in. So off I go to the match. The banners they were talking about read: Moss Side RIDING Stables, phone 0524-791179. For about a month we had folk ringing up trying to book rides. NOT one person rang to send us a horse to train.

TUESDAY March 17

FRED VINER, who owns Sober Lad in partnership with Stan Newman, rang first thing to say he had fallen and torn some ligaments in his leg. For all that he would still be travelling to see his horse run at Leopardstown today.

John Carroll and myself went to Manchester Airport in John's car as I still have no car until tomorrow. Mind you, I could get used to this no driving and no fuel to pay for. Motoring down our lane, two magpies flew over. That was a bit of good luck straight away.

Looking in The Sporting Life our fellow is even money favourite. Jim Bolger's filly Please Widd is second favourite at 7-4. That is the danger, I tell John. Jim has already trained three or four winners. At Manchester, with it being St Patrick's day, the airport staff gave John and I some Shamrock for our button hole-Another lucky omen?

Benny and Sheila Powell, Brendan the jump jockey's parents, met us at Dublin Airport to take us to Leopardstown. Our horse was in the first, which was the richest race on the card at £8,000. Arriving at 11.30am gave us plenty of time as the race wasn't until 2.20pm. Just before we got to the races I saw another pair of magpies.

After walking the five furlongs with John, the first trainer I saw on our return was Jim Bolger talking to Joe Mercer. Normally the first trainer you see has a winner. Jim said I had the race to myself as his filly was lame and doesn't run. Walking round the paddock our man Sober looked good. When John cantered him down to the start I was interviewed live on Irish radio. The ground was a bit on the dead side as it was drying out from being soft. Drawn eight, when the gates opened he flew out three or four lengths clear. Close home he was shortening up a bit but Leopardstown is a very stiff track and the slow conditions made it more testing.

Thankfully he held on to win by a neck. Burmah Castrol, the sponsors of the race, also kindly gave £1,000 to the stable staff of the yard which produced the winner.

John Kent, Sober Lad's breeder, was there to see him. Stan, Fred and their wives, along with a lot more went for a quick drink. We couldn't hang about as we had to catch the 4.0pm flight, although I would have loved to have stayed for the rest of the card and see more of the old faces. Saying our farewells we arrived at the airport 3.45pm, after having quite a hairy drive courtesy of Mr Powell Senior.

Amazingly at Manchester Airport no one knew us. At Dublin Airport nearly everyone did.

I was actually in our house sat down to my tea at half past six. It was easier than going to Leicester or Southwell.

Two points you may be interested in. Firstly fillies only receive a 3lb allowance from colts in Ireland. Here they get 5lb. Secondly, regarding my tie, the one that Ray Gilpin of the Racing Post asked me to wear as a belt the next day. Well, Tracy Piggott, Lester's daughter, said she liked it. She would be a better judge than Ray any day.

WEDNESDAY March 18

IN THE morning racing papers we have nice things reported about our Irish victory.

Alec Russell the photographer came to take photos for the Racing Post of the horses working.

Today we run Gorinsky at Southwell. He should run well as it's the first time he's had blinkers on. The main danger will be African Chimes who won at Southwell last Saturday. Put tomorrow's Doncaster runners, Sabre

Rattler and Echo-Logical through the stalls. Everyone is complaining about the drought and we have to work on the all-weather because of too much rain.

Worked all the horses by 11.30am. Steve Haworth, one of the apprentices, was sent in Jo's car to Doncaster Breeze-Up Sales. Steve and Paul Roberts who went earlier in the box, are riding Preston Guild and the Cragador colt in the breeze-up on the racecourse at 3.0pm. Preston Guild came up the three furlongs with number eight, the Cragador colt. Our fellow looked a real racehorse and went like a good un. Not a bit green and as straight as a dye. Lots of people were looking at him. Tomorrow morning he has to breeze-up again. Then after racing he will be sold at the sales yard by public auction. He is a real nice horse and I am very hopeful of him ringing the bell-that means topping the sales price.

On the way back from the breeze-up I stopped at a bookies to see how Gorinsky fared-second to African Chimes. Steve passed his driving test yesterday so I let him drive when we got to Hartshead Moor Service area on the M62.

Alan and John returned from Southwell and said Gorinsky only got beat half a length.

Wally went on to the train this afternoon to pick up my new car, a now white 1900 Audi diesel from Terry Holdcroft's at Stoke-on-Trent. He has just brought it back. Personally, I am not a great lover of any kind of machine, but this is real nice. The racing colours of Laurel Racing Club and their advert are along the sides with Terry's garage on the front and rear.

THURSDAY March 19

6.0am on Brocklesby morning and it's a lovely sunny day. I am just having a cup of tea, the wild birds are chirping away outside.

Our entry in the Brocklesby, Sabre Rattler, is a lovely colt by Beveled. Beveled is the same sire of the good two-year-old Bit-a-Magic who we trained last year to win a Listed race in Italy. The poor horse was fatally injured at Doncaster the same day we won the Flying Childers with Paris House. It shows how our job is up and down. John and I rode out tomorrow's runners then set off to Doncaster in his car. Jo is bringing my new job later. We have to be at the morning's breeze-up for 10.20 am. Jo and I are staying overnight.

Reading the papers we have got plenty of coverage. The Racing Post have a coloured photo on their front page of yesterday's work, where we have a big bunch of horses hacking back afterwards. There's a nice write-up, too. The Handicap Book has a photo on the front cover of Paris House in the winning enclosure after winning the Flying Childers. My weekly write-up is in The Sporting Life Weekender and Preston Guild is featured in The Sporting Life. Got to the sales yard where John rode Preston Guild, and yet another one of our band of apprentices, Paul Roberts, rode the Cragador colt.

Sabre Rattler, our runner in the Brocklesby, bounced out of the stalls from the number ten berth-the best draw right on the fence. Pinged along until the last furlong only to be headed by Touch Silver and Nominator, to finish third at 4-6 favourite. In the next the £5,000 five furlong sprint, Echo-Logical, with top weight of 9st 7lbs, took up the running in the last twenty yards, but was unluckily beaten a head in a photo.

Sabre Rattler (far side) seen finishing third to
Touch Silver (nearside) and Nominator (centre) in the Brocklesby.

Right after the fourth race, our lovely filly bought by William Hills, was drawn by John McCririck live on television. The proceeds from the raffle, which amounted to £100,000, are to go to the Royal Marsden Hospital. When the racing finished the breeze-up auction began. Our Cragador colt was number eight in.
He did quite well reaching 10,500gns, bought by a wood firm in Scotland. Next horse in was Preston Guild, who, not being bitchy, looked the best in the whole sale. He was bought by Lady Matthews from Jersey, on the telephone, for 21,000 gns. Thankfully Lady Matthews said we could take him back and train him for her. What a relief, as he is a lovely horse.
Tony and Jo Shelton were at Doncaster and were staying in our hotel the Moat House. After our business was done at the sales we returned to the hotel, had a swim and a sauna before joining the Sheltons for an evening meal.

FRIDAY March 20

RANG Alan early on to go through the declarations and the entries, check that the horses were all right and ask who has rung, and what's what. When finished, Jo and I went for a swim. While Jo went for breakfast afterwards, I had a sauna. Who do you think was there again, starkers? Yes, Derek Thompson. He wants to think himself lucky I didn't bring Palacegate Prince in with me. He could have had a nice breakfast.

Jo and I went later to watch the horses breeze on the track. There were half a dozen two-year-olds I would have liked. Thank God we are in the fortunate position that we haven't room. Mind you, I can't remember ever going to a sale and really liking horses and coming home empty handed. So we shall see.

The first race on the Doncaster card is the two-year-old seller with fourteen runners. Classic Storm is our contender. As a foal, the poor little mite had an accident and went blind in her near side eye. Mandy, a little girl in our yard, looks after her and thinks the world of her. In the race the filly went in the stalls last. Always handy, she took it up a furlong out and went on to win by three lengths easy. At the auction she failed to attract a bid. That was a bonus for Derek Ayres, her Isle of Man-based owner. In between races Graham Orange, the Northern PRO and racecourse announcer, asked me if I would have a chat with some patients in wheelchairs who had come from a home near Huddersfield for a day at the races. Not only did I go but I took some jocks with me. They loved it. As it happened, there wasn't a photographer about so Graham borrowed a camera from a lady in the crowd to take a photo of them.

The last race on the card we had Amron in, owned by Roy and Norma Peebles, who absolutely love the little fellow. He won the same race last year. This year he was in the middle until two out. He came through with a lovely run to win easy by five lengths.

Back at the sales I couldn't resist buying lot 98, a plainish looking colt by Exhibitioner who looked a real tough sort and had breezed well.

Robert Aird, one of our Scottish owners, picked out a very well bred colt by Dowsing out of a Try My Best mare. He was a real good sort who worked very well on the racecourse. Not a bad judge Robert, as it was the highest priced lot of the sale. Both Robert and his wife Elaine were keen for me to buy him for them. Let's hope he justifies their faith.

Lots of our owners are staying at the Moat House. With us having a good day we all ate together on a big table. I don't have to tell you we had a good night.

SATURDAY March 21

FIRST thing I rang Alan to get through the daily routine of entering the horses, organising their work, and so forth before he dives off to saddle Cranfield Comet, hopefully to win at Lingfield. He looks quite a good thing, the Life's men have him at 8-13 favourite.

During the flat season I write a Saturday column and tip horses that run in all the televised races. This is my first Saturday back. For the Lincoln I have napped Willie Carson's mount Roseate Lodge. My Next Best is our own

Fylde Flyer in the Cammidge Trophy, so I hope we've got that one right. My third selection is Big Leap in the seven furlong handicap. Had a swim and sauna. In the pool this morning was Rod Simpson and John Francome so as you can guess we had a bit of a giggle. Derek didn't come down as he was busy with the Morning Line on telly.

Charlie runs tonight at Hall Green in a trial for the Grand National. On the front page of the Greyhound Life it reads: "Lisnakill Wish, one of Jack Berry's flying two-year-olds." I liked that.

Jo and I were invited for lunch in the William Hill box. Our two-year-old Two Moves In Front ran unplaced in the first race. Straight after, Graham Wright was presented with the filly he had won in the competition.

I watched High Low win the Lincoln Handicap from Hills' box. The hope of Willie giving me a dream start to the season for my Star punters just wasn't to be. I could imagine my ex-fans throughout the betting shops, tearing their tickets up. "Couldn't tip muck out of a barrow" they'd be saying.

Next race Fylde Flyer is in the Listed race. Listed status means its not quite as good as Group 3 but it has more prestige than a handicap or a normal stakes race.

It's good for horses when they go to stud as they get what we call black type. Although he is only three years old Fylde Flyer actually receives 21lb from some of the older horses. This fellow is a very strong mature colt, so I have thrown him in at the deep end.

In the race John gave him a bit of a chance: two furlongs out he takes it up and in a ding-dong battle he holds on to beat Notley by a short head in a photo at the SP of 8-1. When the result was announced an enormous cheer went up from the contingent of members from the Blackpool Gazette, who have a 400-strong syndicate.

The next race was duly won by my other tip Big Leap, 9-1. Hopefully, after that I have got all my fans back and they are blaming Willie Carson for getting Roseate Lodge beat.

I drove my new car home. It's a bit noisy but I like it and it certainly traps. Alan rang on his way home as did Richard Quinn, Cranfield Comet's jockey. He didn't ping the boxes yet managed to get back in the race to lead. Coming round the turn too fast he carried straight on and lost the race in doing so.

Nothing serious in the injury book. The phone never stopped ringing until about 9.0pm. I read all the mail Ruby had left for me to look at.

Stan Newman rang-Charlie had won at Hall Green. What a dog. Talking of dogs, David Brown, Dave Minton and myself invested today in two coursing dogs. We can look forward to some fun there.

SUNDAY March 22

IT'S a beautiful morning. I am working away, drinking a cup of tea. Not a soul about but the birds singing away outside. Without doubt, it's the best time of the day. Perfect peace.

While we have been away at Doncaster there has been quite a lot of rain here. Two Times Twelve, a two-year-old, who is entered at Catterick on Wednesday was playing about and slipped up in the yard. He has grazed his knees slightly. Thankfully he hasn't broken the skin so he has a good chance of being fit. There is just a bit of puffiness but he is sound. I have told Flash to keep him on the hose-pipe three or four times a day, and keep our fingers crossed.

Tomorrow's Folkestone runners cantered a couple of furlongs to stretch their legs before their long journey in the horsebox. I didn't want to do too much before travelling.

High noon, we had an Open Day for the Fylde Flyer supporters at the stables. It couldn't have fitted in better with their horse winning at Doncaster yesterday. Four coach-loads of people and a few cars rolled-up. It was warm and sunny for them. Peter, one of our lads, had a pair of gloves on when he was showing the horses. I said: "For God's sake man, you don't want gloves on a hot day like this."

"They're not gloves, boss. They're bandages from getting my finger's burnt on Sabre Rattler last Thursday."

We got Flyer out of his box for the people to photograph. He loved the attention.

From the yard the supporters went and took over the Village Hall for a buffet and open bar. We had a question and answer time with me on the stage with the mike. The people loved it. We had a good laugh.

Later in the day I finished writing up my copy for the Weekender, which was about Sunday racing, and answered the phone countless times. Alan and I did the entries for tomorrow as it's an early start for one of us to go to Folkestone.

I rang Sam up in Tenerife. He was in good form. We received a card from him the other day wishing us well for the new season.

MONDAY March 23

WELL done Alan Munro being voted Jockey of the Year. Congratulations also to Richard Quinn for scooping the Racing Post readers Jockey of the Year and to Alex Greaves for becoming Lady Jockey of the Year. It's a long way to Folkestone and I have a fair bit of catching up here to do with having been away two nights at Doncaster. Alan has gone instead of me.

John Curwen's merry men have got the walkers up and the bases are laid with hardcore. It's all being rolled at the moment. The arms are ready to go on the machines. Only the wood fibre needs to be put down and, hopefully, we are in business.

John Carroll has just rung to say he has pranged his car up on the M6 motorway. Thankfully, neither Alan nor John were hurt. Apparently, there is a multiple pile up and they are in the middle. I have arranged with the

Folkestone authorities for Gary Carter to stand-by in case John doesn't get there, which I can't see him doing as he said his car is very sick and where do you hire a car just like that on a motorway?

A load of hay has just arrived, its 12.5 pm and pissing down. I bet it won't be long before the bales are stacked away and the wagon is on its way home.

Just listened to the 3.45 pm race from Folkestone, Arctic Appeal has just won the sprint for us by five lengths. Rang again for the 4.15 pm, but our Critical Mass is not in the first three at 7-4 favourite. It goes to show it's not automatic. They don't all win!

Leicester has been abandoned tomorrow because of waterlogging. That will save us a journey.

What a mess across our front lawn. The electricians have had to dig right across it to enable them to lay a higher voltage cable to get enough power to operate the new walkers.

On Ceefax it mentions about John being involved in a car crash. Lots of people are ringing asking after his well being.

TUESDAY March 24

MICKY HEATON-ELLIS, the trainer, and I leased Camden Belle for a month from Mr Edgeley to run in today's Royal Artillery Gold Cup at Sandown. Seeing as we were both in the RA but having no jumpers of our own, leasing was the only way of giving us a runner.

All our five runners at Catterick tomorrow were jumped out of stalls and galloped for two furlongs on the straight of the all-weather. It's still very wet here and by the looks of this morning's sky we have more rain to come.

The rest of the horses cantered round the ring as at the moment that gallop is as dry as any we have. The reason for this is when we made that gallop we didn't excavate. We built it up on the top of the land with boards twenty two inches high all the way round to hold the four layers of membrane, stone, membrane and wood fibre. We did likewise on the far side of the nine furlong all-weather because, being on the west side of the country, if there is any rain about God seems to wet us first.

Andrew Hoyle, the Lancashire Evening Post Sports Editor, has just rung to say Jim Joel has died. I know he was 97 and had a good innings, but it's still very sad to lose one of racing's finest gentlemen.

Mike Gallemore came for a ride out second lot to give him a blow out for tomorrow's race at Worcester as he also has a scrub in it.

Ruby has just given me the runners and draw for Catterick tomorrow. From our five runners we have three of the worst draws. I suppose someone has to have them but odds would be high for that to happen.

Mark Tompkins, the Newmarket trainer, rang to say Father Time won't be running in the Worcester race tomorrow, as he has hurt his knee. Instead I can ride his other horse Tipperary Azul. Sounds like an Irish Arab. The only problem is its got 11st 8lb. Father Time had 12 stone, so I may have to struggle a bit to do the weight. I am certainly not performing on one of those saddles John rides on at times. They are no bigger than my tea cup.

Would you believe it-Camden Belle has just won the Royal Artillery Gold Cup at Sandown for Micky and I. That is amazing. Most Royal Artillery personnel would give their back teeth to win that race. We go and lease a horse for a month and win it first time of asking.

Looked round the horses at stable time. Then at 6.0pm decided to go round to John Carroll's to have half an hour in his sauna to lose a bit of flab.

Turning the teletext on, it says: "Sound Victory for Ellis and Berry. Trainers Michael Heaton-Ellis and Jack Berry teamed-up to lift the Royal Artillery Gold Cup with Camden Belle. As former gunners they were qualified to have a runner in the race so they leased the horse from Menin Muggeridge and their plan came to fruition.

The 10-year-old stayed on gamely to account for Gaelic Cherry by a length. Heaton-Ellis said: "That was a great training performance by Menin. Jack couldn't be here as he is in the sauna trying to lose weight for the Worcester Celebrity Race."

WEDNESDAY March 25

ON the back page of The Sporting Life there is a lovely picture of the Queen Mum presenting my co-owner Micky Heaton-Ellis with the Royal Artillery Gold Cup, for Camden Belle winning at Sandown yesterday.

We worked all horses on the back straight of the all-weather gallop. The two-year-olds who have run have all come out of their races well, particularly Sabre Rattler. Of the older horses, Paris House is absolutely flying. It's a pity there isn't a decent race for him around at the moment. Another Episode, Sizzling Saga, Amber Mill and Food of Love, all worked exceptionally well today.

Alan has gone to Catterick to look after our five runners. We are very hopeful both our two-year-olds will run big races.

Jo and I are going to Worcester as I ride Tipperary Azul of Mark Tompkins' in the Celebrity Race sponsored by William Hill to aid the Injured Jockeys Fund.

Diane Bain, a student of West Oxfordshire College, watched all the horses work with me this morning. She wrote asking permission to come as she intends to train eventually herself.

Listening on the carphone to Two Times Twelve's race it sounds like he was a bit flat-footed in the stalls. According to the blower he was doing a lot of running about and managed to finish third. We listened to the next two races, Miss Parkes and Oyston's Life. Miss Parkes ran on to finish third. She must have run exceptionally well as she was drawn twenty, right out with the washing. Oyston's Life finished somewhere in the middle.

We got to Worcester in time to watch our two-year-old Lucky Parkes on SIS. She was smartly away, in the first two throughout. She went on two out to win by three lengths easily.

It was good to get with the old jump lads again and Tipperary Azul ran his little heart out to finish seventh. He gave me a smashing ride. It was great fun, I enjoyed it. Elain Mellor rode the winner, with husband Stan second and the inspector of courses, Ron Barry third. Stan probably daren't beat Elain as he might have been cooking his own tea tonight.

To swell the Injured Jockeys Fund further two course bookmakers, Turner and Kendrick and Len Bowman, donated their profits on the race for the cause. The Sporting Life donated the proceeds on all the papers sold today

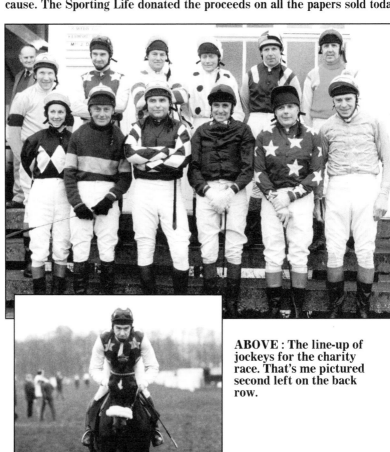

ABOVE : The line-up of jockeys for the charity race. That's me pictured second left on the back row.

LEFT : Here I am finishing a respectable seventh on Mark Tompkins' Tipperary Azul. He gave me a smashing ride. It was great fun.

on the course at Worcester which amounted to £200.

John and Alan rang us on the carphone to say that Two Times Twelve was a bit colty in the preliminaries. John confirmed that down at the stalls he was the same. When the stalls opened he just stood there and lost a lot of ground. In the stalls at home he flies out-he knows the score. John said if he had got his act together he would have won five lengths. I will be having a chat with his owners to see if we can call in the vet and do a little job on him.

THURSDAY March 26

THIS morning before John and I travelled to Wolverhampton we jumped tomorrow's Beverley runners out of the stalls. Alan and I did the decs and entries.

Our place this morning is like Piccadilly Circus. Conveyor Erections, the firm who are putting up the new walkers, have half a dozen or so men working on them, with two wagon loads of parts. John Hoyles, the local contractor, has a tractor and rotovator working on some land we are reseeding. John Curwen, another contractor, is piping a dyke for us. They have machinery and pipes all over the place. What a mess they are making too, especially with the land being so wet. We have just had a ruddy great load of woodfibre dropped for the all-weather, on our car park. Loudvale Haulage are continually carting loads of stone for the pipe job. Also John Whitlow has arrived with a wagon and trailer load of hay.

On the way to Wolverhampton Sir Rupert Mackeson, my publisher, rang regarding "It's Tougher At The Bottom" going into paperback for June. The judge had no problems sorting our horses out. Murray's Mazda was our nearest horse home, finishing fourth. His owner, Murray Grubb, flew with his pal Roy Peebles from Scotland to Birmingham and took a taxi to the course. I've said before it just shows it's not automatic getting winners. On the way back from the races it rained quite heavily.

FRIDAY March 27

THIS is the nicest morning we have had for a while, lovely and sunny but cold. We have just jumped tomorrow's runners out of the stalls and cantered the rest of the horses round the ring.

Yvonne Carr came to see us in connection with Racing Schools and ask Flash about the young staff obtaining certificates of competence. Not very long ago Flash went on a course to Doncaster to see what was required to achieve these. The top and bottom of it is there is no substitute for apprenticeships. Now the apprentices only have to sign a contract for a year. After we have put so much work into showing them the proper way to do things and just when they start to be some good, they move on.

On our way to Beverley John and I go through the form of the runners and Ruby rings through on my carphone with tomorrow's batch. Palacegate Episode looks good at Warwick. Price Rumpus at Beverley goes very well also. They both look to have an outstanding chance.

Requiring some information from the King's Troop, RHA for my weekly write-up, I ask Jo to ring them up. She rang me back without one of the questions being answered as the person she spoke to didn't know. She thought she had been talking to a Major Mainwaring. I asked her if she was sure it wasn't Captain Mainwaring from Dad's Army. Laurel Queen finished second in the first race, a seven furlong handicap. The others ran well enough without putting any money in their owners' Weatherby accounts.

SATURDAY March 28

WORKED the horses, and did the entries for Brighton and Kempton next week, before getting ready to set off for Warwick. Just as I was getting changed we had a phone call from the police. Our horsebox has had a puncture somewhere in Cheshire.

Travelling on the M6 we passed the box about fourteen miles before the Wolverhampton turn off. The time was 11.45am. At that rate Amanda should be at Warwick for 1.0pm. Palacegate Episode is in the first race at 2.15pm.

Jo and John were in my car so we drove straight to the stables and dropped Jo off so she could give our lads a hand when the box eventually arrived. I went to the weighing room and declared. The box arrived before 1.0pm and both horses had travelled well.

In the first Palacegate Episode jumped out fast. Turning into the straight she was clear and went on to win by seven lengths. We wouldn't have had a winner of the first race at Warwick today if Tom Blain, a horse transporter, hadn't kindly given Colin, one of our lads in the box, a hand to change the wheel. Apparently, they had already waited a couple of hours for the tyre service to arrive.

Our other Warwick runner Super Rocky finished unplaced. After the race, as he was pulling up, he stumbled and fell. Unfortunately, the fall broke

John's right collar bone. I must say that there are some lovely people who go racing. As Rocky was lying on the track winded, with the knacker wagon hovering around, Rocky suddenly jumped up. The crowds from every enclosure gave a resounding cheer. It was as if England had scored a goal in the World Cup.

The ambulance took John (left) to hospital so I followed in my car. As I'm struggling to lay up with the ambulance in Warwick town centre, Benny Powell rang on the carphone, as he bred our winner. Cars got in between me and the ambulance, as it went through a red light, and I lost sight of it. Eventually I found the hospital after asking the way.

At South Warwickshire hospital while John was being attended to, I found Jo in the waiting room. We had been planning to go to Hall Green greyhound stadium tonight to see Lisnakill Wish run in a qualifier for the Daily Mirror Greyhound Grand National. Dave Brown had booked a table, as himself and Trish his Mrs, the Viners, and the Newmans were all coming up. Jo and I were to stay the night at the Browns. The nurse came and told us Mr Carroll was being kept in until 5.20pm as he had had 100ml of pethidine. She said he was all right and was having a cup of tea. When John came out looking as white as a sheet and his back up, I didn't have the heart to ask him if he would like to come to Hall Green to watch Charlie run. So we came home.

Dave Brown rang me at home to ask what the problem was and why we weren't there. He promised to ring me back straight after the race. True to his word Dave rang. Our star dog had won by three lengths.

Sonia and Stan also rang to fill me in from their carphone on their way home.

SUNDAY March 29

SUPER Rocky is all right this morning. John had a comfortable night sleeping on his settee. His wife Tracy told me she was trying to keep their daughter Danielle and Midge the dog, off him while he slept. Poor old John has had better weeks. What with crashing his car and now breaking his collar bone. At least he rode a couple of winners.

Amron is our only runner tomorrow. He worked yesterday so he was just led out for ten minutes and had a pick of grass today. Everyone remembered the clocks went forward last night and were here for work on time. I hope the kids (apprentices) remember it was also Mother's Day.

Dave Fish, one of our owners, remembered. He brought his mother to see the horses. When they were walking round the yard it was raining really hard and Mrs Fish got soaked. He did her a great favour. I bet she would have rather had a box of chocolates or a bunch of flowers than being dragged out here on a day like this.

Reading yesterday's Sporting Life I see Diamond Mine, the ex-Peter Savill two-year-old we trained for him, beat Whittingham, another of our ex-trained horses in Italy. When I was in Newmarket the Italian agent Mr Massimi wanted a horse to beat Whittingham, who is that country's joint top-rated sprinter. I advised him to buy Diamond Mine.

Paul Hoffman, who has Westmead Nick with us, a two-year-old and also owns greyhounds, rang up to let me know a bitch of his had pups last night and he is giving me one of her dog pups. Jo will be pleased.

Having walked around the gallops with my dogs I realise just how wet it is. I know down the South they have been crying out for rain-well they are very welcome to some of ours.

MONDAY March 30

IT'S a nice sunny morning but I'm afraid it has rained all through the night to keep the water level up. The amount of rain we have had this year in Lancashire we should never hear of a water shortage again.

Steve Porritt, one of the lads hasn't turned in today. Apparently, the wheel fell off his car returning from home on his weekend off. First lot I led the string round the roads on Palacegate King. We cantered the Hamilton Wednesday runners.

Amron is our only runner today at Newcastle. He is 9lb worse off with Never So Sure, who was third to him at Doncaster, beaten four-and-a-half lengths. Amron (Ronnie), however, is in such good form I still think he will beat him again, even though the papers have Lynda Ramsden's horse favourite. With John breaking his collar bone, Nicky Carlisle steps in for the ride.

At Newcastle it was a bright day but very cold. Walking round the paddock Ronnie is still showing his winter coat and is by far the smallest horse competing.

When they jump off Nicky sits last of the five runners until halfway then he makes a move and takes up the running two out and strides clear to score by six lengths.

RONNIE (Amron) gets a pat from all of us after his convincing win at Newcastle.

Going over Stainmoor on the way home a police car came winging by us with all its gadgets going. A couple of miles further on we came to a complete standstill on both sides of the road. After being stopped for fifty minutes we moved on and saw two lorries had been involved in an accident. One had run into the back of the other. An ambulance passed us and it looked as if the driver who had done the ramming had to be taken to hospital after being cut out of his cab. There was also a fire engine at the scene.

We called in at Ravenstonedale to see Jean and Colin Bradford-Nutter, owners of ours who live there.

When we got back home and put Oracle on the TV Ronnie had a page to himself. Part of the write-up said he shot clear to lead two out and Berry jokingly said: "I hope the handicapper is on holiday and didn't see that."

TUESDAY March 31

BIG headlines in the Greyhound Life this morning, "High Noon as Slippy and Lisnakill Wish Square Up." There was also a photo of Charlie in the Racing Post. Kildare Slippy is the local wonder dog, breaking Hall Green's track record last Saturday. He is clocking times over the hurdles comparable to Flat races. I will definitely have to get from Hamilton to see the race. I was hoping to go to the Amateur boxing at The Savoy Hotel in Blackpool with John Carroll as our yard sponsors a bout. Still it's not possible to be everywhere.

There is also a nice picture of Amron on the back page of The Sporting Life. Birthday greetings in The Post, I see George Slack is 69. Happy Birthday George. He was our stable jockey at Charlie Hall's when I was an apprentice some 38 years ago.

At the moment, it is impossible to go anywhere other than the all-weather with the horses, it's so wet. We are having a lovely mild day now but it has rained virtually all night again. The horses are going well. That Paris House, if I don't get him in a race shortly, he'll explode. The Field Marshal Stakes, a Listed race at Haydock is in a couple of weeks. That would be just a nice pre-outing for the Group 2 Temple Stakes, which is run at Sandown on May 25.

In the afternoon Jo actually got me out shopping with her at the Asda superstore. When she finished clearing a fair proportion of the place we went to the cafeteria for a coffee. I was sat at a table guarding our goods while Jo went for the coffee. A very small frail-looking lady with two walking sticks came by. Two six or seven-year-old kids came running towards her from behind. One of them wanted her walking stick and tried to grab it off her. Without further ado she picked the stick up and gave him such a crack with it on his backside. Then just walked off. The Cheltenham Stewards would have given her a three day suspension for that. I was laughing that much I bet people thought I wasn't a full shilling.

[163]

WEDNESDAY April 1

BE careful you don't get caught today. It's April Fool's Day. There is a real April Fool's Day joke by Ray Gilpin in the Racing Post-Jockey Club approves idea to cut jockeys down to size. The Jockey Club last night gave the go-ahead to set up a sperm bank in Newmarket and will help finance the scheme expected to cost £250,000 a year. A Jockey Club spokeswoman said there are only a few jockeys who can do 7st 7lb. They will apply for women of small stature to produce jockeys of the future. Nicky Carlisle welcomes the move.

Worked the horses before setting off to Hamilton at 10.15 with Paul Roberts, one of our apprentices who rides Bobby on the Bank for Stan Payne in the apprentice race.

Just on the M6 near Carlisle it's raining very heavily. The river has gone right over its bank and there is water lying in most of the fields. There was an announcement on the radio that there is going to be a noon inspection. I took a message on the carphone, my brother-in-law died this morning.

When we arrived at Hamilton the going was very heavy. The stewards announced they would race but without stalls.

In the first race Sabre Rattler, our two-year-old, looked a bomb. John Leech, the starter was winding the two-year-olds up, chewing them about, turning and messing. He told the jockeys to turn round again. Richard Quinn on ours got left a few lengths. On ground like today one can't afford to be left an inch. Rattler got to the front but did too much in doing so and faded over the last couple of strides to finish second, beaten half a length.

Music Dancer in the next also finished second, beaten a length and a half. Our last chance of the day was Tynron Doon, in the seller, who duly obliged by one-and-a-half lengths.

With the hold-ups on the roads and the rain I had no chance of getting to see Lisnakill Wish take on Kildare Slippy at Hall Green. I even gave my boxing ticket to Kevin, one of our Head Lads thinking I was going to Birmingham. I rang Jo up on the carphone to say I couldn't make it.

When I got home and had my tea, I answered and made some phone calls. Trish Brown rang from Hall Green. Yes, Charlie had beaten Kildare Slippy by two-and-a-half lengths. What a dog. That was a great performance because Kildare Slippy has some reputation.

THURSDAY April 2

WE were going to run a two-year-old at Brighton today, Press the Bell but he had a temperature yesterday.

It's just roadwork with the horses today.

At 9.30am Jon Freeman of The Sporting Life came to interview me for his paper's profile. We talked about the horses, their ability and my views. It was quite interesting as Jon is a knowledgeable racing man. He then went on to Aintree.

I rode Fylde Flyer round the roads third lot and he seemed in fine form. He is a very lively horse and loves a buck and a kick.

Graham Orange, one of racing's PROs, rang me to say I am to be presented with a prize at Ripon next Wednesday for being last season's leading trainer there. Please don't let anything stop me that day getting to Hall Green to watch my dog run. That is Grand National night. I have been so unlucky not to have seen him on his last two outings.

In the afternoon, I watched racing from Liverpool on telly. The first race, which unfortunately wasn't on TV, was won by David Nicholson's Carobee. The last time Carobee won at Chepstow on telly I was impressed with him. So impressed with him that I mentioned to David at Cheltenham what a lovely horse he was. I also wrote about him and Richard Dunwoody in the Weekender. For me, if all goes well with him, he could be a Champion hurdler maybe next year.

Read in today's Sporting Life that Mr Jim Joel had bequeathed Keep Talking, his National Hunt Chase winner to Her Majesty the Queen Mother. That was really nice. Let's hope he goes on to win the Grand National for her.

At evening stables Jo asked me to go down to her mother's bungalow as she has had trouble with the central heating. When I opened the door her dog Sam bolted to get out it was that warm. The last time I felt heat like that I was in John Carroll's sauna.

Justin, one of our lads, is going to pick a new lad up from Preston Station at 1.15am. I gave him a few sheets for his trouble.

FRIDAY April 3

AT 7.30am Jo set off in her car to go to Kempton to see our runner there Tuscan Dawn. She is staying overnight with Fred and Gwen Viner as we run Pilgrim Bay at Lingfield tomorrow. Pat Eddery rides the pair of them.

All the horses did a nice long canter round the ring. The new lad who arrived early this morning is a fair size. Too big for us I'm afraid. I'm sure he said he was just over 9st when he applied for the job. He must have put just one foot on the scales.

Just as we set off cantering round the ring second lot, one of the lads got one of the two-year-olds kicked. It's all very well buttering these lads up and pouring out sympathy to them. Sometimes the occasional one can be bloody dozey. I can handle piling the cars up and doing daft things like lads do, but getting the horses hurt through negligence or stupidity makes me lose my rag. It isn't easy ringing owners up and telling them their horse has got kicked because the lad fell asleep. Reading between the lines you can guess I wasn't chuffed with this berk.

John Nixon's men have brought a lot of trees to plant for us. I am just going to show them exactly where I would like them planted around the new walkers. At the moment the walkers look as if they have been dropped out of space or they're some sort of giant meccano set.

Listening on Rapid Raceline to the 1.40pm at Kempton Park, our two-year-old Tuscan Dawn has won in a photo at 8-1. He has done well to win from the number three draw in soft ground in a field of nineteen runners. He had plenty on his plate as high numbers have a definite advantage. Tuscan Dawn is owned by London banker Antonia Taverner and was bred by Frazer Hines of Emmerdale Farm.

Watching Liverpool on the telly I was reminded of the article I wrote in The Sporting Life Weekender about Doncaster fences being too soft, causing the horses to walk right through them. I said at the time it teaches the horse bad habits. Ossie Dale, who is responsible for making the Aintree fences, has gone over the top in tightening up the Mildmay fences too much. Good horses are falling for only minor mistakes. In fact, some of the boys were saying the fences are like stone walls. Come on Ossie, your age and experience should tell you to let them out a bit. No one wants to see the jockeys hurt or the horses on the deck. It was nice to see Red Rum on the box at Don McCain's new yard in Cheshire.

Talking to Pat Eddery on the phone, he said he liked Tuscan Dawn and reckoned he should go on to win more races.

SATURDAY April 4

WHEN we have finished working the horses I am going to the National. Cheltenham Gold Cup Day and the Grand National are my two days out every year. Tonight I am determined to make it to Hall Green to see Sonia's and my flying machine, Lisnakill Wish, run in the semi-final. Although he has the coffin box, number four draw, hopefully he has enough track craft to overcome it.

Alan and I did the entries first thing. That alone is a time-consuming job but it is one of the most important roles of a trainer. We can have the horses jumping out of their skins, but if we enter them in the wrong races it's futile. Keep yourself in the best company and the horses in the worst. That's the way to be patting a few horses on the neck in the winning enclosure.

The two-year-olds worked brilliantly. I couldn't be more pleased with them. Quite a number that haven't run yet are beating the ones that have already won. That's what I like to see. Among the three-year-olds, Fylde Flyer is going well, as is Paris House.

Travelling on the M6 on the way to the National the roads are quite busy. It's a lovely sunny day and the going should be perfect for the big race. After the grief we've been encountering over the Mildmay course these past couple of days, lets hope it doesn't continue today over the National course. Each year it's every jockey's aim to get a ride in the National. Lots of stories go around the weighing room. Mick Batchelor, the ex-jockey, was an artiste at telling tales and winding up the lads. He used to relate a tale about a trainer who had in his care a real hairy beggar with form figures like FFUPUF. The trainer rang up a struggling jump jockey and asked if he would like to ride so and so for him at Hereford on Saturday in the Novice Chase. Word gets around fast about these bone breakers. All the old flannel would be told, like, 'we schooled him over a couple of bales of straw the other day and he was brilliant'. 'This fellow would jump Liverpool backwards'-all the usual nonsense. The jump jockey apologised to the trainer and said he couldn't ride him on Saturday as he was there at Liverpool himself. When the trainer said but you don't ride in the National. The jockey replied, "No, I don't, but I would like to see it."

The course looked in fantastic nick. The minute one gets to Aintree the adrenalin gets going. In the paddock the National horses looked tremendous and a good race it turned out to be. It was particularly nice to see lots of finishers. A good job the race wasn't run on the Mildmay course.

Talking to Geoff Hubbard, who trained Gee-A to win yesterday's Foxhunters Chase, he told me Duffle Coat, a horse he bought from us years ago, to run in the National, is still alive and well, at the age of twenty-three. Red Rum looked fine leading the National runners for today's parade and he's twenty-seven.

Pilgrim Bay, our only runner today at Lingfield, finished fourth.

To get a flyer and not get into traffic problems I left Aintree before the last race-destination Hall Green, Birmingham where I am going to meet Jo on her way back from Lingfield.

When I got to Hall Green it was as busy as Aintree. I have never seen so many people at the dogs. It was packed. Charlie with the poor draw jumped out fast. He was third jumping the first, took up the running on the second bend and galloped on relentlessly to win very easy by seven lengths. His odds were 4-6. He has been drawn in trap two in the final on Wednesday. Kildare Slippy won his heat in the next race and is drawn in the coffin box on Wednesday.

SONIA NEWMAN and me with our wonder dog Lisnakill Wish, after his win in the Daily Mirror Grand National semi-final.

SUNDAY April 5

NOT that I am much of a sailor but I see Oxford won the boat race yesterday.

It's a beautiful sunny morning. That means we will have plenty of owners around today. Not that I mind. In fact, I enjoy it because it's a day when we have time to talk to them about their horses.

At Ripon on Wednesday in the two-year-old stakes race we have two of the six declared. Instead of working these two entries on Saturday we worked them this morning. Normally I would have run the maiden in the race but Palacegate Episode was so impressive in her work I don't think I dare take the chance on Local Heroine's inexperience. George Roper and Bright Gem are both winners.

As expected, we had stacks of people come. Dave Brown brought a contingency up from the Midlands on their way to Kelso to see our hurdler Kinlet Vision, trained by Ken Oliver, perform there tomorrow.

Roy Peebles and his wife Norma came. We are going out with them this evening to the Ryecroft Hall for a meal.

Dave Parker, the amateur rider, spends his summers with us at Cockerham every year. Then in winter he goes back to his father Colin, who only trains jumpers.

Francis O'Hare, a lad who asked me for a job last night at Hall Green, rang to confirm he is still coming next week.

Roy had invited John and Lynne Campion to the Ryecroft as well. They live in our village so John said he would pick us up at 7.30pm.

Jim Mitchell, our neighbouring farmer, has been spreading slurry (cow manure) on our grass gallop which does it good. 7.30pm-I came into the house for a bath. John Campion was already waiting to take us out. I was stinking like a pole cat.

We had the nicest meal you could imagine. It was great. Afterwards Martin, the bossman, got his guitar out and we had a real good sing song-me on the spoons.

On the way back to our house at 1.30am John had some good Irish songs on his tapes in the car. We had a sing song to them. It was a great night. We have worked hard all day, and played hard all night.

MONDAY April 6

AFTER a lovely day yesterday I am afraid it has spoilt itself today. It rained again when we rode out.

On the front page of the Greyhound Life is a very good photo of Charlie jumping the last hurdle at Hall Green well clear of the second Deerpark Jim.

We have quite a busy week ahead with runners all over the place. Alan and I sorted them out with jockeys and all the arrangements. It's a shame John is missing out with his broken collar bone as he's put a lot into these horses through the winter. Hopefully, he will soon be back.

At the moment, with 13 winners, we are joint top trainer with Bill O'Gorman. This coming week last year we had trained nine winners but we went the whole week without having a winner. So we are bang on target to beat last year's total.

Steve Simpson, sports reporter for the Blackpool Gazette, just rang to say somebody had burned down Bechers Brook last night. You wonder what things are coming to. They don't know if it was animal rights nutters or hooligans.

On our way to Wolverhampton where the leading trainer is yours truly, we spot a wagon that has hit the barrier on the side of the motorway. It's lucky to be the only vehicle involved. No one seems to be hurt but there are plenty of police cars.

Just as I pulled up in the car park at the course George Roper, the comedian, rang to fix a date for himself and Norman Collier to do a live act at our after season party in November.

Our only runner today is the two-year-old Trentesimo, who has the services of Pat Eddery.

The little horse ran a good race and started 2-1 favourite, like most of ours do this time of year. He looked like obliging but on this paddy-field like ground he led until approaching the final furlong and then just plodded on to finish fifth, beaten about three lengths. Pat said he's a very nice horse and would appreciate better ground. He'll definitely win races.

We stayed on to watch Kinlet Vision at Kelso on SIS finish fifth of 17 runners. As usual the filly doesn't know how to run a bad race.

I would have liked to have gone to Kelso. Not only to see Kinlet Vision but to have seen Jonjo ride Desert Orchid. I bet these two put a few hundred on the gate.

Reading the evening paper I bought at Wolverhampton racecourse I see Graeme Souness the Liverpool football manager has to undergo a heart bypass operation. He's only 38. It will be a few months before he's back training at Anfield with that complaint. I think I would be looking round for a different job.

Five of our ex-horses ran today. They were all sold at the end of the Flat '91 but unfortunately they all failed to recoup any of their purchase price.

On our way home, driving past the village football pitch, I can see all our lads and lasses out in full force playing soccer. Last week Alan sprained his ankle. They are always getting hurt.

Most of them will probably have done their brains on Trentesimo at the bookies in the afternoon and after stables are now kicking hell out of the ball.

TUESDAY April 7

7.0am Margaret Holdcroft rang to give me a real bollocking for not entering Amber Mill in the five furlong sprint at Newbury on Friday. The way she went on I told her she should stand for Parliament. She never let up. Poor Terry, her husband.

Arazi runs at Saint-Cloud today. What a horse he is. I haven't seen him in the flesh but I will make the effort this year to put that right.

First lot were cantered round the ring. Afterwards, we gave them a pick of lush grass from the middle of the ring. The horses loved it.

Tomorrow's runners were just given a run for a couple of furlongs out of the stalls. Palacegate Episode absolutely flew. The race she is in tomorrow at Ripon looks like cutting up as there are only six entries. Two of them are ours. I am going to run both now as Palacegate Episode should win and Local Heroine should get paid to do a bit of work. Being a stakes race the first four are on wages.

It's sports day at Pontefract, where we have two runners. Cashtal Queen is in the six furlong seller and Tom Piper is in the two-year-old race. Both will be ridden by that good apprentice L Piggott.

Post-time for the first race is 2.45pm. The idea of the late start is to allow the local miners, knocking off the 2.0pm shift, to have time to wash and change at the colliery before going racing.

Nowadays the miners nearly all go home washed and changed. When I was a young lad in Leeds they came home in clogs as black as the ace of spades.

No luck with two runners, even with Lester Piggott's assistance. But the good news is Isotonic won the two-year-old race. This filly was second to our filly Lucky Parkes at Catterick a couple of weeks ago.

On my return from Pontefract there was a message on the pad to ring our vet up about our old dog Bruni. Alan, the blacksmith, had taken him in this afternoon as he wasn't very well. He's very old and he's failing. What's the best for him? Alistair, the vet, said we should put him down. Sad day, but we'll have to do it.

Looking at Teletext I see the wonder horse Arazi trotted up in France. It's good to see the microsurgery to remove chips on his knees was a success. What a worry to his connections that must have been.

WEDNESDAY April 8

GREAT big headlines on the front page of the Greyhound Life again with a lovely coloured photograph of Sonia, Charlie and myself. "Lisnakill for Star Role". He is 11/10 favourite to beat Kildare Slippy in tonight's Daily Mirror/

Sporting Life Grand National for £5,000 at Hall Green.

The Racing Post in their greyhound section have the headlines, "Lisnakill Set To Put Skids Under Slippy," and there's a photo of himself and Jackie Rees, his kennel maid.

Rang John Carroll this morning, he reckons his collar bone is healing but it could be another week before he's fully fit.

Galloped fifty-seven two-year-olds and twenty-seven older horses before setting off for Ripon at just turned 11.0am. We have runners in the first three races.

It's a beautiful warm sunny day travelling to Ripon. If it's like this at home we will be working the horses on grass this Saturday.

When I arrived at Ripon I walked the course as they had had rain overnight. On my return to the paddock a punter said: "That's your job these greyhounds. You're good with them." He must have been backing some of our losers.

The first race Two Times Twelve finished fourth. Immediately after the first race there was a presentation to myself as leading trainer and Dean McKeown as leading rider at Ripon last season. This was organised by Graham Orange, Northern Racing's PR man for the sponsors Black Bottle Scotch Whisky.

Bold Mood was out the back. It was too much for him, carrying 9st 7lb, as a maiden three-year-old. He only beat home one of the twenty runners to compete.

Palacegate Episode absolutely cantered up by twelve lengths beating our debutante filly Local Heroine. Pat Eddery was most impressed with her and said she is as fast as her brother, Another Episode. Jo and I intended driving off to Hall Green straight after the race as we are dinner guests of the sponsors. Dinner is booked for 7.0pm. However, with Palacegate Episode being a syndicate horse with lots of members in attendance Dave Spence, the bossman, invited us to share some champagne with him and the members before setting off.

At Hall Green the stadium was packed to see these two great dogs clash. Jo and I met Sonia and Stan Newman and Mike and Janetta Gallemore in the Executive Bar for a drink before being ushered to our table for a lovely meal while watching the racing. We were introduced to Kildare Slippy's owner, Mr Deeley and trainer Paddy Hancox before the race. Kildare Slippy flew out of the box and jumped brilliantly. Charlie got left a bit at the start but he ran a good race to finish third to Slippy who did a better time than Flat racers do, completing the 474 metres in less than 29 seconds, breaking yet another record. Kildare Slippy is trained locally and the punters have taken him to their hearts and rightly so. It's looking like he is the best hurdler there has ever been. Paddy Hancox and Mr Deeley sent two bottles of champagne round to our table after the race. That was a really nice gesture. Jo and I shared the driving home. When we got in it was gone 2.0am. Well worth it. We have had a lovely day and night.

THURSDAY April 9

ELECTION DAY. Peter Smiles, head of the horseracing police force, has resigned.

It's a lovely day to be going to Hamilton Park, where we have four runners. In today's Weekender-the Straight from the Stable features our yard, giving a rundown on the season's horses, on both centre pages, with a couple of photos of Paris House and Food of Love.

Road work today, except for half a dozen we put through stalls. I rode Palacegate Racing a long steady canter as he gets stuffy if he has any days off.

John Nixon's two men are making a great job of planting the trees. Not only have they put some three deep as a windbreak around the new walkers, they have also made a couple of nice spinneys on our top moss. Hopefully it should attract pheasants and other birds. They have planted a few around the bungalows, wherever there is a bare corner. Beautiful copper beech trees have been planted on the border dividing our land from our neighbouring farmer. When the planting is finished they will have put in something like one thousand trees.

For a future date I have my eye on a small area on our land where I would like to make a pond with a nice island in the middle. I would stock it with fish and buy different kinds of ducks and tempt some wildlife to it.

David Spence, of Palacegate Racing, rang to come with us to Hamilton as he has to pass this way. In the car were Jo and Paul Roberts one of our apprentices who was riding High Principles. We had a good run up to Hamilton. Arriving at the racecourse I saw Tim Riley, the Clerk of the Course, who assured me they were using stalls today and the ground was only soft.

Classic Storm, our two-year-old filly, finished second. In the next race Palacegate King finished third, and in the mile race Laurel Queen came fourth. None of them pulled any trees up but they all ran well.

Arriving back at Cockerham, Jo and I called in the village school to vote. I met up with Alan, David Spence and John Carroll in the Patten Arms for a pint of Murphys and something to eat. John's collar bone is healing nicely and he is going to have a ride out on Monday to make sure it's all right. Then he will probably be back in business on Tuesday at Newmarket for Fylde Flyer.

FRIDAY April 10

CONSERVATIVES are still in power as they won last night's election with a nineteen majority.

On our list of injuries we have a Music Boy colt who isn't named yet. He had been rolling in his box and hurt a foot banging it on the side wall. He's at the vets having an X-ray. This is the worse part of training, telling owners what's happened when a horse gets hurt. Bob Heathcote owns the colt. After ringing Bob to tell him, he wasn't too upset about it. The Conservatives getting back into power must have helped. Bob understands how accidents happen. Look at hospitals all over the country full of people, most of them haven't volunteered to go in. At least, in the orthopaedic section they have had accidents.

I haven't seen any workers down by the horse walkers today. Maybe Mike Burrows has taken the huff as the panelling on the outside has been done in plywood instead of good wood. It's pointless the walkers costing an arm and a leg and spoiling it all by putting crap material in for the sake of saving just a few shillings.

The grass has started to shoot up so fast you can nearly hear it grow. It's more like spring today. Suddenly there is life in the ground.

Everywhere should be drying up shortly and we will be galloping on grass tomorrow.

Put the two-year-olds through the stalls on the open grass gallop watched by John Carroll. He had the job of pulling the handle to let them off, otherwise he would have been wanting to ride the horses. It's hard for him to watch others do his job.

Peter from Geoff Lewis's Epsom yard rang for me to buy their horse in if it's lucky enough to win the seller at Thirsk.

Jo has gone to see to our Newbury runners, Sabre Rattler and Tino Tere. John is trying out his collar bone driving me to Thirsk while I catch up on some paperwork. I walked the course before racing, the going was perfect.

SABRE RATTLER (noseband) and Pat Eddery
beat a competitive field at Newbury.

[173]

We both watched Sabre Rattler win on SIS the £5,000 maiden for us at Newbury, ridden by Pat Eddery.

Preston Guild, our two-year-old making his maiden appearance, finished a creditable third of ten in the first race.

Between Two Fires finished third, beaten a neck and a head, in the second race at Thirsk. Threepence, owned by Robert Sangster, was second for us in the three year old sprint, giving the James Fanshawe-trained filly 12lb. Tino Tere finished fifth of the eleven starters, our only other runner of the day at Newbury.

If John Leech the Hamilton starter saw Oracle tonight he won't be very pleased. Sabre Rattler has a whole page. It says the youngster was most unlucky at Hamilton as the start was by flag and Sabre Rattler was facing the wrong way. I won't go as far as saying he was facing the wrong way but he was five lengths adrift when the starter let the horses go, and on ground as bad as it was that day, the little horse had faced an impossible task.

SATURDAY April 11

AFTER going to bed at 11.45pm it's now 3.0am. I have just got up and made a cup of tea. Often I get up early like this to catch up with all the things I don't have time to do during the normal course of the day. My Jack Russell Olly is flat out next to the Aga cooker in the kitchen, fast asleep. On my mind at the moment is the Music Boy colt of Bob Heathcote's who rolled in his box. Having rung the vet on my return from Thirsk races last night, he told me he has some ligament damage to his hock. Also in the injury book we have Darling Miss Daisy, a three year old filly. She is lame with an injured pelvis. Last season she was trained by Gavin Pitchard-Gordon. Today, being work day for the horses, I want to see if the list needs any adjustments. For the first time in ages we are working on grass.

Racing is now getting into full swing and there are lots of races coming up here and abroad. Now is the right time to absorb them. To get the feel of them so to speak. It's a very important part of the job to use the horses' mileage up properly. They only have a certain amount on the clock and it doesn't register how much. It's impossible to concentrate for four or five hours on this part of the job before I go racing. With the phone ringing, working the horses, looking round them, stall work, and literally hundreds of other jobs, there just isn't the time in the mornings to plan ahead in any sort of peaceful conditions. No matter how many secretaries in the office try to pacify the callers, it's me they want to talk to. I can't remember anyone getting me out of bed to answer the phone but it happens all the time in the yard. I have to have some space to work out where we are going to get the best out of the horses. I am very fortunate I don't waste too much time in bed. All the planning I do I leave on messages on a clip. The important mail is put on my table to sort out. Flash and Kevin, the head lads, fill in the injury book every day with the slightest problem with the horses for me to see. If I have been night racing somewhere like Goodwood and get in about two in the morning I would still sort out all the mail, look at the injury book and tick off every entry before signing the book. Any real problem I go there and then to see the horse. If it's minor I wait until morning stables.

The clip is picked up by Ruby. Any messages or jobs I want sorting out which cannot be done straight away, Ruby writes on her daily sheet to keep me in the picture as when I get back from racing Ruby and Helen, our secretaries, have gone home. We keep in constant touch on the carphone.

It's now 6.25am. I have completed my weekly slot for the Weekender-one story on the wonder horse Arazi, the other on jockeys' betting. I am going out in the yard now. It's a lovely morning and the birds sound in good voice. Fred Viner and Stan Newman came up from Ascot to see their Sober Lad win the first race at Thirsk. Arctic Appeal was second in the next race. These were our only two runners. I went on my own today as Jo went shopping.

On my way back from the races, there were about forty Charolais bullocks turned out in a field near Skipton. They didn't half look well.

SUNDAY April 12

IT'S nearly 6.0am. We've had a drop of overnight rain but it's a nice morning now and the birds are in full song again. You lot who stop in bed don't know what you are missing. It's so peaceful this time of day. People die in bed. If I croaked tomorrow at least I will have had my time even at 54. Some people who die at 80 might have spent a third of their life in bed. They haven't seen it being asleep. Jo does my sleeping. She likes her bed.

Came back from walking the gallops with my dogs. It was great. My gallop men did a good job after ninety-three horses had galloped up the five furlong grass yesterday. All the staff went out and trod the footings in after they finished riding work. The two gallop men then rolled it. There's a lot of pretty Shell ducks around the place at the moment. I spotted a dozen of them sitting out on the top moss this morning. They look a real treat. Olly Oyston and Tiny Tim were pleased to see me when I was on my rounds.

The yard looks really good this time of year. It's all been painted up through the winter. Old Bob, our gardener, has certainly had the brakes off this week. All the lawns are immaculate and the stone troughs around the yards have got nice bedding plants in.

If the weather keeps fair for the next few days and we manage to fence off the new trees I will turn out our cattle. They are getting a bit restless in the fold yard. They sense this time of year they should be out in the fields and we have plenty of grass for them.

Outside our kitchen window overlooking the main yard I have my rabbit hutch. All the dogs are on top of it looking through the windows yapping to come in. I would let them in but they are filthy. When they go on walkabout with me they are in dykes roaming around all over. These Jack Russells are no choir boys. They are little hooligans who get everywhere and into everything. Not a good influence on the rest of the pack.

Lots of people rang and I made countless phone calls as is the usual routine on a Sunday. In the afternoon I watched Manchester United and Notts Forest on the box. Good match it was, too.

Trainer Francis Lee was taking the juice out of me last Wednesday at Ripon because I was wearing a pair of sunglasses. He went on to say he couldn't wear glasses as he broke the bridge of his nose playing football. The way he used to dive in that penalty area trying to kid the referee into giving him a penalty, it's a wonder the opposition didn't break more than his nose.

MONDAY April 13

IT'S BEEN as wild and wet as anything I've known through the night. We have Cranfield Comet, who should run well, and Red Ronnie running at Nottingham. We are also dropping off a filly who's a bit of a nutcase. The owner is picking her up from the course. There are no mental homes for horses, if there were this filly would certainly be an inmate. On the gallops she goes round and round in circles then plants herself. She can run backwards faster than she can forwards. We worked her on Saturday. I could cry faster than she galloped. Yesterday I broke the news to the owner. He was good about it. What would I do with her he asked. Definitely have her put down I said-she's a mental case. It wouldn't be fair to sell in the sales. Some young girl may buy her cheap and end up in hospital. If you breed with her you run the risk of breeding another like her. What else can you do?

We have three runners up at Edinburgh, where our yard is in the lead with the highest number of winners. Murray's Mazda, Two Moves In Front and Between Two Fires, whose owner lives locally and is picking me up at 10.0am to give me a rare lift to the races. John Carroll rode out this morning for the first time since breaking his collar bone last month. He will hopefully get clearance from the Jockey Club Doctor Rodney O'Donnell to ride Fylde Flyer at Newmarket tomorrow.

Just as I was leaving the house for Edinburgh, John rang to say he had spoken to the Jockey Club who had told him there is no point him going to Newmarket as he will need another week. John was distressed to say the least.

Murray's Mazda ran a poor race to finish fourth of the ten starters. Two Moves In Front, a Newmarket-bought colt by Ballad Rock, won by three quarters of a length at 5-1, beating three two-year-olds with a bit of form. Between Two Fires ran a good race, finishing fifth of the sixteen runners.

Watching the Nottingham horses on SIS they were both unplaced. On my return from Edinburgh I answered the phone and made a few calls myself, before meeting up with Chris and Ray Robinson at the Patten Arms to discuss their two two-year-olds, Jessie Ann and Sharisa. The latter is not in the same league as her half-brother Bit-a-Magic who won four races for us as a two-year-old. In fact, both are not much good. At the end of it we decided to run them in sellers or claimers. They may improve enough to win one of these. Hope so, as the Robinsons are a real nice couple.

TUESDAY April 14

AMANDA, one of our travelling head girls, rang up to tell us the horses that she took overnight to Newmarket are in good condition.

It rained all night here and there is lots of water covering the land everywhere.

The horses cantered round the ring in pairs today, except for the few who are running soon. They cantered round the back side of the all-weather. John rode Tynron Doon, I rode Dokkha Oyston.

At 8.15am I had an interview with Timeform that lasted until 10.15am. Made phone calls to Charles St George, David Abell and Bob Heathcote before picking up John Carroll and setting off with Jo for Newmarket just before 11.0am.

Our runner Fylde Flyer is in the 3.40pm. By the look of the race he has

**FYLDE FLYER (right) with Lester Piggott
seen winning at Newmarket from Case Law.**

plenty on his plate. Very seldom are Listed races pushovers at Headquarters.

At the interchange on the M61 and M62 we ran into a hold-up. Two big lorries had been fighting. One ended up on top of the crash barrier in the central reservation. Fortunately, there was no blood flowing.

At Newmarket it was bitter cold but they had a large crowd. John and I dug the doctor out and he passed John fit for Saturday, so he can ride Paris House in the Field Marshal Stakes at Haydock Park. That's good news.

With John on the sick list it enabled Lester to take the ride on our horse Fylde Flyer in the £14,000 Abernant Stakes, a six furlong Listed race. Snaadee, ridden by Pat Eddery, wouldn't go down to the start. He literally walked down very mulishly for five of the six furlongs and held the start up for a quarter of an hour. In the race our fellow jumped out fast and was always in the first three. He took up the running two out and got headed ten strides from the jam stick. Flyer and Lester fought back like a pair possessed to get back up on the last stride to take this prestigious race by a short-head. When the announcement was made that we'd won, there was a great roar from Flyer's many owners who were in attendance to see him perform.

After racing Jo and I went to Gerry and Bridget Blums with our gear. I had a shower and got changed to go to Reg Griffin's flat for dinner. Pat and Caroline Eddery and Willie and Elaine Carson were also guests. We had a super meal, a good chat and a great time.

WEDNESDAY April 15

JOHN CARROLL's birthday today. He is in good company as it is also Mrs Brotherton's 90th. Mrs B put me up a few times years ago when her horses were trained by Bobby Renton. I even managed to get in the winning enclosure for her.

In this morning's Sporting Life there is a good photo of Fylde Flyer winning at Newmarket and a nice write-up.

Went to see the horses who are in the two-year-old sales tonight after racing have a breeze on the racecourse.

Jo and I called in to see Bill O'Gorman for a coffee. Then we went on to Gibsons saddlers for a new pair of riding boots as mine are knackered.

We only had one runner who was unplaced. It was bitterly cold at the races and it was even colder when Jo and I ventured to the sales. When I arrived there I was told the sad news that Nijinsky had died at the age of 25.

Horses are coming out of our ears. Really we are full. It's very difficult, however, for me not to bid at a two-year-old I like. Today was no exception. Number four came in, a smallish colt by Vin St Benet out of a Porto Bello mare. He moved good and on inspection looked clean and sound. My mate Bob Champion was with me at the time the colt came into the ring. In view of the fact that there is no room at the Berry inn, I got Bob to do my bidding as I have refused a couple of horses recently. We are already committed to picking up a two-year-old from Newmarket for Mr Nasib.

Over at Pontefract races Our Mica was third in the two-year-old race. Incidentally, we have won that same race for the past five years with: Restless Don, Almost Blue, Sharp Anne, It's All Academic and Paris House. Our other runner, Tynron Doon, won the seller and was sold at the auction for £6,000. I only got to know this when I arrived back at Gerry's and I rang Alan up. At least the new purchase doesn't have to sleep in my room now.

Gerry, Bridget, Jo, Pat Knight, and I all went to the New Cabaret Club to a dinner and dance in aid of Sharron Murgatroyd, the lady jockey who had a bad accident at Bangor-on-Dee races a few months ago. There was a fantastic crowd there. Most of the racing people who were staying over for the races and sales attended. Over seventeen thousand pounds was realised on the auction alone. Brilliantly done by David Minton. Dave Thom and myself bought the lease on a greyhound for a year. We are going to call him Murgatroyd. I also bought a big ash tray with Nicholas's racing shoe mounted on it. Nicholas was the horse that gave Lester his first winning ride when the great man made his comeback out of retirement.

THURSDAY April 16

AFTER entering the horses for Warwick on the phone with Alan, I told him to offer David Wintle, the trainer, a monkey profit on Tynron Doon. For what he fetched at the auction yesterday I would keep him myself.

Reading The Sporting Life we could have a good day at Ripon with our two runners, Mamma's Too and Amron. Both are paper favourites. It's also a lucky course for us. Last season we trained the highest number of winners at the course.

Reading in the Life this coming season the leading trainer wins a two week holiday in Barbados courtesy of the Asta Hotel where we stayed in January. That's a good prize to win-I wouldn't mind it being me.

Heather Bank and Kingston Brown are our two here at Newmarket. Both have a squeak but don't look as good as our Ripon pair.

To make our nap of runners Lisnakill Wish runs in the 8.33pm at Hove. He looks the best bet at 4-9 in the paper. Jo and Bridget went shopping. I met Pat at the Moat House to catch up with work on this book. We all met up at the races. We watched our Ripon runners on SIS where Mamma's Too finished second and Amron nowhere. In the Ladbroke six furlong handicap sprint here at Newmarket, Heather Bank jumped out well. Always in the first three he took up the running two out and went clear to win by six lengths. The Edward St George owned two-year-old Kingston Brown ran a nice race to finish sixth of the thirteen starters. This fellow is very laid back and will benefit greatly with this race under his belt.

Travelling back from the races the roads were very busy and the police were out in full force stopping the speedsters.

On my return home, I looked at the injury book, the horses work sheets and the mail that needs my attention. All the bills and letters marked Her Majesty the Queen are normally taken care of in the office. Periodically I sign the cheques. There is also a message to ring the vet in the morning about our two patients he has in his care.

Looking through the racing results and news on Oracle Heather Bank gets a nice mention with the headlines: "Lucky Heather for Berry."

Not good news for Lisnakill Wish-he wasn't in the first two. Still, if he never wins again this season he has done his bit. It's unreal how these greyhounds are asked to keep running week after week. Racehorses certainly couldn't stand it.

FRIDAY April 17

GOOD FRIDAY so no racing today, although we still ride out just the same as any normal day. The yard is on a bit of a roll as we have had a winner every day this week and most days last week.

It was great to get back into a pair of breeches and lead our horses on Gorinsky first lot and Dokkha Oyston second string round our ring gallop.

The phone has never stopped today. The owners must be on holiday and I think I'll ring that berk at Cockerham while I have nothing to do.

The Vin St Benet I bought at Newmarket I sold on the phone to David Abell. So that will be one less brown envelope to cope with. Our apprentice, Steve Haworth, had a sit on him for a couple of furlongs. I was very pleased with him.

At lunchtime I rang my partner to find out how our flying machine ran at Hove. The poor chap got brought down on the first bend. Fortunately he is all right. Straight after the phone call I went to see our two patients at the vets.

The Music Boy colt's swelling on his hock has subsided a fair bit and hopefully he should be all right, given a bit of time. The filly, Darling Miss Daisy, was up on her feet and looking quite cheerful. She doesn't move very much but she is eating. So the filly is trying and has not thrown in the towel.

Ray, our spare box driver, who does odd jobs, has just told me we have a blackbird sitting on three eggs in our woodshed. He can't saw the wood up as she's made her nest on the top of the pile. Good isn't it, ruled by a blackbird!

It's nearly 8.0pm. Jo has gone to see her mother and I am stuck in the house waiting for her to come back, answering the telephone every five minutes with all my dogs flat out fast asleep. We are going for a walk and it's starting to get dark. Bugger the phone, I'm going.

On my return I received a fax from Hilary Kerr of the Injured Jockeys Fund. She has checked with the fund and we are in order to go ahead with our Open Day which we are holding especially to send some disabled beneficiaries on holiday to Tenerife during the winter for a couple of weeks.

I tracked down Mike Gallemore, the editor of The Sporting Life at 10.10pm on his mobile phone, travelling on the train from London, seeking some support from his paper. Looking at the calendar I have gone for Sunday, August 2. Let's hope it's nice weather.

Our last Open Day was in 1989 in aid of an extension on the intensive care unit of the Royal Manchester Children's Hospital for which we collected £26,679.93 from hundreds of lovely people. Let's hope we can do as well for this worthwhile cause.

SATURDAY April 18

IT'S rained heavy again throughout the night so I'm afraid we will be working the horses on the all-weather. It's good going on that.

In the Greyhound Life I read that a Kildare Slippy and Lisnakill Wish match, The Sporting Life Showdown, has been arranged for 2nd May at Wimbledon over 460 metres. That's the headlines and there's a photo of these two great dogs. Paris House also got plenty of coverage in the Post and the Life.

John Carroll is back today riding at Haydock after breaking his collar bone. The horses are going great on the gallops. The Dowsing colt I bought for Robert Aird and Bill Robertson is a lovely horse. Today was the first time we have asked him a question and he flew. He has a fare bit of educational work to do yet but thank goodness he looks a real runner. His connections called to see him on their way to Haydock.

PARIS HOUSE (noseband) scoots to victory from Stack Rock and
Sir Harry Hardman in the Beamish Irish Stout Field Marshal Stakes.

Today we have eight runners at three meetings. Jo has gone to Kempton, Alan to Newcastle, me to Haydock, mainly to see Paris House.

Just before setting off for Haydock, Martin, our travelling head man, rang from Newcastle to tell me our two-year-old Westmead Nick has hurt his foot, so he won't run.

At Haydock there was a huge crowd. In the first our two-year-old was fourth. Paris House looked tremendous in the paddock and was so relaxed for the feature event, the Field Marshal Stakes, a Listed race. He went to the front after a hundred yards and stayed on to beat Stack Rock by a length. This was a fair performance for a three-year-old giving older horses weight. When John was lead into the winning enclosure the crowd gave them a nice round of applause.Windpower was fourth at Kempton, the rest also ran.

On the way back from the races we called round to see our two horses at the vets. The Music Boy colt looked a lot better.

Barry Johnson, the vet, was away at the point-to-point, so I will have a word with him tomorrow about them both. Looking at Oracle on the box, I am not the only one who thought Paris House had put up a good show. They had two whole pages dedicated to him.

SUNDAY April 19

LED yesterdays runners out. Paris House's success was so impressive that lots of people and press have rung up to say well done and to enquire where we intend running him next. His win gave us our 21st for the season in Britain. This day last year we had nineteen.

Rang Robert Sangster up in France to have a chat to him about his horses. John Nixon and I had a walk with my dogs round our estate to inspect the new trees that he planted, so that John could price the job up and send me the bill. As soon as we have finished fencing off the trees, which hopefully will be completed by Tuesday, we will turn the cattle out, as we have lots of grass that needs eating off.

It's been a nice warm day here today which inevitably means being inundated with people coming to the yard.

At a recent Newcastle meeting I asked Graham Goode for some information on commentators for my weekly Weekender column as I am always on the lookout for something different to write about. Today he kindly faxed me what I wanted. Arranged with Graham Rossier, the Swiss trainer, for Paul Roberts one of our apprentices to go to Zurich tomorrow for three rides for him there.

Leased a horse to Keith Dunn, of the Marie Curie Charity, for the season. Also arranged during the course of the day for our Warwick horses to stay with Richard Evans, the ex jump jockey who has a stud near Warwick, as the racecourse stables often don't have enough boxes to cater for overnight stays. Alan, Pat, Jo and myself went to the Crofters at the kind invitation of

Bill and Nan Robertson, who are staying there for the weekend and are going onto Newcastle races tomorrow. We had a nice meal and a few drinks. Pat drove back as we drank for her.

MONDAY April 20

ALAN and I did next Saturday's entries. Except for Oyston's Life, who we tried in blinkers, and Palacegate King who cantered, the rest of the horses went on the walkers or were ridden round the roads before having a pick of grass.

Jo has gone to Kempton. Hills Raceaid, the competition horse, runs there. Alan has gone to Warwick, where we run Threepence and Soba Guest. My venue is Newcastle, where our only runner is Make It Happen, a two-year-old having his first run, ridden by John.

On our way to the races we picked up Mel Haughey, who had rung earlier for a lift. We are leading in the trainer's list with runners at both Newcastle and Warwick, so let's hope our luck continues.

There was a very good crowd at Newcastle, which is well deserved. They put good racing on and it's a lovely track. Our two-year-old ran well to finish third, beaten a neck and half a length. A real nice horse this one. I am certain he will come on from the run.

John had a ride in every race so we couldn't get a flyer after our fellow had run. But I didn't mind, it was such a nice day. Hills Raceaid wasn't in the frame at Kempton. Neither was Soba Guest at Warwick. Threepence didn't let us down though, he won the six furlong sprint there.

On the way home we called into Mel's antique shop to look at a working desk he said he had when I made enquiries last week. He actually had two I liked, so he's going to bring them both to our house on Sunday to see which one fits in the best.

TUESDAY April 21

TOMORROW'S runners went out early for a couple of furlongs' spin. The rest cantered and had a pick of lush grass which they thoroughly enjoyed.

Our only runner today is Pilgrim Bay at Warwick, drawn 14 of 14 on the wide outside. In sprints the draw on some courses like here, Beverley and Chester are so unfair. Our fellow has about as much chance of winning from there as I have counting the hairs on my head with a pair of boxing gloves on. Punters should take a bit more notice of the draw on these kind of courses. In fact, Paris House, drawn one of 24 at Beverley, could get beat in a seller, it's so unfair. There is no way the safety factor should be that amount. The authorities should put more emphasis on the horse's chance from poor draws, instead of just the safety factor.

John and I set off at 11.30am for Warwick as our race isn't until 4.15pm. Before we even got 20 miles on the clock the traffic on the M6 came to a halt. Two cars had been in a bump.

Helen rang from the office on the carphone with tomorrow's declared runners. There are only three in the juvenile race at Catterick so we are guaranteed a pay-day, providing we finish.

Just heard on the radio that Benny Hill has been found dead in his flat. Frankie Howerd died only the other day. There seems to be a bit of a run on comedians at the moment.

It was a lovely day at Warwick with a good crowd. I hope it's an upward trend. Whenever I have been racing recently there seem to be plenty of racegoers.

Pilgrim Bay finished fifth. He was going that fast to get a good position at the bend he ran wide. John had all on to drag him round it. He will be better on a straight five.

There were stalls selling their goods in the paddock area. I bought a large stone pig, weighing about three stones, for the garden. John got a spare ride in the last and he was involved in a stewards' enquiry. While that was going on, I drove the car to the stall to pick up the pig. Fortunately, most of the punters had gone, otherwise I would have looked a right berk carrying a pig to the car. Imagine the racing folk taking the juice.

Back home, Jo cooked some pork chops for dinner and between us we had a bottle of wine. Answered countless phone calls, one asking me to do an after dinner speech at a Round Table function.

Swotted up on tomorrow's form and looked through the entries. It's 1.25am and I'm going to bed.

WEDNESDAY April 22

LOOKING at The Sporting Life, we could be in for a good day. Our two Folkestone runners both have a fair chance. So do the three Catterick contenders. Although there are quite a few undulations on this course and a good draw is important, Catterick is a lucky track for us.

The going is lovely at home, thanks to the warm, dryish weather we've had recently. Today's work is on the seven furlong grass gallop. Captain Wilson, the Tarleton trainer, brought a two-year-old to work with ours. Everything went well on the grass. The horses are pleased to get back on it.

The Dowsing colt from Doncaster performed a treat. Robert Aird hasn't got him named yet. Every time he comes up with one Weatherbys won't pass it. It's a problem to me. I wanted to put him in the Heinz 57 in Ireland. The race closed for entries today. Horses have to have a name to be entered. I got Ruby to ring the Irish authorities to see if they would bend a bit and put him in the race on breeding, but they can't.

Arrived at Catterick where it was drizzling with rain. On walking the course the going was perfect. Palacegate King ran unplaced in the apprentices race.

The two-year-old race, which we won last year with Diamond Mine, was easily won by our filly, Lucky Parkes. Watching our next two races on SIS from Folkestone, Arctic Appeal was second, beaten only a neck. Sabre Rattler easily won the two-year-old race for us, ridden by Pat Eddery. Oddly enough, both the Folkestone races were won by us last year with Sizzling Saga and Bit-a-Magic, ridden by Lester Piggott. To add further spice, Sabre Rattler and Bit-a-Magic are both by the same sire, Beveled. Returning to my car in Catterick car park I found a note under the windscreen wiper which read "L C two rides, two winners". L C being Lindsay Charnock, no doubt wanting more rides.

When I got back from Catterick I went to see what the grass was like after working 90 or so horses on it. The gallop men were just finishing off rolling it since working on it from 11.30am. They made a good job, I'm pleased to say. At 8.15pm Jo arrived back from her 662 mile round trip to Folkestone. They have it easy, these trainers' wives, they will do anything to get out of housework.

Watched Frank Bruno and Jose Ribalta, who looked a giant of a man. If I said he looked evil it would be putting it mildly. Ribalta never laid a glove on Frank. In the second round, he was knocked out by Bruno with a beautiful right. I must say I was really pleased to see Jose Ribalta get back on his feet at the end.

It was brilliant for Jimmy White at the Crucible in Sheffield to get the maximum 147 break to bag him £114,000.

The Folkestone box arrived back at 10.55pm.

THURSDAY April 23

LUCKY PARKES has a nice write-up in the two sporting papers. The horses did road work, except for the few we put through the stalls and tomorrow's runners who breezed for a couple of furlongs.

Alan and I got stuck into the entries until it was time for me to pick up John to go to Beverley. We took Jo's mum to her sister's house there and told her we would pick her up after our only runner, Laurel Queen, had run in the 2.45pm race.

Laurel Queen won the claimer by a short-head, starting at 5-2 favourite, which puts us on the twenty-five mark for the season. There was a good crowd at the races today. Not all were punters of Laurel Leisure but a lot were. I am certain racing is on an upward trend and sincerely hope it continues.

Terry Ellis, Pat Eddery's brother-in-law and agent, rang on the carphone to sort out our Bath runners for Tuesday.

I rang home to see how Grey Pride was because the vet did a little operation on him this morning. His main objective in life was shouting at the fillies rather than burning up the gallops.

Our new horse walkers are finished so the firm say, but I'm not satisfied with some of the workmanship. The cage where the horses go in seems too flimsy for me. In fact, there are quite a few things I am not pleased about. I have asked Ruby to write to the bossman to get it sorted out.

All the trees are fenced in now. We have a few more bales of silage for the cattle to eat before they can be turned out to grass. I have had a word with Dave, our local policeman, to tell him we are having an Open Day on August 2, so he can arrange to alleviate the traffic problems. On the first Open Day we held I neglected to advise the police and all our local roads were bunged up good and proper. A policeman came down to the yard and gave me a real bollocking. Gordian Troeller, the bloodstock agent, has rung with an offer to buy Sabre Rattler for the Italians. Taking instructions from his owner, Mr Hughes which I am obliged to do of course, he tells me to keep him. That suits me fine.

FRIDAY April 24

FIRST lot I led the horses round the canter ring on Fylde Flyer and on Langtonian second lot. Both were in good heart. As we were having a pick of grass one of the horses was bucking and kicking and got loose. He came winging by Langtonian. He wasn't loose for long and was all right when we caught him. It's always a lucky omen when a horse gets loose on a race day. But it's even luckier when you catch them and they are not hurt.

Amber Mill and Margaret's Gift, both owned by the Holdcrofts, run at Sandown. Oyston's Life, Dokkha Oyston and General Brooks perform at Carlisle. The going is good at both meetings.

Jo has gone to Sandown and is staying overnight with the Viners, as we run Echo-Logical there tomorrow.

There is always something that has to go wrong. Martin has just rung from Carlisle to say General Brooks, our two-year-old, has spread a plate and has trod on one of its nails. Fortunately, he isn't lame, but I had better get off there now to have a look at him before his race time.

It poured with rain every bit of the journey to Carlisle. John and I went straight to the stable yard to see General Brooks. The foot had bled a little but thankfully it was all right, he was sound. Martin sensibly had put a bran poultice on his foot.

I saw Margaret's Gift finish fourth at Sandown on SIS. Dokkha Oyston won the claimer at Carlisle and General Brooks was second in his race. John didn't have anymore rides so we went straight home after the two-year-old race. I wanted to see the gallops before it gets dark as it's work day tomorrow. We have had a fair amount of overnight rain and it's raining now. I don't want to be cutting up the grass too much. The ground today at Carlisle changed from good to soft.

John is on a low fat diet so he can lose a couple of pounds to ride Paris House in the Palace House Stakes next Saturday at Newmarket where he only has 8st. John's natural weight is around 8st 3lb but Paris is worth starving for.

Got changed into my jeans and rounded up all my dogs. The going was excellent. The rain had done it no harm at all. Halfway back John Carroll came to see what it was like as I had told him what I was going to do on my return from Carlisle. It's good when a yard has a stable jockey. We can discuss things without falling out. John has his own views on the horses and he is not frightened to air them. I like that. No yard will be successful if the jockey just creeps round the boss and tells him only the things he thinks he would like to hear. It's winners we want, not yes men.

SATURDAY April 25

IT'S a beautiful morning. Six runners at three meetings today, Ripon, Sandown and Leicester. We lead in the trainers list at Ripon. Let's hope we are lucky there.

Another Episode, Paris House and Tino Tere worked for four furlongs. What a sight watching these three leg it. Paris House has come on even more from his Haydock run.

We bounced five two-year-olds out of the stalls who have yet to run but are entered up. The rest of the sprinters and two-year-olds worked in pairs up the grass.

David, one of the vets, came to do the tests on Another Episode with him going to run in Italy next Friday. These have to be done and the horse's passport has to go to Weatherbys to be stamped before he is allowed to go. It never rains but it pours. The Warwick police have rung to advise us our horsebox has overheated on its way to Leicester. The RAC are on their way to rescue it. I wish they would ring the racecourse stables instead of me when this happens. They could send another box to pick the horses up. There isn't much I can do on my way to Ripon.

Our day didn't produce any winners but we had a second and two thirds. That wasn't too bad. Had a look at the injury book on my return home and answered a few phone calls before settling down to watch the telly.

A good night for boxing fans. I watched Paul Hodkinson on BBC-1 defend his featherweight title against Steve Cruz, which he did well, delivering a super left hook in the third to knock his opponent out. On ITV at 10.30 John Jarvis challenged Chris Eubank for the middleweight title. Super sharp Eubank knocked Jarvis out, also in the third round.

SUNDAY April 26

YESTERDAY'S box that broke down on its way to Leicester is now in a Coventry garage with piston trouble.

Beth, one of our girls, was leading Andrea's Girl round the paddock when the filly trod on her foot and badly bruised it.

We had yesterday's runners out and gave them a pick of grass. Tomorrow's runners were cantered a couple of furlongs just to stretch their legs.

Mike Burrows called to see the new walkers and is going to do some modifications to the cage parts as they are too flimsy. With the weather being fine and sunny lots of owners came to see their horses.

Dave, the local policeman, came down to the yard to discuss our Open Day on August 2. We talked about traffic problems, an escort to the bank with the takings and the rest of the details.

Peter Chandler, Paris House's owner, rang to have a chat about his horse. Some man Peter. He has the Paris House restaurant on the Woburn Abbey Estate. On the day of the Palace House Stakes at Newmarket, where his famous grey runs, Peter is cooking a wedding lunch before dashing over to HQ. Now that's dedication for you.

Mel Haughey brought the office desks I had seen in his shop last week on the way back from Newcastle.

The North West Racing Club played football against a team of stable lads at Morecambe as they do every year. Some of our gang played for the stable lads who got beat, would you believe it 4-1.

It was good to see my home team Leeds United beat Sheffield United 3-2, even though it was through a Brian Gayle own goal.

Rang up Gianfranco Dettori, Franco's father, to book him to ride Another Episode on Friday in the Group 3 Premio Certosa in Milan.

There was such a banging and clattering in the yard as I put the phone down. Jo and I ran out. It was Price Rumpus cast in his box, having rolled over and got his feet so close to the wall, he couldn't get up. When this happens the horse panics. We have to either roll the horse over, away from the wall, or pull him around by the tail to enable him to get to his feet. On occasions when the feeders go round early in the morning this is a dreaded sight as it means the horse could have been cast there for hours.

MONDAY April 27

ALAN and I got stuck into entering the horses first thing for next Saturday. We enter Monday for Saturday, Tuesday no entries, Wednesday for Monday, Thursday for Tuesday, Friday for Wednesday. On Saturday, our busiest day of the week, we enter for Thursday and Friday. The horses are declared as runners the day before the race. Then on race day at the races we have to declare them not less than three quarters of an hour before their particular race.

Price Rumpus is all right after being cast last night.

On my way to Pontefract, a car and a caravan had jack-knifed on the M62. The caravan was right up on it's backside I couldn't see where the car was.

Eight runners at three meetings today. John has gone to Windsor with Jo, to the first night meeting of the season. When the weather is fine the evening meetings really pull the crowds. Alan has gone to Wolverhampton. All the races look very competitive today. I will be grateful if we manage to get one winner.

Arriving at Pontefract, the course, as usual, looked tremendous. Norman Gundill the Clerk of the Course is keen and conscientious. The two-year-olds in the first race ran without having a pay day. Our other runner Windpower in the feature race absolutely scooted in. This fellow has really improved from his Kempton run when he was fourth. On today's run he could go on to better things as he was so impressive. I received the silver trophy on behalf of Mr Sangster as he wasn't in attendance.

WINDPOWER scoots to win more silverware for owner Robert Sangster, who unfortunately wasn't at Pontefract to see him.

On SIS from Wolverhampton Convenient Moment, a Clantime filly, owned by some barristers, was beaten a neck. High Principles, our other runner there finished third.

Phoned for the commentary of Trentesimo, our two-year-old running in the 6.15pm, on my way home from Ponty. No luck at Windsor. Like I said, I would be grateful for a winner-and I am.

Answered a few phone calls and made a couple more on my return home. Then took my dogs for a walk on the gallops.

Jo rang. She is staying over again with the Viners as tomorrow we have runners at Bath and she can see to them.

See Jenny Pitman and Michael Bowlby were cleared by the Jockey Club of being in breach of the rules over the running of Golden Freeze in the Gold Cup. If that enquiry had been videoed and shown later on in the evening it would have had some viewing audience.

TUESDAY April 28

THE SPORTING LIFE photographer Dan Abraham arrived at 6.45am to take some photos for this book cover.

We cantered the horses in the ring and gave them a nice pick of grass afterwards.

Rang the vet to cut Trentesimo as down at the start last night at Windsor he was behaving like some of our stable lads. It's not that we are barbarians castrating the horses. Some of them are very randy at times. When it's the only thing on their minds they can be more than a handful. In their off or resting periods colts cannot be turned out to grass with the other horses so their freedom is limited. They are better off being cut unless they have the potential of making a useful stallion.

John and I set off for Nottingham where we have Price Rumpus and Langtonian running. There were hundreds of cones out on the A1 to make the traffic flow into a single lane for a couple of miles. There was nothing at the end of it and not a single workman in sight. Motorway roadworks must cost millions in lost man hours for motorists.

It is not possible to have good days everyday. Today was not one of our better ones. Neither of our two Bath horses looked like giving the judge an anxious moment. Nor did our two at Nottingham. Price Rumpus burst a blood vessel in the race and any chance he may have had went. John came into the paddock covered in blood. Nottingham has a new look. They have spent a fortune on their new stand, weighing room and paddock. It really looks nice. John got a spare ride in the last race for Lynda Ramsden so we didn't get a quick start going home.

On the way back John and I were talking about our grey flying machine Paris House in the Palace House Stakes at Newmarket, when two magpies flew across the road in front of us. That's got to be lucky.

I arrived home at 8.0pm and got changed into my scruffs to help Dave Parker and Alan turn all the cattle out for their summer grazing. They were brilliant, bucking and kicking. What a shame though that the next time they come back indoors will be en route to the butchers.

WEDNESDAY April 29

THIS is the first day we haven't had a runner for a while. I'll have more of a chance to be with the horses longer as normally I am very pushed for time to get off to the races. It will make a welcome change from rushing about trying to see them all before tear-arsing off to a meeting.

Paris House and Food of Love did their final gallops with Tino Tere in preparation for the Palace House Stakes on Saturday. Paris House flew. Food of Love has sharpened up a lot from her run at Haydock. She will run a big race at Newmarket.

On the whole the horses worked well. The going here is very good at the moment. Thankfully, it hasn't rained hard for a week or so. Price Rumpus seems all right now. After having a word with his owner Frank Dunne we decided it would be better to send him back to Ireland. Later on we may send him to the States where horses with problems are allowed to run on Lasix, which is a banned substance here.

The cattle seemed nicely settled turned out. Two fillies have also been turned out for a few weeks as they have had sore shins. At this time of year we turn them out in waterproof rugs and if the weather deteriorates, we bring them in at night. The spring grass really does the horses good. We still feed them while they are out-from tumbrils in the field.

At evening stables Bergenia Belle was lame on her near fore joint. Food of Love has managed to get a cut. But everything else was fine.

John Carroll, Alan and I had a meeting in the evening to discuss this morning's work with the horses.

THURSDAY April 30

TWO meetings for us today. Jo will be staying down at Newmarket until I join her on Saturday. John and I are going to Redcar.

Reading the paper I see Willie Carson was given a four-day ban for careless riding at Ascot yesterday. That will stop him chuckling for a while.

The horses went on the walkers or were ridden round the roads, with the exception of tomorrow's four Hamilton runners. Two of these, which were two-year-olds, bounded out of the stalls. The other two just stretched their legs for a couple of furlongs.

I didn't ride out this morning. Not because it was pissing down, which it was, but because Alan and I were too busy with the entries as tomorrow he's off to Italy to supervise Another Episode and I will have to set off early for Hamilton.

George Roper, the comedian, who I have known for years, always tells me a joke when I speak to him. Today's sick joke on the way to Redcar was-Bernard Manning let him down last week in a treble with Benny Hill and Frankie Howerd. (Bernard had just recovered from illness).

Travelling on the M6 it's very foggy. The warning lights are on. Even so silly beggers are flying past us in their cars. We kick on at times, I know, but in these conditions it's stupid. While John was driving I finished my two stories for next week's Weekender. One was about the new facilities and a bit of history on Nottingham racecourse. The other was on Sunday racing.

No luck at Newmarket or Redcar, I'm afraid. I can only hope things improve tomorrow. Watching the Guineas on telly in the packed owners and trainers room I was gasping to get out after Walter Swinburn had won on Hatoof. I got more smoke in my lungs in that few minutes than when I smoked twenty cigarettes a day.

FRIDAY May 1

THIS morning is very wild and windy. Not at all like the first day of summer. Alan set off on his journey to Italy at 5.45 am. In between answering phone calls I am watching tomorrow's runners breeze a couple of furlongs and the two two-year-olds pop out of the stalls. Jo is at Newmarket and the secretaries don't come in until 8.30am to answer the phones.

Nick Lees, the Newmarket Clerk of the Course, rang to ask me if I would ride in a one mile charity race at headquarters on the May 16. My two steeds I rode today to lead the first lots in a nice long steady canter were Dokkha Oyston and Fylde Flyer.

I see in my Sporting bible, Arazi has a poor draw, eighteen of nineteen in tomorrow's Kentucky Derby. Still, he had a bad position in the Breeders' Cup and he annihilated the opposition.

Travelling to Hamilton with John we have given a lift to Lynne Campion, Andrea's mother, as she has Sobering Thoughts running, trained by David Chapman.

Ruby rang on the carphone to tell me one of my tips for the Daily Star doesn't run. I had to pick out another. I do a weekly slot on a Saturday for the Star, which includes tipping a horse in all the televised races. Last Saturday out of six races I tipped two winners and four seconds. It isn't easy, I can assure you. The going was very heavy at Hamilton. Daaniera, the horse I bought at Fairyhouse who is almost white and who I sold to Seamus Purcell unseen at Listowel races when I went there with Tommy and Liz Stack, didn't mind the ground, winning by a comfortable three lengths. Seamus and his son Patrick flew over from Ireland to cast their eyes on him for the first time. I can tell you they liked what they saw.

James Bennett, one of our former head lads who now trains, had a winner with Verro. It's always nice to see our past employees do well. All the rest of our day's runners, including Another Episode in Italy, were also rans.

SATURDAY May 2

IT'S a lot better day than yesterday. Lovely and sunny with no wind.

Paris House runs in the Group 3 Palace House Stakes at Newmarket, Emma O'Gorman is holding her 18th birthday party this evening also in Newmarket, and Charlie (Lisnakill Wish) runs in a match at Wimbledon tonight against Britain's best hurdler Kildare Slippy for £1,500. These two good dogs have the headlines in the Greyhound Life, who sponsored the match.

I rode out first lot on Fylde Flyer with a pair of chaps over my suit trousers as I am after a quick start. Being Guineas Day the roads to Newmarket could be busy. John also wants to be there early to have a sweat in the sauna.

I drove to save John Carroll's energy for Paris House. The roads, amazingly, were quiet.

Our yard has Common Gain and Music Dancer running at Thirsk and Gorinsky at Haydock.

Wasn't it great Rodrigo de Triano winning the 2,000 Guineas with Lester aboard. When Lester rode him back to the winning enclosure Newmarket erupted. The cheers for the maestro were deafening. They must have been heard down in the town. It was wonderful for Robert Sangster to have another classic winner, and for the horse's young trainer Peter Chapple-Hyam.

I am afraid that although Paris House was odds-on to win his near namesake race, he got beat. He ran a good race, in fact, but not good enough, losing to the French four-year-old Monde Bleu by a length.

The only other horse of ours to trouble the judge was Music Dancer for the minor place of third at Thirsk.

Jo and I went to Gerry and Bridget Blum's to change into evening dress for Emma O'Gorman's birthday party. I had to leave Olly my Jack Russell, who had travelled down with John and I this morning, in one of Gerry's stables as he wasn't invited to the celebrations. There were about 150 guests. An absolutely brilliant spread was laid on in a large marquee in the garden. Our table was labelled with my lucky number 8.

At 10.10pm I managed to slide out to my car to ring Sonia Newman, as I arranged, to find out how Charlie had got on. Well, would you believe it, he

WISH I WAS THERE : Lisnakill Wish with my co-owner Sonia Newman (holding trophy). Others pictured include the dog's trainer Phil Rees (left), and Bob Betts (second left) editor of the Greyhound Life.

[193]

beat Kildare Slippy a length-and-a-half in a very fast time. It's a shame these two functions clashed as Charlie received the Greyhound of the Month award and I would have loved to have been present.

The Kentucky Derby live commentary was piped into the marquee for the guests to hear. To everyone's amazement Arazi wasn't mapped.

It was a very good party, dancing to a disco. Jo and I got back to Gerry's about 2.0am and stayed the night.

SUNDAY May 3

IT'S an absolutely beautiful summer morning. I got Olly out of the stable and packed our things in the car. We set off from Gerry's, for home about 6.30am. The whole village of Tuddenham was fast asleep as we drove through. I made a few calls on the carphone on the way and arrived at Cockerham 10.30am.

A few owners came to the yard to see their horses. Most were saying bad luck about Paris House getting beat yesterday. If Paris House had bad luck what about poor old Arazi. He only finished eighth. At least our fellow was second.

Martin, our travelling head lad, gave me an engraved tankard he had collected on my behalf yesterday from Thirsk for the top trainer award of 1991.

It was good to walk round the gallops with my dogs and to see the cattle. Our cattle are great. With us going in and out of the fold yard with the muck from the horses' stables to bed them down in winter, they get to know us. I talk to them and give them all a stroke. So today I had seven dogs and fifty-two bullocks accompanying me round the gallops.

7.40pm Another Episode arrived back from Italy looking well from his holiday. Wally, who took him, came in the house and said the French horse called Irish Source, who won the sixth race at San Siro, was disqualified by the stewards and placed fifth. The punters were not amused and gathered round the weighing room, which has lovely big glass windows looking onto the course. The crowd started to get excited, as Italians often do, and threw stones at the windows until every single one was broken. They shouted for the stewards to come down. The last two races were abandoned by the stewards but they didn't come down to face the mob. Thank goodness we don't carry on like that.

MONDAY May 4

QUITE rightly a great photo of Kildare Slippy being led over the last flight by Lisnakill Wish at Wimbledon on Saturday makes the headlines. The build-up to this Sporting Life showdown was great. There was a near record attendance to see these two great dogs in action. They had printed one thousand extra race cards. It makes my mouth water missing it. Apparently the cheers for Charlie, being their local dog, were deafening when he jumped the last in front of Slippy. Lucky Parkes and Tino Tere flew over a two furlong blow in preperation for Chester tomorrow.

The picture of "Charlie", seen leading Kildare Slippy over the last flight, that appeared in The Sporting Life.

Jo has gone to Warwick with Laurel Delight, our only runner there. This filly has a good draw which is important on this sharp course. She is a half-sister to Paris House. If she wins a few races, her breeding should make her a valuable broodmare when her racing days are over.

John and I are Pontefract bound where Dokkha Oyston and Super Rocky run. We picked up John Brown at Birch services on the M62 on the way there.

Amanda rang up from Warwick to say the course vet thinks Laurel Delight has a touch of ringworm on her girth. He has taken a scraping. If the sample is active we will get a heavy fine if she runs. If she doesn't run we will still get a fine because she has entered the racecourse stables. This filly had a course of Fulcin two months ago as she had a touch of ringworm. Our vet and our head men thought it was inactive. So let's hope it's a negative report from the laboratory. I have only just settled down and got the bandages off, due to burns from the £2,600 fine those prats from the ministry gave me. It's a hard job to make money training horses at the moment. It's even harder to stay within the rules, red tape and regulations.

At Pontefract it was a beautiful sunny day with a huge crowd. Lester Piggott was there fresh from his Guineas win on Saturday. That alone must have tempted some punters to come and see him in the flesh. Lester didn't let them down either. He won on the Reg Hollinshead-trained Eager Deva. The crowd at this popular Yorkshire track clapped and cheered. They loved him.

Super Rocky was second in the claimer, beaten four lengths by Fangio. After the race a Mr Bates claimed him for £6,030. John Brown told me our two-year-old has just won at Warwick. He had watched the race in the Tote betting shop.

TUESDAY May 5

TODAY we had stall practice in the middle grass gallop, right out in the open. Just recently some of the horses, young and old, have not been pinging the stalls as fast as I like them to.

Tomorrow's two Chester runners had a two furlongs spin and went very well.

Reading The Life I see Jane Groves has resigned her post as Clerk of the Course at Southwell and Wolverhampton because of a disagreement with the management. Shame that, I thought Jane did a good job.

Only Chester for us today. Lucky Parkes runs in the first. Tino Tere and Soba Guest in the sprint. We have some good draws round this tight circuit which is very important. Given luck we should have a good day.

While John drove to Chester I finalised my story about the breeders' plight for next week's Weekender. It's hard to find two stories every week sometimes, but I like doing it.

Richard Pitman rang me on the carphone. He's aiming to entertain 450 racegoers at the Grand Hotel Scarborough while we are at York races on the night of May 13th. He asked me if I would go along.

At Chester it was a lovely warm summer day. The ladies looked beautiful in their nice hats and coloured suits. It was also the opening of the underground tunnel between the paddock and the stands. Like most courses I have been to recently, Chester had a large crowd.

Lucky Parkes drawn the best of the six runners in the Lily Agnes Stakes, shot out of the stalls making every yard of the running to win by three quarters of a length.

Joe Heler, the filly's owner, invited Jo and I to the owners' room for champagne. Joe was the master of the Cheshire Hunt for several years. It was his ambition to win a race on his home course and what added to his pleasure even more was that he bred the filly.

Watching the seven furlong race brought back memories of Olly, (O.I.Oyston) going round Chester. If there was some give in the ground he use to bomb out of those stalls and fly around. The only thing the opposition saw was his backside. He absolutely loved the place.

Came home from Chester, answered a few phone calls, (don't know what I would do without the phone) before gathering up my pack. Or perhaps I should say, I went outside, my pack of dogs, apart from Olly, were at the door waiting to gather me up. We went round the gallops for a stroll to see the cattle. My dog Olly arrived back from his visit to the caravan site at just gone nine to watch a racing programme on Channel Two.

LUCKY PARKES (ridden by John Carroll)
beats Risk Me's Girl at Chester.

WEDNESDAY May 6

IT was drizzling all morning as we were working the horses, but living here on this west coast we seem to have got used to it. The horses worked well. Most of them have now lost their old coats and are looking an absolute picture.

Jo and I were invited to lunch at Chester. I sent Jo with John Carroll as John has a jockeys' meeting before racing. Jo can go then for lunch and eat mine as well. Not only because I am busy here with the horses, but because if I don't get a bit of weight off for Newmarket on the 16th, the poor horse will think he is carrying Cyril Smith.

Travelling on the M56 about sixteen miles away from Chester, which is again the venue today, there were four shire horses turned out in a field. In this modern age they were a nice sight for sure.

Our only two runners today ran in the last two races. Both ran well but unfortunately did not give the owners a pay day. Straight after the last Jo and I went to Cheshire to see Joe Heler's two yearlings. He wants us to train them next season. One is a very nice filly half-sister to Lucky Parkes. That one definitely got the JB seal of approval.

We had a lovely supper with Joe and his wife Janet. Their beautiful home was an old monastery which partly dated back to the fourteenth century.

We set off for home about 8.30pm and on arriving back at Cockerham I saw to my mail. After reading the injury book I had a look at the entries for Hamilton from the prestel machine. Doing it this way we get them before they appear in the newspaper. It gives me a start to see what horses are entered. In the Hamilton maiden two-year-old race there are only four entries-two of them are ours! I had better run them both. If there is a walkover the race will be abandoned with the new ruling.

THURSDAY May 7

OUR five runners at tomorrow's three different meetings breezed for a couple of furlongs. One was ridden by Nicky Carlisle, the jockey who rode our Ayr Gold Cup winner, So Careful. He had stayed the night at John Carroll's.

Tim Riley, Hamilton's Clerk of the Course rang to make sure I was going to run both two-year-olds in the four horse entry there on Monday.

We have two runners at Chester today, Margaret's Gift and Never in the Red. Jo and I are going there, then after the two horses have raced we are going to Wimbledon greyhound track for the Stable Lads' Welfare Meeting put on by the sheer hard work of trainer John Dunlop.

Laurel Queen and General Brooks are the Berry representatives at Carlisle.

Margaret's Gift finished fifth in the first race. It was Pat Eddery's first ride back after a four-day suspension for excessive use of the whip. Pat found himself in more hot water for dropping his hands and the stewards relieved him of £250 for doing so.

We watched Laurel Queen finish fourth at Carlisle on SIS before seeing Never in the Red, with top weight of 10st, run a super race to finish fourth. Got to Wimbledon Stadium just as the second race had finished and heard the dog I had sponsored had won. I was presented with a magnum of champagne. Stan and Sonia Newman had booked a table and we had a lovely meal as we always do at Wimbledon. I had a chat with Phil Rees, Lisnakill Wish's trainer, who reported him to be in good heart.

We had a few tricasts and forecasts in all the races. I had one draw but didn't lose a fortune. Really enjoyed the evening, seeing lots of horse and dog racing folk who we knew. After racing, in the Diamond Room, Harry

Beeby, chairman of the Doncaster Bloodstock Sales, auctioned off a lovely framed photo of Remittance Man and Waterloo Boy pictured running in this year's Queen Mother Chase at Cheltenham. It was signed by the jockeys and trainers involved. Also auctioned was a ten month old greyhound by a Derby second and my magnum of champagne.

We set off for home at 10.51pm and when we arrived the car clock for the day's round trip read 571 miles and it's very late-or should I say early, 2.59am.

FRIDAY May 8

WORK hard, play hard. Livestock are not machinery that can be parked. They eat and want looking after. They didn't know that I didn't get in until the early hours of this morning so as usual they were there this morning to see their master bright faced with eyes like pee-holes in the snow.

At 9.30am Paul Buckfield, the manager of the Sussex Stud, and his wife Judy called to watch a two-year-old and Memsahb, who they have in training with us, work.

The rest of the horses did long, easy cantering, followed by a nice pick of grass.

Just before 11.0am John and I set off for Beverley where we run Classic Storm in the seller and High Principles in the five furlong maiden. Jo has gone down to Lingfield with Charity Express, a filly we didn't, or should say, couldn't sell, so we leased her to the Marie Curie Cancer Charity. Alan has gone to Carlisle with Between Two Fires and Kingston Brown, our two runners there. Derek and Mrs Ayres came over from the Isle of Man to watch their filly Classic Storm win the seller by a length. After the race, when the winner has to be put up for auction, we had to go to 4,800gns to retain her. This now is the second seller she has won. Being a two-year-old she is not allowed to run in any more this season.

Charity Express was second at Lingfield to the odds-on favourite. Hopefully, there should be plenty of fun still to be had from her for the people who had bought shares in her for this worthwhile cause.

The meeting at Carlisle was abandoned because of snow storms. When I got back home I made quite a few phone calls as well as answering even more. The phone is the greatest time-waster in our house. Instead of people getting straight to the point you have to put up with all the drivel like: "Good evening Jack it's been pissing down here all day. Martha and I had a whale of a time two years ago at Butlins. How is your cat now after its castration? That son of mine is a swine," and so on. Well, I really need this when I have passed everything in sight on my way home from Beverley don't I? We have had two secretaries knitting in the office half the day who would and could have quite easily told them most of whatever they wanted to know. I need the time to get on with my entries.

SATURDAY May 9

JO has rung from Fred Viners. She stayed there yet again last night. If this continues she will be charged Poll Tax!

It's Cup Final day, Liverpool against Sunderland. I think Liverpool will win and it would be a good tonic for Graeme Souness after his heart operation.

Alan and I battled with Thursday and Friday's entries for next week. Saturdays are by far our busiest.

After galloping our two entries in the four-horse race at Hamilton on Monday, Glowing Value beat Creagmhor who has been third on his only run. With a view to Steve Haworth riding the second string I asked him what his weight was. He said 8st 11lb. With his claim off he would carry 8st 7lb. Steve reckoned by Monday he could get down to 8st 7lb. But I think he can give this race a miss, I don't want him coming into the paddock at Hamilton looking like Mahatma Gandhi.

Diane Bain, the student from West Oxfordshire College, has come for the weekend. She still wants to be a trainer. She has been to several yards to gain experience. It's her second visit here. While watching over sixty horses work out I heard a cuckoo. I wonder if this is an omen for a prosperous season or just a call of a bird heralding spring.

At 11.15am John and I set sail again for Beverley. As I left the house a damn magpie was hopping around on our garden wall. That is a definite sign of bad luck.

Our runners today are not very good. MDM Racer will probably have the best chance at Bath but he has a very poor draw. The weather was miserable at Beverley, raining and very cold. Miss Parkes ran well in the first race, finishing fourth of seventeen. The rest performed just as the magpie had predicted-not today, Jack.

In the last race John rode the winner for Peter Hobbs-at least it was worth waiting for.

SUNDAY May 10

ALAN and I declared the horses early. At 10.0am I have an appointment with the dentist in Garstang. It's a one-off for him to open on a Sunday. He's only doing it because he can't pin me down through the week.

It rained hard during the night but it's stopped now and African Jack has popped his head out. In yesterday's Sporting Life it says Windsor and Wolverhampton are both watering. Up here we have not had more than three dry days on the run for months.

Although we are at this moment in front numerically with winners-thirty one-Richard Hannon, whose horses are flying, and Henry Cecil are breathing down my neck. If we could have the weather warmed up and get less wind and rain, I am sure the horses would benefit. They are fed up with the bad weather. I'm certain we could push further ahead if the horses could train every day in good weather.

In the afternoon the Sun kept on shining and a few owners came to see their horses. A man I met at Pontefract last week came to buy a horse. I showed him Cashtal Queen. He went home to think about it. I don't know if anything will come of it. Lots of people would buy horses if it was merely the purchase price they had to consider. It's the bills that follow that put them off.

Finished my second story for next week's Weekender. It was about surcharges on entry fees.

The old Cock of the North, Billy Nevett died today at the age of eighty-six. He won the Derby three times and rode the Oaks winner in the forties. Billy always stood in the entrance of the paddock at Catterick, Ripon and Thirsk to have a chat with us trainers before we met the owners and jockeys in the ring. If he didn't turn up we would enquire where he was. He was an absolute gentleman. All of us up the North will sadly miss him.

MONDAY May 11

IT'S rained again through the night. Wolverhampton, Windsor and Hamilton racecourses have the company of six of our horses on their tracks today.

Entering the horses for races at Hamilton is pathetic. Every race on the card is for only £2,000 prize money, except for the feature race which is for £2,250. This is 1992. The prize money in Ireland is twice the amount it is here.

There are six race meetings next Saturday so we had to spend more time than usual with the entries. This day last year we trained five winners. It will be very difficult to do that today but most of our runners have got a squeak.

Hamilton is a very lucky place for our yard where between 1988 and 1992 we have trained the winners of 40 races. The next trainer is Bill Pearce with 18 winners for the same period of time. We head the trainer's list also at Wolverhampton with 14 winners, five in front of Reg Hollinshead. Richard Hannon heads the Windsor list with 16. According to Travellers Check in the Racing Post we have travelled 232 miles to Windsor from Cockerham, the furthest distance of any other trainer with runners at the meeting. Let's hope Mr Sydney Mason's Press The Bell is rewarded by Weatherbys having to transfer some prize money into his bank account.

As we were about to saddle our runners for the first race at Hamilton, a message came over the loudspeaker for everyone to vacate the stands. The stewards announced racing would start half an hour later. Some berk had phoned in to say a bomb had been placed in the stands. Fortunately it was a false alarm and racing continued without any further hitches.

Glowing Value, our colt in the first race, won one-and-a-half lengths on the soft going. The other three Hamilton runners were fourth, just missing a pay day.

I watched Two Times Twelve finish second on SIS at Wolverhampton.

John did a repeat of what he'd done on Saturday-he rode the winner in the last race. This time it was for Colin Parker, our amateur riders's father from Lockerbie. On the way home it was absolutely belting down with rain. Andrea Sharp, whose husband Ken shares Between Two Fires with Jack Clayton, drove my car back. She didn't half kick on too. It's a shame she isn't married to John Carroll. They could breed some little Nigel Mansells. Came home and cooked my tea as the bride has gone galavanting to Wolverhampton.

I listened to Press The Bell finish third at Windsor on the Racecall phone line.

Richard Hannon has had another three winners today. That now puts him on thirty three against our thirty two. If he can get another eighteen winners before May 20, he will have beaten our record which is the fastest fifty ever. Looking further ahead, if he can train one hundred before July 17 he will also have beaten our fastest hundred. If he does, it couldn't happen to a nicer man.

TUESDAY May 12

THE Sporting Life cameraman, Phil Smith, was supposed to come today to take photos for a feature on the yard for the paper. However, because of the bad weather and The Life being busy at York it has been abandoned. It has been wet and windy all night. The weather is worse here now than it was in January. No good for the horses at all.

There is a nice write-up in The Sporting Life about Glowing Value putting up a good performance yesterday at Hamilton. Rang our overseas jockey Lester to ride Sober Lad in a Listed race at the Curragh on Saturday. He has already ridden winners for us in Italy and Germany as well as a few places in Ireland, so let's hope Sober Lad gets him in the winner's enclosure this weekend. Only today, the Irish Field rang the carphone to tell me there are eight declared runners in the race and they were interested in who the jockey was for our horse.

Today we just have two runners at York. Gorinsky and Amron are both in the £15,000 sprint. Gorinsky always runs well at York and he actually ran a big race to finish fourth. He earned his owners £657 for doing so. Even for that Nigel Gray, the sprint handicapper, will probably put him up a few pounds. When Heather Bank won six lengths at Newmarket he put him up 16lb. Last week the bloody man gave him a further 2lb just because Master Planner, the horse who came second, won. So although Heather Bank hasn't run since the Newmarket race on April 16, after one race he has gone from 80 to 98.

On the way back from York, John and I stopped off in Leeds to get our hair cut. It's very difficult to find time to do these kind of things with going racing every day of the season.

We received a letter from the Jockey Club today. The scrape the vet took from Laurel Delight at the last meeting at Warwick when she ran was active. I therefore get a fine of £400.

WEDNESDAY May 13

WORKED the two-year-olds four furlongs on grass. Paris House strode up four furlongs with Another Episode and Tino Tere. Paris House seems as well as ever after his Newmarket defeat. Fylde Flyer and Heather Bank both run shortly. They really burned up the turf for a couple of furlongs.

As we were giving the horses a pick of grass after their work, the cuckoo flew over. That's the first time I have actually seen a cuckoo for years.

On our way to York with Jo and John we passed my old school, Victoria on York Road in Leeds. That brought back a few memories. Jo and I are staying overnight at the Grand Hotel, Scarborough for a racing forum as I am on the panel. John is flying down to Kempton for the evening meeting with Wally Swinburn. He rides our filly Mamma's Too. It's soft going there and that should suit her.

According to the car radio it's going to be hot and sunny tomorrow. I hope they're right. My right shoulder has been giving me jip this past few weeks with arthritis. Mind you I suppose it's only to be expected. I have broken it and my right collarbone five times. Some Sun will cheer it up a bit.

York had brilliant sunshine with a huge crowd in attendance. They were all there to see Sabre Rattler get beat a neck in a photograph. He ran a super race, having just got collared in the last few strides. There was no pay day for our other York runner Amber Mill.

After watching Alnasr Alwasheek win the Homeowners Dante Stakes Jo and I set off to Polly Tierney's Etchingham Stud at Slingsby to see a two-year-old owned by Bob Lofthouse which he wants us to train.

Going through the beautiful Castle Howard Estate reminded me of the last time we were through here. It must have been twenty five years ago when Jo and I brought the kids on a picnic. I liked the horse, which was by Dominski out of a Bustino mare. We arranged for our box to pick him up tomorrow as he's already broken and ready to come into training. Polly has installed a camera patrol screen in her kitchen and we watched a mare who is about to foal any time now.

On the way to Scarborough at a place called Ganton, were dozens of sows turned out in fields on both sides of the main road. They had little igloo-type huts for their homes. What a lovely sight that was-most unusual, too.

Looking out of the hotel window I saw lots of kids playing in the sea. It's remarkable the change in the weather. Richard Pitman hosted the racing forum. Andrew Hoyle, sports editor of the Lancashire Evening Post accompanied me in the talk-in to four hundred racegoers. They were a good lot and they enjoyed it just as much as we did.

THURSDAY May 14

LOOKING out of the hotel window the North Sea is bathed in brilliant sunshine. With a heat wave predicted somewhere in the eighties, there is nowhere better to be than York races on a nice day.

First thing this morning I rang Alan up to do the entries and decs. from the carphone as, believe it or not, there are no phones here in the bedrooms. It's a lovely hotel though.

Jo and I were just having breakfast with Graham Thorner and Dick Pitman when one of the punters from the racing party came over to Richard to tell him he was leaving now. He wasn't going to the races today-he'd received a phone call telling him his son had died following an accident. Isn't that sad? We went to my old riding pal Jimmy Fitgerald's so I could ride out to keep me in trim for Saturday.

Our first runner at York, Fylde Flyer, doesn't run until 4.10pm, so close to another old friend of mine, Paddy Farrell and his wife Mary, we dropped in on them. Paddy unfortunately broke his back from a fall on Border Flight in the 1964 Grand National.

At York it was a red hot summer's day with another huge crowd. The ladies were out in their straw hats and summer dresses, adding more colour to the scene.

Fylde Flyer, despite his many followers from the Blackpool Gazette, could only finish seventh in the Group 3 Duke of York Stakes. Our two-year-old, White Creek, ran a creditable race without troubling the judge.

We were invited to a barbecue by John Barrett and his girlfriend Ruth Dix. There's no problem getting there as it's on our way home. John's sister Anne was there too. They have had horses with us for quite a few years now and we are all great friends. We had the most super barbecue out in the open. Jumbo prawns, fillet steak, kebabs, chicken and lots of salads.

It's always good going to John and Ruth's. The first job Ruth does is give me a tour round all the animals. She's worse than me in this field. Not just mares and foals but rabbits running loose, canaries, golden pheasants, bantams, ducks, cats and dogs. Where animals are concerned, you name it she's got it or if she hasn't got it, she had it. If she hasn't had it, she'll get it!

FRIDAY May 15

IT'S nearly 2.0am. All my dogs are flat out fast asleep here in the room. I have just made a cup of tea. Everywhere is peaceful and quiet. Jo is in bed fast asleep. This is the best time for me to take stock. It gives me time to think. Pondering over the last couple of days Amber Mill and Fylde Flyer ran a bit flat at York, as did Mamma's Too at Kempton. I have made a note for them to get scoped and blood tested. We'll also take a worm count tomorrow. They looked super at the races. Amber Mill, in fact, was awarded the best turned-out. Let's hope it's only a temporary setback. Perhaps with the climate going from wild, wet, windy weather to this extra hot couple of days, they couldn't handle it. Anyway, for my peace of mind, I will get these horses checked over.

We gave the horses a nice pick of grass after work and walking among them they looked good. In fact, they look better than ever. They have all come good in their coats. It's a worrying job training racehorses. One cannot get the smug feeling for too long.

John and I are Thirsk-bound where we run Daaniera, Langtonian and Garnock Valley, a colt by Dowsing. This is the two-year-old we bought out of the Doncaster Breeze-Up Sales. He goes really well at home. Threepence and Bergliot run at Newbury.

The Benham Stud rang to let us know that one of our brood mares Hollia had had a colt foal by Clantime. That's good news. It was such a nice day at Thirsk I gave my panama hat it's first outing of the season. Garnock Valley finished third in his race. Daaniera was fourth. The two Newbury horses ran well, both finishing third.

The reports from the horses that got scoped shows they have some viral infection. If this spreads to the others I will close down for a while, give every horse a worming, treat the infection with the vet and put all the yard on Vi Sorbin, a multi-vitamin boost. Let's hope it doesn't come to that, but I will if need be. We have some very good horses and in the long term it's worth it.

SATURDAY May 16

QUITE a busy day for the yard today. Three runners at Thirsk, two at Headquarters, four at Southwell, on the all-weather, three at Hamilton and Sober Lad at the Curragh.

I am galloping off to Newmarket to ride in the celebrity charity race. Others taking part are John Francome, Stan Mellor, Frazer Hines, Wally Swinburn (snr), Tom O'Ryan, Greville Starkey, Edward Hide, Robin Gray, Claire King and Elain Mellor.

Alan and I did the time-consuming job of completing the entries for next Thursday and Friday before I set off with Pat Knight, who's here again for the weekend.

As Pat was driving my car down the A1 to Newmarket we saw a car completely upside down on the northbound dual carriageway. The police were there and two fire engines and an ambulance were rushing towards the scene. No other vehicles appeared to be involved, thankfully, but it was a mess.

Looking at the mileage on this car it's done 9,948 miles. Must be due for a service. I had better give it a day off as it hasn't had one yet. Arriving at Newmarket the first job was to go and get some of the town's famous sausages.

There was a huge crowd already at the races when we arrived and it was early too as our race was the first at 1.40pm.

I was told that John Francome and John McCririck on The Morning Line had read out from the Daily Star that I was complaining about the handicapper over-reacting after Heather Bank's last win. Jim McGrath said the handicapper was justified. I bet the prat doesn't say sorry he got it wrong if Heather Bank finishes out the back. Tomorrow there will be no mention of it. All he will do is talk a lot of balls about something else.

Michael Bell's little filly, which I rode in the race, didn't let herself down on the firm ground. Edward Hide rode the winner and by the way he performed he should be the next to make a comeback. Greville Starkey was second with Stan Mellor third. It was a bit of fun and we all thoroughly enjoyed it.

Sober Lad was unplaced at the Curragh and Clangold I watched run second on SIS from Thirsk.

It was nice to see Rodrigo de Triano win the Irish 2,000 Guineas at The Curragh.

Heather Bank and Windpower were both unplaced in the big sprint at Newmarket. As I had argued, the handicapper putting Heather Bank up 18lb for his last win never gave the horse a chance to win. He handicapped the horse to stop him. The way he treated the second horse, Double Blue, he must be some relation to the owner. That horse has won his four only starts this season. Mr Gray assessed our chap Heather Bank at 9st 7lb top weight, giving Double Blue 13lb. Even Windpower for winning only two races in his life at Carlisle and Pontefract gave Double Blue 4lb and he was only 1lb better in for getting beat five lengths by him at Newbury. Weight will bring horses and donkeys together, and trainers have a right to whinge when the handicapper abuses his position.

From Newmarket Pat and I went on to Southwell. On the way John Carroll rang me on the carphone to tell me how the horses ran at Thirsk. He rode a winner there for Captain Wilson only to be disqualified and pick up a four day suspension.

At Southwell we had a winner, Super Seve and a third. I listened to the commentary from Hamilton where our Music Dancer also won.

SUNDAY May 17

I ENTERED tomorrow's runners. We also had the vet up to scope some more horses as Sober Lad ran a stinker in Ireland. Some of the horses in the yard have a viral infection. We will just have to battle on and isolate certain ones until we get it cured. Rest assured we will work at it.

Ruby, our secretary, gets married today at 2.0pm. I am giving her away as her parents are no longer living.

The photographer took lots of photos of Ruby in our house and in the yard before she set off for Cockerham church. Ruby couldn't have wished for a lovelier day for the wedding. It was brilliant sunshine. I was very warm in my dress suit. I had the same problem a couple of years ago at Royal Ascot in a heatwave. The wedding ceremony went well. The cameraman was there earning his keep at the church and also at the Pickering Hotel near Garstang where the reception was held for about sixty people.

LEFT :
HERE we are at the house-gate leading to the yard before moving off to Cockerham church for the wedding.
Note my dog Olly.

BELOW :
YOURS truly with the bride-to-be, Ruby, and Jo leaving for the church.

It was a very good meal and we had plenty to drink. I gave a speech as did the best man. Ruby and Roger, her husband, received lots of presents, they were still opening them when Jo and I came home at about 8.0pm.

Settling down in my armchair to watch George Cole on the box, the mother of a young lad who came here to work from Hamilton last night was complaining to me on the phone. Her little boy is homesick and wants to go back home. The worse thing ever to happen to this country was when the powers-that-be did away with conscription. When I was called up I didn't like the idea of two years in the forces. I thought I was God's gift to racing. It did me and many more no harm. Nor would it have done the young fellow who is missing his mummy. Soft little begger.

MONDAY May 18

WHAT a beautiful morning, very warm and sunny even at 6.0am. The horses are doing their roadwork without exercise sheets for the first time this season. They looked really good.

The findings on some of the horses that have been scoped have not been good. They have a respiratory infection. One would never expect anything to be wrong looking at them. They look a bomb.

Alan and I did the entries for Saturday where there are lots of meetings with it being the holidays. Then at 10.30am the vet came to do a little operation on the over-sexed Pilgrim Bay.

John and I are Edinburgh-bound today. We picked up Jimmy Fortune at Forton Services to save him his bus fare. Near Biggar we passed through some lovely countryside with lots of woodland. The fields look like they have never seen a plough. Very little arable farming. All the hilly fields had lots of sheep and there were plenty of beef suckler herds. On this warm sunny day it made travelling a joy. Mind you, with such beautiful scenery, you could never describe travelling to Scotland a bore at any time of year.

Today we sampled J Fortune's driving. If the stewards who dish out suspensions to jockeys for dangerous riding think that's bad they should sit in a motorcar with the little buggers.

At the races, again, there was a very big attendance on what you might call an eventful day. In the claimer Buy Nordan broke a leg. Just Baileys fell in the two-year-old race, landing Dean McKeown in hospital with head injuries. Before the start of the apprentice race Minsk carted her young jockey a couple of circuits.

We didn't visit the winning enclosure but we had a second and a fourth of sixteen.

In today's post I received a letter from her Majesty's representative sending me his compliments but regrets my application for vouchers for the Royal Enclosure has been unsuccessful in the 1992 ballot. I will never get to have tea with The Queen.

TUESDAY May 19

IT WAS a very warm and sunny morning. We steady-cantered the horses on our top moss where the grass is just like a thick carpet. Perfect going, ideal for the horses. When they had finished their exercise we washed and shampooed them off. Then we gave them ten minutes pick of grass.

Peter, one of Johnson's vets came to scope some more of the horses. The majority of them have a throat infection. Hence the reason for some of the two-year-olds not quickening or lasting the trip out when the pressure is on. If the two we run at Beverley run badly I will stop running the horses for a week to ten days and treat them all with antibiotics and Vi Sorbin. It would be nice to give all the horses a worming while they were on the easy list. Normally, we worm the horses every month but with such stringent tests after races we don't worm the horses during the racing season or give them anything while they are running.

Thankfully, Dean McKeown has nothing more than concussion from his horrific fall off Just Baileys at Edinburgh yesterday. Another big attendance at Beverley with lots of people with cars picnicking in the centre of the course, a thing I have never seen there before.

Our two-year-old Oscars Quest ran well to finish fourth, but our fortunes didn't last long. Kingston Brown ran moderately in the auction race. This confirms we have the dreaded lurgi.

In view of this I will shut up shop for a while and hopefully get rid of the bugs we seem to have acquired.

On my return from Beverley I had a shower and then took my dogs for a walk round the gallops where I get my much needed space and time to think.

Came back into the house, bent the ears of our vets, Seamus Purcell and Frank Dunne, about these unwanted bugs and the best way of dealing with them.

WEDNESDAY May 20

INSTEAD of working the horses we did as the vet said-just nice steady cantering so the horses get air smoothly without them gasping for it. It's a funny sort of virus in human terms. I suppose we would call it laryngitis. All the horses look well, no coughs or streaming noses. So hopefully, properly treated, it shouldn't take long to clear up. Flash, one of the head lads, went round with the vet to inject every horse with antibiotics. They are to be done again on Friday.

While the horses were ridden out, leaving the stables empty, Alan and a team of the lads dusted the cobwebs and sprayed all the insides of the stables with a pressure spray containing anti-virucidal disinfectant.

Most of the morning, in between lots, Jo and I have spent ringing up owners to put them in the picture. The ones we couldn't get hold of we have faxed or sent them letters. It's always best to tell the owners personally rather than they read it in the papers. Not one owner moaned. In fact, everyone was brilliant. They all agreed that closing up for a while was the most sensible thing to do.

We have made a ring of about two furlongs with shavings from mucking out-just to hack the horses round the bottom land to give them a change. We did a similar thing last year when the going got firm.

I will get my car serviced now. With 10,889 miles on its clock, it's certainly due.

A change for me in the afternoon to be rolling the gallops instead of going racing. While I was driving the tractor all the dogs were following. There was a hare squatting down in the grass. Rodgers, one of the Jack Russell pups, saw it and grabbed the poor beggar. When the hare squealed reinforcements quickly went to Rodgers' aid. The unfortunate hare was dead in seconds.

It was scorching hot at stable time. Just about all the staff were stripped down to their shorts leading their horses out in a paddock for a pick of grass after being groomed. Some of the horses were bucking, kicking and going bananas. They must have heard on the grapevine they were having it easy for a while.

THURSDAY May 21

JOHN HOYLES, our local agricultural contractor, came first thing to cut the grass in a couple of our paddocks. The grass will be round-baled, stacked up and later fed to the cattle when they are in the fold yard. We can then turn out some of the horses that are in training every day. The idea is to get the horses out in the open to enjoy a bit of freedom, more than stuffing themselves with too much grass. I did an interview with Judith Oliver for Pacemaker magazine, mainly about setting up one's own business-what it takes and what I think is required, and so on.

Leading the string first lot on Fylde Flyer round the roads we met, as we were on our way back to the yard, our neighbouring farmer Jim Mitchell's milk cows. About sixty or seventy came stampeding towards us. Fylde Flyer looks a bit like Roy Rogers' horse Trigger. A flashy chesnut with plenty of white about him and also a flaxen mane and tail. He stood his ground as we turned them towards their rightful direction.

Although we weren't racing at Catterick John has a ride for Captain Wilson. There is plenty going on at the yard. The men are still working on the new horse walkers. The fold yard muck is being emptied onto land where the cattle have grazed. New post and rail fences are going up in the paddock near the walkers.

The shaving ring is nearly finished. Hopefully we'll be ready for tomorrow's cantering.

This warm sunny weather has been a Godsend to our local farmers, enabling them to get their silage in uninterrupted. Looking at the Teletext John Carroll rode a winner. Fivesevenfiveo, a former horse of ours won at Goodwood. Super Rocky, another of our exes got beat in a photo at Catterick. It goes to show we do sell winners.

John, Ann Barrett, Ruth Dix, Jo and myself went to the Cottage at Goosenet for a meal. Before the meal we had a stroll around the gardens where there were peacocks and a nice fish pond with huge fish. Bede and Agnes Robinson provided us with a lovely meal.

FRIDAY May 22

HEADLINES in the Life and Post, Berry Shuts Up Shop. It also said that by this time last year we had trained fifty-two winners against thirty-four so far this season. To keep the dust down to a minimum we have put new wood fibre in the indoor school, resurfaced the walkers, swept and watered the lane. The hay has been shaken up and sprayed with a solution of glucose and water. After the horses have steady cantered the sweaty ones are washed off to prevent them sweating up again in this very welcome heatwave. We gave them ten minutes pick of grass afterwards. When we finished with the horses I went to Lancaster cattle market.

There were lots of heifers in calf, cows with calves at foot, but not all that many store bullocks. Most of them were plain beggars. When I buy cattle I like them to be good sorts. It's not much fun looking at something everyday you don't like. They are cheap when you buy and cheap when you sell them. Nine simmental and charolais bullocks caught my eye and finished up at Cockerham.

In the afternoon, I actually cut our front lawn-something I have never had the time to do in years. Alister, one of the vets, came and scoped Sabre Rattler as he's in a Listed race in Italy a week on Saturday. The Italians are keen to buy into him for that race. He was 95% better, that is real good news. It shows the treatment, thank God, is working. I may give him a gallop around Tuesday, then scope him again and see what happens from there.

Quite a few people have offered Jo and I a holiday in their villas while the horses are recuperating. I am not going but I really do appreciate their offers.

Walked round the cattle early evening with my dogs. The new ones have settled in nicely.

The seeds we put in that 30 acres are showing through and the field looks good.

SATURDAY May 23

MY weekly write up and tips in the Daily Star look good today. I have gone for Garah, Magnificent, Pursuit of Love, Romany Rye, Green Lane, Knock Knock and Cee-En-Cee.

Thankfully, the horses are getting better. I rode Fylde Flyer a canter. Just before we pulled up he scooted off again and gave an almighty buck.

The Yorkshire Racing Club came on a stable visit at 10.0am. There were about fifty in all. Some arrived on a bus and a few in cars. They were a good bunch, too. It was a lovely day for them. Around 11.30am they left the yard to go for a day's racing at Haydock Park. I hope they back plenty of winners.

Two of our paddocks are getting the grass baled-up and the fold yard is still getting mucked out.

Sam has arrived back from Tenerife looking as brown as Frank Bruno.

Jo, Pat and myself set off for Appleby at 1.45 pm. Arthur Slack, one of our owners, has invited us there to see the trotting. We were thinking about going to Cartmel but decided to go to Appleby and had a cracking day there. Saw lots and lots of people we knew and I didn't even have on my red shirt. It just shows you can't go far without bumping into horsey folk. Didn't back a single winner but had an enjoyable day.

After trotting we called into Arthur's place at Stonerigg near Hilton. Looking at his teletext I saw I'd tipped a couple of winners for the Star at 9-4 and 3-1. Arthur took us on a tour of his farm and showed us a two-year-old Swaledale ram he bought for £30,000 which was champion at Kirkby Stephen as a shearing in 1991. He also showed us the nicest Limousin and cross Charolais suckler herd you ever did see-forty-three cows all with a good calf at foot. Some sight that was.

We all ended up in the evening with Arthur and his wife Evelyn at the New Inn Brampton for a steak and a pint.

SUNDAY May 24

IT was another nice sunny morning when I went out into the paddocks that got baled up yesterday. Wally had turned the cattle into one of the paddocks to tidy the field up before we turn horses into it.

This heatwave has gone on for a fortnight now. The next thing you know the water boards will be saying they are short of water.

Alan Daly, one of our young apprentices, rode for trainer Paul Blockley at Haydock yesterday. I asked him how he went on-"Great boss, great, had some lovely pies and lemonade in the weighing room," he said.

That's dedication for you. Not many people came to the yard today but lots rang. Owners and the Press rang to get an update on the horses' problems.

Sam asked me to take him to the Manor as he goes up there for an hour or so on a Sunday when he is home.

It's not for bible practice either. If our lads are in there buying him drinks, as they haven't seen him for a while, he could get a bit under the weather. It can't be much fun propped up on a pair of crutches.

Our A Team are still mucking out the fold yard and spreading the muck on the land.

I have faxed next week's stories in for the Weekender-all about racing clubs and our dreaded lurgi. I also had to do my Star tips for the four televised races at Sandown tomorrow. That kept me busy for a while. It isn't easy picking winners. Yet when one's on a roll it sometimes seems like a piece of cake.

MONDAY May 25

WE put some horses on the walkers then rode first lot round the roads. Alan and I made a few entries for Saturday's meetings. The horses seem all right. Monday being a roadwork day we only cantered the ones who were entered. The horses will be scoped before we commit ourselves to running them. If you don't enter, you are not in. It's a bit sickening when I see races go by that suit our horses. There's a five furlong claimer at Redcar today with only four runners. Many horses of ours, overrated by the handicapper, are queueing up for races like that with the £10,000 claiming price we would be quite happy for some of them to change hotels.

Amanda took Sabre Rattler to our vet to have his knees X-rayed. Subject to the vet passing him, I have done a deal in which he will be sold to Italy. A Newmarket vet is coming up in the morning to scope him to see if it's possible for him to run in Italy next Saturday, as that's part of the deal.

Jo, Sam and myself went to our local National Hunt course, Cartmel. It's only a very small track in the Lake District and very difficult to see the racing. However, it's one of the best days out you could get. The atmosphere is something different. If you haven't been to Cartmel you should put that right and pay it a visit. It's brilliant.

It was a scorching hot day. Shirt sleeves order was permitted. The majority of men were in a sunbathing mood and had their shirts off. I am not in favour of punters taking shirts off at race meetings but in this holiday spirit of Cartmel anything goes.

When it was time for the Group 2 Temple Stakes at Sandown and feeling sorry Paris House wasn't in the line-up, I went to the Tote betting room to watch the race on the box. Snaadee, who on his day is a brilliant horse, certainly got his act together. He romped home to score stylishly from Blyton Lad.

Blyton Lad was third in the Palace House Stakes at Newmarket when Paris House was second so, on the book, we should have had a draw today.

TUESDAY May 26

LOOKING at the Redcar card in the racing papers, how on earth does Mick Easterby's Penny Hasset get in a handicap with 8st 2lb in a 0-95, the very bottom weight of all, when she has won five races 0-70 this season alone? Nigel Gray the handicapper has certainly let this one off the hook. If you tackle the handicapper, he will justify his actions by saying she started on a low mark at the beginning of the season. If he put her up at 16lb a time as he did Heather Bank for winning, she wouldn't have long to wait before she wasn't eligible for an 0-70. Even after all her wins she has a 63 rating.

Compare her with Threepence, who won a four runner maiden at Newcastle first time out as a two-year-old in heavy ground: In a further five runs he never gave the judge another anxious moment. This season he won a small graduation race at Warwick on an 87 mark-far too high a mark for what he has done. For winning that little Warwick event Mr Gray put him up to 96. So we cannot even run him in 0-95 races where the likes of Penny Hasset and Mark Johnston's Double Blue can mop up-and they do.

About 7.30am Andrew Edgar, the Newmarket vet, came to examine and scope Sabre Rattler. He reported that Rattler had a slight windgall. Also he still had a bit of mucus inside when he scoped him. He could not therefore pass him fit for the race in Rome on Saturday-which is fair enough.

I had a dental appointment this afternoon. I am still having trouble with my new teeth. The dentist has either got them mixed up with Esther Rantzen's or he wants me to break them in for Red Rum. Whatever, they are certainly a mouthful.

Jo dropped me off as she went on to Preston to pick up her car from being serviced and put mine in for the same. She collected me on the way back.

Today I had to turn down Mrs Cauce's invitation to open their Sale of Work Day at the Rectory on Saturday, June 13, in our village. I'd been asked to perform this duty in aid of multiple sclerosis. Unfortunately, as it's a Saturday, there are meetings at four venues, so I have no chance.

WEDNESDAY May 27

TO see how the horses were fairing we let most of them we felt were all right go five furlongs. We set them off at a steady pace then let them sling along from halfway. Just a couple didn't go very well but this could be because they have only been hacking about and needed sharpening up. Some blew quite a bit probably because they had been missing their gallops twice a week. We had cut their food down to prevent the horses going wrong but even so some of them had got a bit gutty in just that couple of weeks.

John Carroll is serving his suspension out until Friday. It's sad for him as he's just bought a new place with a bit of land. He could do with all the rides he can get at the moment. It's bad enough him missing his rides from our yard without being deprived from his spares through an enforced holiday.

The vet came to scope Fylde Flyer as I have him entered at Lingfield on Saturday in a nice £18,000 Listed race. This time the horse wouldn't let the vet scope him. He went bananas after the last time he was done. Some of the horses don't take too kindly to having a tube pushed up their nose and right down their throats. This fellow was creating so much the vet had to leave him. I will work him properly tomorrow and if he goes well I will risk him. If he goes badly, I will give him more time.

Alan, Wally and Dave, three of our A team went to Cartmel races. Today they have worked really hard fumigating stables and assisting the vets. All our staff have worked their pants off trying to get our show back on the road.

With this very hot weather the new young trees we recently planted are getting a bit burned-up. Martin has been watering them to prevent them from dying. Kevin and I got muck from the fold yard on the tractor and trailer and put half a dozen forkfulls round the base of each tree. It would be such a shame to lose them, they are really nice.

THURSDAY May 28

IT'S a blustery day-a good deal colder than it has been recently and it looks like it's going to rain.

Alan and I have spent a lot of time on the entry forms over the past few days. The Acorn Stakes, a race at Epsom which we have won for the past three years with Boozy, It's All Academic and Memsahb, is coming up soon. I am very keen to find a nice filly to enter to make it four if possible.

Some of the two-year-olds who look like they may be running soon were put through the stalls. Peter, the vet, came to scope a few more horses to see how they are progressing. I have noticed that some of them have been giving the odd cough this morning. Peter says that could be a good sign. It's their way of getting it off their chests. I hope he's right but I don't like hearing any horse cough.

Helen, from our office, has just handed me entries for the Ballyogan Stakes at Leopardstown for Monday-we have Food of Love in. There are only eight in it. David Abell, the filly's owner, could do with a bit of luck. He hasn't had much this season.

Arranged transport with Doug Francis to pick Food of Love up on Saturday night. She will sail from Holyhead to Dun Laoghaire. The journey takes about four hours.

Turning on Oracle as I do every night it was a great shock to learn Charles St George has died. Only the other day he rang me to ask how his brother Edward's horses were getting on and he was in good form.

It's nearly 10.0pm and I have just returned from walking my dogs. Looking at the sky it appears we are in for a storm. We can do with the rain now. It very soon dries up.

[215]

FRIDAY May 29

A YEAR today we had a treble at Newcastle.

The much-needed rain has freshened things up. Tomorrow's runners kicked on for a couple of furlongs up the straight and seemed all right. The rest did long steady work, except for Food of Love, who we put through the stalls as when she last ran at Newmarket she wasn't very sharp off the mark.

Looking in the Greyhound Life, Lisnakill Wish runs at Wimbledon in a Derby qualifying heat. Also, Jo and Gwen Viner have a dog between them called Fred's Lucy, who also runs at the meeting. She has only had one run and was second. Fred Viner rang to see if we required a box for the night. He said we could stay overnight at his house if we wanted to see the dogs run. Tomorrow morning we could go on from there to Lingfield. I declined, as it's work day here on Saturdays, otherwise I would have loved to have gone.

When we finished working the horses, I dived off to Lancaster Cattle Market. It's great to have a banter with the farmers. Today there were lots of stores of good quality on offer. Another nine Charolais bullocks joined our existing herd of 61.

In the afternoon Jo gave me a lift to Preston to pick up my car from Fairview garage. They didn't make as good a job of servicing it as Holdcrofts who washed and valeted the car after they had finished.

When stable time was over, I went with my dogs to make sure the cattle had settled and also to have a word with Olly. Never in his life has he been so big and fat. The old fella looks tremendous.

Charlie wasn't placed and Jo and Gwen's little bitch ran third.

SATURDAY May 30

ALAN'S birthday today. He is in good company as it is also trainer Richard Hannon's. In the Racing Post it said he was 47. I'd better check that out as he looks a lot older. You can't believe everything you read in newspapers.

First thing I worked the Ascot horses. The ground was perfect and they flew. That Palacegate Episode is only small but she hasn't half got an engine. In the past, every year we have had placed horses at Royal Ascot. This year, we have some really nice horses in, so hopefully we may get our first winner.

It's always busy on a Saturday, working the horses, doing two days' entries and going racing, especially when it's as far away as Lingfield is today. It was half past nine before John and I finally got off, leaving my able assistant Alan to work the rest of the horses.

Our only runner at Lingfield is Fylde Flyer. From there John and I are going on to Wolverhampton's evening meeting where we run Cranfield Comet. Oscars Quest runs in a four horse race at Edinburgh where George Duffield deputises for John. It's nice to be racing again, having our first runners for 11 days. A winner soon would give a just reward to the staff at our yard who have put in endless hours for the welfare of the horses and to get the show back on the road.

Travelling on the M6 just before Birmingham there are roadworks on both North and South sides of the road. On the North side, a crash had occurred. Five passing cars with inquisitive drivers in charge were involved in another accident. The first car stopped and the remaining four ran straight into the back of each other.

Later on, on the M25, three more cars had been falling out. This delayed us a further 15 minutes.

At Lingfield it was great to be on the track. Racegoers in abundance told me it was nice to see me back in action and wished our yard well. Watched our two-year-old Oscars Quest on SIS finish second in the Edinburgh claimer to the already three times winner Shadow Jury at odds-on. It was a pleasing performance for owner Peter Savill who would contemplate running Rodrigo de Triano in a claimer if he owned him.

Fylde Flyer looked an absolute picture in the paddock and John Bostock, his lad, was rewarded by getting the £50 best turned out prize. Fylde Flyer finished third, beaten one-and-a-half lengths to the good filly Central City,

HARRY GREEN
receives a plaque
from me.
This gent is an
incredible 101 years
young.

trained by birthday boy Richard Hannon. The next race on the Lingfield card was a 12-runner one-and-a-quarter mile trotting race. I would have loved to have stayed to watch only John had a ride in the 7.45 at Wolverhampton. We had to kick on, on account of the roadworks and the heavy traffic.

On the M40 a Land Rover in front of us hit the outside barrier, skidded and turned completely over. Remarkably and thankfully no-one was hurt.

After the third race at Wolverhampton, I was honoured to be asked by Godfrey Tabiner, the racing PRO, to present a clock to Harry Green, on behalf of the West Midlands Racing Club, who was 101 today. For years Harry was a respected clerk to a number of well-known bookmakers. Except for him being a bit deaf, he was otherwise in good nick.

Cranfield Comet was third in the last, no undue blowing or distress signals. Today's round trip was 561 miles in the car.

SUNDAY May 31

WE have had a nice drop of rain through the night to freshen everywhere up. The sunshine is brilliant this morning.

Laurel Queen strode out for two furlongs. Sharisa and Music Dancer had a lead out. These two are both a bit light-framed and when they worked yesterday they wouldn't have blown a candle out. They are our three runners tomorrow.

With it being such a lovely morning we also led out the Ascot horses for a pick of grass.

Yesterday's runners all ate up and are as fresh as paint. Linda, one of our travelling head girls, rang up from Leopardstown. Food of Love arrived there okay and she is well. Tomorrow she runs in the Group 3 Ballyogan Stakes, a race we won in 1983 with Bri-Eden, ridden by Steve Craine. Would you believe he beat Hot Princess, the dam of Rodrigo de Triano, the English and Irish 2,000 Guineas winner and maybe next Wednesday's Derby hero also, by three-quarters of a length.

Jo and I went to Bearstone Stud in Shropshire, where they held an open day for the Thoroughbred Breeders' Association. I was invited as a guest speaker, along with Nick Musgrave and Bryan McMahon, the Tamworth trainer.

The Bearstone Stud paraded yearlings, broodmares and foals, plus their three stallions, Mon Tresor, Puissance and Monsanto.

It was attended by about 90 people who sat on chairs round the outside of the indoor school to watch the parade. All of the horses looked really well. This wing of the stud itself is a new building which is both functional and pleasing to the eye.

Nick's speech was about VAT and the new levy for 1993. Brian spoke about breeding and National Hunt stock. The theme of my waffle was that far too many moderate mares were being bred from. Consequently, the sales rings are flooded every year with poor quality yearlings. If only breeders concentrated on upgrading the quality of mare they breed from and sent the no-hopers to do different jobs, there would be less young stock for sale each year. The breeder would also get more for their produce. It might not be a bad idea to cut down numbers. Let some mares miss getting in foal, say every third year or so. If women were to breed like some broodmares are expected to, imagine what the human population would be like. This speech, at a Thoroughbred Breeders' get-together, probably wasn't the best place to deliver it. These people deserve a better deal and, after all, it's only my opinion how in some way it might be bettered.

STEVE CRAINE (left) won the Group 3 Ballyogan Stakes at Leopardstown for us in 1983 on Bri-Eden (above), beating Hot Princess, the dam of Rodrigo de Triano. Let's hope our big hope Food of Love can put up as good a show tomorrow and bring back the Ballyogan to Cockerham again.

MONDAY June 1

ALAN has gone to Ireland for Food of Love's race. John and I are off to Redcar where Sharisa, Laurel Queen and Music Dancer are the Berry trio of runners.

Before we left Cockerham we cantered all the horses entered up to Thursday. Normally I would only canter to Wednesday but as they have missed some sharp work over the past couple of weeks, I wouldn't want them rusty.

Riding out, John Carroll told me that last Sunday morning he was burning a lot of rubbish from his new place, getting ready to build some new stables for our sad, sore, sorry, sick, lame and lazy horses not in training, when he had a visit from his new neighbours complaining about the smoke. They even called in the police. Knowing John, he could have had a couple of tyres on the fire. Anyway, it's only been his second week there and it looks like he has already made himself popular with the locals.

Reading in the Racing Post Barry Hills has closed his yard because of the virus. Also Major Hern won't be having many runners as his yard is infected. Ian Balding said in The Sporting Life, in a report about Selkirk's poor showing in France yesterday, that some of his horses were under the weather. I know how they feel

What bad luck for Saltburn trainer Mary Reveley missing out on her first century for winners of the jumps season by just one.

Our Redcar runners didn't have any luck but I am not putting that down to the dreaded lurgi. They just weren't good enough. The good news was that John rode Best Gun to victory for Bill Elsey, the Malton trainer, beating Cantanta, the 3-1 on shot.

On our way home, John and I stopped at the Coast To Coast Fish Restaurant in Kirkby Stephen, a quaint little village in the Eden Valley, where they serve the nicest fish and chips you ever did taste at a price even I can afford (especially when we haven't had a winner.) As JC rode a winner he made a rare move of putting his hand in his pocket.

As soon as we got back home I took my dogs for a walk round the cattle. Doing this I feel like a Kenyan Masai chief-his wealth judged on the value of his stock. They are in a fantastic pasture up to their knees in lush grass.

TUESDAY June 2

AT 4.25am I greeted Food of Love's return home after her fruitless trip to Ireland.

The overnight rain has made our ground perfect. As Two Moves In Front and Laurel Delight are Epsom and Beverley bound tomorrow, we let them sling along for a couple of furlongs. With Epsom being such a fast track they have to be sharp out of the stalls, otherwise they would never get into the race and it would be a waste of time going.

The Beverley and Epsom Thursday's runners did some sharp work. The rest just cantered.

Mike Burrows's crew have now finished work on the new walkers. Most of their bodging has now been put right. Our 'A' team are putting the membrane down over the stone on the whole area around the walkers, after which they will cover it with a foot of woodchip.

It will look really good when we finish it, which hopefully will be in time for Sunday when we have Laurel Racing's Open Day. The trees we planted around a few weeks ago are all in leaf and things are taking shape.

With me being away at Epsom, Alan and I are meeting at 9.0pm to finish off the week's entries, which we have been working on all this morning in between lots. We worked on them until the Racing Game came on telly. This week it was mainly about the Jockey Club. I thought it was very interesting.

Personally, I am not in favour of professional stewards. There are some moderate stewards and there are some very knowledgeable and good ones who do the job wholeheartedly for the love of racing. Our biggest problem is the lack of money we race for. The prize money at the likes of Doncaster, Haydock and some of our other good tracks are at times pathetic. Surely they could do better. It's degrading when the likes of Hamilton, who don't get anything like their crowds, run for more prize money.

Now we have had trotting at Lingfield, I must admit I like it. The flapping association will be next to stage racing on our tracks, as some of the prize money must now be down to their level.

WEDNESDAY June 3

JO picked up the car for our four-day Epsom stay while Alan and I finalised tomorrow's declarations. The bride assured me she had put everything in the car and hadn't forgotten anything, as she has been known to slip up occasionally in the past.

With JC at the wheel of my car we set off at 7.30am. Steve Hagger, Wally's father, picked up my hired suit from Weybridge, who have my measurements, and delivered it to the Epsom stable yard last night. Or should I say I hope he did. I am travelling down to Epsom in a fawn pair of slacks and a white sweat shirt with bold black lettering on the front that reads: "Only elephants should wear ivory." Hardly the attire for Epsom on Derby day.

When we went to collect the badges the first person we saw was Robert Sangster. He was carrying the biggest plastic carnation you could imagine. No doubt he'd been conned into buying it by some gypsy. Handing it over to me he said: "Here, Jack this will suit you better than me."

Our two Epsom runners did not trouble the judge. Dr Devious won the Derby well, giving John Reid his first winning ride in this great classic, and Peter Chapple-Hyam his first Derby win on only his second season training.

That is some achievement.

Jo and I are staying at our Epsom and Ascot Hotel, Fred and Gwen Viners. The four of us went to Chobham to the Four Seasons Restaurant for a meal. It's good there and we often go when in this area.

Our three runners at Beverley evening meeting were all unplaced. Arctic Appeal even went off at 5-2 favourite. It's been hard to get a winner since

JO and myself enjoying the atmosphere
of Epsom on Derby Day.

our comeback from the virus, as is often the case when one wants something badly.

We still have a bit of pressure on. We are often asked at the races: "How are your horses, are you over the virus? You haven't had a winner yet".

We will soldier on. I don't feel suicidal just yet. Although I would love to be patting one of our steeds on the neck in the winner's enclosure soon.

It was sad to hear that Robert Morley died today of all days. He loved Derby Day. It was said he wouldn't take any work on this day. A fact he wrote into his contracts. It was the most important day of the year for him.

THURSDAY June 4

RANG Alan up to declare tomorrow's runners and enter the horses for next Tuesday's meetings, and to have a chat about yesterday's runners and the horses in general. I made a few necessary phone calls on the carphone as I don't like running up Fred's phone bills.

In addition to Tuscan Dawn and Memsahb running at Epsom, we have Classic Storm and Glowing Value running at Beverley.

Pat Eddery cantered Tuscan Dawn down to the start only to find the horse was lame on his near fore-so he was withdrawn.

I bought a 30p pencil from the Timeform man giving him a 50p piece. Having no change we tossed the coin-50p or nothing. Wouldn't you know it, he won the call.

Memsahb got squeezed up at the start and Cradle Days, Willie Carson's mount, nearly edged her over the other side of the track. You could say we have been having a bad run. The nearest thing to winning was Classic Storm who finished third at Beverley.

We had tea at Fred's before all going off to Wimbledon greyhounds where Gwen and Jo's bitch, Fred's Lucy ran. No fairytale ending for Lucy either. She had a few problems in the race and finished last.

FRIDAY June 5

ALAN and I yet again had to get together via BT to discuss tomorrow's declarations and Wednesday's entries.

Reading the sporting papers and studying the form over a cup of tea at Fred's I would say that Charity Express at Catterick was a good thing, if this black cloud wasn't hanging over our yard.

Bergliot, who got her name from a Norwegian Viking Queen, also looks to have an each-way chance at Epsom. And it wouldn't be an impossibility for Andrea's Girl to win for our Sam at Southwell.

With eight runners at four meetings it would be a great confidence-booster if we could visit the winners enclosure sometime today.

When Jo and I set off for Epsom races it was absolutely throwing it down. The ground is now soft. Only a couple of days before the Derby, and they watered the course.

I called at the stable yard just before racing to see how the horses were. Palacegate Episode, who runs in tomorrow's £10,000 Acorn Stakes, where only three have been declared, had a little nick on her off hind leg she got while travelling down here yesterday.

Linda, one of our travelling head girls, had got to work on it leading her out, hosepiping, bathing, praying. She kept an Animalintex bandaged on her leg overnight to keep the swelling down. This morning she is feeling it but only fractionally. Hopefully by tomorrow she should be all right.

Bergliot ran well to finish fifth in a race full of incident as Gorodenka Boy kept dumping Ray Cochrane and Silent Prince wouldn't enter the stalls.

I went to the Press room in the paddock area to give my selections and summary of tomorrow's televised racing for my weekend slot in the Daily Star. While I was in there I saw on SIS the nicest sight I have seen for twenty days. That was Charity Express with John Carroll on board winning the first race at Catterick. There's more. Ten minutes later our Palacegate

Racing won the five furlong handicap at Southwell. Gorinsky also ran a big race to finish fourth in the sprint, so let's hope we are back in business again properly.

We parked outside a paper shop in Ashtead so I could look at tomorrow's runners when Sammy McKeown, who I was friendly with in my army days, and who is also the father of jockeys Dean and Dale, was tapping on the window.

"Come and have a cup of tea. Dale only lives round the corner," he shouted. When we eventually got back to Fred and Gwen's, the old boy opened a bottle of champagne to celebrate our winners.

On Oracle there were two pages with the headlines: "Berry's team back on course," and "Express shows no charity."

The Viners and the Berrys went to the Cloche Hat at Burrow Hill for a bit of a celebration. We had a fabulous night.

SATURDAY June 6

JO AND I got up at 5.45am to go to the Epsom stable yard to see how Palacegate Episode's leg was doing.

It had been raining through the night so the going's bound to be soft.

Even at this time in the morning the traffic on the M25 is quite heavy.

The filly's leg was a good deal better than it was last night. Linda and Steve Porritt had put her on the hosepipe and walked her out for half an hour. Thankfully the leg had gone down a treat.

Borrowing The Sporting Life from Stuart Dalgleish, the Epsom stable security man who I know very well, having served with him in the King's Troop when I did my National Service, Jo and I went to the stable canteen for a cup of tea and a chat with the lads. I often do this when I go to see our horses at the yards. Training horses hopefully hasn't changed me very much. I still like to feel I am one of them.

In the Life's Lifestyles column, Scottish trainer Linda Perratt has nominated me as her racing hero. Thank you very much Linda.

Of the four meetings where we have runners today our yard has the highest number of winners at three of them in the last four seasons.

Palacegate Episode 1-2 favourite to win her race failed to give the Clive Brittain-trained Anonymous the 6lb and was beaten one and a half lengths by her. Not all gloom though as Mr and Mrs Hislop told me their filly is very good and they think a lot of her. They are not bad judges. They owned and bred the great Brigadier Gerard.

At 3.45pm I went up into the BBC Radio 5 commentary box as I had been invited to join Peter Bromley in giving a preview of the Gold Seal Oaks.

User Friendly won, beating the favourite All At Sea. It was great for a British owner and breeder, Billy Gredley, to win this fillies classic. Also for George Duffield the jockey and the in-form trainer Clive Brittain. I was pleased also to see the local horse Pearl Angel, trained by Brooke Sanders, finish third. I bet there would have been some party in Epsom if that lady had won.

Travelling home on the M42 in the centre lane on the southbound side was a car upside down. Just like the one John and I saw last week on our way back from Lingfield. There were three police cars and two ambulances in attendance.

Listened to Murray's Mazda's race on the carphone-he finished second beaten a neck.

Saw the horses back from Epsom at 11.30pm. They had travelled well and looked no worse for the trip.

ANONYMOUS (left) wins at Epsom on Oaks day, beating our Palacegate Episode (right).

SUNDAY June 7

IT'S a lovely sunny morning-a great day for Laurel Racing Club's open day which starts here at 11.0am. Yesterday, some portable toilets were delivered and a tent was erected in the middle of our three furlong cantering ring. Last year, when the club held their open day, it absolutely poured down.

Declared tomorrow's runner. Also made and received lots of phone calls to catch up on things I'd missed during my absence at Epsom. I rang in my stories for next week's Weekender, which were about Mary Reveley being so unlucky getting to 99 winners and missing out on the 100th, and Harry Green, the old boy from Wolverhampton.

People started arriving around 10.30am. We parked their cars in the centre of the ring in lines. There was a disco with the inevitable mike, a bouncing castle and a small house full of rubber balls for the kids which Olly my dog soon found. He was in there with the kids jumping after every ball. He loved it.

Food was plentiful too. Roast beef, hot dogs, ice cream and a licenced bar. It was a really great day for the 800 people who turned up. They were a lovely friendly crowd.

We worked ten horses for their benefit at 11.45am. After which the yard was opened up to them so they could walk round and see the horses.

It's amazing how far away some of the people had travelled from. They came from all parts of Britain and one man came over especially from Southern Ireland.

When everyone had gone, Alan, Wally and Kevin went into the ring with a tractor and trailer to pick up the rubbish to be burned. It didn't take them twenty minutes to clear up. People had gone out of their way to put their rubbish in the bins provided. They even had a collection in a bucket for our staff.

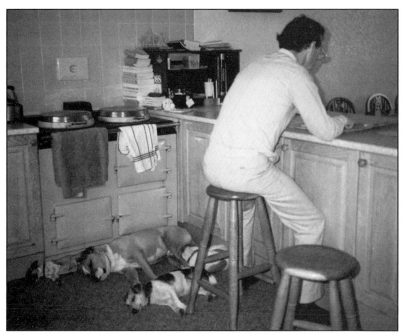

HERE'S me in typical pose in the kitchen :
The master of Cockerham and his hounds.

MONDAY June 8

ON our table top in the extension to the house is a box of cooked sausages and beef burgers that were left over from yesterday's open day. I've given them to my dogs before Jo got them. I hope she wasn't intending feeding me on them to get out of cooking.

Having finished my routine jobs, John Carroll and one of our apprentices Steve Haworth and I set off in my car to pick up our Sam from his flat, before going on to Nottingham. He soon had John and I hanging his washing out on the line in his garden. It's not possible to get away from Sam's without being landed with a job or two. He is the best organiser of work I have ever known.

We run Cranfield Comet in the apprentice race and Tom Piper in the two-year-old maiden at Nottingham. Stan Newman rang on the carphone to let me known Lisnakill Wish did a good trial and runs at Walthamstow on Thursday night.

The roads were nice and quiet today allowing us to get to Nottingham with plenty of time to spare. I wrote my article for the Weekender about our Open Day on August 2 and had a chat with Derek Thompson and Peter Scudamore in the car park.

Cranfield Comet ran a nice race to finish second. Tom Piper, a horse by my favourite sire, Music Boy, pinged the boxes. High Tycoon, the odds-on shot, missed the break and lost too many lengths. Our fellow made all to beat the staying-on favourite by two lengths. I must say that High Tycoon was unlucky.

To add more glory for the owners, Tony Atkins and Brian Piper, who also bred Tom Piper, the European Breeders' Fund contributed a prize of £600 to the breeder of the winner.

We dropped Sam off at his flat on our way home. It had been raining so the lady next door had brought his washing in. I only had to hang his clothes up in the wardrobe and John put some on the airing tank. We were let off the hook lightly.

I had a call from Jim Harris, a friend of mine from our apprentice days. He only owns the two-year-old full-sister to Polytain, the horse that won yesterday's French Derby. He told me he has had so many offers since that he has had to install an answerphone to cope.

TUESDAY June 9

ON a lovely sunny morning we gave tomorrow's runners a blow for a couple of furlongs.

Food of Love in blinkers, along with Echo-Logical, worked for four furlongs. She absolutely flew. The object of putting glasses on was that when she last ran in Ireland she didn't try very hard. I thought I'd try them just to sharpen her up as on her day she is certainly fast enough.

The rest cantered varying distances in pairs. Quite a few were sweating in the heat. They were washed off and led out for a pick of grass.

The yard has only two runners today, both at Pontefract. Press The Bell, owned by Sydney Mason and Sudden Spin, owned in partnership by the Countess of Lonsdale, Marchioness of Hartington, Lady McGowan and Colonel Sir Piers Bengough. As I am in good company today, I have put on my best suit.

When Prince Yazid Saud had his first runner from our yard at Nottingham I put on my double breasted pinstriped suit to look the part. He rolled up in a pair of slacks, a polo neck sweater and a pair of what looked like cowboy boots.

The vets have just had to put Jo's mother's dog down. He had another wobbler. Jo and I gave him to her when he was a pup. The old boy was about sixteen. It's a fair age for a labrador.

At Pontefract races Press The Bell looked a picture. From the best draw he flew from the gate but didn't come round the bend very well. He finished third at 9-4 on, but threw the race away by letting horses through on his inside.

In the extreme heat the day was full of incidents. The ambulance came in the paddock area to collect an elderly man who had been taken ill.

On a day as hot as it was I don't know who would want to eat them but the fish and chip van caught fire.

Most of the noble lords and ladies who owned Sudden Spin turned up to see their charge. Sods law-he ran a stinker and finished last.

Called into Forton Service Station on the way back to buy Jo's mum a bunch of flowers, seeing as she lost her old dog.

WEDNESDAY June 10

WORK day today. Most of the horses went well and appear to have finally rid themselves of the virus.

Tom Beston came to see his two-year-old Two Times Twelve work, as he was in the area on business.

Paris House, who is Ascot-bound for the King's Stand, went very well. Monde Bleu, the French horse that beat him in the Palace House Stakes at Newmarket last month, has won a Group 2 race in France since. In today's Sporting Life it says Snaadee, Sandown's Temple Stakes winner, misses the King's Stand as he's to take up stud duties in Australia.

Jill Campion, my old pal Andrea's sister from our village, came with me to Southwell as their horse Sobering Thoughts runs, and she wanted a lift.

Alan has gone with JC to Hamilton's night meeting, where we have two runners. Nothing looks good from the yard today at either meeting. We will need a rub of the green to get us in the winner's enclosure.

It was Spinal Injuries Association Day at Southwell and to compliment this worthy cause the track was graced with a good attendance.

The facilities at Southwell are the best around now. Ron and Richard Muddle have done a first class job with little help from anyone. In fact, they have had plenty of flak aimed at them. Now they are reaping the rewards from their investment, determination and sheer hard work.

Seeing Cormac McCormack, the bloodstock agent, I asked how business was. He told me: "Not great".

"Even the beggers who never used to pay have stopped ordering now."

Both the horses ran well enough without getting in the frame, to suggest they would win a small race another day.

Pat Rohan, the former Malton trainer who left England to train in the Middle East, was at the races on holiday looking better than ever.

THURSDAY June 11

A MORNING like this it's good to be alive-a brilliant sunny day.

With my dogs I went on the gallops to watch tomorrow's eight declared runners breeze for a couple of furlongs in pairs. Afterwards, we gave them a nice pick of grass. They looked so well hopefully it won't be long before they are on the winning trail again.

Lisnakill Wish is the star choice in big headlines in the Greyhound Life. Roger Jackson is tipping Charlie to win at Walthamstow tonight.

The Life and the Post have front page stories of wonder horse Arazi running in next week's Royal Ascot St James's Palace Stakes, where he will meet English and Irish Guineas winner Rodrigo de Triano.

It will be good for us British to see Arazi run on our shores for the first time. Jo drove the car to Newbury, where our Royal Ascot-bound Wokingham Stakes candidate, Windpower, ran a cracking race to finish third, beaten two heads. He was in front until the last four strides.

Speaking to Robert Sangster, Windpower's owner, in the paddock he said Rodrigo de Triano worked well this morning and is definitely on course for Ascot. So what a race the St James's Palace will be.

The last time I visited Newbury was when Paris House won the £100,000 Sales Super Sprint. Another good day there was when Tod beat the champion sprinter Dayjur in a photo. What a great day that was.

Richard Pitman interviewed me on SIS regarding our next week's Royal Ascot runners and our open day on August 2.

Alan went to Hamilton to take charge of our three runners there. Murray's Mazda obliged for us ridden by George Duffield. Not for the first time John chose to ride the wrong horse in the race. You can see now why jockeys have the reputation of being bad tipsters. Mind you, trainers aren't very far behind them either.

We drove from Newbury onto Chepstow's evening meeting. What a bloody rip-off-the charge to go over the River Severn toll bridge in the car is £2.80, and the man who took my money didn't wear a mask either. I thought the Welsh were famous for rugby, coal mining and singing. It's like the Welsh rhyme: "Taffy was a Welshman, Taffy was a thief, Taffy came to our house, and stole a piece of cheese."

At Chepstow, owners David and Dorothy Mort, who live near the course invited Jo and I to their box for a drink and something to eat before racing. In the claimer Echo-Logical, ridden by Pat Eddery, won by five lengths. I put him in a claimer because with a 96 rating it's difficult to find races for him. Thankfully no one claimed him as he is owned by 400 shareholders from all walks of life who get a lot of fun out of him.

On the way home Sonia and Stan Newman rang on the carphone chuffed to bits because Charlie had won at Walthamstow.

It's 1.50am. I have just seen the horses in from the Chepstow meeting. I will make a cup of tea and have a quick glimpse to see what's happened racing-wise on Teletext before going to bed. I have rather a busy day ahead tomorrow-or rather later today.

FRIDAY June 12

RODE Heather Bank, along with tomorrow's other seven runners just to blow them out. The rest of the horses had a nice long canter round our top moss, where the going on this sacred land is absolutely perfect.

Our Ascot entries look and feel well. Now we have had a few recent winners my confidence is growing. We have some lovely horses entered and it would be great to have a winner at the Royal meeting.

In between lots Alan and I declared and entered the horses. While Jo and I motored to Southwell Ruby phoned over the runners which I marked off in the Life. Did my bit for my Saturday slot in the Daily Star, made some phone calls and answered a few, too.

The yard's eight runners travelled to four different meetings, Southwell, York, Sandown and Doncaster.

At Southwell, Classic Storm won by a neck in the claimer. The other two two-year-olds running for the first time went well. Both should improve from their run.

With the recent hold-up some of the horses, especially the two-year-olds, are short of a couple of gallops. Next week they should be even better.

From the racecourse on SIS I watched Food of Love finish second at Sandown. We then set off for the evening meeting at Doncaster where Daaniera runs in the first race. The level crossing gates were shut leading

CHATTING to the Princess Royal at the Timeform dinner
at York. She did well in replying
to guest speaker John Francome, who was very good.

out of Southwell racecourse. My old guv'nor Charlie Hall used to consider this unlucky. Let's hope that's not the case today.

We arrived at Doncaster a bit early so I walked a couple of furlongs down the track to check the going-it was good.

Daaniera's owner, Seamus Purcell, came all the way from Ireland to see him jump out and hang nearly right across the track, throwing away any chance of winning. His owner's immediate reaction was, "sell him, put him in the sales." After a bit of persuading from me we decided on cutting him to see if that alters his attitude as the horse certainly has ability.

Having changed into my evening suit in the car park Jo and I set off to the Timeform Dinner at York.

It was gone 3.0am by the time I hit the sack. We had a good night at York. The Princess Royal was in attendance and replied to guest speaker John Francome who I might add was very good. The evening was hosted by Timeford Chairman Reg Griffin. He and Jim McGrath work their butts off for this great night year after year.

Lord Oaksey was the Sports Personality of the Year. I had the honour last year.

I was well drawn between Lady Murless and Sally Hall. We never had a dull moment. Both ladies are good company. Peter O'Sullevan auctioned eighteen articles that realised £61,150 for various charities.

SATURDAY June 13

IT'S our Sam's 27th birthday today. John Carroll has taken him to York races in his car, where our runner is Heather Bank in the William Hill Golden Spurs Trophy. John is then going onto Wolverhampton to ride Margaret's Gift, so I'm meeting up with Sam at York, then taking him onto Nottingham with me, where we have three runners. I'm hopeful of getting him back for a pint before closing time at the Manor to celebrate his birthday.

There were two extra passengers in the York horsebox-O I Oyston and Tim his pony. They have gone to Chris Morris's at Malton for a few weeks holiday. Chris looked after Olly for years before she married jockey Stuart. Chris will ride him round the roads for a while to get him in order for me to ride about on our open day on August 2. On that day we are dividing an acre of a paddock into square yards and Olly will be turned loose into the acre. The square where he deposits a set of droppings will give the lucky holder who has paid £5 for the square, the sum of £1,000 in cash.

Heather Bank ran a big race to finish third to the Geoff Lewis-trained Orthorhombus, netting Norman Harper, his owner £2,946 in doing so.

Pat drove the car from York to Nottingham. Travelling on the A1 around Ferrybridge and Barnsdale Bar I have never seen so many poppies. Some of the fields are red all over with them.

The Nottingham horses ran like hairy dogs. Margaret's Gift finished second, only beaten half-a-length, at Wolverhampton. While we were at Nottingham we met Fred and Gwen Viner. Pat drove back with Gwen as the Viners are staying with us for the weekend and Fred came with Sam and me. We stopped and had a feed at a Little Chef near Doncaster. Fred drove my car. While I am talking to JC on the carphone glancing at the speedo Fred's doing 80mph and he's still in third gear with two to go.

Fred went past the M62 turning taking us home via Leeds. He stalled the car at some traffic lights on York Road. The last time I sat in a car with a driver like Fred was my old guv'nor Harry Maw.

SUNDAY June 14

ALL the Ascot horses were led out for half an hour and had a pick of grass. They had done enough yesterday so needed a quiet day.

We just allowed tomorrow's runners to stretch their legs for a couple of furlongs. Daaniera, who ran on Friday, was disappointing. Seamus Purcell rang to tell me to sell him after having second thoughts from the other day. I finished up buying him. I am sure there is good in him, but I will still have the vet perform his operation on him tomorrow. Booked Lester for Sizzling Saga and Nicky Carlisle for Windpower at Ascot. JC's riding the rest. I will only have to get jockeys for Another Episode and Palacegate Episode if we run them.

DINING IN STYLE : Sixteen of us sit down to a special meal prepared by Peter Chandler and his team from the Paris House restaurant. It was absolutely brilliant.

Peter Chandler, Chef de Cuisine at his Paris House Restaurant in Woburn Park and proud owner of Paris House our good sprinter, came today with an entourage of helpers to prepare a meal for sixteen of us. I had bought this at a charity auction on March 15. Our guests were Tom and Nan Bibby, Stan and Sonia Newman, Fred and Gwen Viner, John and Vera Brown, John and Ann Barrett, Ruth Dix, Jo's mum, our Sam and Pat.

Peter and his crew arrived at around 12.0noon. At 1.30pm we started our seven course meal outside on the lawn in our front garden as it was a nice day. We had a lovely meal with beautiful wine. Every single thing, food, drink, cutlery, glasses, cooking utensils, table cloths-all brought by Peter and his crew. They waited on us hand and foot. It was absolutely brilliant. When we had finished I took Peter's staff on a tour of our yards and showed them the gallops.

At 6.50pm they packed everything away in their cars. All of us, except the Viners and the Newmans, who were travelling back to Ascot, went to our local church to the sponsored hymn day, at a fiver a hymn, that had been arranged a few weeks ago. The hymn I chose was "Fair Wave The Golden Corn", a favourite of my mother's years ago. There was quite a crowd in church. I would have thought, as Arthur Daley would say, "It was quite a nice little earner," for Roger our vicar.

MONDAY June 15

RODE all the Ascot horses round the roads for three-quarters of an hour. Then we did a steady canter for five furlongs. The rest of our string just did road work. I organised the vet to cut Daaniera and White Creek in the afternoon.

Brian Durkin, the owner of Tino Tere, came in my car with Sam, John and myself to Edinburgh, where we have four runners. In the first race our two-year-old Make It Happen won by a short head. Tino Tere finished fourth. Miss Parkes finished third and Oyston's Life dead-heated for fourth. John rode the last winner for ex-jump jockey Micky Hammond, who now trains successfully at Middleham.

There were rumours that Bill Pearce, the Hambleton trainer, had committed suicide. I know training racehorses at the moment isn't easy but that is going to extremes. I hope it is only a rumour.

Travelling home, Jo rings me on the carphone to say Helen Inskip, the lady who lives with Bill Pearce, has rung her. Bill has committed suicide and she wants to speak to me. I told Jo to ring her back and tell her I will ring her when I get home in about an hour's time. I rang as soon as I got back. Helen was understandably upset and wanted a bit of advice about keeping the show on the road.

What on earth drove Bill to taking his life when in today's Life and Post big headlines read 'Father Hayes lands the mother of all coups,' and, 'Father's

Hayes gives Pearce Special Lift'. His horse had been backed from 14-1 to 4-1 joint favourite. I would have thought that called for celebrations.

Jo took Sam to his home as he doesn't want to go to Thirsk tomorrow. He wants to watch Royal Ascot on the box, especially the Arazi v Rodrigo de Triano showdown.

I was also hoping to see these two clash tomorrow as we had Garnock Valley in the Coventry but I decided against running a maiden against such good horses. There must be easier things around.

Looking at the injury book just Sudden Spin a bit swollen-he got cut the other day. Palacegate Girl has a knock on a joint and there are a few more trivial injuries. Today we have started the horses on a herb mixture that we mix with honey and squirt 20mls down their throats at the beginning and end of the day. Hopefully it will help the horses recover from the after-effects of the virus.

TUESDAY June 16

THE horses cantered on the shavings gallop today for the first time this season. It was a nice change for them and they enjoyed it. Alan and myself were working hard on the entries from first thing as I will be away for a few days at Ascot.

John and I are Thirsk-bound today where we run Two Times Twelve and Oscars Quest, both two-year-olds. On our journey to Thirsk it was dry but a bit overcast. A few farmers were haymaking. I hope they get it in before the weather breaks. We buy a lot of hay out of Yorkshire. In Lancashire on that West Coast it rains so much that it's difficult to make good hay. In the past we've battled trying to make it. Not now though. The horses, sheep and cattle eat the grass and we buy the hay. By doing this we don't buy rubbish. A horse can't regurgitate. What you put down his neck stays. Therefore it has to be good or the horses will get all sorts of problems. Bad hay doesn't even burn well.

Oscars Quest finished in the middle of the field. John got a spare ride for Bill Pearce's old yard in the second race and won on it. In the next race Two Times Twelve was fourth. This was his first race back since being gelded.

John and I stayed on to watch the clash of the giants, Arazi and Rodrigo de Triano on BBC-1, only to see them both turned over by the Dermot Weld-trained Brief Truce ridden by Michael Kinane with Zaahi second. Lester on Rodrigo beat Arazi into fourth place. From where I was standing in the stands at Thirsk it looked as if LP had just waited a few more strides he would have got a lovely run up the inside-instead he went very wide past horses in the straight.

Looked round the yard a bit sharpish, had a quick shower and changed into my evening suit. Then Jo and I set off to The Pembroke Hotel at Blackpool to the Sportsmans Aid Gala charity ball. It was really good, too. There were a couple of comedians, Mick Miller and Lennie Bennett, singer Bobby Bennett and a few more singers in the cabaret. We had a lovely meal and a very enjoyable night, but it was late when we got back. In this job we work hard and play hard.

WEDNESDAY June 17

GETTING out of bed just gone 6.0am the sun is shining into the bedroom. It's a brilliant summer's morning. The birds are chirping away. They wouldn't be going on like that if they went to bed the same time as I did last night, or rather this morning.

Alan and I finalised the declarations for tomorrow and entered next Monday's horses. Jo and I set off for Royal Ascot at 8.30am. JC had gone earlier in his own car.

Our only runner today is Lucky Parkes in the Queen Mary Stakes. This little filly has had three races and won them all so she has earned a crack at this prestigious Group 3 event. It's All Academic was second in the race the year before last. It would be nice to get a winner at Royal Ascot. We have had quite a number of places but have yet to visit the winner's enclosure-it's the only meeting in Britain where we haven't. The day after the Royal meeting last year at Ascot, we won the Grand Metropolitan with Food of Love. This year we have some live ammunition to fire, although my confidence has been dampened somewhat with the virus still hanging round the yard over the past few weeks. A winner at the Royal meeting would give us a timely boost.

Arriving at the stable yard I got changed into my Ascot gear which had been delivered there by Gwen Viner, who had kindly collected it from Weybridge yesterday. As it was a warm sunny day Jo and I watched the Royal Procession. We then had a coffee and a sandwich before saddling our filly for the Queen Mary. She ran a great race to finish fifth of the thirteen starters, won by Richard Hannon's very small but useful Lyric Fantasy.

Marling won the Coronation Stakes beating Culture Vulture. Colour Sergeant won the Royal Hunt Cup, giving The Queen her first success at the Royal meeting for thirteen years. The ground was very fast. Confirmation of that must account for four course records being broken today.

In the evening the Viners, Jo and I went to the Wheatsheaf Pub at Westend, a village near Ascot. We were entertained there in their lovely garden by a very good jazz band. Afterwards, a buffet was laid on by Fred for his workers whose annual party it was.

THURSDAY June 18

FIRST thing I rang Alan up from my carphone to see how the horses worked yesterday and to have a chat about today and tomorrow's runners, a few jobs that wanted doing and the entries.

Reading The Sporting Life, the Norfolk Stakes, Sabre Rattler's race, looks a competitive event. I'm told Silver Wizard is a flying machine. Niche, owned by Lord Carnarvon and trained by Richard Hannon, the same combination who won yesterday's Queen Mary Stakes, is the only filly in the race. She can really trap, too. Every one of the nine runners has good form.

Jo and I got to Ascot early. Would you believe it, the number on my entry badge was 007. My initials being JB also. Some of the first people we saw were Steve Simpson and a party from the Blackpool Gazette who own Fylde Flyer. Flyer and Sizzling Saga run in the Group 3 Cork and Orrery Stakes. Fylde Flyer was judged the best turned out, earning his lad John Bostock £100.

In the race, Flyer was always well placed and ran really well to finish fourth of the seventeen runners. Sizzling Saga was whipping in for the rest of the field with only a couple of strays behind. Shalford, ridden by Michael Roberts, won in record time.

Drum Taps easily won the Gold Cup for his trainer Lord Huntingdon. This horse at six years old seems to have improved with age.

No luck in the Norfolk for Sabre Rattler. He finished seventh to the Lester Piggott-ridden Niche, only beaten about eight lengths.

In the evening we stayed in and had a lovely meal at the Viners. Fred and I watched the football matches-Holland versus Germany and Scotland against CIS, the Russian team.

FRIDAY June 19

TO GET a better start instead of waiting for the papers to be delivered, I collected them from the shop at 7.0am. Did my work with Alan on the phone. We have runners at three meetings, Ayr, Redcar and Ascot. Two or three horses have a good chance. Today is our last hope for this year of a winner at the Royal meeting.

Fred and I, for a bit of fun, picked out six horses each and have had a £1 Heinz bet.

Before racing, I went to the stables to see if our horse, Paris House, has that mean look about him which he has when he is in good form. I met Tony Lewis from the Daily Star and gave him my views and tips to phone in for my weekly slot in tomorrow's paper.

At 12.30pm Jo and I went for lunch in Tattersalls box as Michael Watt had kindly invited us. We sat next to Maureen and Clive Brittain.

Sober Lad, in the Windsor Castle Stakes, won the best turned out and £100 for his lad, Colin Williams. But he seemed more interested in the fillies during the race, than finishing first past the post.

Windpower ran a good race in the Wokingham to finish seventh of the 29 runners, only beaten about four lengths. The race was won by Red Rosein, trained by Captain Jim Wilson and his lovely daughter, Geraldine.

The Hardwicke Stakes was won by Rock Hopper and Pat Eddery, giving

Pat the honour of being champion jockey at the meeting and the Ritz Club Trophy winner.

Just before the King's Stand Stakes it started to rain very hard. Everyone, dressed in their finery, dived for cover-except us who got soaked waiting in the paddock for the jockeys to mount their horses. Paris House went that fast in the race he cut his own throat. We will definitely have to hold him up somehow next time he runs.

Thankfully, we did have a winner today with Cranfield Comet at Redcar.

Before leaving the course, I recorded a summary for the BBC about tomorrow's Grand Metropolitan.

After racing, the Newmans, Holdcrofts, Forsythes and Berrys met up at Fred's before going to the Four Seasons for a meal. While we were at Freds, the television was showing Coronation Street. All the ladies were still wearing their Ascot hats and, being Street fans, kept them on while Alma and Mike Baldwin tied the knot.

SATURDAY June 20

I AM afraid Fred and I didn't exactly skin Corals yesterday. We just had one winner in our Heinz bet-Cranfield Comet at 4-1.

Alan and I had a chat on the phone about working the horses, did the entries and sorted out the daily chores. Our yard has quite a few runners today.

Reading the paper possibly the best chance is Murray's Mazda at Ayr but I must admit it's an uphill struggle for us at the moment to get the winners.

Jo and I took my hired suit back to Weybridge before we went racing. When we arrived at Ascot we went to watch our Kentucky Dreams on SIS win the 20 runner seller at Redcar. Then we watched Chateau Nord finish second at Ayr, nicely ridden by our apprentice Paul Roberts.

In the Grand Met, both our fillies ran well without troubling the judge. The race was won by Taufan Blu. My selections for the Daily Star this week were Calpella, who won at 13-2, For Mog who won at 11-2, Miss Nosey Parker, who was third at 7-1 and High Tycoon who won at 5-2. Three out of four winners and one placed can't be bad.

On the way to Warwick's evening meeting, where we have two runners, we rang Rapid Raceline to hear Murray's Mazda finish second at Ayr. When we arrived at the course it was a lovely summer evening. The Leamington Spa Silver Band were playing delightful music to a large crowd. Our filly, Laurel Delight, finished second to Mrs West, carrying a 7lb penalty. She was just touched off in the last 50 yards.

In the previous race, Paris House's own-sister Petitesse, trained by Gerry Blum, also ran second. MDM Racer was up with the leaders, going well, but failed to negotiate the sharp bend coming into the straight.

After Warwick we called at Sam's to take him to Cockerham as he hadn't gone racing today.

SUNDAY June 21

WHILE the horses have been a bit off colour with the virus we have been giving them a syrup mix down the back of their throats twice a day, with a big needle-less syringe. When it's time to give them the dosage, all the horses come to their doors looking and whinnying for it just like kids.

I finally caught up with all the phoning and work that had piled up while I was at Ascot.

Tomorrow's runners just stretched their legs for a couple of furlongs. Gorinsky and Bergliot were turned out to grass for a couple of weeks to give them a break.

With it being such a nice day here at Cockerham, we had quite a few owners down to see their horses. In the afternoon my old army pal James Kearsley came. We got the dogs out and went for a walk around the farm and the gallops. James was amazed to see that the 70 cattle were so tame, following us everywhere.

Completed my copy for next week's slot in the Weekender, all about newspaper-owned syndicated horses. We train for two papers, the Liverpool Echo and the Blackpool Gazette.

In the evening, I took Sam back to his house, where we had a can of beer and a game of cards.

MONDAY June 22

FIRST LOT, I led the string on Langtonian. He is entered along with a few others on Wednesday, so we gave them a steady canter.

Alan and I entered horses for six different meetings on Saturday. It's a job we have to give lots of time and thought to in order to give the horses the best opportunity. Years ago horses were handicapped by the handicapper in that particular area. Now it's centralised and all the horses are rated we have to shop around. Like it or not, we are stuck with the rating the man with the pen gives us. We try to anticipate where the best chances for the horses will be. It can cost a fortune entering horses willy-nilly. Plus the fact that there are lots of races now with the added burden of a surcharge, which is often more than the entry fee. It's so unfair. The surcharge is to take account of the possibility of the race being divided. It so seldom happens, they should scrap the surcharge and ballot the horses out.

Jo and I set off at 9.5am to go to Bill Pearce's funeral, which was held at St Oswald's Church at Sowerby, Thirsk. The church was packed. The three hymns selected for the service were Onward Christian Soldiers, Thine Be The Glory and Jerusalem. It was a shame Bill had to go in this way. If he could only have found a shoulder to lean on, things might have been different. Among the wreaths and sprays in the church yard was one in the shape of a Panama hat, just like the one Bill used to wear, with a cigar tucked into the ribbon.

It was so sad travelling back on the A59 to pick up Sam to go to Wolverhampton's evening meeting. Just outside British Aerospace there is always a pot of fresh flowers and the grass is nicely cut. Today there are some lovely dahlias, probably placed in memory of someone being killed there.

Alan has gone to Edinburgh to take charge of our four runners. On the car radio, we listened to High Principles' win and then, in the next race, Classic Storm also won to give us the first two winners.

When we got to Sam's, as usual, Jo and I were put on fatigues. Cleaned his electric shaver (which wasn't before time, no wonder some days Sam goes racing looking like Marten Julian or Axl Rose). Hung out the washing. Put the hoover away. Eventually, we managed to get him out of his house or we would have been late for Wolverhampton, where we have three runners.

Oyston's Life got beat a short head in a 'photo. The three two-year-olds ran well without any success. Two finished fifth on their first runs. Thank God the horses seem to be coming back into form.

TUESDAY June 23

RIDING Fylde Flyer first lot and Sizzling Saga second lot I led the strings a nice long steady canter. No horse racing today for our yard, giving Alan and myself a little more time on the entries.

Lisnakill Wish, however, runs in the 9.15pm at Wimbledon. He has a poor draw, trap four, but for all that, he should still win.

Mike Burrows's gang have finished the new horse walkers. I must say they now look great.

Two loads of new seed hay came straight off the field, which was absolutely brilliant. Another load of the same stuff is being delivered tomorrow. It's been a great year for farmers making hay. These two loads have never seen a drop of rain. That is so important for horses. Cattle can get away with eating moderate stuff but not horses.

One of the shaving canters has got very deep. We are having to take it all up with tractors and put it into the muck spreaders to spread in the field where the grass was recently cut for the cattle. We are going to renew the canter with sand-more expense. It's a very costly job, maintenance for gallops when they are owned by the trainer. In some racing centres, gallop charges are paid to the person or company who own the gallops. In this case, it's us and the cost seems never ending.

In the afternoons we turn our fillies and geldings out in the paddock for a couple of hours. At stable time they are all brought in. Then, when the colts have been groomed, they are led out for a pick of grass. They love this and so do the lads, they can have a fag and a bit of crack with each other.

When stables were over, I had a shower then my tea, followed by a walk with my dogs to see the cattle and the horses that have been turned out for a mid-season break.

Just before 10.0pm, Stan and Sonia Newman rang to inform me Charlie had won. Out of 15 open races, he has won ten. What a dog.

WEDNESDAY June 24

IT'S work day and we have rather a busy schedule ahead so I got up early. Even at 5.0am all the dogs are on the lawn in front of the house waiting for me to let them in. This very firm ground looks like being here for a while so I have sorted out a few more horses to join those on their break.

Four horses are going to the sales at the end of the month. We will bring them in today from the field to get tidied up. Not all of them are going because they are moderate but costs are the deciding factor nowadays. If they don't look like having a pay day in the forseeable future, people can't afford to keep them on.

While we were working the two-year-olds on our near side straight in threes, one of them, Quality Brand, owned by Frank Dunne, broke a pastern. We had to get the vet in to put him down. It's always a rotten task to ring the owners to give them such bad news. Thank goodness it doesn't happen often.

Sam and I set off in my car to Carlisle. We have two runners and the going is hard. The seven races have only attracted thirty-seven runners.

Trentesimo our two-year-old in the first won by one-and-a-half lengths, beating Dahliz an odds on shot from Tom Jones' Newmarket yard.

Our other runner, Murray's Mazda, for some unknown reason reared up in the stalls as they opened and got left. You win some, you lose some.

I collected Sam from the weighing room and set off for the evening meeting at Chester to see to our two runners. There was a huge crowd there. Chester is a beautiful little course. The staff keep the flowers and the lawn looking immaculate. On a warm summer evening like tonight I couldn't imagine a better place to be.

John was driving his car with George Duffield riding shotgun when they got stopped for speeding on the M6 by a plain clothes car.

Gone are the days when the cops had a bit of fun chasing speeding offenders. It's all under the belt nowadays. More's the pity the same effort can't go into catching muggers, rapists and the like.

Amber Mill ran a good race to finish fourth in the sprint. Our two-year-old, Miss Whittingham, finished third in her race.

THURSDAY June 25

HAPPY Birthday to that grand old lady Dorothy Laird the Lady Jockeys' Association President who is 80 today.

Since the virus a few of our horses have got a bit burly through missing a few gallops. Although it's road work day, to get some of the fat off , these horses then did a long steady canter led by me on Cee-Jay-Ay.

Tomorrow's runners breezed for a couple of furlongs, watched by Oaks winning jockey George Duffield as he had been staying overnight with John. He didn't ride out as he said he had forgotten his jodhpurs-some story.

Another load of seed hay and a load of wood fibre has just rolled up. Also a film crew have arrived to shoot the new horse walkers. It's a fantastic sight mind-twenty four horses going round on the walkers together.

The fuel tanks are getting filled up with diesel and the joiner has come to measure up the front room for the new bookcase to go in. It's a real hive of activity round here today.

The dry hot spell in Cumberland has certainly taken its toll on Carlisle racecourse. It was bone hard, just like a road. Having said that Laurel Queen battled on gamely to record her twelfth win by a head for the Laurel Racing Club, who have over two thousand members.

Our other runner, Chateau Nord, also found the official hard going at Carlisle no problem and won the five furlong sprint, kindly sponsored by Norweb. In addition to sponsoring the race they gave £25 to the best turned out horse and mementoes to the owner, jockey and trainer of the winner.

Returning home I switched to oracle on the box. It read : "A brace of winners for Berry" and had a few nice lines to say about Laurel Racing Club.

After tea I went for a walk with my dogs and the cattle. Honestly, these bullocks are something different. The minute I go to the gate and shout them they come galloping up from all directions. I didn't get back into the house until nearly dark but it was great. This switches me off-I love it.

The thirty acres we reseeded is knee high now. It won't be long now before we get John Hoyles the contractor to cut it and round bale it to store and feed the cattle in the winter.

I didn't get to bed until late as I worked on my piece for the Weekender. The main topic was about what the Timeform Organization do for charities.

FRIDAY June 26

FOR A change, we steady-cantered the horses three times round the three-furlong ring. It's very warm this morning and there are a lot of midges flying around. Quite a number of the horses were sweating, so we washed them off.

First Slice, owned by the Cheveley Park Stud, runs for the first time at Newcastle tomorrow. We put her, accompanied by Make It Happen and MDM Racing, in the stalls.

After riding out two lots, we declared tomorrow's runners then Alan and I got on entering the horses for next Wednesday's three meetings. I tried my hardest to get finished so I could go to Lancaster Cattle Mart, but failed as the phone never let up.

One call was from Councillor Peter Pimley, wanting my views on establishing a racecourse on the beach at Knott End, like they do at Laytown in Ireland. Another was to let me know that my old pal Jack Allen from Pontefract is in hospital very ill.

I never managed to get a long enough gap to slide away.

With Jo gone to Newmarket to see to Cranfield Comet (who finished out of the money), Linda, one of the travelling head girls at Lingfield is in charge of Palacegate Racing. It would have been nice to switch off for an hour or so before going to Newcastle evening meeting as it means I don't have to leave until 3pm.

Whilst travelling to Newcastle I rang Racecall phone line and was delighted to hear that Palacegate Racing, with Gary Carter aboard, had won. With a bit of luck Garnock Valley could bring us our 50th win of the season.

Like most days recently it was warm and sunny at the races with a lot of people in attendance.

Never in the Red didn't try very hard in the Gosforth Park Cup, beating only a couple. He used up more energy eating his breakfast than he did in the race.

The two-year-old, although starting odds-on, ran no sort of a race and finished only fifth of the eight runners. It's a great leveller, racing. The race was won by So So, ridden by Alex Greaves-her 100th winner. This is a tremendous achievement for a girl because they certainly don't get the same opportunities as the lads.

SATURDAY June 27

BEFORE setting off for Chepstow with Jo and Pat, where Echo-Logical runs, I watched the first lot at work. It's very dry everywhere at the moment. In fact, we haven't had rain for about three weeks. The new trees we put in are taking a bashing with the drought and we are back working the horses on the all-weather.

On our 208-mile journey to Chepstow, Eileen Allen, Jack's daughter, rang on the carphone. Her dad had passed away just before 8.0am. Poor old Jack, he had been ill for a long time.

Hardly a day goes by when we don't come across some sort of an incident on our travels. Today, motoring on the M5, we could see a lot of black smoke drifting over the carriageway in the distance. When we got closer, we discovered it was a car parked up on the hard shoulder. Smoke was belching from under the bonnet.

Those robbing Welsh beggars were at it again, nicking our £2.80 to cross their bridge. They must have raked in thousands of pounds since the last

Chepstow meeting.

At the races there was a huge crowd, mainly in shirt-sleeves as it was a very hot day. Echo-Logical duly won, making him our 50th winner of the season. This day last year we had 78, but I'm not complaining. Seeing as we have had the virus, it's good to get back on the winning trail.

Looking down from the stands it was interesting and unusual to see seven women clerking up for the bookmakers. You never see that many up North. We went for a drink with the directors of the course after the race. Talking to Rodger Farrant, he told me there were 120 coaches here today.

Then, just before setting off for our next destination-Wimbledon to see the Greyhound Derby and Lisnakill Wish run-we had tea with Dorothy and David Mort.

We arrived at Wimbledon dog track around 8.0pm. Being guests of Mike and Janetta Gallemore, we were able to watch the racing while having a lovely meal.

Charlie ran his little heart out to finish third. It's brilliant going to the dogs. The only drawback is it's so far from home. It makes it such a long day. We didn't get back until 4.0am-it's nearly time to start work.

SUNDAY June 28

SENT Murray's Mazda out of the stalls and let Tuscan Dawn go with him for company. On his last run at Carlisle, Murray had problems in the stalls and Tuscan Dawn hasn't run for three months, having been a bit dicky on and off.

The rest of tomorrow's runners were just led out, having worked yesterday. Had a couple of hours on my old pal the telephone. This has to be the biggest bind of all. I know we have it to do, but if I wasn't careful I wouldn't see any horses for the damn thing.

Les Eyre, who trains jumpers, is building a new yard. He came to ours to see if he could get some ideas for his when he starts building and laying his gallops down. Surely that's a compliment.

Watching the Irish Derby, St Jovite easily turned the Epsom form around with Dr Devious to win the £355,000 by twelve lengths.

John Carroll also had a winning ride on Ancestral Dancer in Italy.

Quite a number of owners came today. As I've said before, warm weather fetches them out. In the afternoon I walked round the cattle with my dogs. Everywhere is getting parched and dried up. It's great to walk around in the nice warm weather but the vegetation badly wants some water. Our all-weather gallop is getting very powdery now, although we keep putting on new fibre. The top and bottom of it is just too dry. All the pounding it gets with the horses, it breaks down the fibre when there is no moisture.

Ivor and Colette Rivenaes came from Ascot to see their filly Bergliot and are staying at a local hotel. Jo and I went out with them to the Crofters for a meal.

MONDAY June 29

WE HAVE quite a busy day ahead, eleven runners at four meetings. Four of them at Hamilton, where normally we are very lucky with our runners.

Looking at the score of the trainers with runners, we have had forty-three winners from 1988 to 1992. The next best trainer on the list is Mark Johnston (below), with thirteen.

After doing my chores, declaring entries and riding out first lot, I set off for Pontefract on my own. One of our lads will bring my car back as John and I are going on to Hamilton by plane for the evening meeting. John came up from Newmarket where he stayed over from his Italian trip.

I arrived at Pontefract the same time as one of the ambulances. Racing cannot start until the two ambulances have arrived at the course. This is in case one has to leave to take an injured jockey to hospital, or perhaps a punter who may have been taken ill, leaving one remaining on the course.

Margaret's Gift, our two-year-old, ran well to finish second, beaten a length by Alasib, a smart newcomer of Mohammed Moubarak's (right).

Windpower also ran, but he never got a chance as he was always boxed in on the inside.

John and I were to have a taxi waiting for us outside Pontefract's owners' and trainers' entrance. The lady driver, however, had gone to the wrong gate. Not only that, she managed to get us lost finding the airstrip near Sherburn-in-Elmet. Finally we found it and boarded the single-engine plane and landed an hour and a half later at Cumbernauld about twelve miles from Hamilton racecourse. There was a taxi waiting for us when we arrived and this fellow knew his way.

In the first race, Creagmhor, our two-year-old, was found to be lame down at the start and was withdrawn. Chateau Nord was third and Miss Parkes was second.

High Principles was third at Wolverhampton and Tuscan Dawn was third at Windsor. A winnerless day, but a few places. John Carroll and myself got a lift home from Steve Meylan, one of our owners, and arrived home just gone 12.0midnight.

TUESDAY June 30

LET'S hope it's a case of quality rather than quantity as we have only Classic Storm running at Chepstow today.

Alan went with JC, not because I begrudged the toll charge over the Severn Bridge, although I must admit that it is a bit steep.

Leading first lot on Fylde Flyer for a long, steady canter, we then put four two-year-olds through the stalls.

The Bishop of Blackburn came down to have a look round the yard, along with Roger, our local vicar. They were late, so I missed them as we had four horses in the Doncaster Sales and time was running out on me.

Between Two Fires fetched 2,500gns, the top prize of the bunch. Not much for a winning filly over one-and-a-quarter miles. I would have thought she could make a nice hurdler. Still, there were lots of horses that either didn't sell or were sold for very little money.

Once, when we were at the sales, a woman came to look at a filly of ours in her box. As the woman was trying to feel her legs the filly wouldn't keep still. Angela, our girl, was amazed when the woman stood back and gave the horse an almighty kick in her stomach. Angela said: "Get out, you old bag. We didn't bring the filly here for you to kick the shit out of her."

At 2.0pm Liz Beeby kindly let me listen to the race from Chepstow via Racecall on her phone. Classic Storm, our two-year-old filly, won again for the fifth time.

On my way home, Jo rang on the carphone. We have had the fire chief down to inspect and make sure everything is in order for our Open Day on the 2nd August.

Stopping at a garden centre near Leeds, (I went this way home for a change from the motorway), there were two women serving at the shop. They had a nice tri-coloured Jack Russell terrier with them.

"How old's the bitch?" I asked, making conversation. "About sixty-four," she replied, thinking I was asking about the old lady.

It was absolutely belting down coming along the M61-first rain I have seen for a long time. Would you believe it, the rain stopped about four miles before Cockerham where we desperately needed some.

In the garden centre I had bought two brown stone squirrels. After I had finished my tea, I pruned the apple tree on our front lawn and tied the squirrels on the branches as if they were climbing. They look great. I'm really chuffed with them.

John Hoyles, the agricultural contractor, came to see if the new grass was ready to mow so we had a walk round with my dogs to inspect the job. It's doing well, but wants another week or so.

It's 10.40pm and it's started to rain. Great.

WEDNESDAY July 1

THE overnight rain we had wasn't sufficient to make any impression on the going.

Paris House and Threepence worked on the moss. All the rest worked on the all-weather.

Today's weather is a lot cooler but no sign of rain. Cashtal Queen and I Do Care run at Warwick. Palacegate Prince is our only other runner at Catterick.

Some joker on the front page of today's Life is giving forth on handicappers not being influenced by trainers, and form books taking priority over the address book. Horses should be handicapped to have a fair chance of winning not handicapped to stop them from winning no matter who trains them or how much they cost.

Whenever I confront a handicapper who has over weighted one of our horses, and I have many times, they always wriggle out of it and justify their views. Not once have they said: "Yes, I'm sorry, I have got it wrong!"

It's a pity they can't take some of our phone calls from the owners who ask: "Why can't we win with it? Get rid of the useless bugger or I am going to send it to so and so."

It's a hard job keeping the owners happy at times, especially when they get their monthly bill which often leaves them short even when they've had a winner.

Today, on my way to Catterick I called into my old school, Victoria in Leeds, as it was the reunion of ex-pupils, to mark the closure of the school 1904-1992. It was fascinating looking at the records of who had the cane from the headmaster and for what. In the report book it gave the name, and the punishment, like two strokes for spitting through the railings, for swearing, for bullying, for smoking and various other crimes. Many times I had the cane but only for being late. Therefore that minor offence wasn't registered.

At Catterick evening meeting there was a good crowd. The night was cool and overcast. Palacegate Prince ran third in the Palacegate Racing Selling Stakes. The race was sponsored by his owners, so there was no fairytale story to tell there.

THURSDAY July 2

AFTER putting a couple of two-year-olds through the stalls, stretching the legs of tomorrow's runners for a couple of furlongs, doing the entries with Alan, Jo and I set off to Pontefract to plant my old pal Jack Allen.

We gathered at St Thomas's Church, near Pontefract where there were about fifty mourners. The service was conducted by the vicar, who had a lovely Yorkshire accent. He led the service with sincerity and feeling. The 23rd psalm was sung as was the rousing hymn "Praise my soul the King of Heaven." Following the hearse to the cemetery and passing the Queens Hotel brought back memories of when I was Jack's best man at his marriage to his second wife, Bess.

After the funeral we headed off to Catterick where we had two, two-year-olds running in the second race, one of them was Laurel King whose owners sponsored the race. Once again no pipe dreams for the sponsors as their horse wasn't in the frame.

General Brooks on the other hand not only earned his owners Mr and Mrs Hibbert £235 for being third but also Steven Porritt the best turned out horse in the race.

Jo at the wheel and me riding shotgun we headed for our home county course, Haydock Park, where we had five runners for the evening meeting. The trend continues as in recent meetings, and again there was a large crowd. Unfortunately in the six races there were only thirty runners but this was possibly due to the firm going.

Sizzling Saga won the six furlong claimer by seven lengths, carrying 9st 13lb. In doing so he broke the track record previously held by this season's Royal Ascot winner of the Jersey Stakes, Prince Ferdinand.

I am very pleased to state both Sizzling Saga and Amber Mill won the best turned out for their handlers Peter Farrell and Kathy Boothman.

After racing we were invited to supper in the Director's Room which was very enjoyable.

FRIDAY July 3

IT WAS late this morning going to bed. I struggled with my copy for next week's Weekender which was about the Jockeys' Association of Great Britain, of which I was a founder member. It all came good in the end but my eyes must have been like pee-holes in the snow. That Fylde Flyer knew I had an early morning when we led out the string-he was bucking, kicking, pulling like a train in the much welcomed rain.

For a change we sent Heather Bank, Chateau Nord, Windpower and High Principles for a few days swimming to an equine centre near Settle.

Alan went to Southwell. Jo went to Beverley. I collected Sam from his flat and headed for Haydock where we had Trentesimo and Our Mica running in the two-year-old races.

It poured with rain and did no favours for the attendance. It was one of the smallest crowds I have seen at Haydock for a long time.

Trentesimo ran a good race to finish second. We had better luck in the seller, Our Mica won for the first time for owners Mr and Mrs Mike Dodds who are such a lovely couple. Fortunately there was no bid.

After racing it was still raining. We were given permission to work Paris House on the course, fitted out with a grackle noseband to see if he could be held any better. He had Another Episode, Nifty Fifty and Mamma's Too for company over the five furlongs. By now the going was soft but the horses went well. I was most impressed by Another Episode, he made Paris House pull all the stops out to beat him.

Dropped Sam off at his flat on the way home and had a cup of tea with him. Saw on Ceefax we drew a blank at Beverley and Southwell, still you can't win them all.

There was a fax waiting for me at home, confirming my book "It's Tougher At The Bottom" is going out in paperback for August.

SATURDAY July 4

FOLLOWING the rain we have had over the last couple of days we have now got some decent going again to work the horses properly. Racing starts early at Beverley, my venue, which puts me under a bit of pressure getting off on time with today being a work day. For Thursday and Friday there are eight meetings to work out the entries for.

Travelling on the motorway branching onto the M62 there were three cars stopped on the hard shoulder. At least a dozen Sikhs or Moslems were holding a meeting.

It looked as though one of the cars had broken down, probably over-loaded with weight. Either that or they had just got out for a stretch.

Police cars were in full force stopping speeding offenders on the M62. I honestly wonder whether the authorities want the cars never to exceed 70mph? Think of the revenue they would miss out on in fines. Now the big brother cameras are out in force on most major roads the police may be left to get more important results hunting out the real criminals. The poor motorist has always been an easy target.

Heavy rain at Beverley made the going very soft. Laurel Queen was entered in the Ladies Amateur race. She hates soft going so I withdrew her.

In the first race Kentucky Dreams ran a stinker in the seller but he couldn't go a yard in the ground. This didn't put off a man called Williams who must have seen Kentucky Dreams win at Redcar last time out when he beat nineteen others in the race. Colin Bradford-Nutter, his owner was cut up a bit as he also bred the horse. To him I suppose it was like selling one of his kids.

Our other runner, Memsahb won the three-year-old featured race. She relished the give in the ground. Glowing Value ran third in the Cock of the North, a Listed two-year-old race at Haydock.

Sefio was third in the two-year-old race at Nottingham's evening meeting.

Peter Manning, whose hotel we stayed at when on holiday in Barbados, came back home from Beverley with us to stay at our house for the weekend.

In the evening we all went to the Crofters for a meal and the food was great.

SUNDAY July 5

BACK TO the nice weather again, another beautiful morning.

We cantered tomorrow's runners just to stretch their legs, except for a couple of two-year-olds that haven't run yet. We just bounced them out of the stalls.

At breakfast time, we had that many folk in the kitchen it was more like 'Jack's Cafe' than Moss Side Racing Stables.

Took my dogs for a long walk round the estate to see the cattle. I'm afraid there are about 14 beasts fit and ready for the butcher. The drought has played havoc with the new trees. I had been hoping the recent rain might have revived them but obviously it wasn't enough.

A microlight club near us brought some aerial photos of our yards, houses, gallops and such. They were really good, I was impressed.

MOSS SIDE . . The place where it all happens,
from a birds point of view.
I think this aerial photo is really good.

Lots of people came today and I cannot remember the telephone being busier.

Colin Baxter, a neighbouring farmer, came to look around the yard with a couple of his relations who were farmers. We were sat on the garden wall, overlooking the main yard, talking about horses, farming, cattle for over an hour. It's great having a banter with the old farmers.

Walked round and saw all the horses. Believe it or not, it isn't very often I get the chance. We have 114 horses stabled. If I spent two minutes with each horse, it would take at least three hours, 48 minutes to get round them. Stable time is only from 4.0pm until 6.0pm. To make it possible to get around the yards we have two headmen, plus Alan and Jo my assistants, to sweep for me. In addition, we have one yard man, three travelling head persons, two office staff, a feeder and a helper, as well as a gardener.

A report is done every evening on the horses in a report book. If anything is wrong I go and see the horse. If it was possible, I would be like Henry Cecil from Newmarket and not go racing so much. But up North, owners like to talk to the organ-grinder and not the monkey.

Diane Bain, a girl student trainer, has arrived to work as a pupil for a few months, to learn the ropes. So if you have seen her with me at the races, I have not been lucky enough to be having it off-it's strictly business!

Peter, Diane, Jo and I went down to the Patten Arms for a pint. A nice change it was, too.

MONDAY July 6

VERY busy entering for next Saturday's meetings. Diane, the pupil, is a nice girl and very keen. My jaws ache answering all her questions as we were watching tomorrow's runners breeze a couple of furlongs.

Dave Parker, our amateur, drove John and I to Edinburgh as he rides Chateau Nord in the bumper, where there are four runners. The other three riders are girls.

Yet another large crowd in attendance at the races and with a nice family atmosphere. In the corner of the paddock area are plenty of amenities for the kids, like bouncing castles and ball games.

In the first race Dave got a good view of the ladies' backsides, finishing last. On SIS I saw Clangold run fourth of the 11 runners from Leicester.

In the maiden two-year-old race, Press The Bell won, beating our other runner First Play on her debut in the same race. She did well to take third place.

Miss Parkes was third in the seller.

Sandra Williams, the Racecourse Judge, gave me the list of the racecourse officials who are riding in a team at our donkey derby.

For the return journey home, JC and I elected Mr Parker to chauffeur us as he doesn't have as many outings as we have.

Listening to the Racecall commentary on the carphone, Two Times Twelve was second at Windsor to the odds-on Kamaatera.

When I arrived home, I saw to the mail, had a look at the injury book then spent another few bob ringing up the commentary services to listen to Rhett's Choice, who runs in my name. She is a filly by Beveled that never got sold on. That's the recession's fault. With the amount of juvenile winners we train, one would think they would be good to sell but it isn't always the case. The filly ran third of the nine that went to post. Thankfully, all our horses have run well today.

Jo took Sam to Ripon as he loves a bit of crack with the jockeys in the weighing room. John, Mark Birch, George Duffield and David Nicholls look after him. Sometimes he has a sauna. Tonight he came back-he had only fallen in the shower. He had gone in on his own and cut his cheek as well as giving himself a lovely black eye.

TUESDAY July 7

DECISION day on whether we run Paris House in the July Cup on Thursday. The problem is he is far too keen when the starting gates open. He goes that fast he burns himself out. To settle him and to help him to get Newmarket's six furlongs we put the grackle noseband on him we tried at Haydock, and let him pop quietly out of the stalls with two more horses for company. Thankfully he did it well and JC is pleased with him. I've read that the two French horses are not coming over so there may only be five or six runners. I have made my mind up he can run. Races are not won by horses staying in their boxes. Diane, my pupil, Steve Simpson, the Sports Editor of Blackpool Gazette and myself went to Newmarket as we run Fylde Flyer with his old pal Lester on board. They have teamed up only twice previously and won both times.

Arriving at the July Course on a lovely day with an exceptionally big crowd, Fylde Flyer, looking a picture in the paddock collected £50 for his lad John Bostock. Lester's record got tarnished but Flyer ran a big race to finish fifth with top weight of 9st 7lb. Lester said we should look for a conditional race for him. I would agree with that, too much weight will slow even trains down.

While at Newmarket I was interviewed by the radio and asked my views about Sunday racing.

Clive Brittain won the Cherry Hinton with a very nice filly Sayyedati, the only maiden in the race.

The much improved Saddlers' Hall won the Group 2 Princess of Wales's Stakes to maintain this season's unbeaten record of four out of four runs.

Listening to the 4.55pm race on my carphone I helped swell the funds of Tony Fairbairn, the boss of Racecall phoneline, in order to hear that Daily Sport's Gift finished fourth on his debut. One of the first jobs I did on my return home from the races was to turn to Oracle on the box for the day's happenings. It was with great sadness I read Pat Taaffe had died at the age of sixty-two. Pat was famous for his riding of the Cheltenham Gold Cup winner in 1964, 1965 and 1966-on the mighty Arkle, as well as every other prestigious jump race in the English and Irish calendar. He was a brilliant horseman and an absolute gentleman.

WEDNESDAY July 8

WE are back working the horses on the all-weather as the ground is as firm as ever again.

Redcar's evening meet has the honour of the company of Julie Krone, America's top lady jockey. The world's most successful woman jockey in fact. Born in Michigan, USA, 29-year-old Julie is 4ft 10 1/2in in height and weighs 7st 2lb. She has ridden in some 14,360 races and rode the winners of nearly 2,500. Some performance! Hopefully she can add another one to her remarkable total as she rides our first time out two-year-old Cockerham Ranger.

The VAT inspector came to look at the books. Would you believe it, I actually sold him a £5 square in the Olly pad for our Charity Open Day next month.

Diane and I went to Redcar. Jo was going to come only she had to do some shopping. Not clothes this time but food for the house. Racing every day as we do often makes that job difficult.

There was a huge crowd turned out to watch Julie Krone at Redcar's evening meeting. As much as we need rain it always comes when you don't want it. The rain came tumbling down, but even the miserable wet weather couldn't dampen the spirits of the diminutive bubbly Julie. She won the first

**JULIE KRONE and I discuss the merits of
Cockerham Ranger, who she rode to victory in the maiden race.**

race named in her honour, the Julie Krone Maiden Stakes, on the Moubarak-trained Al Karnak. Richard Whitaker provided the New York star with a winner in the fourth race with Gant Bleu.

The next race she had to sit out with it being an apprentice event. Claire Balding kept the flag flying for the girls by riding the winner. Julie's turn came to partner our debutante two-year-old we couldn't sell-Cockerham Ranger. He looked cool as a cucumber and like a million dollars in the paddock. When Julie saw him she said, 'he looks like being my third winner'. She bounced him out of the stalls, took up the running a furlong out to win nicely by a couple of lengths. I can tell you that her record in riding all the winners she has is not all luck. The lady is a good jockey. Joanna Morgan the Irish champion and Susanne Berneklint the Swedish leading lady unfortunately drew a blank but they rode very well.

My congratulations must go to the imaginative and forward thinking Redcar racecourse Chairman Lord Zetland, Sandy Brook and Yvonne Stapleton for making it possible for the Northern racegoer to see in the flesh the world's most famous lady jockey.

To end a good night Stan and Sonia Newman rang me on the carphone. That brilliant dog won the 9.0pm at Romford.

THURSDAY July 9

JC WINGED Never in the Red up the gallop for a couple of furlongs. If he put the same sort of effort into his races as he does at home we would visit the winning enclosure now and again. Red is a professional dodger. What an actor he could make.

A fax was waiting in the office from the Department of Transport North West Regional Branch asking if I could give a speech on safety to kids under 14 regarding the importance of wearing crash helmets when riding.

July Cup day at Headquarters where our flying machine Paris House runs for the first time over six furlongs. I am sure he will run well if we can get him anchored early on in the race.

Before setting off for Newmarket Alan and I did the decs and entries. I watched first lot do a nice long steady canter then got changed into the herringbone suit I had made by Andrew Vass, the tailor from Blackpool. It's beautiful material but the berk who made the trousers up could have been Stevie Wonder. I went to the shop so many times for fittings Vass's neighbours probably thought I worked there. In the end as a peace offering the boss actually gave me a jacket.

Travelling to Newmarket Diane drove. John had a good kip in the back. We met up with Pat Knight, who is a member there, and we all went to the TNT horse charter firm's tent, where we had very kindly been invited for lunch. Very nice it was too.

Paris House ran a very good race to finish fifth in the Group 1 July Cup. After the race we were invited for afternoon tea in the Bunbury rooms at

Peter Chandler's table. (Paris House's owner).

John rode Superbrave for William Jarvis in the Bunbury Cup then flew off with Willie Carson to Chepstow to ride our Tuscan Dawn in the 8.0pm race. Listening to the live commentary on the carphone on the way home the little fellow finished second to Mistertopogigo.

Picked up our Sam from his flat and brought him home.

FRIDAY July 10

TODAY we had the pleasure of David Nicholls riding out for us as he stayed with John last night on his way back from Chepstow's evening meeting.

Alan and I did the entries in between lots. If I am not careful, I could spend more time with entries than with the horses.

Jo has gone to Lingfield as Domes Of Silence and Trentesimo run there and she is staying over with the Viners as Sober Lad competes at the same venue tomorrow.

Having got my jobs done, I wangled it so I could go to the cattle market for a couple of hours and have a bit of crack with the old farmers. There was some nice stock in and that is fatal for me as 17 of them will be making their way up to Cockerham.

Before Diane and I set off for Chester I listened to Never in the Red run second in the Tony Budge £12,000 Sprint at York, putting £2,712 in owner Robert Airds' bank account.

The wagon driver dropped the cattle off in the field at the bottom of our lane. Their heads are all down happily eating grass. Since the fall of the hammer they have been penned up and had a worming injection at the mart before travelling home. So they have been put through a fair amount of stress today. From now on, it's all plain sailing for them.

It's a lovely afternoon, Chester should have a bumper crowd.

Cee-Jay-Ay ran in the first, an apprentice race, ridden by one of our kids, Steve Haworth. There were 18 runners. Being Friday night the roads were bad and three apprentices were late, which was fortunate for Alan Daly, another one of our kids who was there, as I managed to get him a spare ride in the race. Cee-Jay-Ay ran well to finish fifth.

Echo-Logical, our other runner at Chester, finished fourth with the top weight of 9st 7lb and the worst draw on the outside. His last two starts were wins in condition races so, all in all, he ran well.

Having a chat with trainer Alan Bailey, he told me when his horse, O'Donnell's Folly, died in the starting stalls at the last meeting at Pontefract, the stewards asked him if he could throw any light on the matter as to why the horse did it. Alan said: "Sorry, I can't. He's never done it before."

Alan, who seldom uses a sentence without the "f" word in it, added he didn't even swear.

Would you believe one of his two-year-olds is named Finmental. work that one out!

SATURDAY July 11

STAYED up early in the morning to write two stories for my slot in the Weekender, which were about Julie Krone at Redcar and advertising on jockeys' breeches.

Watching the horses work, the majority of them went well. Thank God, we seem now to have the virus behind us at long last.

Sizzling Saga must have known he broke the course record at Haydock's last meeting. He is flying up the gallops now. In fact, I have been so impressed, I've entered him for the Group 1 Haydock Park Sprint, which used to be the Vernons. If he does the same time as before, he shouldn't be far away. He didn't know the race was a claimer unless someone told him and he went that fast hoping to get a change of homes.

At 1.15pm it was raining quite heavily on our way to Chester. Along the M6, just before the M56, the traffic came to a standstill as there had been a crash. Thankfully though, not a serious one. Two miles further down the road, however, on the opposite side of the motorway, there was an awful-looking crash with a few cars involved. One in particular was very badly crushed and had a number of firemen around it with cutting gear, trying to get what looked like a woman out. The fire brigade, in my estimation, are the tops. On my travels I have seen them in action many times.

Another Episode finished fourth in the claimer and Windpower finished second, just touched off in the last few strides by the Alan Bailey trained Never So Sure to give him a double, which was a welcome change of luck for him.

Watching SIS from York, Arctic Appeal was third and Sabre Rattler was second. We haven't had any winners today but they have all run well.

On leaving Chester's course, the declarations lady told me last night's meeting had a record crowd with nearly 19,000 paying punters. Making further enquiries about the actual attendance figures, I was told it was 18,723, which is a record for an evening meeting. Tattersalls had to close the gates before the first race when the 5,000 safety limit was reached. This sort of thing happens quite regularly in Hong Kong. But for it to happen in England bears out what I have been saying all along, that I have witnessed large attendances recently and I sincerely hope the trend continues.

On our return journey everything was back to normal where the crash had been earlier. I hope that poor lady is all right. River Fire was unplaced to Foolish Heart at Southwell evening meeting, giving Michael Roberts his 100th win of the season.

Listening on Raceline, it was a great relief to hear our debutant two-year-old Allegrissima won the 7.0pm at Southwell.

SUNDAY July 12

GETTING up early as on a Sunday it's so quiet I get quite a bit done and it gives me some space. I have written a piece for the Weekender about handicapping. The men with pens won't like it but they don't have to earn their keep, trying to train winners. In fact, how they treat some horses, they earn their keep trying to stop us training winners.

After stretching their legs, Alan and I declared tomorrow's runners at Windsor, Wolverhampton and Edinburgh.

John Carroll, Wally, Alan and his pal Kevin Dewhurst hired a helicopter and arranged for it to land on our gallops and take them to Silverstone to see the British Grand Prix. As they were waiting on the gallops, someone from the helicopter firm rang to say they couldn't dare set off as it was too windy and heavy rain was forecast somewhere on their route. Too late to drive down, they all went to John Carroll's house to watch the race on his telly.

Robin and David Galbraith, who owned a moderate horse here, were told by me that he will have to change his address. Instead, I would lease them Cockerham Ranger. Anyway, they came down to sign the relevant papers today.

Michael Dickinson, who now trains in America, rang me up for a chat as he's over here for a holiday.

For the first time in a few days I have had time to take my dogs and walk round the estate to inspect the cattle and generally see how things are doing. Walking round the horses at stable time is almost a thing of the past at the moment as most race days I attend a meeting. With Flash and Kevin, our head men, the job is well covered. Tonight's stables went great, not once was I called in to answer the phone. Since we had that horrible virus we made the honey and garlic tonic up for the horses. We still give them their 20ccs either end of the day. They love it and start whinnying when it's taken round.

I was pleased to see Nigel Mansell won the 28th Grand Prix of his career.

MONDAY July 13

WE PUT Another Episode in the stalls, seeing as he threw the race away at Chester last Saturday by sitting on the back of the gates and getting left. Not much chance of him getting left today, he flew out of the traps like you know what off a shovel.

Breezed tomorrow's runners for a couple of furlongs. Cantered about half-a-dozen who seem to have put on a bit too much condition from having an easy time when they had the virus. The rest did road work.

JC, Sam and myself went to Edinburgh. On the way, driving through the fells on the M6, the RAF planes were flying very low, no doubt training or on manoeuvres. It reminded me of last Friday after Chester races. Barney Curley, Michael Roberts and Jimmy Quinn were all involved in a plane crash. As they were taking off, for some reason, they ran out of runway and landed in a ditch full of horrible, stinking green water. Jimmy couldn't swim so Barney carried him away from the plane in case it caught fire. Barney must have looked like Duncan Goodhew coming to the rescue, doing the breast stroke down the dyke with Jimmy on his back.

Another good crowd on a nice sunny day at Edinburgh, where one of my fans presented me with a lovely Pierre Cardin red shirt.

First Slice, our two-year-old, let her followers down by half a length in the first, but Laurel Queen soon recovered their money, winning at 3-1. We also had a bit of luck with Mamma's Too at Wolverhampton. I watched her on SIS just get home by a short head. Pat Eddery certainly earned his fee. The ground was cutting up after the much needed rain.

Our other Edinburgh runner, Royal Meadow, ran fourth. John flew with Kevin Darley to Beverley to ride Classic Storm for the yard in the 8.5pm race.

At precisely 6.40pm on my way back from Edinburgh I was interviewed live on the carphone for Radio Lancashire on the subject of racing and our Open Day on August 2.

The Racecall phone-ins are ideal for racing folk who want to listen to the night meetings. Two Times Twelve finished second at Windsor. But better news from our little filly with the one eye-Classic Storm. She won again, making her score six wins and bringing ours up to 60. She has now got to be favourite for the Channel 4 Trophy-the award for the horse with the highest number of victories in a season.

TUESDAY July 14

FIRST two lots did long, steady canters, led by me on Fylde Flyer and Langtonian. Some of the two-year-olds who haven't run yet were given stall work.

Beverley, Leicester and Folkestone will have the presence of J Berry runners today.

Reading in the Life I see David Hayes is the first trainer to train three hundred winners in a season in Australia. That's going some.

Travelling to Beverley with pupil Diane at the wheel in beautiful sunshine. It's plain to see the East Coast must have had some real storms recently, as the grain crops are flat to the ground.

Another large crowd at Beverley. The course looked in tremendous condition and the going was perfect.

Bold Mood and Memsahb ran moderately but our two-year-old Margaret's Gift, running out of the dreaded number one stall, soon had the smiles back on our faces. I have been going to Beverley races since I was fifteen and I haven't seen many sprinters win from that box. So I was more than pleased with her winning the maiden by a couple of lengths ridden by John, who had to suffer a couple of hours in the sauna as well as foregoing his morning cornflakes to do the eight stone weight. The filly is owned jointly by Mrs Holdcroft and Mrs Forsyth, who are both called Margaret. Their husbands bought her for them as a Christmas gift-hence the name Margaret's Gift.

On my return from Beverley I see on Oracle that gentleman Jim Joel, who died last March, left the bulk of his forty-one million pound fortune to charity. It will be a sad loss for National Hunt racing not to see the famous black and red colours on the racecourses this winter.

After catching up on all the racing news I rounded up my dogs and went for a look at the gallops, all ready for work day tomorrow. I moseyed around the cattle and the horses we have turned out for a rest. Then, after seeing our horseboxes return from Folkestone and the evening meeting at Leicester, both of which were fruitless journeys, I went to bed.

WEDNESDAY July 15

WITH overnight rain to take the sting out of the ground, we worked the horses on the grass in threes. It's nice to get back on proper gallops instead of the all-weather. A few of the horses are getting sore heels on the all-

**RUNNING INTO A STORM : John Carroll
brings home Palacegate Prince to win the first race
seller at Southwell for the 'Corporation'. When one of the
syndicated horses runs the crack in the paddock is great.**

weather because we have topped it up with new wood fibre and it hasn't got bedded in yet. We have to be so careful how we treat sore heels and cuts as some ointments contain camphor and, if it gets into the horse's system, like it did with our Meine Vonne Lady when we treated her sore heels with Pettifers healing gel, it can, in fact, lead to disqualification.

It was raining as John and I were travelling to Southwell. Some roadworks on the A1 held us up for quite a while-they seem never ending on that stretch of road near Doncaster. To add a little more frustration to the day, both railway crossings near the course were closed.

Palacegate Prince, our two-year-old in the first race-a seller-duly won. At the auction John Lucas, who is famous for pulling bids out of the sky or bouncing them off the walls, set the bidding off. Knowing John of old, I stood next to him. I never saw where the bid came from so I asked him who was the phantom bidder. He replied "a man on the racecourse, who didn't wish to be seen bidding", asked him to do the business for him.

On behalf of the owners of Palacegate Corporation, I bought that horse back for £3,600. The way he ran today he should win again. The crack in the paddock when one of the syndicated horses runs is great. One day, a lady told Gary Carter, who was riding one of the Palacegate horses, that he was her favourite jockey and that she had a photo of him hanging in her living room. She said that if he won on their horse today she would move it into the bedroom and he could come and see it whenever he liked.

Our other two runners didn't collect any prize money but ran quite well.

My car has got 22,222 miles on the clock.

THURSDAY July 16

HEADLINES on the front page of the Life, 'Lucas Antics Upset Berry' and there's a photo of Palacegate Prince winning, alongside another photo of John Lucas conducting the auction with some of the horses' owners and myself. When asked who started the bidding, Lucas said he was commissioned from outside the ring.

Made tomorrow's runners stride out for a couple of furlongs. Alan and I did the entries. Ruby, our secretary, came in with the mail to show me I had won two £50s on the premium bonds, plus a threatening letter from Tony Antoniades. The rest of the mail was of no consequence, although there was plenty of it.

Gerry Blum rang, posing as Mr Lucas the auctioneer-a right practical joker, our Gerry.

Only Hamilton and Catterick have our presence today-both are very lucky courses for us. At both meetings, our yard has had the most winners with runners today. We are 12 in front of David Barron with 32 at Catterick. Pat Haslam is next on the trainers' list at Hamilton with 13 to our 43.

This time last season we had our 100th winner at Hamilton with Our Fan. We have a couple of winning chances today but, being on 62, we couldn't possibly get near last season's score. A more realistic aim would be to train 100 for the season.

Jo and I watched Two Moves In Front at 10-1 beat our other runner at Hamilton, Tuscan Dawn, the 2-5 favourite, from the Tote Credit betting office, then we dashed out to watch Langtonian finish second here at Catterick.

Glowing Value was second at Catterick as was Daily Sport's Gift at Hamilton.

PHANTOM OF THE AUCTION : John Lucas, the Southwell auctioneer, conducts the bidding on Palacegate Prince. I'm standing next to him but I can't see where the bids are coming from. Fortunately, I bought the horse back for the Corporation for £3,600. The way he ran today he should win again.

It was good news to hear the Jockey Club disciplinary committee had reinstated Steve Norton's Mr Confusion in the Magnet Cup at today's hearing. It shows there is justice.

On our journey home, Jo and I called in to see Mel and Sheila Haughey at Kirkby Stephen before moving on to see Colin Bradford-Nutter, our owner who lives in the next village, Ravenstonedale. I promised Colin I would call as his Kentucky Dreams was claimed out of a seller at Beverley on July 4 and, seeing as they bred the horse, his wife Jean would like him back. There's more. Mrs Bradford-Nutter went into hospital yesterday with heart trouble so I wasn't exactly looking forward to the meeting as I don't even know where Kentucky Dreams went.

Thankfully, the Nutters were in good form and they had a message on their answer machine that their horse was at Ron Thompson's at Doncaster and, for a £1,000 profit, they could have him back. I told Jean to let them get stuffed and finished up leasing our filly, Rhett's Choice, to them for free. She has only run once and was third.

FRIDAY July 17

CHRIS MORRIS rang up to tell me she was sending Olly to Thirsk to meet our box as he was coming back off his holidays. I will be glad to see the old fellow. Chris's little girl Arryanne who is four, told her playschool teacher Olly is a lovely kind horse, but Timmy, Olly's pal, is a little bastard. He bites and kicks.

I had an appointment with an osteopath in Blackburn as I have been having a bit of trouble with my shoulder recently. Seeing Jimmy FitzGerald, who rode jumpers the same time as I did, hobbling round Southwell last Wednesday he should have been coming with me.

I was back in the yard to watch second lot canter. Dave Lindsay, a traveller, came to the yard, flogging his wares. He told me Jonathan Haynes, an ex-jump jockey who broke his back a few years ago and is now paralysed and in a wheelchair, parachuted out of a plane to raise money for charity. When have they had enough?

It's ex-jump jockey Michael Scudamore's 60th and Ernie Fenwick's 51st birthdays today. I bet they don't feel like jumping out of an aeroplane.

Sam has a young lady he met in Tenerife staying over here for a holiday. I am taking them to Hamilton's evening meeting with me. They are booked into a hotel for the night and coming back with me tomorrow from Ayr. I don't know how they are going to get from Hamilton to Ayr but knowing Sam he'll probably hitch-hike on his crutches.

Stopping on the way up for diesel I thought the mascot on my car, which I have had for years and swap from car to car, was looking slightly tilted. When I tried to straighten it up it broke off completely. Listened on Racecall to Lucky Parkes getting beat in a photo by Night Melody, owned by Peter Savill-the very same horse who beat Glowing Value only yesterday at Catterick. Peter's other two-year-old, Second Colours, who beat our Daily Sport's Gift yesterday at Hamilton, also turns out again there tonight. We oppose him this time with Make It Happen.

Peter buys horses to race and not to look at. We have trained quite a few winners for him in the past. Unfortunately, I upset him last yearling season, hence the name Savill is missing from our owners list. Nevertheless, I still admire the man.

A huge crowd saw Murray's Mazda at 7-4 on, finish fourth of the six starters. In the next Peter Savill's Second Colours won again-a good performance it was, too, for with yesterday's penalty he carried 10st. Make It Happen could only finished third.

Over the Tannoy a voice asked for Jack Berry, the trainer, to please go to the weighing room. That was to inform me someone had backed their car into mine.

In the last race Chateau Nord whipped the other four runners in. We have had better days. Still there is always tomorrow.

To end this eventful day as we were travelling down the A74 we got stopped by the police for a routine check. Arrived home 12.30am.

SATURDAY July 18

NOT a very good start to the day. As Alan and I are making the entries Flash comes in to tell us Windpower is lame, just before he was due to set off to run in the £15,000 sprint at Ayr.

Then, while I was watching the horses work, we were about halfway through when for no apparent reason Gloddaeth Isa broke a leg and had to be put down.

On my way to Ayr races, travelling on the M6 near Carlisle, there was an awful looking crash involving four cars that were all in a bad state. About ten miles from the races the offside wheel started screeching very loud. A stone or something had been caught in between the brake pad and the brake disc. At the garage where I stopped the man said it would go if I just turned the radio up a bit more, and took no notice of it.

I rang Racecall to listen to the Newbury Sales Super Sprint which as I thought, the Queen Mary winner, Lyric Fantasy won easy.

Never in the Red ran a big race on the top weight of 10st, just failing to hold off the late challenge of the almost white Absolution by a length-and-a-half, giving him 11lb. In the next race, my day started to improve. Laurel Queen won in a photograph beating Inseyab, who was third to her at the last Edinburgh meeting. Our game little mare has now won three races on the bounce and thirteen in all for her many owners, members of Laurel Leisure Limited.

On our return home, with the car full with Andria and Sam and John at the wheel, JC's grand prix driving style very soon got rid of the squeak with the stone. It was raining quite heavily on the way back. Around Southwaite Services we listened on the phone line to General Brooks, from our yard, finishing third at Wolverhampton's evening meeting.

SUNDAY July 19

GOT up early to ride my old horse Olly out. I gave him a short canter and he loved it. He was brilliant. Just like old times. I am certain the old fellow would still win races. He is in such good form.

After doing all the jobs, like getting tomorrow's runners out and declaring, I had a 10.30am appointment with Alan Bate, our new bank manager, and Ian Bolland our accountant. After driving round the whole estate and walking round the yards, I think Alan went away feeling his money was quite safe. Bruce Jackson from the Racing Post rang for any views on the flying filly Lyric Fantasy's super sprint win yesterday. I told him with 7st 8lb in the Group 1 Nunthorpe Stakes the filly will think she has got loose and Lord Carnarvon may as well book his holidays now. It would take Nigel Mansell in his pepped-up Renault to beat her.

Picked Sam and Andria up for dinner. We invited Jonathan Haynes round to join us. We all piled in my car and did a tour of the gallops and looked at the cattle. Jonathan was pleased to see everywhere as he used to ride out for us on a weekend before he left school. It brought back memories for him. Jonathan is the subject of one of my Weekender articles today. Very good it was too. This young man's courage is incredible. He told me about the days when he used to ride beach ponies on Morecambe sands as a seven-year-old and then showjumpers when at the age of 12 he won the junior championship at Hickstead. He also trained as a boxer as a youth. He is going to do another parachute jump from 10,000 feet on our open day, weather permitting on August 2. He was contemplating doing a bungie jump. Don't some mothers have them, eh?

We had a lovely dinner of roast beef, Yorkshire pudding, potatoes, three veg, apple pie and ice cream, cooked entirely by my Mrs, who is a super cook. We opened a couple of bottles of wine and had a good chat. It was great.

MONDAY July 20

IT'S THE birthday of my old pal, Paddy Farrell.

On today's agenda: stalls work for the two-year-olds that haven't yet run and for those who are a bit iffy. We also included Another Episode to make sure it wasn't a fluke the other day when he didn't do his old trick and sit on the back of the stalls. He's in a race at Sandown on Wednesday evening and it's got his name written all over it, if he gets his act together.

Nottingham and Ayr have the pleasure of our horses today, with four at both meetings. Looking at the papers, it will be a bonus if we collect a prize at Nottingham's evening meeting. Jo has gone to look after the horses there and no doubt she will be giving some of her new clothes an airing. She is forever buying clothes on her shopping sprees.

We look to have a couple of lively chances at Ayr, my favourite racecourse. This day last year we had a double.

As John and I were setting off I saw a damned magpie at the bottom of our lane. That's not a good omen.

Charlie Smith, the sports editor of the Daily Record newspaper, has kindly invited Mr and Mrs Berry for lunch at the races. If I can find a substitute there for Jo I might take her to lunch in Jo's place. One thing for sure, I won't be taking another man. I wouldn't like people to think I was bent. We had a lovely lunch. I was drawn next to Scotland's leading trainer, Linda Perratt.

There was a huge crowd of 9,114 paying people and the meeting attracted top jockeys like Lester Piggott, Willie Carson, Pat Eddery, Michael Roberts and John Reid.

Miss Parkes ran a bit flat in the first race. When she got back to the racecourse stable she had a touch of colic. Cee-Jay-Ay didn't try. Cockerham Ranger worried himself to death in the stalls and got so sweated up he came back from the race like an ice cream. He must have been expecting to see Julie Krone and John Carroll frightened him. Our last chance, Garnock Valley, looked all over the winner until the Tom Jones-trained Dahliz ran him out of it in the last stride by a head.

It's not the first poor day I've suffered after seeing a single magpie. No bonus came from Nottingham either.

TUESDAY July 21

ALTHOUGH I don't usually have many hours sleep, last night I had enough to dream I had a ride in an invitation race and the horse only had 10st. Stan Mellor (below) had a ride and his horse was set to carry 11st 9lb. I had been starving myself so much to do the weight I looked like Mahatma

Gandhi. I pleaded with Stan to swap me rides as he could have done 10st easy but he wouldn't. I was so weak, a valet on either side of me had to help me into the paddock. I then woke up in a muck-sweat.

We cantered the horses on the grass. With the drop of rain we have had recently it has made the going perfect. Paris House did a nice swinging canter, along with Sizzling Saga and went well in preparation for his tilt at Goodwood's Group 3 King George Stakes.

John and I are Edinburgh bound. We picked up Jimmy Fortune at Forton Services to save him a few bob and to keep him company. In return for the lift, I let him drive my car. Some driver he was, too. He ran over two kerbs on corners and stalled the car at a set of traffic lights.

On the way, we passed about three dozen motorbikes with foreign registered number plates. They looked as if they were attending some rally. They don't know how lucky they were. You should have heard Jimmy talking to fellow Irishman and jockey Jimmy Quinn on his portable telephone, you would have been in stitches.

Allegrissima, owned by Peter Chandler of Paris House fame and his neighbour, Lord Howland, won the two-year-old claimer by two lengths. In the other two-year-old race, our runner Drumdonna, ran a nice race to finish third on her debut.

It's a long haul back from Scotland and that's the fourth time I have been there in the last five days.

Arriving home at 7.30pm, I changed, gathered my dogs up and went round the stock and the horses turned out in the fields.

WEDNESDAY July 22

FOR a change I got up to feed the horses at 5.0am with Neville and Dave. Let's hope it's quality and not quantity today as we only have two runners, Another Episode at Sandown and Rhett's Choice at Redcar.

Sorted out the entries with Alan. All the horses worked in pairs on the grass. I only saw tomorrow's runners as I had another appointment with the osteopath in Blackburn at 8.45am. I had been asked by the Department of Transport to attend a meeting at Briercliffe near Burnley regarding the importance of children under fourteen wearing headgear whilst riding their ponies. After taking ages to find the place, as it was way out in the sticks, a young woman there told me the meeting had been cancelled as someone connected with it had broken his ankle.

John Hoyles, the contractor, is round bailing those seeds we put down. With it having 10 per cent barley in it this grass will be super feed for our cattle through the winter.

Sam and Andria went racing to Redcar with Jo and I. Alan went to Sandown with John.

Arriving at Redcar at 6.0pm it meant we were in nice time to hear the commentary in the Tote Credit from Sandown. Another Episode was five lengths in front with a furlong to go only to get collared by Walk in the Park. The good thing about that was the winner is trained by Rod Simpson, who was reported in the papers to be really struggling to survive even having to lead his horses up himself to save money. Racing cannot afford to lose characters like Rod.

We had a long wait before our filly Rhett's Choice ran, as it wasn't until the last race. She had the best draw but missed the break and had three or four attempts to get through a gap. Joe Fanning saw an opportunity open up and dashed through the gap which finally came on the inner and won by a length. This win compensated Jean Bradford-Nutter who has been given Rhett's Choice on a free lease after being so upset at her horse Kentucky Dreams being claimed last meeting at Beverley.

We didn't get home until 12.30am after taking Andria and Sam to his flat.

THURSDAY July 23

HAD a canter on old Olly, he was brilliant. I am getting him fit for our open day as that day I ride him to get around everywhere. His fans, and he has plenty, like to see him. You have no chance of seeing him down as a runner in your morning paper again. Although I am sure he could still win a race.

Just two runners again today, both at Hamilton, Palacegate Prince in the two-year-old claimer and High Principles in the six furlong handicap.

In the two-year-old race there were only three left in. First Play of ours was going to run but her owner rang up to ask me to take her out as he couldn't be there to see her run. It's a pity. She looked as if she would have won the race doing somersaults.

On the way to Hamilton I finalised my copy for my slot in next week's Weekender. It's about Jonathan Haynes the ex-jockey who broke his back riding at Southwell in 1980. Jon has agreed to do a parachute jump for charity at our Open Day on August 2. This week's article is about the rough treatment some horses receive from the handicapper. It will probably raise a few eyebrows but what the hell-it's true.

I don't know what's happening to us lately, but we were on the course at Hamilton a full hour before racing started. I walked a couple of furlongs down the track. The going was good to firm but there was lots of grass which made a nice cushion. Alec Ferguson, the groundsman, does a good job.

Our first runner, Palacegate Prince won easily, High Principles our other runner won the Arthur Balding Sprint by a length. I was particularly pleased to win this race as when we first started training near Doncaster Arthur Balding was our neighbour. I also rode a few jumpers for him when I was riding. High Principles is looked after by our apprentice Paul Roberts, who must get a lot of credit for this fellow's success. In the past the horse was very stroppy, but young Paul loves him and has coaxed him along. The owner, Mr Heathcote, recognised this fact and has given Paul a couple of rides on him in races. Not only did High Principles win the race, he also earned Paul £30 for the best turned out. On the way back home I had every intention of calling in at the Shap Wells Hotel near Kendal for the wedding reception of Kenny Slack, who's parents have Snowgirl with us. But, on reflection, what was the point, I couldn't drink and drive.

John and I therefore kicked on home, where I changed, rounded up my dogs and went to the thirty acres where they are still baling, wrapping and carting the grass. They packed up after 10.0pm when the light went.

FRIDAY July 24

GOT up early to start on my copy for next week's issue of the Weekender, where I talk about advertising on jockeys' breeches. I also did my bit for tomorrow's Daily Star. Having finished I went out into the yard to give the feeders a hand, the time being 5.15am.

We have lots of horses entered for four meetings. I just breezed them for a couple of furlongs to give them a blow. The rest of the string cantered steady round the three furlong ring three times and then were led away for a pick of grass.

The contractors are still wrapping bales of grass and stacking them. They got nearly four hundred bales-that should see the cattle through the winter.

Met JC on the Manor car park at 12.30pm to go to Carlisle, where our two runners, Oyston's Life and Margaret's Gift both ran third in their respective races.

I mentioned to Johnny O'Hara about the possibility of him going on holiday to Tenerife with our ex-jockeys for the winter holiday we are hoping to fund from our open day. The poor fellow was so touched he started to cry.

John and I picked up jockey Kevin Darley for a mad dash as our two-year-old First Slice runs at Ayr in the 6.45pm race. Laurel Queen and Soba Guest also run there.

We arrived half an hour before the first and we passed everything in sight. When we pulled up in the car park the car must have had stomach ache. It was pinking and making some weird noises. When I trade it in for a new one no doubt the garage will say when they sell it: One careful owner.

First Slice only beat one. Laurel Queen, the star she is, won her fourth race on the trot. Soba Guest was third, but only three ran. Taking a peep in the Tote Credit Office Trentesimo had won the first race at Pontefract's evening meeting for us. We've had a good day.

Went to my hotel, Fairfield House, as I am staying overnight with having runners at Ayr tomorrow. It's great here. First thing I had a swim, a jacuzzi, then a fifteen minute sauna. I had rung to ask Linda Perratt at just gone six this morning, if she would book me a room in Fairfield as I hadn't got the number and Linda doesn't live far away. She only booked me the four-poster bridal suite. And me on my own.

I had a lovely meal. Afterwards, talking to the manager, I find they've got the receivers in as they can't make a go of it. What's it all about.

SATURDAY July 25

FAIRFIELD is a lovely hotel overlooking the sea. First thing in the morning the seagulls are in good voice. The day started a bit dull and we have had overnight rain but the going should still be good for today's racing.

Ringing home I hear everything is all right. Paris House went to Pontefract to have a spin after racing. Gary Carter rode him and said he went well, that should put him just right for Goodwood's King George next week.

You would think I see enough horses at home but I still rode out for Linda Perratt first lot. It was good to have a bit of a chat to the lads. Linda has a couple of the old school to ride out for her. They go on about days gone by and a lot of old timers they mention I actually knew-that pleases them. Most of the youngsters don't want to talk about old timers. If it were possible they would ride out with walkmans under their crash helmets. We rode on the back stretch of the racecourse and the going was perfect.

Before I came back to my hotel to do the entries on the phone with Alan, I decided that while I was in Ayrshire I would drive out to have a look at the cottage where Robert Burn's was born in 1759. In good nick it was, too. The great man was only 37 when he died.

On my return to the hotel I finished my work then went straight into the swimming pool and sauna for an hour. It was brilliant.

We have sixteen runners today at four meetings, so hopefully we should visit the winner's enclosure somewhere. The law of averages says we should. At the racecourse I watched SIS from Wolverhampton. Two Times Twelve got beat a head to finish second. Better luck with Charity Express, who is leased by the Express Marie Curie Racing Club. Never in the Red was third in the valuable sprint at Newcastle. Two Moves In Front was fourth with 9st 7lb top weight in the nursery. You may have thought this fellow had been named after Peter Savill, the owner of the recently retired great old campaigner Chaplins Club. Echo-Logical won the claimer and on the very last second before claim time was up Mr Savill arranged for a man to put a claim in on his behalf for our chap. Martin, our travelling head lad was holding the counter claim in his hand as the bell rang time was up. Too late.

Our yard won the award for training the most winners on the Scottish circuit-a very large bottle of Courvoisier cognac.

SUNDAY July 26

TOMORROW'S five runners cantered for a couple of furlongs to stretch their legs to make sure they were all right. To help us over our virus we used some potion that is made in France. Jonjo O'Neill told me at Ayr yesterday that his horses have the virus, so I have arranged for him to come over this morning to pick some up. It's always good to see Jonjo, he is a star man.

At 10.30am Jo, Pat, Diane and myself set out on a historic occasion-Doncaster's first Sunday race meeting. Before leaving, I had made countless phone calls and answered just as many. One important call I couldn't get through was to the Liverpool Echo to let them know their horse was subject to a claim yesterday. I will probably get some flak from the 400 punters who owned him. Still, he did them well. He cost 8,200 guineas as a yearling, won twice as a two-year-old and three times as a three-year-old so they have had plenty of fun with him racing.

Travelling on the M62 we passed yet another caravan turned over while being towed. The number of caravans we have seen smashed up this season alone must make them a very hazardous risk on the roads.

On arriving at Doncaster racecourse to an enormous crowd of some 23,000 people, the atmosphere was electric. I have never seen so many young people at the races. I just hope they keep on coming. Jo and I were invited to Coral's box where we had a very nice lunch. Desert Orchid, Teleprompter and Red Rum were at the course. Rummy, for a 27-year-old who had been seriously ill in January, looked tremendous.

Going down in the record books with the first winner on a Sunday in British racing is Lady Butt's Savoyard, ridden by Walter Swinburn and trained by Michael Jarvis. The prize money was very good and went right down to sixth place. We had four runners but it was not to be for our yard to go down in the history books as a winner trained by J Berry.

The huge crowd were all well behaved and smartly turned out. It was a most enjoyable day. John Sanderson, the Clerk of the Course, and his staff, did a first class job. All we need now is for the Government and the relative authorities to get the laws changed so we can race in earnest and let the people who want to go racing on a Sunday, go racing.

Came home and watched John Wilson in Austria on his 'Go Fishing' programme-it was brilliant.

HISTORIC moment as Lady Butt's Savoyard wins the first
Sunday race in Britain, ridden by Walter Swinburn,
watched by 23,000 racegoers at Doncaster.

MONDAY July 27

IT'S my old pal ex-jockey Joe Sime's 69th birthday today and also Harry Sprague's 72nd. He was the jockey who rode the 1956 Champion Hurdle, Doorknocker, who I looked after as an apprentice at Charlie Hall's.

Roadwork today for the horses but we cantered about a dozen that are entered in races up to Wednesday. We also did stall work with everything that hasn't run or has been laid off a long time.

On an absolutely beautiful sunny day John and I picked up John Nixon, the owner of Beanshoot, as Sefio and her are our two Newcastle runners. Travelling over the moor at Brough and looking down on the Eden Vale Valley on a day like this is a spectacular sight and the natural dry stone walling in this part of the world is a pleasure to see. John Nixon, who is a member of a cycling club, normally goes racing on his pushbike. He actually set off today on it but turned back as he felt unwell. It's 135 miles to Newcastle. I felt unwell at the thought of biking that distance.

In the first race Beanshoot cantered down to the start only to be found lame when she arrived and therefore couldn't run. It's a good job John Nixon came with us in the car or his return journey would have felt like 531 miles. Saw Palacegate Racing finish second on SIS from Lingfield. Then watched Sefio in the flesh ridden by Joe Fanning finish last in the nursery. Some good came out of the race as JC, who couldn't do the weight on Sefio, ended up riding the winner, Tarnside Rosal, for Malton trainer Jimmy Etherington. That put John on the fifty mark for the season.

Passing through Kirkby Stephen it was 7.10pm. We stopped for some fish and chips. While the two Johns went and ordered I stayed in the car and listened on Racecall Phoneline to the 7.15 race from Wolverhampton where we had our filly Convenient Moment, owned by a few barristers, running. Smartly away, according to John Turner, the commentator, she disputed the lead until one and a half furlongs out, then took up the running and won to register the 73rd winner of the season for the yard. This little filly hasn't run for ninety-one days as she suffered quite badly with the virus. There isn't very much of her to start with but she is a gutsy little thing and a little good 'un is better than a big bad one.

TUESDAY July 28

SOME days it would be easier getting out of Alcatraz than getting away from the yard. I was hopeful of setting off for Goodwood at 8.0am. But it was more like 8.45am by the time Alan and I had got the declarations and entries ready for when the secretaries arrived. Answered the phone, watched the horses work and did countless other jobs. When I went out to the car Jo was already in it. Olly, my dog, followed me hoping to get in, too. He often comes with me but not today, seeing as we are away a few days. Not taking no for an answer he followed the car down our lane hoping I would soften up as I have done on numerous other occasions. I couldn't today though. The car clock had 285 miles on it when we pulled up on Goodwood car park. On a glorious day Heather Bank finished fourth of the thirty runners in the Stewards' Cup beaten about two-and-a-half lengths. If the damned handicapper hadn't raised the horse a colossal 18lb for winning first time out at Newmarket he would have been there abouts and I can assure you Mr Harper, Heather Bank's owner could have done with the money. His business like many others has had problems in the recession.

Watched on SIS as Food of Love got beat a head at Beverley by Ron Boss's Walking Possession.

Just before the last race Jo and I went to our hotel, the Inglenook at Pagham, where we always stay on our Goodwood trips. Along with the Sheltons, Viners, Forsyths, Holdcrofts, Campbells and Richard Evans, racing correspondent of The Times newspaper.

We all ate our evening meal on a large table. Before they all got drunk I collected £500 from them to sponsor Jonathan Haynes' parachute jump on our Open Day.

I had already collected from John Nixon. Richard Evans is also going to put a line or two in his paper about our Open Day so hopefully we should get a spin off from that. It was rather late when we hit the sack from talking about racing but it was good.

WEDNESDAY July 29

FIRST thing, I rang Alan for a chat about the horses' work, our entries and declarations. When we got breakfast over with we sat in the hotel's large country garden as it was a nice warm sunny morning. The owners Edna, Wally and son Tony are animal fanatics and they have all kinds of animals, birds and fish. At the rear of the garden is a paddock where a young lady from the village keeps the ex-racehorse twenty-two-year-old The Caseystan with a pony that was rescued from slaughter.

I drank tea with Geoff Lester of The Sporting Life and Richard Evans in the garden until it was coming out of our ears while studying form for a couple of hours after which, not a fraction wiser, we set off for the races.

Glorious was the right word for Goodwood. The sun was blazing down all day. It was so hot the gentlemen were allowed to remove their jackets. On entering the course there was a very good steel band playing Island In The Sun. In the Group 1 Sussex Stakes Marling gave a very game performance to hold on by a head to beat Selkirk in a driving finish.

In the last race Major Hern introduced a lovely American bred filly called Liyakah to win. We are definitely going to hear more of her. Our Garnock Valley ran a blinder to finish third to her.

Called in the stable yard to see tomorrow's runners who travelled down earlier today. Paris House looked a bomb. Then I had a chat with Stuart Dalgleish, my King's Troop pal, who now works on Racecourse Security down the south.

Racecall line benefitted yet again from me ringing up to hear our Palacegate Sunset finish second at Southwell's evening meeting.

Had a nice carvery meal at the hotel. Nearly all of the residents are racing people. Tonight was Karaoke night and I don't have to tell you we had some fun. Jimmy Byrne and I were first to sing the Kenny Rogers number Lucille. Jimmy's the person who helps me when I buy the yearlings at the sales. He looks after all the documentation, vetting, transport and the like. John Sexton, Richard Evans and Geoff Lester, for the Press, had a go but I'm afraid they will definitely have to keep their day jobs if they want to continue eating.

I called it a day just after 1.0am. Our bedroom was above the room where they were singing and at 2.0am it was still going strong.

THURSDAY July 30

ALAN and I got together on the phone first thing to have a chat about how the horses worked yesterday, the transport arrangements for the runners, the declarations and the entries. Told Alan to sort some cattle out for the market tomorrow. Also talked about a few details for Sunday's Open Day and a general chat about everything, seeing as I have been away.

After breakfast Jo and I walked round Wally's animals and through the orchard. Their apples are twice the size of ours at home. We settled down to read our sporting papers for a couple of hours in the brilliant sunshine.

Before I set off for Goodwood races I rang Ruby to make sure she had arranged for the parachute club to come and jump on our Open Day. Had she got a definite Yes for the Jonathan Haynes drop to go ahead-she had.

At the races it was a sweltering hot day. Once again the rule was relaxed regarding the wearing of jackets in the Richmond Enclosure.

There was some real good racing which boasted three Group 3 races on the same day's card. Maroof won the Lanson Champagne Vintage Stakes, Further Flight won the Goodwood Cup, Freddie Lloyd won the King George Stakes where Paris House ran a dismal sort of a race only beating three home. In the Lavant Nursery, which we have won for the last two years with Amber Mill and Heather Bank, the handicapper was making sure it wasn't going to be three years on the trot by giving Two Moves In Front top weight of 9st 7lb. By putting up Jason Weaver to claim 5lb and to the annoyance of JC, our horse finished fourth. It was supposed to be Quiz night after dinner at the hotel. Geoff Lester of The Sporting Life and I were to take on two bookmakers. But by 11.20 pm Geoff hadn't made a move so Jo and I went to bed. Last year the bookies beat Geoff and me. They asked questions like "what did they call the lad who led up the horse that finished second in the 1987 Lincoln Handicap, and what price was the horse?"

After last night I was glad of a breather.

FRIDAY July 31

SPENT most of the morning on the phone to Alan organising and making the final arrangements for the Open Day. Did the tips for tomorrow's Star, napping All At Sea for the Nassau Stakes. We are booked in here tonight but in view of having so much to do at home for Sunday Jo and I are going home straight after Sabre Rattler and Palacegate Episode have run in the Molecomb Stakes.

Benny Powell, of the Swordlestown Stud, rang on the carphone with a proposition to stand Paris House as a stallion next season in Ireland. Benny also bred Palacegate Episode as he did her full brother Another Episode who was second in the Molecomb last year to Sahara Star. Low numbers in the sprints have been fading from halfway every day so I walked onto the course to see if I could detect any difference in the going. To be fair I couldn't.

In the Molecomb we have one horse drawn one and the other on the outside in the number eleven stall. John Bostock, Palacegate Episode's lad, was £100 better off for her being awarded the best turned out. She ran a big race to finish second to the Ray Guest-trained Millyant with the Royal Ascot Norfolk Stakes winner Niche in third. The finishing order for the draw was 8, 11, 7.

MILLYANT (right) seen winning at Goodwood. Our filly
Palacegate Episode (noseband) comes second.
Further back is Royal Ascot heroine, Niche.

Peter Manning came back from Goodwood with us in the car. He is staying with us for a few days.

Travelling back home on the M42 there was a very nasty looking accident involving three or four motor cyclists and two cars on the outside lane. The ambulance men were stretchering people into the ambulance. Two young men were laid flat out on the road motionless, they didn't look good.

The traffic as usual on a Friday was very busy. During one jam we listened on Racecall to Domes Of Silence run third at Edinburgh. This particular hold-up was caused by yet another caravan turning over. It was completely wrecked. With all the hold-ups, crashes, roadworks and busy traffic it took six-and-a-half hours to get home.

SATURDAY August 1

IT'S nice to be home, back among the horses. Rode out Olly first lot. Second lot my mount was Fylde Flyer. The way he went he is well named.

The phone's never stopped ringing this morning, mainly with people asking how to get to Cockerham for our Open Day tomorrow. People are so kind- we have already got £705 for the Jonathan Haynes sponsored parachute jump.

Would you believe it after the sweltering weather of the past few days at Goodwood it's raining. God I hope it doesn't tomorrow.

Peter Manning, John and myself set off at 11.30am for Thirsk where Glowing Value gets us off on the right foot by running in the first race. Soba Guest and Oyston's Life both run in the six furlong three year old seller Ladies Race. We have won this race for the last four years. Allegrissima is in the last.

It turned out a lovely sunny day at Thirsk with a large crowd. Quite a lot of the racegoers were young people, which is nice. Playing to the punters was the Tom Roberts Jazz Band and the racecourse executive had really gone out of their way to make it a family day, with a creche for the kids plus roundabouts, swings and a bouncy castle. A raffle was held and the tickets were put in the original Dusty Bin of the Ted Rodgers telly series. Not to be outdone I have borrowed him for our Open Day so we can do likewise. Lots of lovely people gave me money for the Olly Drop or to sponsor Jonathan's jump.

Glowing Value was third but we managed to keep our record intact for the Ladies Race-Soba Guest ridden by Diane Jones won. Gratefully, there was no bid for the winner. Oyston's Life was third, ridden by Linda Perratt. Allegrissima was unplaced as were our two Goodwood runners Laurel Queen and Amber Mill.

John went to his house with Lindsay Charnock as he is staying overnight at John's. Lindsay is riding work for us tomorrow as well as riding in the Donkey Derby.

Called round to see Sam and had a game of cards with him. Afterwards I picked-up a Chinese from the shop in Garstang for Jo, Pat, Diane, Peter and myself. The girls are all busy preparing for tomorrow.

About 10.30pm I went to watch the finish of Rambo First Blood II on the telly. There were so many things in the film against poor old Rambo you would have thought it was produced and directed by Geoffrey Gibbs and Nigel Gray.

SUNDAY August 2

THANK God it's not raining, just a bit overcast. Let's hope it keeps fine and everything goes well. The Open Day was to start at 11.0am, only people were ringing up as early as 8.0am to ask what time we started, where is it, how do we get there, and the like. One gentleman even asked what kind of shoes he should wear.

Around three-and-a-half thousand people came, from Land's End to John O'Groats. They paid £5 per car entry and the two charming girls who took the fivers from the people were Pat Knight and Diane Bain.

People bought programmes, raffle tickets, tombola tickets, sponsored jockeys to ride donkeys, sponsored the actual races, sponsored Jonathan Haynes who so bravely parachuted 10,000 feet from a plane. They were so considerate to bid at the auction for prizes people had so kindly donated.

We worked eighteen horses, ridden by some of our best jockeys. We had a bouncy castle and everything you could imagine. Even Jimmy Byrne got on the microphone in between Henry Beeby's superb auctioneering and sang The Crystal Chandeliers. I can put my hand on heart and say not one person moaned or grumbled about a single thing-they spent their money and really enjoyed themselves. All of our staff worked their weekend to make sure the day was a success. All the people who ran the various stalls, and there were lots of them, did a marvellous job. The racing clubs all contributed by giving money, prizes and their time. Peter Manning, who manages the Asta Hotel in Barbados, kindly gave for the auction a holiday for two at his hotel for a fortnight. I have been to his hotel so I can assure the purchaser, Dean McKeown the Northern Flat jockey, he will have a super time.

There was plenty of good food and drink. I would like to thank the parachuters, the police, the firemen and Yorkshire Television for lending us the original Dusty Bin for our raffle. Unfortunately, I cannot mention

**PRESENTATION TIME : The open day at our yard means
a busy day for myself and stable-jockey
John Carroll (right) and all the staff at Cockerham.**

[275]

everyone. However, for all you lovely people who contributed to making our day a success, from the bottom of my heart-thank you. A special thanks to Adrian Ross on the mike, he was priceless.

We haven't arrived at the exact figure yet but we have already got over £12,000. Considering it was also Tom Jones, and Luca Cumani's open days today, that can't be bad. Later in the evening Peter, Jo and I went to the Patten Arms for a pizza, a pint and a game of dominoes.

MONDAY August 3

GOT up really early and gave Neville and Dave a hand to feed the horses. This is a nice time of day. The horses are always pleased to see someone first thing and they are, of course, ready for their breakfast.

Alan and I did Saturday's entries. Echo-Logical is entered at Brighton next Thursday. I wonder if any of his many past owners and followers from the Liverpool Echo will go to see him run. They used to follow him about with great enthusiasm.

Diane had last week in the office, today she is driving JC, Peter and myself racing. We are doing the two, Ripon this afternoon and Nottingham tonight.

Classic Storm runs at Ripon, seeking to win her fifth race on the trot. But she is up against it attempting to beat Lord Olivier of Willie Jarvis's (pictured left). He was only one length behind Satank and that horse went on to win the Windsor Castle Stakes at Royal Ascot. If we do win that man Savill from the Cayman Islands will probably be sniffing around the claiming box. Some people would take the headcollar off a nightmare.

Arriving at Ripon it was very windy but that didn't put those Yorkshire racegoers off. They love their racing. In the claimer Classic Storm ran third to the easy winner Lord Olivier. Our other runner, Grey Pride, also finished third in the two-year-old maiden.

We left Ripon racecourse in brilliant sunshine to set off for the evening meeting at Nottingham. Getting onto the A1 we had a lovely view of the White Horse on Sutton Bank.

When we arrived at Nottingham I looked at the car's little face on the clock. It read 26,614. The car hasn't been very well recently but he's booked in to see the "doctor" on Wednesday for a check-up and service.

Inside the racecourse punters were greeted to the sounds of the Calverton Colliery Welfare Band.

In the nursery Palacegate Prince wasn't up to the step-up in class and therefore only beat one home. Windpower, our other runner in the sprint, never got his act together at all. We left immediately after the third race and were home for 9.15pm.

TUESDAY August 4

MANY happy returns of the day to the best loved lady in the land, the Queen Mum, who is 92.

Last March, at the Doncaster Breeze-Up Sales, we bought a lovely Exhibitioner colt. We got him going nicely and turned him out. He looked like making an ideal three-year-old. I named him Glensdale Grove, after the street I was born in. This morning he was playing about with his three pals in the field and ran into the hedge and didn't get the brakes on early enough. He hit a post and ruptured the muscles in his back so badly the vet had to put him down. In the past, thank goodness, it's been such a rarity to lose a horse. Yet this year this is our third. Now we've got the three, let's hope it's the last for a long time to come.

After riding the first two lots out and making the declarations with Alan, Jo and I went to pick up our Sam and Andria to take them to the airport. Andria is going back home to Tenerife today.

We only run Westmead Nick at Nottingham so I'm going to go with Jo and help with the shopping. With so many people stopping at our house recently, being away at Goodwood and the Open Day yesterday, we have had a bit of a run on the freezer and the pantry. In addition to the shopping I've had to move round all the furniture in the house. I am definitely going racing tomorrow-it's getting too much like hard work round here. At stable time I went round the horses in the evening. There are four or five we put on the walkers for half an hour before giving them a canter, as they are a bit burly. By exercising them twice a day we can control their weight better. In the past a couple of this sort have blown up in races. Being here to see all this actually happening and getting among the horses as they are led out for a pick of grass is a nice change for me.

It started to rain after stables and now we have the Open Day behind us I wouldn't mind it raining for a day or two.

After we finished dinner I had a couple of games of cards with Sam then I worked on my story for the Weekender. This week's is about last Sunday's Open Day.

Later, watching the Olympics, on the telly, I was enthralled with the heavyweight lifting. It was stunning. Those big lads were lifting well over four hundredweight. It's truly remarkable.

WEDNESDAY August 5

IT'S been raining all night which is just what the good doctor ordered. Today is crunch day on the whip rule, regarding where and how many times it is permissible to hit a horse. Steve Cauthen meets the Stewards of the Jockey Club for this never-ending saga about whip abuse. Headman Flash was telling me as we went to work the first lot that Philip, his four-year-old son, has to have an operation today to remove ten teeth. The poor little mite has ulcers on his gums.

The rain had got nicely in the ground, making it good going on our grass gallop where we worked the horses today. With today's venue, Pontefract, only ninety-two miles away I was able to watch all the horses work, do the entries with Alan and not be under as much pressure as some days.

After watching the morning work and digesting some of the horses' recent runs, I have marked up a few to be changing hotels shortly in order to make room for the yearlings we shall very soon be buying.

Sam stayed at our house last night. On the way to Pontefract we called in to his flat near Garstang, so he could change into his suit and put a Bic razor in his shirt pocket to have a shave with while he has a sauna with the jocks who are fighting the flab.

There was a good crowd at Pontefract-and so there should be. Norman Gundill, the Clerk of the Course, works his butt off for the place.

In the five furlong sprint our filly Food of Love had a day off and only beat two of the six home. Debutante two-year-old Killy's Filly was second to Goodbye Millie.

On our return from Pontefract Mike Torpey, who was in charge of the Liverpool horse, Echo-Logical, rang on the carphone. He is getting a bit of flack from the members about losing their horse. I told him I would give him a lease on Daaniera, a horse I bought earlier from his owner Seamus Purcell. Mike will ring tomorrow with a Yes or No.

Dropping Sam off at his flat, I had a coffee and a few hands of cards with him.

Watching Oracle I was amazed to see Steve Cauthen has received a further six day suspension from the Disciplinary Committee. I bet there is plenty to say about that in tomorrow's Life and Post.

THURSDAY August 6

JUST as I expected-headlines "Steve Cauthen is hit for an extra six" said The Life. "Six more for Cauthen," quotes the Post. It seems such a shame. Steve is one of the kindest jockeys to ride a horse. No facial changes are apparent as he kicks and chases his horses along.

This month our yard won the Whitbread Stable of the Month award for the highest number of best-turned-out horses.

I didn't ride out today, seeing as it's only road work, and I had plenty of other things to do-such as meeting Keith Dunn, the manager of the Marie Curie horses, regarding horses for next year.

On our way to Pontefract, in Jo's car as my fellow has gone for a service, it's a beautiful sunny day. Our two-year-old Beanshoot runs for the first time in a four horse race. There is another large crowd at the races. I met my old pal

Jack Allen's widow, Bess, and had a nice long chat with her.

My book, "It's Tougher At The Bottom" was on sale in paperback and it appeared to be selling quite well. The hard-back edition has already sold 10,000 copies, making it one of racing's best sellers.

Beanshoot finished third but the poor little mite didn't cope very well with the firm ground. I had Pat, Diane and Sam with me and, after our race, we took Peter to Doncaster Railway Station to catch the London train as he goes back to Barbados tomorrow.

On our way back home along the M62 motorway a policeman stopped to change a wheel for a lady motorist whose car had a puncture. Good for him. We dropped Sam off at his pad and then went home to a lovely meal cooked by Jo. I finished off my copy for next week's Weekender. It's funny, I work like mad on it then when it comes out. I think of all the things to say when it's all too late.

FRIDAY August 7

WE HAVE quite a number of horses entered in races tomorrow. They breezed for a couple of furlongs, while Alan and I did the entries. The rest of our horses cantered in pairs round the top moss where the ground is perfect. Three racecourses will have the presence of six of our string today. For me, the best chance is Arctic Appeal at Haydock's evening meeting.

Jo, John and myself travelled to Redcar in my car, which is feeling much better for being serviced yesterday. En route the phone never seemed to stop ringing. One call was about me sponsoring three ducks for £50. The proceeds would be used to send some disabled kids from Lancashire on a holiday. I forgot to ask the lady whether she intended racing or flying the ducks.

While John was driving I did my tips for tomorrow's televised races for the Star. Last week I tipped Vallance, a 5-1 winner, but that's not a meal ticket forever. Let's hope I tip some more today.

Our travelling head lass Linda and one of our lads, Peter Farrell, were returning Dusty Bin to the Redcar racecourse office. If you remember, we borrowed it for our Open Day. They were each holding a handle. Colin, Wally Carter's travelling headman, saw them and said, "Martin (our other travelling head lad) doesn't look very well, where are you taking him?"

Palacegate Prince, from the worst draw (number one), was beaten a head in the seller by First Option, owned by Peter Savill. I suppose this was an opportunity to get my own back on him for claiming Echo-Logical at Ayr's last meeting by running him up at the auction-but that's not my style.

In the feature race, the five furlong handicap, Mamma's Too looked a picture. She won best turned out, too. Even with top weight she battled well to beat Bodari a head. A neck further back was Super Rocky who we bred and trained but lost in a claimer at Pontefract, where he was second.

We gave Willie Ryan a lift from Redcar to the Haydock Park night meeting where our first runner, Hills Raceaid, was in the 6.40pm. Travelling to Haydock we listened on the carphone to Convenient Moment get beat a head by Aberlady.

Although the fields weren't very big at Haydock, there was a big crowd at this popular course. Our three runners all got in the frame but we didn't have a winner, although Arctic Appeal won the best turned out award.

In fact, all our six runners today ran well. We've had one winner, three seconds, a third and a fourth. There's no danger of the bookmakers closing my betting account. I thought Arctic Appeal, who was beaten two-and-a-half lengths, was quite a good thing today. Let's hope my Star tips fare better tomorrow.

SATURDAY August 8

GOT up early with Alan to do the entries. It's a workday and we are at five meetings so I wanted to kick on.

In the post a letter arrived from the Horserace Writers' Association inviting me as their guest of honour at their annual dinner at Ayr on September 18. I feel very honoured and I'm looking forward to going.

On the gallops, working the horses, it was very dark and wintery. The activity was like Piccadilly Station, with all the horseboxes passing the bottom of the gallops going to all parts of the country with today's runners.

Pat and Diane came with me to Haydock, where I had an appointment to meet Keith Dunn of Marie Curie to help pick the winner of a competition. I was ten minutes late for the presentation to the winner because of the heavy traffic and the rain belting down on the M6 motorway. All the cars had their headlights on.

Our only Haydock runner, Never in the Red, was unplaced in the Coral Handicap Stakes. Half a Tick, trained by Paul Cole won the Group 3 Rose of Lancaster Stakes. Haydock's chairman Bill Whittle asked me if I would present the trophies to the owner, trainer and jockey of the winner of the Juddmonte Claiming Stakes, which was won by the 1989 Cambridgeshire winner Rambo's Hall.

Straight after the race Diane, Pat and I set off for our next venue, Southwell. While travelling, with the aid of the carphone I listened to Laurel Queen finish second at Ayr and Oyston's Life finish third at Redcar. An hour and a half earlier Rhett's Choice was also second.

The track at Southwell had had lots of rain on it. Normally the wet makes the Fibresand track faster, especially when it's rolled. Today it was just like wet sand without fibre. It was very slow. Horses were flat to the boards as soon as the stalls opened. Jockeys were complaining it was impossible to ride a proper race and came back absolutely plastered in wet sand.

Our horse, Palacegate Sunset went off at 5-2 favourite ridden by Alan Mackay, because JC couldn't get back from Redcar in time, and only beat a couple in the seller. Robert Stopford, the stipendiary steward, did a fair job of winding up the stewards by wheeling Alan and me in front of them to explain the dismal performance. He said the racegoers would like to know. There wasn't a single racegoer at Southwell who didn't appreciate the horse couldn't go a yard in the mud-like going. Besides, he needn't have had me in, the jockeys ride the horses. The "Stipes" should get the trainers in if they are under suspicion of stopping horses from winning. I would have carried him home if it had been at all possible.

SUNDAY August 9

IT'S Tony Budge's birthday today. I know this as I read it in yesterday's Racing Post. Tony (below) hasn't sent me an invite to his party, although I do recall going to a party at his house near Worksop a couple of years ago. In the great big hallway there were literally thousands of stuffed birds in cabinets.

Made lots of phone calls to owners I haven't seen or spoken to for a while. Today, Jo and I have been invited to lunch in Cheshire by Reg and Jenny Leah. They own one of our rare jumpers-No More The Fool (Jessie).

While we were travelling down on the M6 in heavy rain we noticed that the traffic on the Northern-bound side was at a standstill for miles because of a five-car crash. Three police cars and an ambulance were frantically trying to get through the traffic as this particular part of the motorway didn't have a hard shoulder. When an accident like that happens it just proves how dangerous the motorways are without emergency routes.

Arriving at Reg's we had a couple of jars at their local pub followed by a very nice lunch. We then had a look at his brood mares and foals. One of the mares, Sharp Anne, we trained to win seven races.

On the way back home it was still raining, with many fields submerged in water. Sam was at our house having his tea. Afterwards we had a few games of Nap, a card game we play. Sam wanted to go to his house. He was walking with the aid of his crutches and carrying his suit on a coat hanger. It's tough enough for him with trying to cart things as well. Down he went and got a nasty cut on his forehead. Jo cleaned him up and after I got him to his flat we had a hot chocolate and watched the closing ceremony of the Olympic Games from Barcelona. The Clint Eastwood film, Play Misty came on the telly. He got stuck into that, so I made my way home.

MONDAY August 10

YESTERDAY'S rain has freshened everywhere up. The birds are in full song and it's a lovely morning.

Reading the papers, I see Mr Brooks, ridden by Lester Piggott, won the £70,175 Grosser Preis von Berlin, a Group 3 race in Germany. Doesn't it make our prize money look poor?

Richard Hannon also trained the Heinz 57 winner in Ireland, with Pips Pride. Michael Roberts has now gone 22 winners clear of Pat Eddery in the race for the Jockey's title.

Tomorrow's entries ran along for a couple of furlongs on the grass. Today we only have See Us There at the Ripon 'night shift'.

The venue for me is Doncaster Sales, where we have Bold Mood, Andrea's Girl and Lawnswood Quay in. Judging from the unusually high number of people attending the sales, I can only think the nice warm sunny weather has brought them out-unless it's just somewhere to go for the day. Whatever the reason, they certainly don't go to spend money. The prices the horses were fetching were really poor. Bold Mood was sold for 1,300 guineas and Lawnswood Quay for 3,100. I didn't sell Andrea's Girl as she didn't reach the modest reserve I put on her. I am sure she has improved of late, so we will keep her for a bit longer.

Here I am surveying the ruins
of my old yard at Almholme.

After the sales, Pat and Diane, who came with me, went to see our old yard at Almholme, near Arksey, where we first started to train. When we first rented it off John Massarella, who trained the great show jumper Mr Softee, it was really run down. Jo and I, along with our couple of staff worked our pants off to get it nice. Seeing it now, all derelict and falling down, is a crying shame. Crikey, I wished I hadn't gone.

While we were there my old mate Alec Coates, who farmed the adjacent land, stopped for a chat when he spotted me. He was really chuffed at seeing me again after all these years.

On the way home we called on Sam and had a Chinese meal and a bottle of wine before dropping him off at the Manor to have a jar with our crew.

When everyone had gone to bed, I wrote my piece for the Weekender, which is about Southwell Racecourse.

TUESDAY August 11

ALL our horses cantered on the top moss. With no day racing for us, and with this being the only weekday we don't have to make entries, I was able to ride out three lots. My mounts were No More The Fool, Gorinsky and Fylde Flyer. It was great. After all these years of riding you would have thought I would have become more of an office boy than a saddle tramp. Not a bit of it.

In the Life I see there is a crisis meeting involving senior Jockey Club officials this week regarding the surface of the Southwell track. I think it would make more sense if they had a meeting with the firm who sold the Muddles the Fibresand, and got it renewed.

Although Catterick was an evening meeting Jo, Diane, Sam, John and I set off early as Jo and I were sponsoring a pony half an hour before the first race. The pony race was organised by trainer Wilf Storey in aid of the injured jockey Sharron Murgatroyd, in whose name the race was named. The brave lady was there in person. Our pony was called April Fool and was ridden by John Lowe. John Carroll rode the top weight with 9st 7lb. He set off at a blistering pace and held on to win by three-quarters of a length from Autumn Celeste ridden by Alex Greaves. April Fool finished out the back but it was a lot of fun. The pace they went was unbelievable. John said he would have got a place in the seller on Pirate, the pony he rode. That says a lot for our horse Coffee Mint, who finished towards the rear of the field in that event.

Our Mica and Daaniera ran fourth and fifth in the nursery but both went well enough to suggest they would win again before the season is out.

It was nice to see ex-jump jockey Pat McCarron at the races. That's the first time I have seen him since he packed up through injury over twenty years ago.

WEDNESDAY August 12

WITH the rain we keep on getting here at home the going is good. When I finished working the horses and doing the entries with Alan, I set sail for Beverley with Diane and Sam. John went in his own car as he is going on to Epsom to ride some work for Wally Carter in the morning.

Beverley is one of the very few courses I am not keen on. It is so unfair. Horses with low draws in a big field have very little chance. If the punters went down to the five furlong start at Beverley and saw the amount of ground the low-drawn horses have to make up, they would think twice before they backed them.

On the way to Beverley on the M62 it was raining cats and dogs. However, a few miles before we got to the course it cleared up and turned out to be a nice day. The seven races had attracted seventy-two declared runners and the management were duly rewarded with a large crowd.

Our pupil, Diane, who has very thin legs, had asked Jo to get her a pair of tights on one of her shopping trips. Jo must have got her a pair of cheap ones with very little elastic in them. She was following me around with wrinkles round her ankles. All she needed was a hat on her head and she would have been a dead ringer for Nora Batty.

Our two runners ran quite well, although none of the punters were impressed. Laurel Etoile was 10lb out of the handicap. Yesterday, when our office phoned the trainers with the top weights they were told they weren't running. Our horse was therefore going to be in the race on a handicap mark. At five minutes past the deadline time to take horses out, at 10.5am, John Dunlop's office rang to say they were now running their horses after all. That's how it came about.

At Beverley I was asked by a phoneline if I would speak about next week's York meeting for a few minutes, and if I had the option of training one of the Ebor entrants which one would I pick. My choice was Matador. In appreciation of the few minutes of my time they gave me a bottle of Lanson Black Label Champagne.

We dropped Sam off at his flat prior to getting him a pizza for his tea in Garstang.

THURSDAY August 13

IN THE Sporting Life is my story about the all-weather surface being worn out. The reason this story appeared in The Life was because when I originally asked Mike Gallemore, the editor, if I could change my Weekender article, which he already had about our Open Day. He said he liked my story so much he wanted to use it in The Life. I'll have to do another story now for The Weekender. I will need to put my thinking cap on. Last night was a wild one with howling winds and rain. The dogs were barking like mad. Looking around, I can't see any damage but it was awful, just like a night in a Frankenstein movie.

Coming back off the gallops from stretching the legs' of tomorrow's runners', I picked the first mushrooms I have seen this year. Pat Knight said they were delicious as she ate them for her breakfast.

Nora Batty, sorry, I mean Diane, and I set off for Beverley at 11.30am. The traffic was really heavy on the M6-it took three-quarters of an hour to do the first 22 miles. We got to the course, however, in enough time for me to make out my placepot on my racecard and pass to Diane for her to put it on, as the jockeys were already mounted in the paddock.

After the first race, as we were saddling our runner for the second, Diane said to me: "Would you like the good news or the bad news first?"

"The good", I replied.

"Well, at the moment your first horse is up. The bad news is I was too late to get it on."

Trentesimo ran a good race to finish third.

In between racing, lots of people were commenting on the fibre-sand track at Southwell, on account of my article in today's Sporting Life.

In the sixth race I had put Romoosh, at 3-1, in my placepot to beat the odds on favourite, Mimique. This would have made my 'should-have-been' placepot winnings £308.

Still, what you have never had, you never miss.

FRIDAY August 14

I GOT up early this morning in order to have a good look at the entries to see if we could poach a race or two. The winners are slow coming in at the moment-it seems we have to battle for every victory. Mind you, after having the virus I suppose we are fortunate to have put the show back on the road. I have worked on my Weekender script and my tips for tomorrow's Daily Star and it's only 5.15am. I am just waiting for Neville to get up and I will give him a hand to feed the horses.

We ride out the next day's runners very early, before first lot pulls out, to make sure they are all right before they set off on their journey racing. This morning I rode one of tomorrow's Lingfield runners, Palacegate Racing, and he flew.

Before Alan and I got on with the entries and declarations I rode Jessie out. This season he is as big as a bull and with a bit of luck he could do well novice chasing. Hopefully, we will have him ready for our local jump meeting, Cartmel.

Olly, my dog, and I set off for Southwell. We got there with time to spare as I wanted to see Bob Lee, the fencemaker, as we could do with some new fences. I've lent ours to Judy Eaton and for the few times we use them we can share. However, I just feel I would like some of our own again. I also wanted to get there early to walk the course with Alan Daly, one of our kids who rides Soba Guest in the apprentice race. There was some trotting racing before the first race. The race was won by Evelyn Slack, the owner of Snowgirl. Allegrissima ran well to finish second of the fifteen runners. I told young Alan, who has had about half a dozen rides, to keep his whip in his left hand, as he is drawn twelve of the twelve runners, which is the best draw right on the fence. This will stop him wandering off the rails. As Alan was going out of the paddock he said: "Do you mind if I take the whip down to the start in my right hand, boss?"

The horse ran a good race to finish third.

The traffic, like most Fridays, was hectic on the way home.

Good news from Romford-that star dog of ours, Lisnakill Wish, won again tonight. He is now on schedule for the Irish Grand National.

SATURDAY August 15

HOPEFULLY, we should have a winner somewhere today. We have had a fairly lean week. I am going to Newbury where Palacegate Episode and Threepence run. Jo is going to Lingfield and Alan is going to Ripon.

A quick glance at the Life and Post and I see it's Princess Anne's birthday. Alan and I entered the horses for next Thursday and Friday. I then watched first lot work. Sizzling Saga and Fylde Flyer galloped five furlongs with Paris House. God, did they trap. Diane, and one of our ex-apprentices, Willie Hollick, who now works for Alan Bailey, came with me. Willie wanted a lift to Newbury, as he has a ride, so he came up and stayed in the hostel last night. Diane is a good driver, which gives me more of a chance to work and do my phone calls. She likes driving and I hate it.

On the way, we stopped for some sweets at a service station. Willie was in the queue behind us. Diane and I went to the car and drove off. Willie was running round the car park after us like a mad thing, thinking we had forgotten him.

Dave Thom the Newmarket trainer, who is an old pal from our riding days together, rang on the carphone to ask me if I would saddle his filly, Yes, in the fourth race, the sprint.

Although I would be finished after the second, I intended staying to watch the Geoffrey Freer £75,000 Group 2 race. Even being 225 miles from base it was no trouble.

There were lots of people at Newbury races. Our filly, Palacegate Episode, looked so small against the other five in the St Hugh's Stakes Listed Race, which we won last year with Mamma's Too. In the race she flew out of the stalls and was never headed to win by five lengths, giving Gary Carter an easy win.

Threepence had top weight of 9st 7lb although I don't know what he'd done to earn it, could only finish in the middle of the field.

Geoffrey Freer, who was a Senior Jockey Club Handicapper and also the Clerk of the Course at Newbury prior to Captain Toller, would have been disappointed with the turnout in his race-only four runners, Michelozzo, Rock Hopper, Sapience and the eventual winner, Shambo, trained by Clive Brittain for this wife Maureen. It was Michael Roberts' first day back from a few days off through injury.

Dave Thom's horse, Yes, finished second, ridden by another or our ex-apprentices, Kim McDonnell. Diane and I then watched our two-year-old filly Lucky Parkes win the feature race from Ripon, the Hornblower Stakes, on SIS.

Passing Knutsford on the M6, about 100 geese flew quite low over the motorway heading east. A few miles further on we drew upsides Gordon Richards' horsebox, driven by Martin Todhunter, on its way back from Bangor-on-Dee. We wound our windows down to ask each other how we

had fared. They had two winners.

Looking at Oracle on my return, Palacegate Episode has a page. It says how I told the Press boys the filly is so fast it's like sitting on an electric shock.

SHE might look small but she's big-hearted : Palacegate Episode, seen winning impressively at Newbury.

SUNDAY August 16

GOT up early and took my dogs for a walk round the gallops to inspect the ground after the pounding they took during yesterday's workday, and also to see Olly and the cattle. It is light so I might find a few mushrooms. Only three of tomorrow's runners who tend to be a bit stuffy had a burst, just to stretch their legs. The others were led out for a pick of grass.

Gorinsky, who is entered at York on Tuesday got a cut yesterday while working. I suppose he could have done with some penicillin but I daren't let him have any as it will still be in his system. I told Flash to put him on the walker for an hour and put an animalintex poultice on and just hope the leg doesn't flare up. That little filly, Palacegate Episode, was led out for a pick of grass.

A gentleman from Pakistan called Ahmed Ezziz, trading in the name of International Business Corporation, wanted to buy some cheap horses to

HAPPY RETURNS: The cattle are having a good tuck in as Olly, my Jack Russell, and I go on walkabout.

race in that country. I sold him Cashtal Queen. He said the horse didn't have to be very good, just cheap. Cashtal Queen doesn't look as if she has trained on this year so she may as well eat into his rations as opposed to ours.

Norman Gundill, the Clerk of the Course at Pontefract, came to visit us with his family and his mother-in-law, Mrs John Massarella from whom we rented our first yard when we trained near Doncaster. When Jo and I finished showing them round the yards and the gallops we took them to the Orchard Restaurant at Broughton for lunch. We have known each other for some twenty odd years. It was good to talk about old times. On the way back home we called in to see Tom Bibby, a dairy farmer, who is a part owner of Mamma's Too and a few more horses in our yard.

Ruby, our secretary, has got herself in foal, and is therefore leaving soon. We'll miss her. She's brilliant. Ian Bolland, our accountant, has been on the lookout for a replacement. We are also being sued by our local farmer, Bill Sutcliffe, for a bit of fencing a loose horse broke through. I thought the bill he sent us was exorbitant. The case is coming up shortly so I am liaising with Ian over the matter.

MONDAY August 17

BOTH the sporting papers give Palacegate Episode and Lucky Parkes good write-ups for their wins last Saturday with the Post putting photos of both events in their paper. While we were riding out first lot some of us went for a long canter and the heavens opened. We got absolutely soaked to the skin. John Carroll went early to Hamilton as he wanted to lose a couple of pounds in the sauna for a horse of Lynda Ramsden's in the first race.

Dave Bamber, the Blackpool footballer who was second top goal scorer last season in the Football League and Cup with 36 goals, and owns a share in Oscar's Quest, came with me in the car. Dave is on the easy list at the moment, recovering from a broken ankle.

Speaking to JC on his carphone on the way to Hamilton he was telling me he got yet another ticket on Saturday from the police for overtaking on a road with an unbroken white line. If we ever get going well enough to afford a plane I will make sure we get a pilot. What damage could he do in the sky?

With us going out for lunch yesterday I put the Sunday joint in the bottom oven of our Aga with the intentions of taking it out on our return. Jo has just rung me to say it's burnt black and it's the size of an Oxo cube.

Racing at Hamilton always has a nice atmosphere. In fact, that can be said about all Scottish racing. It was a warm sunny day. We had four runners, High Principles being the first in the third race. Directly after the first race I attended a meeting regarding the compulsory scheme of declaring overnight jockeys. Never mind what they said at the meeting, it's yet more hassle for trainers and, to be honest, we have enough of that.

High Principles finished in midfield but Arctic Appeal won the next for us. Our two two-year-olds ran in the sixth race. Pilgrim Bay was first and our other runner, Oscar's Quest, was last.

As I had a bit of time Diane and I had a placepot again. Mine came up and thankfully this time the Nora Batty ringer put it on in time.

When I got home I looked at the injury book. Memsahb has some poison in her hoof. I Do Care is lame. Domes Of Silence has a swelling on the knee. Palacegate King has a knock on a joint. Not bad from around nearly 100 horses stabled at the moment. I bet Martin Pipe or Gordon Richards in their jump yards have a lot more.

Looking at Teletext my placepot paid £14.20. For a £32 investment I wouldn't have thought that was very good.

9.0pm I received a phone call from the Warwickshire police. The box that took Tuscan Dawn to finish unplaced at Windsor had broken down on the M40. A piston had blown. We have arranged with my old jockey pal Richard Evans who lives only twelve miles away to pick the horse up. The horsebox is to be towed back to Cicely Motors, the Mercedes people of Blackburn who service and repair our boxes and Tuscan Dawn is to be brought home tomorrow by Mark Sanderson, a local transporter.

TUESDAY August 18

IT'S the first day of York's Ebor meeting today and we have no runners-which is a bad start for us as last year our yard won the Ritz Club Trophy. Gorinsky was a declared runner in the six furlong handicap only he got balloted out. Except for tomorrow's runners all the other horses cantered round the top moss. I rode Jessie. Everyday he gets a bit better, so hopefully we will have him on top hole for Cartmel on the 31st of the month.

Lucky Parkes went home for her winter break in her owners' trailer, which she didn't want to go in. It took a few of our lads to literally lift her in.

Chris Marriott came today about taking over Ruby's job when she leaves on account of her being pregnant. When we were finished I went to Garstang for a couple of hot meat and potato pies and some cakes then went on to Sam's place to watch the racing with him from York on the telly. The Juddmonte International Stakes was a great race with some really good horses in. The likes of Derby winner Dr Devious, Guineas winner Rodrigo de Triano, the brilliant mare Kooyonga and the other good mare Ruby Tiger, who has won races in five different countries. What a remarkable race it turned out to be. Lester and Rodrigo won by a length from All At Sea. The crowd really got behind the connections of this great horse, owner, trainer and jockey when they entered the winner's enclosure.

When telly racing finished Sam and I went home for evening stables. On my arrival I was greeted with the news that Rodgers, one of my Jack Russell pups, had been run over in our lane. Peter one of the lads had buried him so at least I was spared that task.

Tuscan Dawn, and the two girls who took him to Windsor, finally arrived home about 4.30pm.

About 7.0pm, as we were just finishing our tea, there was an almighty banging and clattering in one of the seven boxes near the house. It was Allegrissima who was cast. We managed to roll her over to get her up. Thankfully she hadn't come to any harm. It's always a worry when a horse gets cast during the night in case he or she lames themselves when kicking and thrashing about.

WEDNESDAY August 19

I WORKED Paris House over two furlongs with Another Episode and Food of Love to give him a good blow for tomorrow's Nunthorpe Stakes Group 1 race, the race he came second in last year to Sheikh Albadou. The work for the rest of the horses was going well until about the third last lot, when John Carroll lost an iron on Laxey Flyer, fell off and twisted his knee. He couldn't drive his car home so our secretary, Helen, had to take him. Let's hope it's not too serious. We got Richard Quinn to stand by for today's York rides.

Within threequarters of an hour three agents had rung for his rides. These fellows don't believe in taking prisoners. It shows how things have changed. When I was riding, if a jockey rang a trainer up to poach a ride off a fellow jockey he would have been threatened with being put over the rails.

On the way to York John rang my carphone, he has hurt the ligaments in his knee and will be out of action for a few days. I have booked Steve Cauthen for Paris House tomorrow through John Hanmer, Steve's agent, who rang the carphone as soon as he'd heard John was hurt.

York's Ebor meeting is absolutely brilliant. As well as having a big crowd there was some great racing with the best horses in the business running. Palacegate Prince, with his substitute jockey aboard, finished fourth of the twenty-one runners. User Friendly won the Yorkshire Oaks, owned and bred by Bill Gredley. Hopefully that will help cheer Bill up somewhat as, only ten days ago, he lost his wife. It was great for the North to see Quick Ransom, trained by Mark Johnston and ridden by Dean McKeown, win the Tote Ebor Handicap. In the Listed Roses Stakes, the race Another Episode won for us last year, our good luck continued. Pat Eddery substituted for the unfortunate JC to win by a length, giving the yard it's 80th win of the season. Before the race, as we were saddling Sabre Rattler, his owner Henry Hughes asked me if we should get him gelded during the winter. I told him if he wins today, No. So horses really do understand what we are talking about.

Today was a day of incident. Michael Hills, Lester Piggott, Philip Robinson and George Duffield narrowly escaped a mid-air crash when their Piper Seneca was approached by six fighter planes, missing them by only feet. Then there was an electrical fault which caused a ten minute delay to the start of the Yorkshire Oaks.

On the way back from York we were invited for dinner to John Barrett and Ruth Dix's, near Burley. Ruth, as I have mentioned before, is worse than me for animals. I ended up travelling back home with a pair of white fantails in a cardboard box on the back seat. She's also given me an address where I can buy a labrador pup to replace old Bruni, who died a few weeks ago.

THURSDAY August 20

DID the decs and entries as usual and rode out Jessie first lot. I gave him a long canter as I don't want him short of work for Cartmel. These jumpers need lots of long steady work. It's not easy for Jessie working on his own for most of the time as most of our steeds wouldn't get two miles in a horsebox. A film crew came to the yard to film our new walkers in action.

Jo, Diane and myself went to York where at 12.30pm we had an invitation by Mr and Mrs Greely, sponsors of the Keeneland Nunthorpe Stakes, to join them for lunch in the Shirley Heights suite.

There was a huge crowd on the Knavesmire, and a good band were playing on entering the course. There were some fine horses running in first class races and the punters really appreciated it. The Group 2 Lowther Stakes was won by Niche, the third home in the Molecomb at Goodwood. One wonders how good the winner, Millyant, really is-seeing that second-placed Palacegate Episode won the St Hugh's Stakes at Newbury and Sabre Rattler won the Roses yesterday here at York. The Molecomb has certainly turned out to be a good race.

Lyric Fantasy won the Group 1 Keeneland Nunthorpe Stakes being the first two-year-old to do so for thirty-six years. Her rider Michael Roberts lived on a toast and Bovril diet for several days in order to ride at 7st 8lb. Paris House ran a good race to finish sixth.

Both Niche and Lyric Fantasy are owned by Lord Carnarvon and trained by Richard Hannon.

In between races at York, Jo and I were kept busy watching our four runners, on SIS, perform at my favourite racecourse, Ayr. They ran out of their skins for us, recording three wins by Another Episode, Laurel Queen and Drumdonna. Cockerham Ranger, our other runner, was second. Fylde Flyer was fifth in the last at York.

We had a glass of champagne in the car park with Terry and Margaret Holdcroft before motoring to Jim Harris's Carlton Stud at Malton to see our two brood mares and foals, I Don't Mind and Hollia. The foals are by Puissance and Clantime and looked really well. Olly, my dog, was in his element chasing after the rabbits in a field there.

FRIDAY August 21

RANG John Carroll to see how he was. There doesn't appear to be any chance of him riding before Monday. Apparently, yesterday Peter Savill, the North's leading owner, put a frivolous claim in for our winner Laurel Queen. It was reported in the papers that Laurel Queen was a threat to him winning his fifth Channel 4 Trophy. That is a trophy for the horse with the most wins in a season. If Laurel Queen, or any others from our yard, win the trophy I will ask our owners if Mr Savill can have it and I will also buy him a dummy to go with it. Mr Peter Savill's antics were mentioned in both the Life and the Post. Lots of people have rung, including trainers, telling me what a nice man Peter Savill is.

A letter came the other day from Mike Gallemore asking me if I would ride in a series of charity races, ex-jockeys against the racing Press, starting in October. Every time I get a chance to ride I do and as it's no good riding in these races half fit, I rode three lots cantering today to get prepared.

On my way to Chester with Diane and Sam I swotted away for tomorrow's televised races Star tips. I don't know whether they sell any more papers or not but people often mention them at the races. I have to admit it gives me great pleasure when my nap pops in.

As always, the Chester course looked like a picture postcard. Ron Walls and his team do a first class job on the course and the facilities there are first class. They were rewarded with a hot day and a huge crowd.

I watched on SIS in the Tote Credit Club Mamma's Too finish second at Sandown to Rod Simpson's Walk in the Park. Local Heroine, who was bred by her owner Linda Meylan, was running for the first time in four months as she has been suffering with sore shins. She was out of the gate like a shot and made most of the running to win by a length. With it being a European Breeders' Fund race the trustees of the fund awarded Linda a £1,000 prize for breeding the winner.

Racing was delayed after the third due to a fuse blowing in the PA system. Our only other runner, Charity Express, finished third in the nursery, running a big race.

Travelling home on the M6 the traffic was like it is every Friday nowadays-hectic.

Arriving home the white doves have settled in our dovecote. I just hope the cats don't get them. I settled down in the evening with a bottle of lager to write my piece for the Weekender-all about the declaration of overnight jockeys.

This time of the year we sell quite a few horses on in order to make room for the yearlings. Tonight, Amanda, one of our travelling head girls, brought an empty box back from Sandown as a Mr Purcell had claimed Mamma's Too for £15,000.

The dogs were barking and going bananas outside. When I went to see what was the matter with them, I discovered that the pilot of a microlight "plane" had run out of petrol and landed in one of our fields. He was coming towards the house in his spaceman-type outfit to tell me he'd just dropped in.

SATURDAY August 22

THIS morning, for a change, we worked on the round gallop and took the horses for a nice pick of grass afterwards.

Two lovely horses came from Colin Tinkler-Oxrib and Ribox. The owner asked me the other day at York if I would take them to train. I told him I wasn't keen as it's not my style to take other trainer's horses. He said if I didn't take them they would still leave Colin's yard anyway. So, after having a word with Colin about the matter, I agreed to take them. They were just arriving as Jo, Diane and myself were leaving for Chester. We picked up Sam on the way there.

We have Never in the Red, Rhett's Choice and Glowing Value running at Chester and, at Ripon, we have Gorinsky, Laxey Flyer and Classic Storm.

In the Nursery, Glowing Value, with top weight of 9st 7lb, ran a brilliant race. He took up the running two furlongs out, and was in front for every yard except on the line. Beaten a short head by After The Last, ridden by Willie Carson who, around this sharp course, should have a 10lb penalty. He is that good.

Rhett's Choice ran third to two very useful two-year-olds in the graduation race. I watched Gorinsky on SIS in the Tote Credit Club finish second in the £20,000 six furlong Great St Wilfrid handicap, earning his owners £4,630. At the moment, our horses are running out of their skins.

On our way home from Chester it started to rain. Mind you, I'm not grumbling. With the dry warm weather we have had over the past few days the ground is firming up again.

Listening to Classic Storm's race on the Racecall line in the car I could hear an almighty cheer go up from our lot when our little filly hit the front 100 yards from home. This is her seventh win of the season. What a bargain she's turned out to be, costing only 2,500 guineas when we bought her at Newmarket. Although she has sight in only one eye she is so tough.

Looking at Teletext, I tipped just one winner today but lots of outsiders were winning on the box and not many others tipped the winners either.

Jo went off to Asda to do the shopping for the week as they open late on a Saturday night. Diane went to Garstang to get a Chinese takeaway for us.

Duncan Sasse, the Newmarket trainer, rang and offered £50,000 for Glowing Value to race in Italy. He wants him for a Listed race but the entries close on Monday.

SUNDAY August 23

AFTER the rain, everywhere has freshened up. The birds are singing and it's a beautiful day. I asked one of our lads to take the bricks away from the dovecote entrance to feed them and let them have a quiet look around their new surroundings. I told him to do this before going home at evening stables. What does he do? At breakfast the berk takes the bricks straight off and the doves were last seen going flat out towards Lancaster.

It's now 8.0am. One of our tractors has just passed the window towing one of our staff's cars. It's in need of intensive care so badly I honestly can't recognise it to tell you who it belongs to.

No More The Fool (Jessie) and Cee-Jay-Ay went in our box to Gordon Richards to have a school over hurdles and fences and to allow Neale Doughty to have a sit on them. Neale rides our few jumpers whenever he can.

The new fences I bought on my last visit to Southwell haven't arrived yet as Bob Lee, the fence builder, hasn't quite finished them.

Guess what? I've just heard one of our staff has broken a shoulder-I wonder how?

I rode Grogfryn for a couple of furlongs as she is our only runner tomorrow. She flew. JC's wife Tracy rang to say John is okay for tomorrow.

Walked round and fed my cattle, they look super. Unfortunately, 20 of them are going to market on Friday. It's getting time to buy yearlings and we could do with some money in the bank. With this recession it's very hard to get paid by some of the owners. I don't want to be going to Doncaster Sales on the eighth of next month to LOOK at the yearlings. I want to go there to BUY some.

Jessie jumped brilliantly over the fences. Neale hopes Gordon hasn't got a horse in Jessie's race at Cartmel so he can ride him. So do I, as Neale is a good jock and a great lad.

At 7.0pm, Arthur and Evelyn Slack, the owners of Snowgirl, arrived and brought with them some aluminium racing plates they got from Australia. They have a cushion welded onto them to stop the jar when the ground is firm. I will give them a whirl through the week. Arthur and I walked round our cattle as he is a good stockman. In fact, I have bought lots of cattle off him from time to time. We also joist sheep for him through the winter.

I watched John Wilson on "Going Fishing" on the telly. This programme is a dream to watch. John was in South Africa this week. He makes the programme so interesting it's nearly like being there, helping him pull the fish out of the water. I love it. It's brilliant.

Diane and Pat went up to bed about 8.30. Jo followed around 10.30 so I brought my dogs into the front room. They all sat round the open fire and I started my Weekender story on OJOCS. Perfect peace.

MONDAY August 24

ALAN and I did the entries for the Saturday Bank Holiday. We had quite a few meetings to enter including Cartmel, our local jump course, for Jessie and Cee-Jay-Ay. To keep Jessie on the move in preparation for Cartmel I cantered him one and a half miles steady on the all-weather. Normally he would only have been doing roadwork.

Daaniera, the two-year-old I bought from Seamus Purcell, has gone in the Nottingham box with our runner Grogfryn. A prospective buyer, who intended coming yesterday to see him, couldn't make it so we are taking the horse to see him. We have to be fairly versatile nowadays as it's very easy to get left behind.

Lisnakill Wish runs in the 9.45 tonight at Canterbury. Jo has gone to Ragdale Hall, a health farm, until Friday with Josie Shelton, a pal of hers from Jersey. So everybody's out and about today.

In the first race at Nottingham there were seventeen runners, Grogfryn ran a good race to finish sixth in a very competitive race.

Colin Davey, who had the interest in Daaniera, brought along a pal of his, a barrister called David Nicholes. They both liked the horse and are having half each. Being almost white Daaniera is a miniature Desert Orchid. He has a bit of ability and he should give them a lot of fun.

John drove back from Nottingham while I kept my eye on the speedo. We dropped him off at his house as his car went in for its MOT today. He has a lovely place. It's the first time I've seen his new empire since he moved in.

Lord Mostyn didn't go to Nottingham, so I rang him to let him know his filly ran well and to make sure he was all right with him not going, as he is a smashing old boy. Stan and Sonia Newman rang from Canterbury, our flying machine has only won again. That is his sixteenth win from twenty-five runs this season. What a dog.

TUESDAY August 25

AFTER leading out yesterday's runner and stretching the legs of those who run tomorrow, the main lots cantered in pairs, four lengths apart round our top moss. It's a spectacular sight to see them working round this way in a figure of eight on the top moss with the horses silhouetted on the horizon. Two loads of wood fibre were delivered to top up the all-weather just as Diane, Sam and I were setting off for Pontefract, where our sole runner is Two Moves In Front.

John has gone on early as he and his wife, Tracy, who acts as his agent, want to see the OJOCS roadshow, which comes into force next month.

Pontefract is one of the most popular courses in the country, so, as expected, there was a very big crowd on their Timeform Day. In fact, the Timeform Organisation have generously sponsored six of the seven races.

In the Timeform Futurity race, Two Moves In Front could only finish fourth of the five horses that faced the starter, but in doing so collected £222 for his owners. He also won the best turned out award, putting £75 in his lad Steve Haworth's pocket.

Diane Gundill, wife of the Clerk of the Course, invited me for tea in their private box. Would you believe who I was drawn next next to around a huge round table?-none other than John Lucas, the auctioneer who I crossed swords with at Southwell for plucking bids out of the sky a few weeks ago.

On the way home along the M6 the traffic came to a standstill. A big wagon had stopped in the middle lane and there were lots of police trying to sort it out.

Bill and Nan Robinson, who are part owners of Two Moves In Front, are staying at The Crofters. I told them I would go round there for a drink this evening if I got the time. However, by the time I had finished my phone calls, had something to eat, it was 9.20pm so I thought I'd better give it a miss.

There was a lot of rubbish on TV so I finished my Weekender copy on OJOCS then went to bed.

WEDNESDAY August 26

WITH the overnight rain the ground was good and as I didn't set off to Redcar until after 11.0am I was able to watch all the horses work.

Alan and I still had quite a lot to do on the entries as today was the closing day for Bank Holiday Monday and there are lots of meetings.

This recession has really taken hold in places. Arthur Campbell rang to tell me that Miami Bear, one of our few jumpers, won't be coming to us this season. He won his last race over fences at Southwell and the winnings hardly paid for a couple of months training bills. It is a sorry state of affairs.

In the first race at Redcar, Soba Guest ran in the British Racing Schools Handicap for apprentices. Steve Porritt, one of our lads who was having his first ride, gave Soba a nice ride to finish third.

It started to rain and continued throughout the day, making the firm ground very slippy for the horses coming round the bends. Inside the straight, four or five horses slipped badly. Fortunately none fell but they were lucky. The next two races were run up the straight and the stewards sensibly abandoned the last race.

Travelling on the A66 two cars had been falling out. One of them was halfway up a bank. Both cars were in a very bad shape. The police were there sorting things out.

Bryan McMahon, the trainer, rang me up for a whinge about handicappers. By the time he'd finished, my jaws ached. I am glad it was he who rang me. He was on that long I would have had to put the training fees up to pay for the call.

Around 10.0pm some punter from Bolton rang me up. He was telling me about a 'system' he had worked out. He was on a roll and what did I think? He was a nice fellow. I was let off the hook at 10.25pm.

After that I got a can of lager out of the fridge and sat down to read my Sporting Life and weigh up the form of the horses we have declared later on in the week.

THURSDAY August 27

FOR a change, I didn't go to Edinburgh today-Alan went in my place. I have to have the odd day at home to catch up with things. Judging by the number of phone calls I've had passed through to me via the office, I think some little bird must have been telling everyone I was in residence.

Sometimes it's hard to keep out of the news in the sporting papers. Today, Peter Savill has written yet another letter in the Life about me and claiming races. A couple of punters have also written in. Ian Carnaby wrote a nice article in the Life about Mr Savill, so Ian can take some flak now.

Headlines in the Post, "Berry is critical of OJOCS". I hope this is soon defused, otherwise I will have to go racing wearing a back pad and crash helmet.

It was great to spend a couple of hours in the yard among the horses instead of travelling. I managed to have a good look around the stock. The winter lambs arrived today for us to joist for Arthur Slack. Good sorts they are, too. It's always nice to see the animals in the fields and the place well stocked.

I went shopping this afternoon. I had every intention of getting measured for a couple of new suits in Kendal by a tailor I go to, because if I don't go quickly I'll be looking like yer man Compo in the TV series, 'Last of the Summer Wine'. However, it poured down so I just went to Lancaster to get a few things I wanted for the house and I never got to Kendal.

In the evening, Kevin, Neville and myself met up with Brian Durkin to go to Bernard Manning's Embassy Club in Manchester. Boy, he was brilliant. The entire place was in hysterics. My sides honestly ached with laughing. I hadn't got over one joke when he hit us with another. I really thought I was going to throw a wobbler. The cabaret show was also great. We had a real good sing song together. It was brilliant.

In our job everything is done so prim and proper, it's good to let your hair down once in a while.

Coming home through Manchester on the Mancunian Way there was a blown-up, life-sized doll tied to the railings. I had all on to keep Neville in the car.

FRIDAY August 28

WITH my chaps over my suit trousers I rode out Jessie for his final spin before his big day at tomorrow's Cartmel, a meeting I look forward to every year.

Music Dancer and Fylde Flyer perform at Newmarket today. I have a car-full going down with me-there's driver Diane, Pat and Wally, nursing his broken shoulder.

Travelling on the A1 near Blyth, yet another car had turned completely round with the caravan upside down. The amount of these we have seen this year makes one wonder if they are safe on our roads.

We arrived at Newmarket where I met up with Jo and her pal Josie, fresh from their health farm visit. I must say they both looked very well.

Fylde Flyer ran a brilliant race in the Hopeful Stakes, a six furlong Listed race, to finish third to Rose Indien and Hamas. There were five three-year-olds of the 13 runners in the race. Amazingly, three of them finished first, second and third.

Colin Davey, the young man I sold Daaniera to, asked me if I would go to Brickfield Stud while I was in Newmarket to see a yearling he owned.

Said cheerio to Jo as she went on to look after our tomorrow's Goodwood horses. I went with Colin in his car and met our gang at the Moat House afterwards to come home. Colin's yearling, by Glint of Gold, was a big backward type that looks like needing a bit of time. Needless to say it's not coming to Cockerham. Not yet, anyway.

In the car we had a swap round for the journey home. Wally is staying overnight and coming back in the horsebox tomorrow after Charity Express runs. Steve Simpson, of the Blackpool Gazette, and John Bostock, Fylde Flyer's lad, are coming back with us. John starts his holidays tomorrow but he didn't want to miss out on taking his horse racing-that's loyalty for you. The roads are busy as usual on a Friday and, with having to go and see that yearling, we didn't arrive home until 9.20pm.

SATURDAY August 29

FIRST thing, Alan and I entered the horses for Thursday and Friday. Linda rang from Goodwood as did Amanda from Newmarket, to let me know the horses who stayed overnight are all right. We have a policy that the travelling head lads and lasses always ring up early in the morning to tell us how they are-just in case a horse got a knock, travelled badly, didn't eat up or whatever.

We worked the horses in threes on the back stretch of the all-weather as I didn't want to cut up the grass gallop after the recent heavy rain. We had a tractor standing by to harrow and roll the all-weather after every 24th horse had gone up, in order to keep it in good nick. With the rain today it rode really well.

We have six runners at four meetings and two or three have a good chance. We haven't had a winner all week so let's hope we have a rub of the green today. I am going to Cartmel to see Jessie run. Although we only ever train the odd jumper nowadays, I absolutely love it. In winter, I often have a day at Wetherby, Uttoxeter or Carlisle, even when we don't have a runner. To say I am geed up about going to Cartmel, my first jump meeting of the year,

JESSIE seen on his way to an emphatic victory at Cartmel.
He never touched a twig. It was a really nice way to start the jump season.

would be an understatement.

Cartmel is such a picturesque course, right on the edge of the Lake District. There was a nice friendly crowd and every other person I came across seemed to ask why I wasn't at either Newmarket or Goodwood. The course was in beautiful condition. Jessie walked round the paddock looking like a million dollars. Kathy, his lass, had plaited his mane and tail and she was rewarded by being judged as having the best turned out.

Jessie gave an exhibition of jumping that was a pleasure to watch. Making most of the running, he won by two-and-a-half lengths. Jessie's owners, Reg and Jenny Leah, who have owned him since a yearling, absolutely adore him. Jenny was a nervous wreck during the race but my day was made by having a winner at our local track.

Watched Laurel Queen on SIS run a great race at Newcastle to record her seventh win of the season. She slightly missed the break but got a nice run up the inside to get up close home by a neck. This win now puts her in front for the Channel 4 Trophy.

Trainer Don (Ginger) McCain was lucky he didn't get locked up at Cartmel. He was walking around with a huge split in his trousers until he sent someone to the car for his mac.

Looking at Teletext, my Star telly tips did quite well, netting three winners, including Mamdooh at 11-2.

GINGER McCAIN : Racegoers at Cartmel saw more of the Cholmondeley trainer than he had intended, until a mac from his car saved his blushes.

SUNDAY August 30

WITH it being Bank Holiday Monday tomorrow there are lots of race meetings to prepare for. What a job getting the jockeys sorted out. We run nineteen horses at five different meetings. I must have boosted BT's profits with our phone calls this morning. When we run so many, very seldom do we have many winners. Let's hope tomorrow is different.

It was very wild and windy here at Cockerham. When I took Sam home after lunch it was high tide. I could tell as the beck at the bottom of our lane was full of water right to the top of its banks and the marsh was flooded on the opposite side of the road.

It rained every bit of the day. At stable time a couple of us went round to check all the drains to make sure they were all running. Last year in the main yard a drain got blocked and water flooded into the bottom boxes. What a mess that was.

Annie and George Atkinson came to see their horse Ultrakay. They were the only visitors we had today.

Kevin, one of our head lads, told me his young lad Adam had broken his collar bone yesterday playing football in the garden. Heather, the wife of Flash, our other head lad, is due to foal any day now, so he went to Cartmel yesterday but only for Jessie's race. His in-laws stood in for him while he was away. In the evening, I watched John Wilson in "Go Fishing". He was still in Africa and caught a huge catfish, weighing in the region of 60lb on a 15lb breaking strain line. It took him well over an hour to land the monster catch.

MONDAY August 31

IN The Racing Post, All Our Yesterdays reads for August 31st, 1982, "Jack Berry saddled his 100th winner when eight-year-old Bri-Eden, ridden by George Duffield, won the Handicap Sprint at Epsom". Let's hope we celebrate by winning the same race today with Never in the Red.

Jo and Pat went to Newcastle, Alan to Wolverhampton and the travelling head-lads and lasses saw to the other meetings. Diane, John and myself went to Ripon. On a Bank Holiday it is always a bit of a strain on the staff at home with so many away racing.

John and I were reading the papers when Diane slammed on the brakes. Too late, though. We hit the car in front that had also stopped suddenly as a Volvo car and trailer had stopped in front of him. Then there was another almighty bang as the car behind ran into the back of my car, lurching us forward to have another bang at the car in front. All the cars needed a bit of surgery. The only minor injuries were to two little kids in the car that hit us. They bumped their heads, thankfully not badly. One had a big lump on her head. The man in the car we hit was crying his eyes out because it was his father's car.

Waiting for the police, and exchanging insurance details, lost us so much time that John Carroll jocked off Diane Bain in the driver's seat. As he has little feeling for motor cars, we burned the road up to try and get there in time for the first race, in which John had a ride on Petraco for Liam Codd. But even with all JC's efforts at the wheel we arrived at Ripon just in time to see G Parkin ride Petraco to finish third, beaten less than a length.

With all the ammunition we fired today, only Allegrissima hit the target. We did have a few placed horses up and down the country, though.

I managed to arrange with Terry Holdcroft, who I bought my car from, for it to go into hospital tomorrow and for a loan of another until it's better.

TUESDAY September 1

EXCEPT for Palacegate Episode, Gorinsky and Windpower, who breezed along for a couple of furlongs as they run at York tomorrow, the remainder of the horses cantered round the all-weather ring. We put a visor on Windpower for the first time as in his last race at Nottingham he didn't concentrate very hard.

Given normal luck Another Episode and Arctic Appeal, who both run in condition races, should have a good chance of winning for us today. They may not be very good prices but that isn't too important. If they were 33-1 that would suggest we have made a poor job of placing them. John, Diane and I picked up Sam from his flat to go to Ripon races in Jo's car. Jo took mine and changed it on the way to Epsom with Pat. Travelling to Ripon no less than seven cars had concertina'd into each other on the M6 without any assistance from Diane.

Today at Ripon, in the three-year-old and upwards five furlong handicap, Murray's Mazda has top weight with 9st 10lb. Last time he ran fourth of six in a bad seller. In fact, out of his total of thirteen runs he has won one poor Hamilton seller. Yours or Mine has won her last two races and with a penalty has only got 8st. She is the Sporting Life's morning favourite at 11-4. Murray's Mazda at 16-1 is the outsider of the eleven runners. He is one horse who will be lucky to ever win another race, but the owners love him and want to keep him in training. He has so little ability. I feel like taking him up the road and running away from him, or give him to Nigel Gray, the handicapper, as he also likes him.

It just shows there are no certs. Arctic Appeal, at 1-2, got beat in the first. I watched Another Episode oblige at Epsom on SIS. I don't want to be brash and say I told you so, but I hope the sprint handicapper Nigel Gray watched the 5.0pm at Ripon on SIS to see Murray's Mazda finish tailed off last of the eleven runners. Diane drove us home and got a clear round.

In the mail when I got home was a letter from an eighty-five year old lady who had included a self-addressed stamped envelope. She is a follower of the yard who lives in a home for the elderly at Garstang and she hasn't been too lucky with our horses recently. Could I please tell her one I think will win.

WEDNESDAY September 2

IT rained all night and with today being a work day it's still raining. In preparation for work the horses went on the horse-walkers with hoods and waterproofs on. They looked like the Klu Klux Klan. We didn't gallop them for results, we just worked them in threes up the back straight of the all-weather.

Jo, Pat, Diane and I all went to York. Later on we are booked in at the North

Pier Theatre, Blackpool, to see Russ Abbott. On the way there I rang my old pal Joe Sime as the old boy hasn't been very well recently. What a good jockey he was and a gentleman to boot.

As usual, there was a good crowd at the Yorkshire meeting. The first of our three runners, Palacegate Episode in the second race for two-year-olds, reminded me of the Nunthorpe at York last meeting where Lyric Fantasy was so minute. Palacegate Episode is also very small-just 14.2 hands in fact. Not to be outdone by her full brother Another Episode, who won the race last year, she fought on gamely to beat Satank, the winner of the Windsor Castle Stakes at Royal Ascot, by a neck.

PALACEGATE EPISODE seen bravely holding off
the challenge of Royal Ascot winner Satank.

In the £20,000 six furlong feature race Gorinsky ran well to finish third of the sixteen starters. Our other runner, Windpower, finished in the middle. I had a drink with another pal of mine Eddie Gray who used to play for my old team Leeds United. Eddie owned Zamanda with some of the other Elland Road squad when we first started training near Doncaster.

On our way to the North Pier for the Russ Abbott show we stopped for a sandwich at Hartshead Moor service area on the M62.

Russ Abbott's show was really good and we all enjoyed it. Although we only live some twenty miles away, except for going to the boxing functions and a few dinners during the year, we seldom get into Blackpool. Arriving back just gone midnight, I flicked through the racing news on Teletext and was sorry to see one of the leading jockeys in Australia, thirty-year-old Noel Barker, had died from a heavy fall at Randwick racecourse, Sydney.

THURSDAY September 3

ROADWORK for the horses today, except for Jessie, with me on board, and the next few days' runners who we cantered. Afterwards they all had a nice pick of grass in one of our paddocks.

Alan and I wrestled with the entries before John and I set off for Wolverhampton where we run Cranfield Comet and Noteability. Jockey David Nicholls' young son, who had been staying at John Carroll's house for a few days, came with us to get a lift back home.

At Wolverhampton John had an outside ride before ours ran, which gave me time to write my copy for next week's Weekender which is about claiming races.

Just before I went to collect the tack for Cranfield Comet there was an almighty crack of thunder and two or three flashes of lightning. The heavens opened and I got absolutely soaked as my mac was in the car. It must have given Cranfield Comet quite a shock as he isn't normally gifted with a very big heart, but from halfway in the race he never looked like getting beat and went on to record our 90th win of the season. Unfortunately, I wasn't brave enough to risk a fiver on him and he paid 20-1 on the Tote.

Mrs Jones, the Oswestry trainer's wife, asked me if Jo was at home putting her feet up as she wasn't with me. I told her I hoped so as it's a lot cheaper than her going shopping.

In the last race, the second division of the two-year-old seven furlong maiden, Noteability ran a fair race to finish fifth of the eleven runners. The form looked good enough to win a small claimer or seller.

Diane leaves us tomorrow. She has worked hard here for the past nine weeks and we have enjoyed having her. I rang my trainer pal Tommy Skiffington up in Garden City, New York, to get her on a year's course with him as his assistant. Needless to say Diane is over the moon.

FRIDAY September 4

IT WAS gone 2.0am when I finished my story on the claiming races for my slot in the Weekender. It's now 7.0am and I am waiting for Bob, our gardener, to bring the papers in. He's normally here by now so there must be some sort of hold-up. Eventually, I rang up the Post Office in our village and discovered it was the Racing Post which hadn't arrived and Bob was hanging on for it.

Diane left today. It has been a real pleasure to work with her. On leaving, saying cheerio to us all, she couldn't stop the tears from falling.

Phil Tuck, the ex-jump jockey came for a ride out and went on with us to Haydock races. That man is wasting his time, he could make a living by doing impressions of G W Richards. He can take him off better than Gordon can himself.

It was very cold at Haydock but there was still a large crowd. Due to the heavy going the horses with low draws in the sprints came up the middle of the course and finished tailed off.

Daaniera was the nearest horse we got to troubling the judge and he could only finish fifth. Tino Tere, in the last race, hit his mouth on the stalls and knocked a couple of front teeth out.

When Jo went to the owners and trainers car park for her car in order to pick Sam, Phil and myself up, she discovered someone had broken into it. Gone was her compact disc player and radio.

On the way back home we dropped Sam off at his flat and went onto the Chinese take-away to get our tea. Over a bottle of wine back home we had a good laugh with Phil.

Amanda picked up half of the chase fences I bought at Southwell the other week on her way back from Newmarket.

SATURDAY September 5

IT WAS a nice warm day working the horses. Cockerham Ranger, Glowing Value and Garnock Valley were flying. Jessie did a nice piece of work with his half-sister, Laurel Queen.

The kitchen boiler sprang a leak and there was water all over the place. Through the night Flash had to take his wife Heather into hospital as she was getting ready to foal. He rang up around 11.0am to tell us she had an 8lb filly and both are well.

Alan has gone to Thirsk to look after Chateau Nord and Palacegate Prince. Jo and I picked up Sam to go to Haydock, where we have a few runners. I am hopeful rather than confident about the prospects of having a few winners today. Any winner that comes our way will be a bonus.

There was some very good racing at Haydock and so there should have been-there wasn't a race valued under £5,000. The Group 1 Haydock Park Sprint had £100,000 added. Sheikh Albadou beat Mr Brooks and our own Sizzling Saga ran a sound race to finish sixth. His owner David Abell collected £450 place money. It was a winnerless day for the yard but no doubt we will bounce back. We'll be having another go on Monday. We very nearly took Glowing Value to Florence for tomorrow's race but we bottled out.

Checking my Star telly tips I had a good day selecting Aitch N' Bee, who won at 14-1 and Mr Confusion at 4-1. I also went for Sayyedati in the Moyglare Group 1 Stakes in Ireland, who obliged at 11-10. My nap, Liyakah, ran at Kempton but didn't win. I saw this Major Hern-trained filly win at Goodwood on her debut, beating some useful two-year-olds, including Carbon Steel, who won yesterday at Haydock.

SUNDAY September 6

DECLARED the horses for Hamilton and Wolverhampton. It was the first day of OJOCS when we had to declare the jockeys with Weatherbys at the same time we declared the runners at the overnight stage. Only Richard Hills had to be declared to ride Press The Bell, because it was a late booking and all the jockeys' agents had already declared our other jockeys. Unless it was because of the system being new or what, which I hope it is, but it took at least five minutes to confirm the booking. If the trend continues it will cost us a fortune in phone calls. Let's hope they don't install an 0898 number.

Having received an invitation for lunch at the Middlethorpe Hall Hotel at York by the directors of Tattersalls, Jo and I set off in her car at 10.30am. This time she didn't grumble about my dog Olly coming. Jo normally complains about Olly's hair falling out. He nearly always comes with me in my car. She's not got over having her compact disc nicked last Friday at Haydock and I've been crowing about the fact that no one has pinched anything out of my car with my dog being in it. I have had my country and western tapes in my cars for years. But Jo reckons I don't have to take Olly as no one would take them even if I left the car doors wide open. That's taste for you.

Arriving at the beautiful Middlethorpe Hall, built for Thomas Barlow, a master cutler in 1699-1701, we had a splendid lunch. All the other Northern trainers and their wives were there and we were able to have a bit of a chat with each other. It was most enjoyable. That's more than I can say about the weather as it rained nearly all the time.

On my return home I flicked through Teletext for the racing news to see if Arazi had won the Prix du Moulin de Longchamp. But he hadn't even run because of injury. Good news though, Henry Cecil's All At Sea won the race, giving Henry his first Group 1 winner of the season.

MONDAY September 7

AFTER tomorrow's runners breezed a couple of furlongs I rode Jessie for a mile swinging canter on the all-weather and he was great.

Alan and I got the declarations and entries ready for Ruby to phone them in. I made and answered a few phone calls before meeting John on the Manor car park at 10.30am to set off for Hamilton.

We have runners at both today's meetings, Hamilton and Wolverhampton. Our yard leads the winners' table on both courses.

Arriving at Hamilton on a very wet day with gale force winds blowing, the crowd was a bit sparse, which was only to be expected. John had three spare rides before partnering our Oyston's Life in the sprint. But they didn't tear any trees up. In the next race Dokkha Oyston finished third to the leading Scottish trainer Linda Perratt's pair, Francis Anne and Diet.

Watched SIS from Wolverhampton and saw our filly Dutch Dancer run well for a long way on her debut. We had a far better run in the Nursery from Laurel Delight, who popped out in front from the word go and stayed there to win by four lengths.

On our way home we called round to the stable yard to pick up Gerry Blum as he's staying with us tonight and travelling back to Carlisle races with Alan tomorrow.

Like most people in racing I watched the Panorama programme about our ailing industry. The Government is milking it to death and the bookmakers aren't putting enough back. But if they don't take heed soon it will be too late.

Paris House is entered for the Scarbrough Stakes on Wednesday at Doncaster. He seems to have been a bit flat these past few days, although he worked quite well on Saturday. He beat Food of Love in a gallop and at home she is very fast. I think I will rough him off until next season. He has been in training a long time and he probably wants a holiday.

TUESDAY September 8

WELL this is where it all started last year-the first day of Doncaster Yearling Sales. It so happens it's two days earlier than last year. I have had a few hours looking through the catalogue over the past week and have got one or two yearlings printed on my mind I am keen to see.

It's just gone 6.0am so I rode out Jessie and gave him a long canter. Looking at tomorrow's Scarbrough Stakes at Doncaster it doesn't look a very hot race. I told John to have a sit on Paris House for a couple of furlongs with blinkers on and he flew. One has to be versatile in this job. We now run him tomorrow.

Jo has packed her car up with all our gear. We are booked into the Moat House until Friday. We set off at 7.45am in the lashing rain for the St Leger Sales. At the sales, trade was a bit slow. People were talking of the depressed state of racing. Taking most of the gloom in my stride I got my head down and bought lot number 35, a Belfort filly for 2,000gns. Nine lots later a nice-looking colt by My Generation was heading for Cockerham for 3,800gns. I then bought a colt by one of my favourite stallions, Music Boy, looking a dead ringer for his dad. But the one I had been waiting for, the half-brother to Sabre Rattler, lot 161, came in looking a million dollars. He topped the day's sale price at 27,000gns bought by you know who. Thankfully, I sold three-quarters of him within the hour. No doubt that will please the bank manager as this time of year he gets a bit on edge. A Mr McCreery asked us to train a nice Bustino colt that didn't fetch his reserve. Two Moves In Front kept up the good work at Carlisle by winning the two-year-old race for us.

Returning to our hotel I went and had a swim and a sauna. Linda Perratt, Liz and Harry Beeby and a few others were down there, along with a couple of young girls, probably looking to see if Derek Thompson was there.

Harry Beeby kindly invited Jo and myself for dinner and we had a most enjoyable evening.

HERE I AM leading the horses in after
work on the all-weather gallops.

Jack Berry's year of 1992

A YEAR IN RED SHIRTS opens on September 10, 1991 and closes on September 8, 1992. The significance of the dates is the start of the Doncaster yearling sales. That's when Jack Berry's season really begins, selecting his youngsters for the forthcoming campaign.

An integral part of the Berry success story is his remarkable eye for a racehorse. He relies heavily on his inbuilt radar system to pinpoint the potential winner. It's the Berry factor in finding horses with that indefinable ability to win races.

Having bought the ammunition the business turns to training his sights on the target. Recently he has hit the mark with increasing regularity, topping one hundred winners in each of the last four years.

1991 was a record year for Jack Berry. He was leading trainer numerically and came close to becoming the first person to train one hundred two-year-old winners in a season.

1992 started equally well. By the end of April his horses had won 27 races, among them three Listed events, well up with his previous year's schedule.

On May 16 he had a double, Music Dancer winning at Hamilton and Super Seve scoring on the all-weather at Southwell. Then the virus struck, bringing the yard to a standstill. He had no alternative but to shut up shop. It was twenty days before Jack was back in the winner's enclosure, at the double again, with Charity Express at Catterick and Palacegate Racing at Southwell.

Although Moss Side was back in business the virus had left its mark. Many of the horses took time to come round to their early-season form. But the Cockerham team plugged away. Soon the horses started to fire again and the winners began to flow.

In July the yard had twenty-two winners, including a treble on the 13th at Beverley, Edinburgh and Wolverhampton and doubles on the 23rd, 24th and 25th.

It was a victory for perseverance, and dogged determination not to be beaten by the virus that had laid flat so many yards around the country.

When Jack realised that another record was out of reach he accepted that the only realistic target was another century of Flat winners for the year. In the event, he took the total to 107 for 1992, a remarkable achievement in a year of setbacks and racing's worst recession.

It is not easy to keep the momentum going in the final weeks of the Flat season with exposed two-year-olds and sprint handicappers, but it turned out to be a most productive period for the yard.

Palacegate Touch completed his hat-trick at Newmarket on October 3 and although he then found the competition a bit hot in a Listed race at York, three wins from five outings was a more than satisfactory return in the grey's first year.

Two days later there was almost a 1,988-1 treble for the stable at Warwick, Convenient Moment and Cee-Jay-Ay popping up at nice prices and Langtonian finding just one too good in the last.

Heather Bank, who had started the season by trotting up in the Boldboy Sprint at Newmarket, ended the year on an equally high note when returning to Headquarters to beat Fascination Waltz by two and a half lengths in the Olivier Douieb Memorial Handicap (Oct 17).

Threepence was another to come good in the autumn, notching up a quick double at Chester (Oct 20) and Lingfield (Oct 26), and Jack rounded off his turf season in some style at Hamilton (Nov 3) when saddling Soba Guest and Anusha to complete a double.

The last winner of the year was the speedy Another Episode, who added to earlier successes at Ayr and Epsom when just holding on for a short-head victory on the all-weather at Lingfield (Dec 16).

So ended another successful year for Jack and Jo and the Cockerham team, scoring a fourth consecutive century of winners. It will be another year in red shirts in 1993 for Jack Berry, striving for a fifth hundred — and another tilt at the record book.

MIKE GALLEMORE
Editor
The Sporting Life

List of J Berry's Flat Winners in 1992

MEETING	HORSE [AGE]	JOCKEY	SP	PRIZE
		Jan		
1 Southwell (A.W)	Palacegate King [3]	L Charnock	8-1	2,030.00
10 Southwell (A.W)	Palacegate King [3]	R Cochrane	11-2	2,186.80
15 Southwell (A.W)	Palacegate Racing [3]	J Carroll	4-1	2,167.20
17 Southwell (A.W)	Palacegate King [3]	J Carroll	5-1	2,167.20
		March		
20 Doncaster	Classic Storm [2]	J Carroll	5-1	2,070.00
Doncaster	Amron [5]	N Carlisle	7-1	3,840.00
21 Doncaster	Fylde Flyer [3]	J Carroll	8-1	9,218.75
	Cammidge Trophy (Listed Race)			
23 Folkestone	Arctic Appeal (IRE) [3]	G Carter	11-4	2,259.00
25 Catterick	Lucky Parkes [2]	J Carroll	4-5F	2,387.20
28 Warwick	Palacegate Episode (IRE) [2]	J Carroll	4-1	1,932.00
30 Newcastle	Amron [5]	N Carlisle	13-8	2,820.00
		April		
1 Hamilton	Tynron Doon [3]	L Charnock	16-1	2,500.40
3 Kempton	Tuscan Dawn [2]	Pat Eddery	8-1	2,539.60
8 Ripon	Palacegate Episode (IRE) [2]	Pat Eddery	30-100F	2,488.80
10 Newbury	Sabre Rattler [2]	Pat Eddery	100-30	3,980.00
11 Thirsk	Sober Lad (IRE) [2]	G Carter	6-4F	2,584.00
13 Edinburgh	Two Moves In Front (IRE) [2]	G Carter	5-1	1,563.50
14 Newmarket	Fylde Flyer [3]	L Piggott	9-1	10,234.00
	Abernant Stakes (Listed Race)			
15 Pontefract	Tynron Doon [3]	G Duffield	3-1F	1,884.00
16 Newmarket	Heather Bank [3]	Pat Eddery	6-1	7,570.00
18 Haydock	Paris House [3]	J Carroll	3-1	8,893.75
	Beamish Irish Stout Field Marshal Stakes (Listed Race)			
20 Warwick	Threepence [3]	G Carter	4-1	3,003.00
22 Catterick	Lucky Parkes [2]	J Carroll	5-6F	2,476.80
Folkestone	Sabre Rattler [2]	Pat Eddery	1-2F	2,364.00
23 Beverley	Laurel Queen (IRE) [4]	J Carroll	5-2	2,402.40
24 Carlisle	Dokkha Oyston (IRE) [4]	J Carroll	9-4	2,206.40
27 Pontefract	Windpower (IRE) [3]	G Carter	6-1	3,785.00
		May		
1 Hamilton	Daaniera (IRE) [2]	J Carroll	5-1	2,499.50
4 Warwick	Laurel Delight [2]	G Carter	9-4	2,588.80
5 Chester	Lucky Parkes [2]	J Carroll	Evens F	5,530.00
8 Beverley	Classic Storm [2]	J Carroll	9-4F	2,598.40
11 Hamilton	Glowing Value (IRE) [2]	J Carroll	10-11F	2,260.80
16 Hamilton	Music Dancer [3]	L Charnock	15-8F	1,660.00
Southwell (A.W)	Super Seve (IRE) [2]	Dean McKeown	11-2	1,725.00
		June		
5 Catterick	Charity Express (IRE) [2]	J Carroll	5-2	2,186.80
Southwell (A.W)	Palacegate Racing [3]	G Carter	12-1	2,265.20
8 Nottingham	Tom Piper [2]	J Carroll	7-1	2,511.00
11 Chepstow	Echo-Logical [3]	Pat Eddery	40-95F	1,548.00
Hamilton	Murray's Mazda (IRE) [3]	G Duffield	9-2	2,206.40
12 Southwell (A.W)	Classic Storm [2]	G Carter	10-11F	2,265.20
15 Edinburgh	Make It Happen (IRE) [2]	J Carroll	4-11F	2,414.40
19 Redcar	Cranfield Comet [3]	G Duffield	4-1F	3,752.50
20 Redcar	Kentucky Dreams [2]	G Carter	14-1	2,422.00
22 Edinburgh	High Principles [3]	J Carroll	2-1	2,169.00
Edinburgh	Classic Storm [2]	J Carroll	Evens F	2,050.00
24 Carlisle	Trentesimo (IRE) [2]	J Carroll	5-2	2,477.80
25 Carlisle	Laurel Queen (IRE) [4]	J Carroll	6-1	2,343.60
Carlisle	Chateau Nord [3]	J Carroll	6-1	2,128.00
26 Lingfield (A.W)	Palacegate Racing [3]	G Carter	6-4F	2,499.20
27 Chepstow	Echo-Logical [3]	G Carter	Evens F	2,984.00
30 Chepstow	Classic Storm [2]	J Carroll	11-8F	2,322.00

[311]

July

2 Haydock	Sizzling Saga (IRE) [4]	J Carroll	7-2	1,590.00
3 Haydock	Our Mica [2]	J Carroll	3-1	2,167.20
4 Beverley	Memsahb [3]	J Carroll	3-1	3,557.50
6 Edinburgh	Press The Bell [2]	J Carroll	Evens F	2,192.00
8 Redcar	Cockerham Ranger [2]	Julie Krone	3-1	1,520.00
11 Southwell (A.W)	Allegrissima [2]	J Fortune	7-2	1,213.50
13 Beverley	Classic Storm [2]	J Carroll	2-1JF	2,820.00
Edinburgh	Laurel Queen (IRE) [4]	J Carroll	3-1	2,374.00
Wolverhampton	Mamma's Too [3]	Pat Eddery	3-1F	2,469.00
14 Beverley	Margaret's Gift [2]	J Carroll	13-2	3,002.00
15 Southwell (A.W)	Palacegate Prince [2]	J Carroll	5-2F	2,385.00
16 Hamilton	Two Moves In Front (IRE) [2]	Dean McKeown	10-1	2,280.00
18 Ayr	Laurel Queen (IRE) [4]	J Carroll	6-4F	2,262.00
21 Edinburgh	Allegrissima [2]	J Carroll	5-2	2,211.00
22 Redcar	Rhett's Choice [2]	J Fanning	15-8F	2,070.00
23 Hamilton	Palacegate Prince [2]	J Carroll	8-13F	2,343.00
Hamilton	High Principles [3]	J Carroll	9-4CF	2,499.20
24 Ayr	Laurel Queen (IRE) [4]	J Carroll	10-11F	1,523.00
Pontefract	Trentesimo (IRE) [2]	G Carter	11-4	2,259.00
25 Ayr	Echo-Logical [3]	J Carroll	2-5F	2,169.00
Wolverhampton	Charity Express (IRE) [2]	G Carter	7-2	2,364.00
27 Wolverhampton	Convenient Moment [2]	G Carter	11-4	1,604.00

Aug

1 Thirsk	Soba Guest (IRE) [3]	Miss D Jones	3-1	2,553.00
7 Redcar	Mamma's Too [3]	J Carroll	11-1	3,143.25
15 Newbury	Palacegate Episode (IRE) [2]	G Carter	5-6F	8,941.00
	St Hugh's Stakes (Listed Race)			
Ripon	Lucky Parkes [2]	J Carroll	4-1	5,026.00
17 Hamilton	Arctic Appeal (IRE) [3]	J Carroll	2-5F	2,290.00
Hamilton	Pilgrim Bay (IRE) [2]	J Carroll	2-1	2,346.00
19 York	Sabre Rattler [2]	Pat Eddery	13-2	14,100.00
	Roses Stakes (Listed Race)			
20 Ayr	Another Episode (IRE) [3]	G Carter	1-3F	2,221.50
Ayr	Laurel Queen (IRE) [4]	G Carter	9-4F	2,263.50
Ayr	Drumdonna (IRE) [2]	S Wood	33-1	2,368.50
21 Chester	Local Heroine [2]	G Carter	14-1	3,687.50
22 Ripon	Classic Storm [2]	G Carter	4-1	2,448.00
29 Newcastle	Laurel Queen (IRE) [4]	J Carroll	11-1	4,077.50
31 Wolverhampton	Allegrissima [2]	G Carter	8-1	1,884.00

Sept

1 Epsom	Another Episode (IRE) [3]	G Carter	1-2F	2,238.00
2 York	Palacegate Episode (IRE) [2]	J Carroll	2-5F	4,844.00
3 Wolverhampton	Cranfield Comet [3]	J Carroll	20-1	2,595.00
7 Wolverhampton	Laurel Delight [2]	G Carter	5-1	2,637.00
8 Carlisle	Two Moves In Front (IRE) [2]	Dean McKeown	7-1	1,786.00
15 Yarmouth	Palacegate Touch [2]	G Carter	20-1	2,973.00
17 Lingfield (A.W)	Cranfield Comet [3]	G Carter	7-2JF	2,811.60
26 Haydock	Palacegate Touch [2]	L Charnock	7-2	4,050.00
28 Hamilton	Palacegate Sunset [2]	L Charnock	14-1	2,742.00
29 Newcastle	Cranfield Comet [3]	J Carroll	9-2F	2,490.00

Oct

3 Newmarket	Palacegate Touch [2]	J Carroll	7-1	6,368.00
5 Warwick	Convenient Moment [2]	J Williams	16-1	2,994.00
Warwick	Cee-Jay-Ay [5]	P Roberts	8-1	3,870.00
17 Newmarket	Heather Bank [3]	G Carter	20-1	8,740.00
19 Edinburgh	Dokkha Oyston (IRE) [4]	J Carroll	11-1	1,976.50
20 Chester	Threepence [3]	G Carter	7-1	3,912.00
26 Lingfield (A.W)	Threepence [3]	J Carroll	Evens F	3,106.00

Nov

3 Hamilton	Soba Guest (IRE) [3]	J Carroll	6-1	2,301.00
Hamilton	Anusha [2]	J Carroll	5-4F	2,448.00

Dec

16 Lingfield (A.W)	Another Episode (IRE) [3]	G Carter	7-4F	2,385.00